D0776208

THE BEST
PLAYS
OF 2014

THE BEST PLAYS OF 2014

Edited by Lawrence Harbison

APPLAUSE
THEATRE & CINEMA BOOKS

An Imprint of Hal Leonard Corporation

Copyright © 2015 by Applause Theatre & Cinema Books

All rights reserved. No part of this book may be reproduced in any form, without written permission, except by a newspaper or magazine reviewer who wishes to quote brief passages in connection with a review.

Published in 2015 by Applause Theatre & Cinema Books
An Imprint of Hal Leonard Corporation
7777 West Bluemound Road
Milwaukee, WI 53213

Trade Book Division Editorial Offices
33 Plymouth St., Montclair, NJ 07042

Permissions can be found on page 395 which constitutes an extension of this copyright page.

Printed in the United States of America

Book design by Lynn Bergesen

Library of Congress Cataloging-in-Publication Data

The best plays of 2014 / edited by Lawrence Harbison.
    pages cm
 ISBN 978-1-4803-9665-4 (pbk.)
 1. American drama--21st century. I. Harbison, Lawrence, editor.
 PS634.2B48 2015
 812.608—dc23
                    2015023214

ISBN: 978-1-4803-9665-4

www.applausebooks.com

Contents

Introduction
vii

The Country House
by Donald Margulies
1

Dinner with the Boys
by Dan Lauria
78

Mala Hierba
by Tanya Saracho
145

Our Lady Of Kibeho
by Katori Hall
201

When January Feels Like Summer
by Cori Thomas
293

Year of the Rooster
by Eric Dufault
353

Introduction

This volume contains six terrific new plays produced during the 2014 calendar year (as opposed to the 2013–2014 theatrical season), which featured a plethora of new plays—on Broadway, Off-Broadway, and in regional theaters, so I had many to consider. I chose the plays that I feel were the most significant. And, let's face it, the ones I liked the best.

The Country House, the latest from Pulitzer Prize winner Donald Margulies, lit up Broadway in a fine production by Manhattan Theatre Club at the Samuel J. Friedman Theatre. It starred Blythe Danner as a fading film and theater star performing at the Williamstown Theatre Festival. It's set at her house in Williamstown, where she lives with her brother when she's in town. He's a Vanya-esque failed actor and soon to be failed playwright. On the occasion of the death of her oldest daughter, family members converge to remember her. There's her other daughter, a surly college student who's unimpressed by the theater and its practitioners, and the widower of her oldest daughter, a former theater director who's left the theater behind to become a successful film director. He's brought along his new wife, which makes things awkward, particularly for the brother, who once had a fling with her when they acted together at the Humana Festival and who still carries a torch for her. Also in the mix is a handsome film star slumming in theater in a production of *The Guardsman*, who is invited by Ms. Danner's character to stay at her house. All the women make a play for him. Margulies's play is a wonderful Chekhovian portrait of theater people, with echoes of *The Seagull* and *Uncle Vanya*, which I, and many other critics, found entrancing.

Dinner with the Boys was the biggest hit in the history of New Jersey Rep. It's a mafia comedy written by TV actor Dan Lauria (best known for playing Jack, the dad, on *The Wonder Years*). The fact that Mr. Lauria starred in the production certainly helped ticket sales, but the theater's audience (and the critics) really took to the play itself, which sold out its entire run, sold out its extension, and sold out tickets for people to see it live-streamed while sitting in the lobby. The play's about two aging mobsters, Charlie and Dom. Charlie's a hit man; Dom is the mob family's cook. They are in disfavor with the family don, Big Anthony Junior, having refused to carry out a hit on another wise guy, named Leo, because he was their best friend. They have been ordered to go to a house the family owns in Northern New Jersey while Big Anthony Junior, who whacked Leo himself, decides their fate. They have also been ordered to cook and eat Leo, who Big Anthony Junior whacked. Also in the mix is Uncle Sid, the family's accountant, who has figured out where Charlie and Dom are because he has started seeing bills come in for the house. Big Anthony Junior arrives and informs them that one of them is to whack the other. What do you think they do? This mordant comedy is one of the most hilarious plays I have seen in many a moon.

Mala Hierba marked the stunning debut of a talented new playwright, Tanya Saracho, and was a hit at Second Stage's Uptown series. It's about a woman named Liliana who's married to a very wealthy, rather shady man who abuses her physically, psychologically, and sexually. She can't dump him, though, because he is supporting her destitute family. In a cry for help, she's asked her former lover, Maritza, who now lives in Chicago, to come down to South Texas. Maritza wants her to come to Chicago with her. Will she? Also in the mix is her callow stepdaughter Maritza, and a common-sense housekeeper named Yuya, who urges Liliana to suck it up and endure her husband's abusive behavior. *Mala Hierba*, which means "bad seed," is a heartbreaking comic drama about a woman at the end of her rope.

Katori Hall continued to prove that she is one of our major playwrights with her astonishing *Our Lady of Kibeho*, produced by Signature Theatre, based on the true story of three Rwanda girls who claimed to be able to see and hear the Virgin Mary, much to the consternation of the woman who runs the Catholic school where they are students and the local bishop. When a legate from the Vatican arrives to investigate, they wind up convincing him by what can only be described as a miracle. Eventually, they become local celebrities of sorts, and pilgrims start coming to Kibeho. On the Feast Day of the Assumption, the Blessed Mother appears to the girls to deliver a terrible prophecy: "The hills of Rwanda will run with blood."

Ensemble Studio Theatre had two hits in 2014, Cori Thomas's *When January Feels Like Summer* and Eric Dufault's *Year of the Rooster*, both of which the theater revived for a second run, a highly unusual occurrence Off-Broadway. Ms. Thomas's play is a comic drama that follows the stories of two African American teenage boys and an Indian widow who took over her husband's bodega after he died. She's joined by her brother, who is going through sex change procedures to become a woman. Eventually, all the stories intersect, with the possibility of love for one and all.

Year of the Rooster is a non-realistic comic drama about a hapless middle-age man who works at a McDonald's, and who is training what just may be the greatest fighter rooster who ever lived, a bantam bad boy named Oedipus Rex. If his rooster wins the big match against a longtime champion, it just may be his ticket to fame, fortune, and escape from McDonald's. Oedipus Rex, by the way, is personified by an actor costumed like a rooster would be if his was into punk.

So here you have comedy, drama, comedy-drama; realism, non-realism— something for everyone! It is my hope that you will want to produce these plays. If you do, break a leg. Anyway, I promise you six great reads.

—Lawrence Harbison
Brooklyn, New York

THE BEST PLAYS OF 2014

THE COUNTRY HOUSE

A New Play by
Donald Margulies

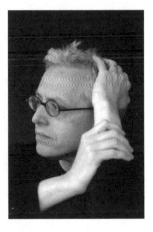

Note: This is the Broadway version of *The Country House*, which differs slightly from the acting edition published by Dramatists Play Service.

For Dana Morosini Reeve

Production History

The Country House was originally commissioned by Manhattan Theatre Club. Lynne Meadow, Artistic Director, Barry Grove, Executive Producer, with funds provided by Bank of America.

The Country House was produced by Manhattan Theatre Club on Broadway at the Samuel J. Friedman Theatre from October 2 to November 23, 2014, with the following cast:

Cast

SUSIE KEEGAN: Sarah Steele
ANNA PATTERSON: Blythe Danner
MICHAEL ASTOR: Daniel Sunjata
ELLIOT COOPER: Eric Lange
NELL MCNALLY: Kate Jennings Grant
WALTER KEEGAN: David Rasche

Creative Team

Directed by Daniel Sullivan
Scenic Design by John Lee Beatty
Costumes by Rita Ryack
Lighting by Peter Kaczorowski
Sound by Obadiah Eaves
Original Music by Peter Golub
Fight Direction by Thomas Schall
Production Stage Manager: James FitzSimmons

Characters

SUSIE KEEGAN, twenty-one, a college student, the plainly lovely daughter of a recently deceased actress named Kathy and

WALTER KEEGAN, sixty-six, a successful film and stage director;

granddaughter of **ANNA PATTERSON**, the matriarch, a great and famous actress; and

niece of her late mother's brother, **ELLIOT COOPER**, forty-four, a failed actor and aspiring playwright.

MICHAEL ASTOR, forty-five, a ruggedly handsome, charismatic actor and longtime family friend, who has become famous playing a doctor on a hit TV series.

It is the family's first gathering since Kathy's death, and Walter has brought along his new actress-girlfriend, **Nell McNally**, early forties, an intelligent, inscrutable beauty.

ACT I
Scene 1: Friday afternoon. Scene 2: Later that night.

ACT II
Scene 1: An afternoon a few days later.
Scene 2: Later that night.

INTERMISSION

ACT III
Scene 1: The following day.
Scene 2: Later. Dusk.

ACT I

A century-old house in the Berkshires, near Williamstown, Massachusetts, it has long been the summer home of a family of theater people. Bought for a song four decades ago, it has changed relatively little over the years, and what improvements that were made were done piecemeal. Still, it is not without charm. Secondhand furnishings, collected over decades, somehow work in concert to convey cozy, Bohemian chic. (Look closely and you will see the decay.) Warped wooden shelves are crammed with mildewed, summer-reading paperbacks; arts and crafts made by two generations of children on rainy summer days; box games, a motley assortment of sporting equipment. Vintage posters from the Williamstown Theatre Festival and framed, faded production stills adorn the walls. Screened French doors open onto a brick patio and a garden. A kitchen, dining room, and bathroom are accessible; a staircase leads to a warren of bedrooms on the second floor.

Scene 1

[*At rise: A humid, overcast afternoon in early summer.* Susie, *barefoot in a black cotton dress, comes downstairs with earbuds in, listening to music. She chooses a photo album from the bookshelf and sits on the couch. We hear (but* Susie *does not) a car pull up on a gravel driveway, its motor turned off, a car door shut.* Anna, *sunglasses on, makes her entrance carrying canvas bags of groceries.*]

ANNA [*Entering.*] Darling, I can use a hand. [*With bags.*] Hello-o-o?

[ANNA *comes closer, startling* SUSIE.]

SUSIE God, Granna, you almost gave me a heart attack!

ANNA How do you expect to hear anything, those stupid things in your ears?

SUSIE You could have at least made your presence known.

ANNA I entered the room. I am not one whose entrances go unnoticed. Except, apparently, by my own granddaughter. Come here, you.

[ANNA *opens her arms to* SUSIE, *kisses the top of her head.*]

I haven't seen you in so long.

SUSIE You saw me winter break.

ANNA Feels like ages. You. Are a lifesaver. Thank you so much for opening the house.

SUSIE You're welcome.

ANNA The very thought of walking into this empty house . . .

SUSIE I know.

ANNA Something, isn't it? Rooms so alive with someone . . . once she's gone . . . all that's left is stuff.

[ANNA *regards* SUSIE.]

SUSIE What.

ANNA You look more and more like your mother.

SUSIE I look *nothing* like my mother.

ANNA When did you get here?

SUSIE Last night. One of my suitemates gave me a ride from New Haven.

[SUSIE *brings the bags into the kitchen.*]

ANNA [*Calls.*] How can you wear black on a hot summer day? It makes me sweat to just look at you.

SUSIE [*Offstage.*] That's a fallacy, you know.

ANNA Who said? Black is a heat magnet. And it's depressing.

[SUSIE *returns.*]

I need you to run lines with me later.

SUSIE Do I have to? I read horribly.

ANNA You do not. You read wonderfully.

[*Remembers to ask.*]

Whose Porsche is sitting out there?

SUSIE Dad's. Doesn't it just cry out "Male Menopause"?

ANNA [*Lower voice.*] Is he here?

[*Meaning upstairs.*]

SUSIE Went for a run.

ANNA [*Surprised.*] Your father's running?

SUSIE See: Porsche above.

ANNA Did he bring the girlfriend?

SUSIE Oh, yeah. What kind of man brings his girlfriend to his dead wife's family's house? And what kind of woman goes with him?

ANNA What's she like?

SUSIE [*Shrugs.*] Beautiful.

ANNA And Elliot . . . ?

SUSIE Uncle Elliot is napping. Uncle Elliot naps.

ANNA Your Uncle Elliot naps . . . far too much.

[*She picks up a discarded liquor bottle.*]

What are you doing inside on such a gorgeous day?

SUSIE Waiting for *you.*

ANNA Well, go! Shoo! Shouldn't you be out having unprotected sex with people your own age?

SUSIE I'm with people my own age all year long.

ANNA So what? It's summertime! You know, I just got a look at some of this year's apprentices. They're adorable.

SUSIE They're *always* adorable.

ANNA You should hang out with them.

SUSIE Why? They're all actors.

ANNA What's wrong with actors?

SUSIE I hate actors.

ANNA You do not hate actors. Your whole *family* is actors.

SUSIE Exactly.

ANNA Very funny. Speaking of actors . . . Guess who I just ran into at Wild Oats.

SUSIE Who?

ANNA Michael Astor.

SUSIE [*Blushes.*] You're kidding. What was he doing there?

ANNA He's doing a play up here.

SUSIE I know. What was he doing at Wild Oats?

ANNA Shopping for food.

SUSIE Michael shops for food? Doesn't he have, like, little assistants who run errands for him?

ANNA Maybe in LA he does. He was by himself. Posing for people's iPhones.

SUSIE *That* must've been a scene: Michael Astor in produce.

ANNA *I* actually got a lot more looks than *he* did. I didn't recognize him right away; he's grown some sort of mustache.

SUSIE Eew.

ANNA He was supposed to move into his sublet today but there were bugs or something. They were going to put him in some board member's house—that awful woman with the high-decibel voice—I said absolutely not, he was staying *here*.

SUSIE [*Distressed.*] Here?!

ANNA For one or two nights.

SUSIE One or *two*?

ANNA Until they can fumigate his sublet.

SUSIE How could you do this to me?!

ANNA What am I doing to you? You *love* Michael.

SUSIE I *do* love Michael. In theory. And on television. That doesn't mean I want him staying in our house. . . .

ANNA I thought you'd be thrilled.

SUSIE He's rich. . . . Couldn't he stay at a hotel? What about The Williams Inn?

ANNA Michael Astor is not going to stay at The Williams Inn—not when he has us.

SUSIE The least you could have done was ask me first.

ANNA Excuse me? This is still *my* house, young lady. I thought it would be festive having him here.

SUSIE   "Festive?!"

ANNA   Given the circumstances. He'll be a welcome distraction.

SUSIE   [*Vulnerably.*] But . . . I thought this was going to be, you know: just us. Immediate family.

ANNA   Oh, honey.

SUSIE   We were going to keep it low-key, look through photo albums and stuff.

ANNA   We *are* keeping it low-key.

SUSIE   No, now thanks to you we have guests to entertain. Michael, Daddy's girlfriend . . .

ANNA   Michael is hardly a guest who needs to be entertained.

[*A car on gravel.*]

SUSIE   Oh, my God!

ANNA   Stop being such a drama queen.

SUSIE   I come by it genetically. [*Car door slams.*] Wait. Where's he gonna sleep?

MICHAEL   [*Offstage.*] Hello?

SUSIE   Shit.

ANNA   [*Brightly.*] In here!

[MICHAEL *enters, with an Italian leather duffle, a bag with bottles of wine and flowers. He indeed sports a mustache.* SUSIE, *blushing at the sight of him, tries to be invisible.*]

MICHAEL   Anna.

ANNA   Michael. Welcome, darling. You remembered how to get here.

MICHAEL   Of course I remembered. These are for you.

[*He kisses her cheek and presents her with the flowers.*]

ANNA   Aren't you sweet! Thank you!

[*He sees* SUSIE *for the first time.*]

MICHAEL   That *can't* be little Susie. . . .

ANNA   It certainly is. . . .

SUSIE   [*Waves wanly.*] Hi, Michael.

MICHAEL   The Susie *I* know is twelve years old. *Look* at you! Are you in college yet? God, you must be.

SUSIE   Yes, I'm in college; I'm practically a college *graduate*.

MICHAEL   *Now* I feel old. What are you majoring in?

SUSIE   Religious studies with a minor in psych?

MICHAEL   Interesting, coming from a family of heathen actors.

SUSIE   It's called reaction formation.

ANNA   Susie's the sane one. Always has been.

MICHAEL   Never got the acting bug?

SUSIE   You mean like scarlet fever or the plague?

ANNA   Ha.

SUSIE   Weren't you just in Africa?

MICHAEL   How did *you* know?

SUSIE   *People* magazine. It's not like it was a secret. . . .

MICHAEL   Oh. Right.

ANNA   Were you shooting a movie or something?

MICHAEL   No no, I go a couple of times a year. To Congo, actually. We're building schools there.

ANNA   Oh, *that's* right. . . .

SUSIE   Isn't that awesome? You've been doing it for a while now, right?

ANNA   Darling, why don't you see if Michael would like something to drink?

SUSIE   Michael, would you like something to drink?

MICHAEL   Why, yes, Susie, I would.

[*He produces a bottle of Pellegrino from a bag.*]

On ice? With lemon?

SUSIE   We don't have lemon.

[*He presents one from the bag.* ANNA *hands her the flowers.*]

ANNA   I'll have the same, dear. Thanks.

SUSIE   Anything else? I'm like a little serf around here. All I need's a little babushka.

ANNA   Shoo!

[*She goes.*]

MICHAEL   She's great.

ANNA   Susie? She's a rock.

MICHAEL Elliot here?

ANNA Napping, apparently.

MICHAEL And Walter . . . ?

ANNA Out running. *With* his new lady friend.

MICHAEL Good for Walter.

ANNA When do you start rehearsal?

MICHAEL Tuesday. You?

ANNA We follow you onto the main stage, so not for another three weeks or so.

MICHAEL What are you going to do up here, take it easy?

ANNA Learn my bloody lines, *that's* what! He used a lot of words, that Mr. Shaw.

MICHAEL Back to Shaw.

ANNA Yup.

MICHAEL *Which* one?

ANNA *Mrs. Warren.* I'm a tad long in the tooth for Mrs. W, but what the hell, it's summer theater. PS: I'm terrified.

MICHAEL Why? You're an old hand at this.

ANNA Key word: "old."

MICHAEL No. . . .

ANNA The noggin's not as reliable as it used to be, my dear. Just when I think I've got it down—*pffft!*—right into the ether.

MICHAEL Happens to everybody.

[ANNA *has taken a framed photo off the wall to show him.*]

Will you look at that: *Candida. How* many years ago?

ANNA Twenty . . . four? What a marvelous Marchbanks you were.

MICHAEL Look what a boy I was! I could be that boy's *father!*

ANNA Don't talk to *me* about getting older. When you're *my* age, *you'll* still get the girl. *I'm* lucky if I get to play Grandma.

MICHAEL I had such a crush on you. . . .

ANNA And every girl and boy was in love with *you.*

MICHAEL I couldn't believe my good luck: playing love scenes with *Anna Patterson!*

ANNA   "Eugene: why are you so sad? Did the onions make you cry?"

MICHAEL   Your memory is going? Yeah, right.

ANNA   Lines I memorized twenty-five years ago are not the problem.

[*She touches his face.*]

"Poor boy! Am I so cruel? Did I make it slice nasty little red onions?"

[*They look at one another. Silence. A spark?* MICHAEL *isn't sure.* SUSIE, *oblivious, returns with drinks.*]

SUSIE   What's for dinner?

ANNA   They had these beautiful rib eyes; I thought we'd throw them on the grill.

SUSIE   [*Sarcastic.*] Great.

ANNA   What.

SUSIE   I don't eat meat, remember?

ANNA   Oh, of course.

SUSIE   How come nobody around here ever remembers I'm a vegetarian?

ANNA   I forgot. Forgive me.

SUSIE   It's hostile, Gran, it really is.

ANNA   Oh, please. I can't keep track of all your fads.

SUSIE   "Fads?" I have a gluten allergy. A gluten allergy isn't a fad, it's a diagnosis. I *can't* eat gluten and I *don't* eat meat. What's so difficult to remember about that?

ANNA   Who even *heard* of gluten till a few years ago?

[*To* MICHAEL.]

Did you?

[*He shrugs.*]

Now it's the scourge of the nation.

MICHAEL   [*Whispers, to* SUSIE.] I don't eat meat, either.

SUSIE   Ha! Michael doesn't eat meat, either!

ANNA   You don't? How stupid of me! I didn't think to ask.

MICHAEL   Don't worry. I'm sure there'll be plenty for me to eat. Hey, where should I put my stuff?

ANNA   Susie'll show you.

SUSIE   Where?

Anna   I thought you could give Michael *your* room.

Susie   Oh.

Michael   You don't have to do that. . . . Where will Susie sleep?

Anna   Down here. On the couch.

Michael   No, no, I'll sleep down here.

Anna   She doesn't mind.

Michael   I'm more than happy to sleep on the couch.

Susie   This is actually a much better deal, believe me: My bed sucks.

Anna   You're not really going to let Michael sleep in the living room. . . .

Michael   I don't mind! Really!

Susie   He doesn't mind!

Anna   Well, I'm not going to argue with you.

[Anna *gives* Susie *a look as she exits to the kitchen.*]

Susie   I hope you don't think I'm a brat. 'Cause I'm really not.

Michael   Not at all. I crashed many a night on this couch. Back in the old days. I'm kinda looking forward to it.

[*Pause.*]

I was crazy about your mother, I hope you know that.

Susie   I know. You were lovers.

Michael   What?! Who told you *that*?

Susie   *She* did. Before she died she told me about *all* her lovers.

Michael   Jesus. That must've been some conversation.

Susie   It was.

Michael   We met *here*, you know. At Williamstown.

Susie   I know.

Michael   Not much older than you are now.

Susie   Uh-oh. This isn't gonna be like *Mamma Mia* or something, turns out you're my real father?

Michael   [*Laughs.*] Uh, no. Not that I know of.

Susie   So what's with the mustache?

Michael   What, you don't like it?

Susie   Truthfully?

MICHAEL   Yeah.

SUSIE   Looks stupid.

MICHAEL   [*Amused.*] Stupid?!

SUSIE   You asked me what I thought!

MICHAEL   Yeah, but "stupid"?!

SUSIE   Why'd you grow it?

MICHAEL   For the play I'm doing.

SUSIE   What play is it?

MICHAEL   *The Guardsman.*

SUSIE   Never heard of it.

MICHAEL   It's old. It's a comedy.

SUSIE   Is it funny? Or is it one of those old comedies that isn't funny?

MICHAEL   No, it's funny. Kinda. I wanted something light.

SUSIE   Your character has a mustache?

MICHAEL   It doesn't say specifically.

SUSIE   Then why did you grow one?

MICHAEL   That's how I saw him.

SUSIE   With a mustache.

MICHAEL   Yeah. It helps me find my character.

SUSIE   You need facial hair to find your character? That's lame.

MICHAEL Why? Olivier loved noses, prosthetic noses. . . .

SUSIE   Yeah, but that was Olivier.

MICHAEL   Thanks a lot.

SUSIE   No offense. I mean, who are you fooling? You're one of those actors, no matter what you do, you'll always be you.

MICHAEL   I'm not sure how I should take that. . . .

SUSIE   I guess that's what it means to be a star.

MICHAEL   What.

SUSIE   You give people pleasure just by being *you.* They don't care what play you're in or what part you're playing, all they care about is seeing *you.* In the flesh. Like, when my grandmother walks out onstage?

MICHAEL   Yeah . . . ?

Susie   I love looking around at the audience. Everybody's beaming. Just at the sight of her. They *love* her. You feel their love for her. Give the people what they want.

Michael   What.

Susie   You! Michael Astor! Not some character with a stupid mustache. Besides, you have a nice upper lip.

Michael   You think I have a nice upper lip?

Susie   Oh, come on, you know you do. God.

Michael   What.

Susie   Actors. You're all alike. No matter how beautiful and famous you are . . .

[*He laughs.*]

What.

Michael   You're funny.

Susie   Gee, thanks. What do you care what I think, anyway?

Michael   I care very much.

Susie   Why?

Michael   [*Shrugs.*] I like you. I'm fond of you.

Susie   Eew.

Michael   What.

Susie   "Fond."

Michael   What's wrong with "fond"?

Susie   You're fond of dogs. Or Indian food. How do you know you're fond of me? You don't even know me.

Michael   What do you mean I don't know you, I knew you in utero!

Susie   Yeah, but that's not the same as *knowing* me.

Michael   You're a tough house, you know that?

Susie   So what happened with you and your girlfriend?

Michael   What?!

Susie   Didn't you have like a bitter breakup?

Michael   How do you know these things?!

Susie   It was like everywhere! What *is* it with you and those gorgeous skinny models, anyway?

MICHAEL   What do you mean?

SUSIE   They all have, like, this disturbingly wide gap between their legs that doesn't even seem anatomically possible.

MICHAEL   Okay.

SUSIE   I mean, they're incredibly picturesque. But they don't seem very . . . I don't know, *substantial*. I guess substantial isn't what you're looking for, huh. You just want women who are functional and decorative.

MICHAEL   Alright . . .

SUSIE   I mean, if you were seriously looking for a wife and the mother of your children, you could have any woman in the world. . . . But I guess you're not there yet. Look at my dad: He was like forty-five when I was born, so there's hope for you.

MICHAEL   [*Quasi-amused.*] Who *are* you?

[ELLIOT *comes downstairs.*]

ELLIOT   Susie, why'd you let me sleep so late? I *told* you to wake me up!

SUSIE   I'm sorry! I forgot! I was busy!

[*She points to* MICHAEL.]

ELLIOT   Wow! Look who's here!

MICHAEL   Hey!

SUSIE   [*Exiting, calls.*] Gran? Uncle Elliot's up!

ELLIOT   I *heard* you were going to be up here. . . .

MICHAEL   Drove up this afternoon.

[*The men embrace.*]

ELLIOT   [*Re: the mustache.*] What the fuck is *this*?

MICHAEL   It's just . . .

[ANNA *enters with a vase of flowers.*]

ANNA   [*Entering.*] Hello, darling, have you rejoined the living?

[*She offers* ELLIOT *her cheek, which he kisses.*]

ELLIOT   Hello, Mother. Look who the cat dragged in!

ANNA   Not the cat, dear, little old me. I found him at the supermarket.

ELLIOT   The *super*market? With all us mere mortals?

MICHAEL   Fuck you.

ELLIOT   Where you staying?

MICHAEL   Here, apparently.

ELLIOT   [*Unpleasantly surprised.*] Oh!

[*Looks at* ANNA.]

Wow!

MICHAEL   The house I was supposed to move into, they'd set off this toxic insect bomb in it; started choking the minute I walked in. So, until they can air the place out . . .

ANNA   [*Returning to the kitchen.*] I *insisted* he stay with *us*!

MICHAEL   Persuasive woman, your mother.

ELLIOT   You're telling *me*.

MICHAEL   Hey, I told your mom: I am so sorry I didn't make it to the thing for Kathy.

ELLIOT   That's alright. You sent flowers . . . and all that food. . . .

MICHAEL   I should've been here.

ELLIOT   You were shooting. What actor wouldn't understand that? Kathy certainly would. . . .

MICHAEL   I should've come last summer. I kept telling myself there'd be time.

ELLIOT   We all did.

MICHAEL   I'm one of those people who has a hard time with hospitals.

ELLIOT   [*Faux analytical.*] And yet you play a doctor on TV. Hm . . .

MICHAEL   I know. Ironic, isn't it?

ELLIOT   She died *here*, actually.

[*Meaning this room.*]

MICHAEL   Oh.

ELLIOT   Put a hospital bed right here. Facing the garden. Just as she wanted. My beautiful sister. Gone.

MICHAEL   Unbelievable.

ELLIOT   *I* can't believe it and I was here when she died. "After a heroic battle with cancer." Isn't that what they like to say? *What* "heroic battle?" Cancer beat the living shit out of her.

MICHAEL   I'm sorry, man. I know what she meant to you.

ELLIOT   Thanks.

MICHAEL   Have you seen Walter?

ELLIOT   Is he here?

[MICHAEL *nods.*]

Must have arrived while I was napping.

MICHAEL   Apparently he's out jogging.

ELLIOT   [*Chortles derisively.*] Jogging?! He has a girlfriend. Do you know he has a girlfriend, my brother-in-law?

MICHAEL   Uh-huh. So I heard. Have you met her?

ELLIOT   No, not yet. This is her debut.

MICHAEL   Ah.

ELLIOT   That didn't take very long, did it. My sainted sister barely in the ground and that sonofabitch—

MICHAEL   [*Calming.*] Now, now.

ELLIOT   How's *your* love life? No, don't tell me.

MICHAEL   I haven't been in love with anybody in a long time.

ELLIOT   Really? What about that last model-hyphen-girlfriend of yours?

MICHAEL   That was just . . . There are all these women parading through my life who are too willing, too accessible. Sometimes I feel like I'm being used for sex so they'll have a story to tell their friends.

ELLIOT   [*A beat.*] Yeah, I *hate* when that happens.

MICHAEL   Yeah, well, a steady diet of that isn't very nourishing. You begin to feel not so good about yourself. How have *you* been?

ELLIOT   Well, I wasn't exploited for sex and luck into a hit series, if *that's* what you mean. You want to know what I *am* doing?

MICHAEL   What.

ELLIOT   [*A beat.*] I'm writing.

MICHAEL   What do you mean?

ELLIOT   I'm writing!

MICHAEL   *What* are you writing?

ELLIOT   I'm writing a *play*, actually.

MICHAEL   A play! Really! A full-length play?

ELLIOT   Yes. A full-length play. Why? Is that so hard to believe?

MICHAEL   No, it's just, I didn't know you wrote plays.

ELLIOT   I didn't; this is my first.

MICHAEL   Congratulations.

ELLIOT   Well, not since I was twelve; Kathy and I would put on these little skits for the amusement of our mother, the queen. But this play: it's as if it had been inside me all along, it practically wrote itself. I've found my calling, Michael, I really have.

MICHAEL   Wow, that's exciting.

ELLIOT   You're the first person I've told, so keep it on the q.t. I haven't had the guts to say it out loud before: I'm a playwright. I. Am. A playwright. I'm ready to give up acting.

MICHAEL   Really!

ELLIOT   Well, that's not entirely accurate: In order to give up acting I have to have *been* acting. Announcing that I'm ready to give up *auditioning* doesn't have quite the same impact.

MICHAEL   I'd love to read it. Can I?

ELLIOT   I'm almost done; I still haven't cracked the last scene. Hoping to have a reading while I'm up here.

MICHAEL   Oh, yeah?

ELLIOT   It's good, Michael, I think it's really good.

MICHAEL   I'm sure.

ELLIOT   Why are you sure?

MICHAEL   You're a bright guy. . . .

ELLIOT   Not every bright guy can write a good play.

MICHAEL   True. But you've been around theater all your life. . . . It's in the genes.

ELLIOT   Are you patronizing me?

MICHAEL   What? No! I'm trying to be encouraging!

[*Smiling.*]

Jesus, Elliot, what the—!

NELL   [*Off, calls.*] HELLO? CAN SOMEONE HELP?!

[WALTER's *ad-libbed offstage protests are heard.*]

WALTER   [*Offstage.*]. I can do it. . . . It's not such a big deal. . . . (etc.)

[MICHAEL *runs out.*]

MICHAEL   [*Offstage.*] What's going on?

WALTER   [*Offstage.*] Michael . . . !

MICHAEL   [*Offstage.*] Hello, Walter.

[WALTER *enters being assisted by* MICHAEL *and* NELL. NELL *and* WALTER *are in running clothes.* ELLIOT *is stunned when he sees* NELL.]

WALTER   . . . Didn't expect to find *you* here.

ELLIOT   [*Passively.*] Mother? Susie? Something's wrong with Walter.

[ANNA *and* SUSIE *run out.*]

ANNA   What happened?!   **SUSIE**   Daddy?!

[*Overlapping introductions are made and* WALTER *is ministered to by everyone but* ELLIOT, *who remains on the periphery.*]

WALTER   Some entrance, huh? Anna!

ANNA   Hello, darling.

WALTER   Whataya know, the gang's all here.

SUSIE   Sit him down here.

NELL   He has a bad knee. I never should've let him run. . . .

WALTER   It's my own damn fault.

SUSIE   Would ice help? I'll go get ice.

WALTER   [*To* SUSIE.] Thanks, kiddo.

[SUSIE *goes.*]

ANNA   [*To* WALTER.] What did you do to yourself?

WALTER   Fucking knee.

ANNA   Poor Walter. Why didn't you call? We would've come to fetch you.

NELL   We didn't have our phones.   **WALTER**   Didn't take our phones.

[SUSIE *returns with a bag of frozen peas.*]

SUSIE   Well, that wasn't very smart, was it.

ANNA   It was an emergency. You could've knocked on someone's door.

NELL   That's what I told him. He refused.

WALTER   My fucking knee went out! It's not like I had a heart attack. . . .

SUSIE   What if you did?! You could have . . . !

NELL   Miss Patterson, I have to say . . . I am such a fan.

ANNA   Oh, thank you, dear. Tell me your name again?

NELL   Nell.

ANNA   Nell. Right.

MICHAEL   [*Attempting levity.*] I'm not a doctor, but I play one on TV. . . . May I . . . ?

WALTER   Well, it's a little tender.

[MICHAEL *palpates* WALTER'S *knee.*]

Ow!

MICHAEL   Sorry!

ANNA   I think I have Vicodin. You want a Vicodin?

WALTER   May not be a bad idea.

ANNA   [*To* SUSIE.] Honey, go look my medicine cabinet.

WALTER   I should go lie down.

[SUSIE *runs upstairs ahead of* MICHAEL *and* ANNA, *who help* WALTER.]

MICHAEL   [*Extending his hand.*] I'm Michael, by the way.

NELL   I know who you are. Nell McNally.

MICHAEL   Nice to meet you, Nell.

[WALTER *tries to get up.*]

NELL   Oh, honey . . .

WALTER   Sorry to be such a gimp. Bet you never thought life with me would be so exciting.

NELL   I knew.

[*As he goes past,* WALTER *notices* ELLIOT.]

WALTER   [*Surprised.*] Elliot!

ELLIOT   Walter.

WALTER   I didn't see you there!

[ELLIOT *waves in greeting. Ad-libs as the others go upstairs.*]

ANNA   Careful on those stairs, they're uneven. . . .

MICHAEL   Walter, I never told you how sorry I was about Kathy.

WALTER   I know you were, champ.

MICHAEL   [*Offstage.*] I wish I could have made it to the memorial. . . .

[ELLIOT *and* NELL *are alone. Pause.*]

ELLIOT   [*A la Bogart.*] "Of all the gin joints in all the towns in all the world . . ."

NELL   Hello, Elliot.

ELLIOT   So *you're* the new girlfriend. How do you like that?

NELL   How've you been?

ELLIOT   How've I been: Gee, let's see. . . . Eleven years? A couple of years ago: Okay. Last year? Not so hot.

NELL   I'm sorry about your sister.

ELLIOT   Yeah, thanks.

NELL   I should have written you.

ELLIOT   That would have been nice.

NELL   I'm sorry I never got to work with her; she sure was a wonderful actress.

ELLIOT   Lucky for you, though, huh, Walter bein' a big Hollywood director an' all.

NELL   I should go see how he is.

[*She starts to go.*]

ELLIOT   [*Derisively.*] Jogging!

NELL   [*Stops.*] What?

ELLIOT   The man is, what, sixty-six years old?

NELL   That's not old.

ELLIOT   Running around outside in his brand-new little jogging suit? In ninety-degree heat?

NELL   It isn't ninety degrees.

ELLIOT   He's lucky he didn't have a massive coronary. Or a devastating stroke.

NELL   He's an incredibly *vigorous* sixty-six year-old, if you ask me.

ELLIOT   I *didn't*. Ask you.

[*A beat.*]

Where've you been?

NELL   I moved to LA.

ELLIOT   [*A la Palin.*] How'd that work out for ya?

NELL   Episodic work here and there, a few pilots that didn't get picked up. . . .

ELLIOT   How is it possible?

NELL   What.

ELLIOT   You're lovelier than ever.

NELL   I'm not.

ELLIOT   Eleven years, for you, have been a gift.

NELL   Hardly.

ELLIOT   Time . . . has only toyed with me, made me more foolish. You . . . ?
Only more exquisite.

[*Pause.*]

Nellie . . .

NELL   Don't.

ELLIOT   Did all those weeks in Louisville . . .

NELL   Elliot . . .

ELLIOT   . . . doing that terrible play . . . mean nothing?

NELL   Of course not.

ELLIOT   We were inseparable! Every day for weeks! Onstage and off!

NELL   We made the most of a bad situation, that's all; made it *bearable* for
each other.

ELLIOT   No no, more than that, more than just bearable: *Bliss.*

NELL   Bliss?

WALTER   [*Off, from upstairs.*] Nell?

NELL   [*Calls.*] Yes? Need anything?

WALTER   [*Offstage.*] Only you.

NELL   [*Calls.*] Be right there.

ELLIOT   Tell me something: When you took up with Walter . . . I'm
curious; this is fascinating. Surely you knew he and I were related.

NELL   Of course I knew.

ELLIOT   Did you even bother telling him about Louisville. . . .

NELL   Yes.

ELLIOT   . . . or was it such an insignificant blip in your life it wasn't worth
mentioning?

NELL   No, I told him.

ELLIOT   So when you knew you were coming here, you didn't think
preparing me might have been the right thing to do?

NELL   "Preparing" you?

ELLIOT   A postcard? An e-mail? "By the way, I'm fucking your dead sister's
husband?"

NELL   Don't be disgusting.

[*She starts for the stairs; he follows.*]

ELLIOT   Hey ...

NELL   Frankly, I didn't feel I owed you an explanation.

ELLIOT   Oh, really? Why's that?

NELL   We were colleagues, Elliot.

ELLIOT   Colleagues! We weren't just "colleagues" ... !

[*Sudden and piercing.*]

I loved you!

WALTER   [*Offstage, from upstairs.*] Nell?

ELLIOT   I was in love with you!

[*Genuinely, but it can't help sounding patronizing.*]

NELL   You have to make peace with this, Elliot. Walter's asked me to marry him, and I told him I would. Now if you'll excuse me, we'll see you at dinner.

[*She goes upstairs, leaving him dumbfounded.*]

End of Scene

Scene 2

[*Later. Dusk.* ELLIOT, *wearing a "kiss the cook" apron, enters from the patio, followed by* MICHAEL, *who has shaved off his mustache.*]

ELLIOT   It's the first anniversary! That's why we're here!

MICHAEL   Shhh

ELLIOT   [*Lowers voice.*] Does my mother suggest that maybe it's not such a good idea to bring the girlfriend? No! "Bring her along!" she says. Why? Because she loves Walter. Like a son, she says. Never mind they're practically the same age. . . .

MICHAEL   She is beautiful, the girlfriend. . . .

ELLIOT   "Beautiful"? "Beautiful" is too banal a word for what she is. "Radiant" is what she is. "Incandescent."

MICHAEL   Okay. What's the story?

ELLIOT   The story is . . . there is no story. I could have had her, I let her get away. The end.

MICHAEL   When?

ELLIOT   Eleven years ago. We did a play together. In the Humana Festival. You ever been to Louisville in February?

[MICHAEL *shakes his head.*]

We were like sole survivors of a nuclear winter. Clung to one another for dear life. Breakfast, rehearsals, drinks after the show. Did everything but sleep together. It was like—

MICHAEL   You didn't sleep together?

ELLIOT   Sometimes we slept in the same bed but, no, we never slept together—slept together.

MICHAEL   Why not?

ELLIOT   She had a boyfriend back in New York.

MICHAEL   How many weeks?

ELLIOT   Six?

MICHAEL   You shared a bed with this . . . "incandescent, radiant" woman . . .

ELLIOT   I know, how quaint, right?

MICHAEL   . . . for six weeks . . .

ELLIOT   Not every night . . .

MICHAEL   . . . and you never slept with her?!

ELLIOT   I was ecstatic just to be with her. If you can imagine such a thing. Talking. For hours on end. Laughing. She has the most joyful laugh, Nell. Making her laugh was one of the greatest pleasures of my life. Seeing her now? With him? You'd never know she was capable of such joy.

[*We hear voices on the stairs.* MICHAEL *signals for* ELLIOT *to quiet down.*]

Fuckin' vampire. Sucked the life-force right out of her.

[NELL *helps* WALTER *down the stairs.*]

WALTER   Not too late to trade me in for a younger model, you know.

NELL   Not a chance.

WALTER   Why should you be saddled with an old man?

NELL   I'll be old soon enough. Watch: Five years, the bloom'll be off the rose.

WALTER   'L never happen.

[*He kisses her cheek.*]

[ANNA *enters from the kitchen and hands* ELLIOT *a platter.*]

ANNA   Elliot?

[ELLIOT *takes the platter and goes out to the grill; she returns to the kitchen.* NELL *gets* WALTER *settled into a chair.*]

MICHAEL   How's the patient?

NELL   Upright

WALTER   For the time being.

MICHAEL   Here, let me, uh . . .

WALTER   I can manage.

NELL   Let him, Walter, stop being so proud.

[WALTER *relents;* MICHAEL *helps him into a chair.*]

MICHAEL   Hey, gotta earn my keep around here; may as well start now.

[*To* WALTER.]

There you go. . . . How's that?

WALTER   Thank you.

NELL   Hey, didn't you have a mustache?

WALTER   Oh, yeah!

MICHAEL   Susie talked me out of it.

WALTER   Susie, honey, could you uh . . . ?

NELL   I like this better.

MICHAEL   I do, too.

[SUSIE *moves the ottoman closer so he can elevate his leg.*]

WALTER   Thanks, kid.

[*She starts to go. He takes her hand to stop her.*]

Hey. How's my girl?

SUSIE   [*Unsmiling.*] Awesome.

[SUSIE *brusquely extricates her hand and moves away.* MICHAEL *opens wine, serves.* ANNA *enters from the kitchen with a bowl of nuts.*]

NELL   [*To* ANNA.] I love your house.

ANNA   Yeah? Don't look too close. It's sort of like me: it needs work.

WALTER   I was telling Nell about this house, teeming with actors, all summer long, year after year. Everybody came to Anna's.

NELL   Sounds fabulous.

ANNA   It had its moments.

MICHAEL   I even remember some of them.

[*She makes room on the sofa; he joins her.*]

WALTER   [*To* MICHAEL.] Hey, I haven't seen you since your series took off!

NELL   Yes, congratulations!

MICHAEL   Oh, yeah, thanks.

ANNA   I didn't realize it was still on the air.

SUSIE   Still?! It's huge!

MICHAEL   Just wrapped season three.

ANNA   I had no idea.

[ELLIOT *returns from the patio with a foil-wrapped platter of steaks.*]

MICHAEL   Damn thing's taken over my life: Our schedule is insane, and when I'm not shooting, they've got me promoting the show!

ELLIOT   You're not complaining, are you?

MICHAEL   No. . . .

ELLIOT   Because that would be in really bad taste.

[ELLIOT *exits to the kitchen.*]

MICHAEL   I used to think, if I only got a series . . . I'd have it made. I'd never have to worry about anything again.

NELL   Isn't that what every actor thinks?

ANNA   Are you an actress, dear?

NELL   Yes. . . .

SUSIE   [*Sotto.*] I told you that.

[ANNA *shrugs.*]

NELL   I feel like such a fraud telling Anna Patterson I'm an actress.

ANNA   Aren't you sweet. Might I have seen your work?

NELL   Not unless you watch shows intended for pre-adolescent girls. I went from "Hot Neighbor" to "Single Mom" seemingly overnight.

ANNA   Ah.

[ELLIOT *returns from the kitchen, lingers on the periphery.*]

WALTER   Nell's a wonderful actress.

ANNA   Ah!

NELL   Walter . . . You don't know that . . .

WALTER   I've seen enough to know. She's just being modest.

ELLIOT   Isn't it funny how people always say that?

WALTER   What.

ELLIOT   "She's a *wonderful* actress." It's not enough to say that she's an actress, no, she has to be a *wonderful* actress. As if the quality of actress she is, is a reflection on *you*.

WALTER   In this case, it happens to be true.

ELLIOT   I know; we worked together.

WALTER   That's right!

ANNA   You did?

[NELL *nods.*]

When was that?

NELL   Years ago.

ELLIOT   Remember that play I did? In the Humana Festival?

ANNA   Vaguely.

ELLIOT   I did a play? Eleven years ago? In Louisville?

ANNA   I can't keep track of every play you've ever done.

ELLIOT   There haven't been that many.

ANNA   [*To* MICHAEL.] You're a detective or something? On your show?

SUSIE   [*Shocked.*] Granna! Do you honestly not know?

MICHAEL   [*Feigned offense.*] I'm Dr. Alec Matheson, chief of extraterrestrial medicine on *Lunar Pod VI*!

SUSIE   You know, Granna, going around saying how you don't watch TV. . . . It's not even pretentious anymore . . .

ANNA   Why thank you, dear.

SUSIE   . . . It's just plain out of it.

ANNA   I know, everyone's always telling me all the great stuff I'm missing.

SUSIE   You are!

WALTER   You really are.

MICHAEL   Well, my show isn't one of them.

NELL   Oh, I like it.

MICHAEL   Why?

NELL   It's a guilty pleasure.

MICHAEL   Which is another way of saying it's not very good.

NELL   No . . .

ANNA   I hope it's made you rich.

MICHAEL   [*Equivocal.*] It's made me rich. . . .

ANNA   Good!

MICHAEL   The next two years'll make me *very* rich.

ANNA   Even better.

WALTER   And here you are, back in Williamstown, right on schedule. Where *all* ambivalent successful actors come for absolution.

MICHAEL   Guilty.

WALTER   Return to their roots, remind themselves why they got into this business in the first place, work their asses off—for nothing—then fly home to Hollywood, cleansed and virtuous. The Williamstown Cure: Better than a high colonic! Cheers.

[*He raises a glass and drinks.* MICHAEL *does, too.*]

MICHAEL   Cheers.

WALTER   *What* play are you doing up here again?

MICHAEL   *The Guardsman.*

WALTER   Molnar.

MICHAEL   Right.

WALTER   Old chestnut.

MICHAEL   Young director.

ANNA   They're all young.

WALTER   So it seems.

ANNA   This boy director who's doing *Mrs. Warren* . . . Everyone was telling me I *had* to work with him, how brilliant he is.

WALTER   Maybe he is. We were all young once.

ANNA   We shall see. You're so good with Shaw, darling. Remember the time we had on *Candida*?

MICHAEL   Uh-huh.

WALTER   I had a ball directing that show!

ANNA   You must give me notes on *Mrs. Warren.*

WALTER   Sure. Who's your Vivie?

ANNA   Some TV actress.

MICHAEL   Hey, watch it!

ELLIOT   I don't envy *her*. Mother eats ingénues for breakfast.

ANNA   I do not.

ELLIOT   It's true, Mother, you always choose a designated victim, on every production you work on, some underling you can project all your anxieties onto.

ANNA   That's a very uncharitable thing / to say. . . .

ELLIOT   Usually the ingénue. Sometimes the dresser. The green p.a. working for nothing. . . .

WALTER   So your boy director . . .

ANNA   You should see him! He barely shaves!

WALTER   You met with him?

ANNA   I had lunch with him at Orso.

WALTER   And?

ANNA   He was lovely, but so *serious*. Like a grave little prodigy.

WALTER   If you were so unsure about him, why'd you say yes?

ANNA   Because I had to, darling. I had to get back to work. It was time. It'd been a whole year since Kathy . . . Time to get back to the only thing I know how to do. I figured what better place than here? Either that or go insane.

WALTER   I know what you mean.

[*A solemn pause.*]

MICHAEL   I'm looking forward to reading *Elliot's* play.

[**ELLIOT** *shoots him a look.*]

ANNA   Play? What play?

MICHAEL   [*Realizing his faux pas.*] Oh, shit.

WALTER   Elliot, have you written a play?

SUSIE   Have you, Uncle Elliot?

ELLIOT   [*Daggers at* MICHAEL.] Thanks a lot.

MICHAEL   [*Sotto, to* ELLIOT.] I'm sorry, I assumed it was common knowledge.

ELLIOT   Why would you assume *that*? I *told* you . . .

WALTER   I want to hear about this play!

ANNA   Yes, tell us!

ELLIOT   There's nothing to tell. I'm writing a play.

WALTER   A full-length play?

ELLIOT   Yes, a full-length play.

ANNA   Mm! Isn't that wonderful.

ELLIOT   Two acts and everything. I even typed it myself. See? This is why I didn't want to tell you people.

ANNA   Who are you calling "you people?" We're your family! Since before when are we "you people?"

ELLIOT   Since the day I was born?

ANNA   Oh, you.

ELLIOT   Everybody gets that tone with me.

ANNA   What tone?

ELLIOT   "A play! Wow! Isn't that marvelous!" Like I'm a moron or an out-patient or something.

MICHAEL   Jesus, Elliot. . . .

SUSIE   Oh, Uncle Elliot. . . .

ANNA   Oh, God. . . .

WALTER   That's all in your head, champ.

ELLIOT   Oh, yeah? All in my head?

WALTER   I think it's *super* you've written a play.

ELLIOT   Super.

WALTER   Yes. I'm jealous. It's quite an accomplishment.

ELLIOT   You're jealous? Of me?

WALTER   That you actually had the discipline to sit down and write a full-length play? You bet I am. What can you tell us about it?

NELL   Yes, what's it about?

SUSIE   Yeah, Uncle Elliot.

ELLIOT   I don't really feel comfortable talking about it.

NELL   Oh, okay.

ELLIOT   Playwrights shouldn't discuss their work. It's so . . . reductive. The work should speak for itself.

WALTER   You've written *how* many plays?

ELLIOT   One.

WALTER   Uh-huh. Have you *heard* this one yet?

ELLIOT   Actually, I'm thinking of having a reading while I'm here.

ANNA   Good idea. With whom?

ELLIOT   Well, I was thinking all of *you.*

ANNA   Oh!

ELLIOT   I got some excellent feedback on the first act. . . .

WALTER   Oh, yeah?

ELLIOT   People who were really blown away by it.

WALTER   Who?

ELLIOT   What?

WALTER   *Who* was blown away by it?

ELLIOT   Knowledgeable people. Who read a lotta lotta scripts.

WALTER   Who, exactly?

ELLIOT   This guy at my agency for one. Very smart kid. Really knows his stuff.

WALTER   An intern?

ELLIOT   [*A beat.*] So?

[*To* SUSIE.]

Went to Yale, actually. Ethan somebody?

SUSIE   [*Shrugs.*] They're all named Ethan.

MICHAEL   [*Changing the subject.*] So: Nell—right?

[*She nods.*]

How did you meet Walter?

NELL   [*To* WALTER.] Can I tell them?

WALTER   *I* have nothing to hide.

NELL   We met at Starbucks.

SUSIE   Eew, you're kidding.

NELL   I know.

ELLIOT   Didn't see *that* coming.

WALTER   I'd just finished auditions for the picture I'm about to do. . . .

ELLIOT   You mean people actually audition for those things?

WALTER   . . . and there, sitting at a table outside, was this . . . angel, crying into her latte.

ANNA   Oh, dear.

NELL   Soy latte.

MICHAEL   Why were you crying?

NELL   Let's just say I was having a bad day.

MICHAEL   What happened?

NELL   It's too trivial to go into. Actor stuff: I was up for a pilot; I didn't get it. I told you it was trivial.

MICHAEL   What was it?

NELL   Some police-procedural thing I didn't even want—that's the thing, I didn't even want it and it still felt like the end of the world. And I started sobbing big existential tears. People looked at me like I was crazy, mothers moved their children away.

Then this lovely, compassionate man offered me a napkin and sat down and asked what was wrong, and we talked, for hours, till the sun went down, and he told me about the terrible loss he was going through, and that his *family* was going through, which was a gift, really, because it certainly put my ridiculous crisis into perspective—and it was only then that I realized who this wonderful man was.

WALTER   What can I say? I was enchanted.

[*They kiss.*]

ANNA   [*Put off by the kiss; to* SUSIE, *signaling.*] Shall we . . . ?

SUSIE   Okay, I made a gigunda salad for me and Michael and for anybody else who abhors the murder of animals.

ANNA   And on that note: Dinner is served!

[*The* COMPANY *files into the dining room,* MICHAEL *walks beside* NELL.]

MICHAEL   [*To* NELL.] I want to hear more about your existential crisis.

NELL   [*Amused.*] Why? It's not terribly interesting.

MICHAEL   Oh, I don't know about that. . . .

[ANNA *slips her arm through* MICHAEL's.]

ANNA   [*To* MICHAEL.] You sit by me.

[*They exit;* ELLIOT *and* SUSIE *follow* WALTER.]

ELLIOT   So, Walter: This new picture of yours. What is it? *Truck Stop Three*?

WALTER   *Truck Stop Four*, actually. There's already been a *Truck Stop Three*.

ELLIOT   Oh, of course. How could I forget? They're so distinct from one another.

[WALTER *shakes his head and exits.*]

SUSIE   [*Enjoying his sarcasm.*] You are so bad.

ELLIOT   Can't you just see it, twenty years from now . . . ? "Walter, what are you working on?"

[*Imitating a doddering* WALTER *as they start to join the others.*]

"*Truck Stop 19: Attack of the Long-Haul Living Dead!* Where these tractor-trailers—a whole fucking caravan of 'em—loaded with nuclear bombs—and toxic chemicals!—are making these hair-pin turns—in the Rockies! And all of a sudden, this big honking alien-zombie mothership crashes into the mountain. . . ."

[*He makes an exploding sound as they exit.*]

End of Act One

ACT II

Scene 1

[*A few days later. Morning.* NELL, *in running clothes, comes downstairs and stretches before a run.* MICHAEL *emerges from the kitchen with a mug of coffee, surprising her.*]

MICHAEL   Didn't mean to sneak up on you.

NELL   I thought you'd left for the day.

MICHAEL   I'm about to. I just made a fresh pot . . .

NELL   No, thanks. I can't drink coffee before a run.

MICHAEL   [*Nods, then.*] Don't mind me . . .

[*Meaning, continue warming up.*]

NELL   I'm good.

[*A beat.*]

Today's your first day on *The Guardsman*.

MICHAEL   Yup.

NELL   Excited?

MICHAEL   Yeah, I am, actually. I still get that first-day-of-school feeling, whenever I start anything.

NELL   *That's* refreshing. Means you aren't jaded.

MICHAEL   Not about *acting*, anyway.

Nell   I envy you. This business has done nasty things to me, things I'm not terribly proud of.

Michael   How so?

Nell   I'm constantly looking over my shoulder to see who's the new "me" coming up behind me. And resenting them. And wishing them ill. I used to be a much nicer person.

Michael   I think you're a very nice person.

Nell   What makes you think that?

Michael   [*Shrugs.*] Just a hunch.

[*Pause.*]

So, I understand congratulations are in order.

Nell   What do you mean?

Michael   Aren't you and Walter getting married?

Nell   Oh! Yes. How did you know?

Michael   Elliot.

Nell   We are. Susie doesn't know yet; Walter hasn't found a good time to tell her.

Michael   [*Nods, then.*] Walter is a lucky man. First Kathy. Now you.

Nell   I'm the lucky one.

[*A beat.*] You know? I'm not a mystical woo-woo sort of person but we were fated to meet that day; I really believe that. We rescued each other. The love he had for Kathy . . . ! I found it incredibly poignant.

Michael   Poignant? Is that what you look for in a lover? Poignancy?

[*She smiles, shakes her head.*]

What.

Nell   You really think I'm so weak?

Michael   What?

Nell   So susceptible to your irresistible charm?

[*Pause.*]

Michael   As a matter of fact . . . I don't think that at all.

[*Long pause.*]

Nell   Well . . . Have a great first day.

Michael   Thanks. Enjoy your run.

NELL   Will I see you later?

MICHAEL   Oh, I'll be here.

[NELL *nods and goes.* MICHAEL *puts his script and stuff into a small knapsack and he, too, exits.*]

[*Time shift: Later that morning.* ANNA *enters with a tray of iced tea, followed by* SUSIE, *who reads from a copy of Mrs. Warren's Profession.*]

ANNA   [*With English accent.*] "Don't you be led astray by people who don't know the world, my girl. The only way for a woman to provide for herself decently is for her to be good to some man that can afford to be good to her."

[*A slight hesitation.*]

SUSIE   [*Prompting.*] "Ask any—"

ANNA   I know! I was acting!

SUSIE   Sorry.

ANNA   If I need a line, I'll call for it, okay?

SUSIE   Yes, Gran, sorry.

ANNA   "Ask any lady in London society that has daughters; and she'll tell you the same, except that I tell you straight and she'll tell you crooked. That's all the difference."

SUSIE   [*English accent.*] "My dear mother: you are a wonderful woman: you are stronger than all England. And are you really and truly not one wee bit doubtful—or—or ashamed?"

ANNA   "Well, of course, dearie, it's only good manners to be ashamed of it: it's expected from a woman. Women have to pretend to feel a great deal that they don't feel. Liz used to be angry with me for . . ." Line!

SUSIE   ". . .plumping out the truth about it."

ANNA   ". . . plumping out the truth about it. . . . Plumping out the truth about it." Plumping, plumping, plumping. "She even said—"

SUSIE   "—used to say—"

ANNA   What?

SUSIE   "She used to say—"

ANNA   "—used to say"— shit!—"that when every woman could learn enough from what was going on in the world before her eyes, there was no need to mention it—"

SUSIE   [*Parsing it out.*] "no—need—TO—TALK—ABOUT—IT—to—her."

ANNA   You don't have to shout! I may be old but I'm not deaf!

SUSIE   Sorry. I'm sorry.

ANNA   Where was I?

SUSIE   "Plumping out the truth about it."

ANNA   After that.

SUSIE   ""She used to say . . .""

ANNA   [*Quickly, to catch up.*] "She-used-to-say-that-when-every-woman-could-learn-enough-from-what-was-going-on-in-the-world-before-her-eyes,-there-was-no-need-to-mention-it—"

SUSIE   "—TO—TALK—ABOUT—IT—"

ANNA   Fuck! Give me that.

[*She snatches away the script.*]

I'm not ready to run this.

[ANNA *looks over the script. Pause.*]

SUSIE   I can't believe Michael left this morning without saying good-bye.

ANNA   He didn't leave. It's his first day of rehearsal.

SUSIE   You mean he's staying here again?

ANNA   Yes.

SUSIE   I thought he was supposed to spend a night or two.

ANNA   He was.

SUSIE   It's already been four. Isn't his house aired-out yet?

ANNA   Apparently not to his liking. Are you going to let me study?

SUSIE   Sorry.

[SUSIE *watches* ANNA *concentrate on the script. Silence. Do you realize this is the quietest it's been here for days?*]

ANNA   Shhh.

[SUSIE *gets a photo album and begins to leaf through it, distracting* ANNA.]

I don't know how you can look at that. If I see a picture of her somewhere, I have to turn away, quickly, before my brain can tell me whose face I'm looking at. I go through each day trying not to think about her, but I have lapses, I do, I forget she's gone, and want to tell her something, and have to remind myself: Oh, that's right . . . So I play this game with myself. You know what I do?

[SUSIE *shakes her head.*]

I imagine she's working, off on location, shooting a movie.

SUSIE   Where?

ANNA   Someplace magical and far away. One of those remote islands in the Pacific with white-sand beaches and turquoise water; and cloudless, sky-blue skies. And this little island is so off the grid, she can't contact us; as much as she'd like to, she can't. But it's alright because she's having such a marvelous time.

SUSIE   [*Smiling.*] Mm.

[NELL *returns, sweaty and breathless, from her run.*]

NELL   Phew, it's getting humid out there!

[*Sees* SUSIE *return the photo album to the shelf.*

Oh, I'm sorry, am I interrupting something?

ANNA   Not at all. You've rescued me from learning my lines.

NELL   Have you seen Walter?

ANNA   [*Refers to the patio.*] Out there. He hasn't budged.

NELL   [*Sees* WALTER *asleep outside.*] He's sleeping.   Poor baby. His knee kept him up all night.

[SUSIE *walks past* NELL.]

Don't go. Not on my account.

SUSIE   I've got stuff to do anyway.

NELL   Susie . . .

SUSIE   Only my family gets to call me Susie.

[SUSIE *is gone.*]

NELL   I can't seem to say the right thing.

ANNA   Give her time. It's a lot all at once.

[NELL *nods, serves herself iced tea. She sees the Shaw script.*]

NELL   So. *Mrs. Warren's Profession.*

ANNA   Uh-huh.

NELL   I did *Pygmalion* in acting school.

ANNA   Oh? Where was that?

NELL   DePaul? In Chicago?

ANNA   I know where DePaul is.

NELL   Some people don't.

[*A beat.*]

You know? *You* have the career I used to dream about.

ANNA   *I do?*

NELL   Yes. The way you go from stage to film and back to stage again . . . You're a Broadway star.

ANNA   There are no Broadway stars, dear. Not anymore. Oh, there are stars on Broadway but they're not *Broadway* stars. In the old days, every season there'd be the new Gerry Page play, or the new Julie Harris. *They* were Broadway stars. Those days are over. I was born in the wrong era, I'm afraid.

NELL   Why do you say that?

ANNA   *I* can't get something on.

NELL   I can't believe that.

ANNA   My TVQ isn't high enough, my agents tell me. "Do more TV." If I did a series like our friend, Michael . . .

WALTER   [*Entering from the patio.*] Do it.

ANNA   Hello, Walter.

NELL   Hi.

WALTER   Hello, my darling.

NELL   How're you feeling?

WALTER   Old.

ANNA   Join the club.

NELL   How's the knee?

WALTER   Better. I'm gonna have to get the damn thing replaced, no getting around it. But it's going to have to wait till I'm done shooting this picture. I can't tell you how much I'm looking forward to being on set with a bum knee.

NELL   Anna was just saying how she can't get a play on Broadway. I can't believe that.

WALTER   I can.

ANNA   There are no real producers anymore. People with vision. And balls.

WALTER   You can't blame the producers.

ANNA   Why can't I?

WALTER   They have to sell tickets. Can't have them losing their shirts. Then there'd be *no* plays on Broadway.

ANNA   You're quite right, Walter. Why don't you send me out to sea on a fiery barge? Now. Before I'm even dead.

WALTER I wouldn't dream of doing that.

ANNA I'm a throwback. Isn't that awful? To live long enough to be a throwback? A leading lady without a stage. My audience—the matinee ladies and their poor husbands—is dead or dying or going deaf. And I fear I'm not far behind.

NELL No, you look fantastic.

WALTER You do!

ANNA You mean for my age.

NELL I mean for any age.

ANNA I've done a little sprucing up, I admit, a little spackling and sanding here and there.

NELL Well, I'm your audience, too, and I'd love to see you do just about anything.

ANNA Why, thank you, dear.

NELL Would you excuse me? I'm pretty grungy, I've got to take a shower.

[NELL *kisses* WALTER; ANNA *averts her eyes.*]

WALTER Bye, darlin'.

[NELL *goes upstairs. Pause.*]

Thank you for hosting her. I know this can't be easy.

ANNA She's lovely, Walter.

WALTER Isn't she?

ANNA I suppose you'd like my blessing.

WALTER Of course I would.

ANNA I have nothing against her. It's the fact of her I have trouble with.

WALTER I know. It's—

[SUSIE *returns, and heads to the front door.*]

SUSIE Oh. You're awake.

WALTER Hey. Where you going?

SUSIE I promised Gran . . .

ANNA That can wait.

WALTER I feel like I haven't gotten to see you since I got here.

SUSIE Maybe that's 'cause you haven't gotten to see me since you got here.

WALTER Whose fault is that?

[Anna *gives* Susie *a look ("He has a point") and goes to the kitchen so they can be alone.* Susie *reluctantly sits.*]

Thank you.

[*Pause.*]

So? Tell me how you are.

Susie   Fine.

Walter   How are you really?

[Susie *shrugs, doesn't look at him.*]

[*Pause.*]

How'd your term end up?

Susie   Two A's, two A-minuses.

Walter   Great, but that's not what I'm asking.

Susie   You pay my tuition. . . . Don't you want to know if I'm wasting your money?

Walter   I meant . . . I know you were feeling blue.

Susie   Of course I was feeling blue, my mother died. I miss my mother.

Walter   I know you do, kiddo. So do I.

Susie   Really?

Walter   Of course I do. You think I want to forget your mother?

Susie   How could you bring her here?

Walter   Susie.

Susie   How could you bring her to this house?

Walter   I ran it by your grandmother; she said it was okay.

Susie   My grandmother? What about me? Don't I get a say?

Walter   Of course.

Susie Walter   Yeah right.

Walter   Give Nell a chance. Let down your guard. You'll see. She's a fantastic woman. There's a lot about her that reminds me of your mother. They would have liked each other; I mean it, they would have been friends.

Susie   [*Just dawns.*] Oh shit. You're not going to *marry* her. . . .

Walter   Sweetie . . .

Susie   Really, Daddy? Are you really going to *marry* her?

WALTER   Honey . . .

SUSIE   Mom's barely been gone a year.

WALTER   I know, the speed of all this surprised me, too.

SUSIE   Couldn't you live together? Why do you have to run and get married? She's not pregnant, is she?

WALTER   No. Your mother spoiled me: I *like* being married. I like the comfort it brings. I missed that.

[*A beat.*]

This was the only time I could introduce you; I know it's awkward. . . .

SUSIE   You think?

WALTER   I didn't know what else to do! I go back to LA next week, start shooting on the fifteenth. . . . You know how crazy things get. . . .

SUSIE   Oh, I know.

WALTER   Then you go back to school . . . and before you'd know it, we wouldn't be seeing each other again till Thanksgiving or Christmas. I didn't want all that time to go by before you got to meet her. I'm really sorry.

[*Pause.*]

After we buried your mother . . . and I was back in that big house . . . My life felt pretty much over. Certainly my happiness. It was hard for me, too, you know.

SUSIE   I know.

WALTER   Maybe you *don't* know. The minute I saw Nell . . . I felt something I thought I'd never feel again.

SUSIE   You sound like a Lifetime movie.

[*He gives up. Pause.*]

WALTER   We used to be able talk, you and I. Didn't we? I'd drive you to school, way the hell out in Studio City? Sitting in traffic on the 405? We'd talk about everything! I couldn't get you to shut up!

SUSIE   It's easy to talk to your parents when you're in the car, driving. Nobody has to look at each other.

[*A beat.* WALTER *gets an idea.*]

WALTER   Come. Let's go for a ride.

SUSIE   No, I can't. I have to run these errands for Gran.

[*She starts to go; he joins her.*]

Walter   I'll go with you.

[*She thinks about it.*]

Susie   On one condition.

Walter   What.

Susie   You let me drive the Porsche.

Walter   What?!

[*She shrugs ("Take it or leave it.")* Walter *considers it. Pause.*]

Oh, what the hell . . .

[Walter *tosses her the keys. As he limps out with* Susie:]

Walter   The clutch is very sensitive. . . .

Susie   I know how to drive a stick; you taught me. . . .

[*Time shift. Late afternoon. A gentle rain.* Elliot *hurries downstairs holding his unbound manuscript; he's packing it in a satchel when* Nell, *wearing a mac, enters from the patio.*]

Nell   Nice rain. I love that earthy smell.

Elliot   I finished my play.

Nell   Congratulations.

Elliot   I was up all night writing. It was fantastic: I finally figured out how it should end.

Nell   Good for you.

Elliot   You stare at a blank page for days and all of a sudden you know just what to do.

[*They look at one another for a beat.*]

I'm gonna go make copies.

[*He starts to go.*]

Nell   Elliot.

[*He stops.*]

Elliot   Yeah?

Nell   I owe you an apology.

Elliot   Me?

Nell   I *should* have let you know about me and Walter.

Elliot   Wow.   You mean we weren't "just colleagues?"

Nell   I was being disingenuous. Of *course* we were friends.

ELLIOT   [*Joking.*] I'm feeling a little light-headed; you mind if I sit down?

[*He sits on the sofa.*]

So I'm not crazy?

NELL   I didn't *say* that. I said we were friends.

[*She laughs. Pause.*]

ELLIOT   Who would have thought you'd come back into my life this way? *Deus ex* Walter.

NELL   I know, right?

ELLIOT   Do you ever imagine what might have happened if I'd made a move all those years ago?

NELL   No.

ELLIOT   That might have changed everything. But, no, I was too afraid of bursting the bubble. I couldn't risk it. Not for something as fleeting as lust.

NELL   Enough of the hapless, hangdog routine!

ELLIOT   You think I put this on? You think I would choose to be this way? It's exhausting being me. I wouldn't recommend it to anyone.

NELL   You know? You were funny when I met you. You made me laugh.

ELLIOT   You thought I was funny?

NELL   You know I did. Whenever I feel the slightest twinge of affection towards you, you . . .

ELLIOT   You feel affection?

NELL   Oh, stop it. You're your own worst enemy, you know that? I wish you would just—

[*He kisses her mouth. She recoils.*]

Elliot! No!

ELLIOT   I'm sorry, I'm sorry.

[*She moves to the staircase.*]

Don't go.

NELL   [*As she runs upstairs.*] Just when I thought I could have a civilized conversation with you . . . !

ELLIOT   [*A beat; shouts after her.*] Why would you think that?

[*He gets his satchel and goes out the front door.*]

End of Scene

Scene 2

[*Later that night. A roiling and rumbly summer night; a thunderstorm is brewing. The* COMPANY, *drinks in hand, enters the living room after dinner.* MICHAEL *is speaking. The others listen intently, except for* ELLIOT.]

MICHAEL   [*Entering.*] The civil war is so insane. . . . I mean, these tribes are killing each other over fishing rights! Who has the rights to fish in certain ponds! These kids have nothing. No hope. No families. They watch their fathers dragged away, never to be seen again, their mothers raped. Brutalized. Kidnapped. The rebels put guns in the boys' hands and turn them into soldiers when they're as young as six.

WALTER   Six! My God.

MICHAEL   And the girls, well, you can imagine what happens to them.

SUSIE   Uch . . .

WALTER   So, once they're rescued from the rebels . . . ?

MICHAEL   Get 'em into schools. Problem is, there are no schools. They've been burned to the ground, or washed away during rainy season. So we build them.

NELL   You literally build them?

MICHAEL   Uh-huh.

NELL   With your own two hands?

MICHAEL   With my own two hands.

ANNA   Isn't that marvelous?

ELLIOT   [*To* SUSIE.] You got any weed?

SUSIE   What?! No!

MICHAEL   If we can give them a safe haven . . .

ELLIOT   [*A new idea; to* SUSIE.] Ooo, where'd your mom keep her stash?

SUSIE   [*Annoyed.*] I don't know.

ANNA   Elliot!

[ELLIOT *looks around the room.*]

MICHAEL   A safe haven where they're allowed to be kids, not soldiers or sex slaves, and teach them basic skills that might give them a shot at a living wage, they might just have a chance in hell.

NELL   Oh, Michael, that is so . . .

ANNA   [*Sotto, to* ELLIOT.] What are you doing?

ELLIOT   Looking for Kathy's medical marijuana. There's got to be some left.

MICHAEL   This one boy . . .

ELLIOT   Tah-dahh!

[ELLIOT *finds a plastic bag with weed and proceeds to roll a joint.*]

ANNA   Really, Elliot. Not in front of Susie.

SUSIE   Are you kidding? Far worse was done in my presence.

ANNA   Where? At school?

SUSIE   By this family! In this house!

NELL   [*To* MICHAEL.] You were saying about this boy?

ANNA   Sorry, Michael.

SUSIE   [*To* MICHAEL.] Sorry

WALTER   Please. Go on.

NELL   Tell us about that boy. Please.

MICHAEL   He wouldn't speak, or make eye contact. But I sat with him, a few minutes every day I was there, and talked about baseball, soccer, whatever I could think of, and had no idea if anything was getting through to him.

[*A beat.*]

On my last day, I was saying my good-byes, he came up to me—

[*He chokes up.*]

I'll never forget this. He looked up at me—really looked at me, for the first time—and held out this piece of paper. . . .

[*To* NELL.]

He was giving me a present. Something to remember him by. He . . .

[*He's moved.* NELL *is, too, and spontaneously touches his hand, which doesn't go unnoticed by* ANNA.]

NELL   [*Gently.*] Go on.

MICHAEL   He made a drawing. Of the two of us. I still have it.

[*He and* NELL *share a moment.*]

ELLIOT   [*Takes a hit; derisively, to himself.*] Oh, brother.

ANNA   Can I get anyone more wine?

[NELL *removes her hand from* MICHAEL's.]

WALTER   How much does a school like that cost?

MICHAEL   Twenty-five thousand.

WALTER   Where do I send a check?

MICHAEL   Oh, I'll get you the info, don't worry.

WALTER   I'm serious.

MICHAEL   Hey, man, so am I!

ANNA   Bravo, Michael! What a godsend you are!

MICHAEL   No, no. There are people who devote their *lives* to this stuff. I'm just there to help shine a light on it.

ANNA   [*Genuinely.*] Aw . . .

WALTER   We send our checks and buy our tables at fund-raisers, but you actually go there. . . .

NELL   It's true.

ANNA   If more people were like Michael, we . . .

[*The* OTHERS *agree.*]

ELLIOT   [*Loudly, above the murmurs.*] Jesus! You sound like a fucking public service announcement!

SUSIE   Uncle Elliot . . .

ANNA   Elliot. Really. Must you?

ELLIOT   Spare me the self-congratulation.

NELL   That isn't fair.

ANNA   [*To* MICHAEL.] Don't pay attention to him, he's jealous.

ELLIOT   It's all about you! Saint Michael of the Congo!

MICHAEL   It's not about me at all! You don't get it! I lose myself in this work. That's what I love about it.

ELLIOT   You go to the Congo the same reason you come to Williamstown: To feel better about yourself.

WALTER   Jesus, Elliot . . .

MICHAEL   Oh, is that what it's about? Feeling better about myself? I feel better knowing I've done something for the greater good, so yeah.

NELL   [*To* ELLIOT.] What's the alternative? To do nothing? Like you? I'm not saying I'm any better but Michael is saving lives; he's actually doing some good in the world.

SUSIE   Yeah.

MICHAEL   [*To* NELL.] Thank you.

ELLIOT   Of course you think that, that's what he wants you to think.

ANNA   [*To* ELLIOT.] Put. That. Away.

ELLIOT   Anybody want some . . . ?

[*He offers the joint to* SUSIE, *who swats him away.*]

MICHAEL   I'll take a hit of that.

[ELLIOT *passes the joint.*]

SUSIE   [*Admonishing.*] Michael . . . !

MICHAEL   What.

[*He takes a hit.*]

ELLIOT   You and your rich and famous friends . . . you pick your pet causes but it's . . .

MICHAEL   Cut me some slack, man. I figured, if I'm going to be a celebrity or whatever the hell you want to call what I am—I used to be an actor but now I'm a celebrity—then I'm going to put it to good use. Y'know?

ANNA   Hear, hear.

MICHAEL   I refuse to be a prisoner in my own house, behind gates and security cameras. I don't want to live like that. I want to be out in the world and do something. Something that matters. What else am I gonna do? Stay home and party all the time? Fuck around, put shit up my nose? I tried all that; believe me.

SUSIE   You did?

MICHAEL   Lost a good year, year-and-a-half of my life to it.

NELL   [*To* MICHAEL.] What happened?

MICHAEL   It's not worth going into.

[*Rumbles of thunder. Lights brownout, then restore. Oos.*]

WALTER   It's definitely trying to do something out there.

[ELLIOT *stands and clinks his wineglass to get their attention.*]

MICHAEL   [*To* ELLIOT.] Yes . . . ?

ELLIOT   May I have your attention, please?

[ELLIOT *continues clinking for a few seconds after everyone is quiet.*]

MICHAEL   Yes?!

ELLIOT   I suppose you're wondering why I called you all here today. . . . Our father, Art—I mean, Leonard—who art in heaven or wherever the hell he ended up . . .

ANNA   What are you doing?

ELLIOT   It's a good thing Dad didn't live to bury his only daughter; it would've killed him. *Bu-du-bum.* But seriously, folks . . .

[SUSIE *gently tries to rein him in.*]

SUSIE   Why don't we go upstairs?

ELLIOT   I don't want to go upstairs.

[SUSIE *reaches for his glass which he brusquely pulls away. More rumbles. Storm approaching.*]

NELL   [*To* MICHAEL.] Front's coming through.

ELLIOT   Lest we forget why we're here . . . I'd like to propose a toast. To the missing woman. The woman who is missed. Conspicuous in her absence. To Kathy. One year gone. But not forgotten.

[*The* OTHERS *raise their glasses in an awkward toast.*]

OTHERS   [*Not in unison.*] To Kathy!

[*A loud crack of thunder followed by a flash of lightning and torrential downpour.*]

WALTER   Here it comes!

ANNA   It's raining in! Close the doors!

[SUSIE *closes them.*]

MICHAEL   Wow, it's really coming down!

NELL   I love storms like this! I've been in LA too long!

[*Lights flicker and go out entirely! Collective gasp.*]

WALTER   Oh, shit!

ANNA   Oh, no!

ELLIOT   Aha! Kathy's revenge!

[*Ad-libbed pandemonium in the dark.*]

ELLIOT   Where have we got flashlights?

ANNA   I don't remember.

ELLIOT   You don't remember?!

ANNA   Check the kitchen drawer that has everything.

SUSIE   The hurricane lamps!

ANNA   Oh, damn, I left windows open upstairs.

MICHAEL   I'll go.

[*He goes upstairs by the light of his iPhone, followed by* ANNA. *Vignettes play in light provided only by flashlight, hurricane lamp, iPhone, or candle. Time is contiguous; we shift minutes, sometimes seconds between scenes. Steady rain. Rumbles and flashes of lighting. Time shift.* WALTER *and* NELL *snuggle in a chair by hurricane-lamp light.*]

WALTER   Elliot's in rare form tonight.

NELL   It's alright. I can handle Elliot.

WALTER   I shouldn't have brought you here. It was selfish.

NELL   No . . .

WALTER   I had to be here. For Susie.

NELL   Of course you did.

WALTER   How are you holding up?

NELL   Okay. I feel a little like Joan Fontaine in *Rebecca*, but aside from that . . .

WALTER   Am I a terrible man?

NELL   Yes, you're awful.

[*She kisses him; their kissing progresses. More thunder.*]

WALTER   [*Remembers.*] Oh, shit!

NELL   What.

WALTER   I left the top down on the Porsche!

[*He hobbles off, cursing his pain.*]

NELL   Walter! Wait!

[NELL *goes after him.*]

[*Time shift:* MICHAEL *enters, followed by* ELLIOT, *and begins to get ready for bed.* ELLIOT *dons a windbreaker.*]

MICHAEL   Why must you be so fucking cynical?

ELLIOT   Earnest, holier-than-thou bullshit does that to me. You're not running for student council president, for crissake!

MICHAEL   What the fuck does that even mean?

ELLIOT   You don't need to play up the activism to impress girls!

MICHAEL   I'm not "playing up" anything.

ELLIOT   If this is what helps you get laid . . .

MICHAEL   Whoa! First of all, this may come as a shock to you but I need very little help getting laid, thank you. And, secondly, I certainly don't need to exploit women's sympathy to do it. When did you get to be such an asshole?

Elliot   [*Shrugs.*] I've always been kind of an asshole. I mean, really, when you think about it.

Michael   Y'know? You may be onto something there. . . .

[Elliot *starts to go.*]

Where are you going?

Elliot   I'm gonna do a little gardening.

Michael   Elliot . . . !

[Elliot *exits to the garden with his flashlight.* Michael *gets bedding from a trunk and prepares to make up the couch.* Susie, *in a nightshirt, comes downstairs by the light of a hurricane lamp.*]

Susie   Want help?

Michael   Sure.

Susie   I wish you didn't get stoned with him.

Michael   What? I had one hit!

Susie   Don't encourage him. In any way. Please? His drinking is bad enough but he shouldn't be self-medicating, especially not while he's taking anti-depressants.

Michael   *He's* taking anti-depressants?

Susie   Isn't everybody? Well, they don't seem to be working. For him, I mean. Me, I swear by them.

[*A beat.*]

My mother made him promise, on her deathbed, he would clean up his act but he hasn't even tried.

Michael   I'm sorry; I didn't know it had gotten so bad. Your grandmother hadn't said anything.

Susie   Of course not. She's in denial about everything. Will you promise not to encourage him?

Michael   Yes I won't encourage him.

Susie   Please, Michael, I mean it.

Michael   I said yes! You worry too much, you know that? It's not healthy for a person as young as you to worry so much.

Susie   I worry about everyone. That's what I do.

[*A beat.*]

What did you mean before about your lost year?

MICHAEL   [*Shrugs.*] That's what it was. Typical Hollywood insanity. My first taste of success, I went a little crazy. Thankfully, I realized I was going crazy and did something about it.

SUSIE   And you've been okay?

MICHAEL   Reasonably, yeah.

SUSIE   If you ever find yourself there again . . . Will you let me know?

MICHAEL   If I ever do? Yeah. Yeah, I will.

SUSIE   Good.

[*Pause.*]

MICHAEL   I can do the rest, I'm keeping you up.

SUSIE   I don't care.

MICHAEL   We should get to sleep. We've got Elliot's reading in the morning.

SUSIE   Yeah. Okay. Good night.

MICHAEL   Good night.

[*She starts to go but stops.*]

What is it?

SUSIE   [*With difficulty.*] The last few nights? Having you here? Sleeping under the same roof? Knowing you're right there. . . . In the flesh. Breathing. It's almost too much. I mean . . . I've thought about you . . . that way . . . from the first time I started thinking those things.

MICHAEL   Susie . . .

SUSIE   That's a little girl's name. I'm not a little girl anymore.

MICHAEL   Sweetie, you should go to bed.

[*She lingers for a moment before disappearing into the darkness.*]

[*To himself.*]

Oh, boy . . .

[*Time shift:* MICHAEL *takes off his jeans, sets them down on a chair.* ANNA *comes downstairs holding a candle, a pillow tucked under her arm.*]

ANNA   [*Like a hotel maid.*] Housekeeping.

MICHAEL   Hi.

ANNA   I thought maybe you could try a different pillow tonight. This one [*the one in use*] has lost so many of its feathers. . . .

MICHAEL   I hadn't noticed.

ANNA   You've really been okay down here? I feel like such a bad hostess.

MICHAEL   It's been fine, really.

[*She puts her hand on his chest.*]

ANNA   Great to have you here, Michael.

MICHAEL   Great to be here.

[*She touches his cheek.*]

ANNA   It's a comfort to me. Really

MICHAEL   I'm glad.

[*Pause.*]

ANNA   Well . . . Good night.

MICHAEL   Good night.

[ANNA *snatches the pillow she delivered as she heads back upstairs. He raises an eyebrow.*]

[*Time shift:* MICHAEL, *stretched out on the couch, is illuminated by his iPhone.* NELL *comes downstairs by the light of her iPhone, sees him.*]

NELL   Oh.

MICHAEL   Hey.

NELL   Sorry. I just . . .

MICHAEL   That's okay.

NELL   I didn't mean to disturb you.

MICHAEL   You're not disturbing me.

NELL   I wanted a glass of water.

MICHAEL   Help yourself.

[*As she goes to the kitchen:*]

Could I have one, too?

NELL   [*Offstage.*] Sure.

[*She returns with two glasses of water, hands him one.*]

Thanks.

[*They both drink.*]

NELL   Well . . . good night.

[*She starts to go.*]

MICHAEL   Sorry if I went on before.

NELL   [*Stops.*] What?

MICHAEL   About Congo.

NELL   Not at all. I found it inspiring.

MICHAEL   I can't help it; once I get started . . .

NELL   If I had something like that in my life . . . that really mattered . . . I'd want to share it with people, too.

MICHAEL   I didn't want to make you feel bad. . . .

NELL   You didn't. You just got me thinking. We get so caught up in our own little dramas . . . we forget that we share the planet with people whose lives are truly hellish. It's good to be reminded that we can make a difference. Even if it's convincing *one* boy that someone in the world cares what happens to him.

MICHAEL   That boy did more for me than I could have possibly done for him. To him, I wasn't famous, I was just a man who showed him kindness.

NELL   Didn't you want to be famous?

MICHAEL   Are you kidding? I wanted it so badly. . . . I can't remember *why* it was so important to me but it was. My self-worth was all tied into my being famous. Then . . . one morning you wake up on one of those glorious LA mornings, with someone beside you you don't love, in a house you once dreamt about, only now it's *your* house but it doesn't *feel* like your house and probably never will. And you drive to the studio in your super-energy-efficient car, and memorize pages of inane dialogue for which you're paid a *stupid* amount of money and . . . You do that enough mornings . . . You begin to wonder . . .

NELL   . . . if that's what you really wanted.

MICHAEL   That's right.

NELL   *I* understand.

[*A beat.*]

MICHAEL   I think you do.

[*They look at each other in sexually charged silence.*]

NELL   I should go up.

MICHAEL   Stay. Talk.

NELL   Walter will wonder where I went.

MICHAEL   Walter is zonked out on Vicodin.

[*She stands to go. He stands and takes her hand, stopping her.*]

Stay.

[*They look at one another. He steps closer, when suddenly, power is restored! The lights go on—revealing* ELLIOT, *flowers in hand,* ANNA, *and* SUSIE, *who have been eavesdropping from the shadows, unseen by one another.*]

ELLIOT   Oops.

[*He chucks the flowers and leaves. Abashed, the women go their separate ways, leaving* MICHAEL *alone.*]

CURTAIN

END OF ACT TWO

INTERMISSION

ACT III

Scene 1

[*At rise: The following morning.* MICHAEL *is unmaking his bed.* SUSIE *warily comes downstairs and helps him.*]

MICHAEL   Morning.

[*Silence.*]

SUSIE   What were you thinking?

MICHAEL   I *wasn't* thinking.

SUSIE   Not with your *brain*, anyway.

MICHAEL   I'm sorry you all had to see that.

SUSIE   I'll bet you are. I'll bet *she* is, too.

MICHAEL   Nell did nothing wrong. I asked her for a glass of water. . . .

SUSIE   Uh-huh.

MICHAEL   Look, whatever it *appeared* to be, it was my fault; I take full responsibility. Please don't punish *her* for it; she's a good person.

SUSIE   What about you? Are you in the habit of hitting on other men's fiancées?

MICHAEL   I'm really not. I don't want you to get the wrong idea.

SUSIE   Too late.

[ELLIOT *comes downstairs carrying his scripts, sees* MICHAEL.]

ELLIOT   Is it safe?

[MICHAEL *feels the chill but doesn't respond.*]

[*To* SUSIE.]

Could you make sure your grandmother's up?

SUSIE   Okay.

ELLIOT   Thanks.

[SUSIE *goes back upstairs.* MICHAEL *takes out his bag to pack.*]

Where do you think you're going?

MICHAEL   I thought it would be best if I, uh . . .

ELLIOT   Un-uh. Not so fast, Romeo. I need you for my reading.

MICHAEL   Don't you think maybe we should do it some other time?

ELLIOT   Oh, we're doing it. You promised. We arranged it around your fucking schedule.

[ELLIOT *hands* MICHAEL *a script.*]

You're the lead. Congratulations.

[WALTER *enters from the kitchen with a tray of coffee mugs and a carafe.*]

WALTER   [*Brightly.*] Show time! Boy, I'm really looking forward to hearing this play!

ELLIOT   Where's Nell?

WALTER   I'll get her.

[ANNA *and* SUSIE *come downstairs.*]

ANNA   Tell me again: *Why* are we doing this so unconscionably early?

SUSIE   Michael has rehearsal.

ANNA   Oh, that's right.

WALTER   Good morning!

[WALTER *hands* ANNA *a cup of coffee.*]

ANNA   Thank you, darling. I don't know about you but I slept miserably last night.

WALTER   Not me. I slept like a baby.

[*Calls.*]

Nell, honey? Are you coming?

ANNA   What about you, Michael? How did *you* sleep?

MICHAEL   Not very well.

ANNA   Oh, what a shame.

WALTER   [*Calls.*] Nell? Here she comes.

[NELL *sheepishly comes downstairs, all eyes on her.*]

NELL   Sorry.

[WALTER *kisses her cheek.* ELLIOT *distributes scripts.*]

ELLIOT   I highlighted everybody's lines.

ANNA   How thoughtful.

[ELLIOT *offers* NELL *a script, teases her by withholding it before handing it over. She takes a seat.*]

WALTER   Alright, let's get this show on the road, shall we?

ANNA   Yes, let's.

ELLIOT   Okay.   I'll read stage directions. Ready?

WALTER   Ready.

[*They open their scripts.*]

ELLIOT   [*Reads.*] "The Descent of Man." Working title. "A new play by Elliot Cooper."

[*They turn the page.*]

"Act One. Scene One. The curtain rises on a house in the country. A forty-year-old man addresses the audience."

[*He gestures to* MICHAEL *to begin.*]

[*Curtain.*]

[*Curtain rises on the scene about two hours later. Except for* ELLIOT, *the company's body language suggests annoyance and boredom have set in.*]

ELLIOT   [*Reads.*] ". . . and the curtain falls. End of play."

[*He closes the script. Pause.*]

MICHAEL   That's it?

ELLIOT   Yeah. That's what "end of play" means.

ANNA   Well! That was . . .

WALTER   Yes! Bravo!

[*He claps. Others join in, tepidly.*]

NELL   Congratulations.

ELLIOT   Thanks.

MICHAEL   [*To* ELLIOT.] Wait. He kills himself?

ELLIOT   Uh-huh.

SUSIE   Excuse me, I have to go pee.

NELL   Me too.

[Susie *goes to the upstairs bathroom;* Nell *to the one on the first floor.*]

MICHAEL   So . . . at the end . . . The mother is dead; he's killed her.

ELLIOT   Right.

ANNA   I'm parched. [*To* WALTER.] Would you like some water?

WALTER   Yes, please.

[*She goes.*]

MICHAEL   He's taken pills and the house is engulfed in flames. Burning rafters falling all around them.

ELLIOT   Yeah . . .

WALTER   How are you going to pull that off onstage?

ELLIOT   What.

MICHAEL   That was my question.

WALTER   Burning down the house. I mean, it's a great image. . . . In a movie you can do that and it'll look spectacular. Onstage, though . . .

ELLIOT   I know the difference between stage and film, Walter. I don't know, some designer'll figure it out. They love that stuff.

WALTER   What happens to it now?

ELLIOT   I try to get it produced.

MICHAEL   Where you gonna take it?

ELLIOT   I don't know. Walter, where would *you* take it?

WALTER   I have no idea.

ELLIOT   Think. You must have *some* idea. . . .

WALTER   I wouldn't know who to approach.

ELLIOT   Oh, come on, you know everybody and everybody certainly knows you. . . .

WALTER   Not really; not any more. I'm out of touch with the theater scene; I haven't done a play in years. It's a whole new generation. These kids don't know who I am. Or was.

[ANNA *returns with her and* WALTER's *drinks.*]

Your *mother* would be a much more reliable source.

[ANNA *glares at* WALTER.]

ELLIOT   Mother?

ANNA   You *are* going to do some more work on it first, though, right?

ELLIOT   Yeah . . .

ANNA   Aren't you?

ELLIOT   Why, you didn't like it?

ANNA   I didn't say that. I assume you'll want to do more work on it before you start sending it out.

ELLIOT   You didn't like it.

ANNA   Elliot, it's your first draft of your first play! You can't write one play—the first draft of a single play—and expect it to work right off the bat.

ELLIOT   So you're saying it doesn't work?

ANNA   All I'm saying is, darling, writing plays is a very difficult pursuit.

ELLIOT   Really? I had no idea.

ANNA   Just because someone writes a play doesn't make them a playwright.

ELLIOT   Wow.

WALTER   She's right, champ.

ANNA   I think it's marvelous you found yourself a hobby.

ELLIOT   A hobby?!

ANNA   Something that really gives you pleasure.

ELLIOT   This isn't a hobby, Mother. It's a calling.

ANNA   Being a *play*wright, darling? A *play*wright? Acting isn't demoralizing enough, you choose *play*writing?

ELLIOT   The nerve of me! The arrogance!

ANNA   [*To* WALTER.] Help me out here.

WALTER   Go ahead. You're doing fine.

ELLIOT   That—a talentless schmuck like me!—

ANNA   Oh, God . . .**MICHAEL**   Elliot!

ELLIOT   [*Continuous.*]—might have something illuminating to say about the human condition . . .

[ANNA *emits a scoffing sound.*]

Are you laughing?!

ANNA   No.

ELLIOT   You think that's funny?

ANNA   I don't think it's funny, no.

ELLIOT   That's right: Writing plays is off-limits to someone like me. Only a chosen few have the right. What am I but a mere interloper?

ANNA   Oh, darling, why is it so important for you to be an artist?

ELLIOT   *Why?* Because artistic accomplishment is the only way to feel anything resembling *love* around here!

MICHAEL   Calm. The fuck. Down.

ELLIOT   Fuck you, Michael. *You're* one to talk about self-control!

[MICHAEL *throws his hands up and exits to the patio.*]

[*Continuing, to* ANNA.] Why can't you be supportive for a change?

ANNA   I *am* being supportive.

ELLIOT   No, you're not.

ANNA   Darling, if you announced that you wanted to become a . . . I don't know, a massage therapist or a—

ELLIOT   *Massage* therapist?

ANNA   —a high school *English* teacher. Bravo! What a noble profession. But deciding at your age that—poof!—you're a playwright?! It's magical thinking, darling, it really is.

ELLIOT   You think if you throw in a "dear" or a "darling" it mitigates every hateful, demeaning thing you say to me, don't you.

ANNA   Do you think it's easy telling your child the truth? Do you? Shall I pretend your play was a work of genius? Is that what you want? Lies? I can lie; I pretend for a living.

Marvelous! Absolutely brilliant! All it was, was a childish attempt to get back at me! To embarrass me!

ELLIOT   That's right, it's all about you!

ANNA   You insist on turning me into this . . . gorgon, this monstrous mother. You take pleasure in it. What a sick exercise: I can't believe I was a party just now to my own vilification.

[*To* WALTER.]

How does he do it? *He* behaves abominably and *I'm* the one who ends up feeling guilty!

[*She exits. Silence.*]

ELLIOT   *You've* been awfully quiet, Walter.

WALTER   You're not interested in what I have to say.

ELLIOT   That's not true, I'm very interested. I want your feedback.

WALTER   Artists *say* they want feedback but the fact is: They don't, not really, all they want is praise. I've lived long enough to know. . . . People who beg for your opinion—not just about art, about anything—what they *really* want is validation of the choices they've already made.

Someone'll ask, "Which color do you think I should paint my living room? The blue or the green?" "I like the green." "Well, I'm going with the blue." What's the point in my saying *anything*? It won't matter one way or another because you've already made up your mind. And that's fine. But don't act like you give a shit what I have to say.

ELLIOT   Yeah, well, you're wrong: I do care.

WALTER   You do, huh.

ELLIOT   Yes.

WALTER   What is it about you, Elliot, this gift you have for self-mortification? You practically insist that people hurt you. Alright, I can do that. You want to know what I thought of your play?

ELLIOT   Yes.

WALTER   I thought it was appalling. Okay? Amateur. Masturbatory. Shall I go on? For our friendship's sake, please, let's just drop it.

ELLIOT   Friendship? What friendship? We're not friends, Walter. We *were* in-laws. Now that Kathy's gone, are you anything to me anymore? Except an irritant? A pebble in my shoe? In all the time we've known each other—that you've been part of this family—have you ever, once, used me in anything?

WALTER   Oh, Jesus. *

ELLIOT   Have you?

WALTER   What is this: "What have you done for me lately?"

ELLIOT   What have you done for me—ever. Some dipshitty little part. A walk-on. Anything.

WALTER   You know my policy: I never work with family.

ELLIOT   That didn't stop you from working with Kathy. . . .

WALTER   She was my wife.

ELLIOT   I hate to tell you but your wife is your family. And Mother? How many times have you worked with Mother?

WALTER   Your mother is one of the all-time greats. Of course I'm going to work with her.

ELLIOT   And what am I to you? Huh? Just another schmuck actor?

WALTER   You need to pull yourself together, champ.

[WALTER *gently touches* ELLIOT's *shoulder;* ELLIOT *brusquely pulls away.*]

ELLIOT   You need to fuck off . . . champ.

[*Pause.*]

WALTER   You think coming in to audition is hard? Try sitting on the other side of the table for a change. Actors I've known for thirty, forty years—people I started out with, people I admired—schlep in to read. Angry. Desperate. Cracking too many jokes, laughing too hard. Pushing it. You smell flop sweat the way a dog smells fear. It's *awful* seeing people you care about so exposed, just horrible. I've sat there when *you've* come in, Elliot. Failure and aggression follow you into the room. Like a storm cloud. With this Fuck-you, I-don't-need-you chip on your shoulder. The vibe you give off . . . You don't *want* the job.

ELLIOT   Is that right.

WALTER   You think you *should* want it; you go through the motions. But you don't. Not really.

ELLIOT   And why is that?

WALTER   Because if you got the job you'd have to deliver, and you're terrified that you won't be able to do it. You'd bomb out. Or, worse, you couldn't cut it and I'd have to fire you.

[*A beat.*]

No one wants to work with you, Elliot. You've done a very good job of making yourself radioactive. You're on everyone's life-is-too-short list.

[*Pause.*]

ELLIOT   I idolized you, Walter. You know that?

WALTER   Elliot, please.

ELLIOT   When Kathy first brought you around . . . ? I thought: "Wow: Walter Keegan, the famous director: How cool is that?" And to be an intimate of yours?—your brother-in-law?!—I felt so damn proud. And then . . . When you started making shlock . . .

WALTER   Okay, here we go.

ELLIOT   First that scatological teen comedy . . .

WALTER   Coming-of-age story.

ELLIOT   You wish. And when you stopped directing plays altogether . . . I felt so betrayed.

WALTER   Betrayed? How did I betray you?

ELLIOT   By selling out!

WALTER   Grow up, Elliot. Selling-out is a young person's idea. An adolescent's romantic notion that in order to be an artist you need to starve and suffer; commercial success is the devil's work. Well, I say, nuts to that.

ELLIOT   You were the paragon of artistic success!

WALTER   I was the paragon of nothing! I was a pragmatist who got sick of filling my calendar just to make enough to scrape by, and wanted to make some real money for a change!

ELLIOT   How does it feel knowing that you'll be best remembered for pandering to the puerile impulses of fifteen-year-old boys?

WALTER   It feels fine! If you think I've lost any sleep over this . . . I have nothing against fifteen-year-old boys; they're as legitimate a demographic as any. Fifteen-year-old boys have made me rich. I am indebted to them. Call it pandering if you like. I call it commerce. I provide a product to a vastly appreciative audience.

ELLIOT   My God. "Product." Listen to you! The old Walter would have been sick to his stomach.

WALTER   I *am* the old Walter. Same guy! I made this choice, long ago, no looking back, no regrets. What should I regret? The work onstage I didn't do? Not a chance. Starvation is not a virtue. I've tried it. It takes just as much energy and imagination making good, commercial entertainment than it does to make so-called art. So why not get paid for it? I discovered there will *always* be fifteen-year-old boys, an endless supply, *ad infinitum*, who go to the movies to watch all the cool different ways you can blow stuff up. I happen to like that, too.

ELLIOT   But what have you contributed to the world but pollution? At least when you worked in the theater . . .

WALTER   Ah, the thea-tuh, the thea-tuh. If I hear one more time how I abandoned the fucking thea-tuh . . . The grandiosity of theater people! Who have convinced themselves that what they do is of a higher order than all other forms of make-believe! What an odd pursuit, when you stop to think about it: Grown people shouting in rooms missing a fourth wall?

ELLIOT   Your *Winter's Tale* in the park . . . When Hermione came back to life . . .

WALTER   I hate to tell ya, that wasn't me, that was Shakespeare.

ELLIOT   It *was* you! It was beautiful!

WALTER   And where is it now, this beauty? Gone! Evaporated. The way of all ephemera.

ELLIOT   Ah, yes, what comfort that must bring: *Truck Stop 3* will live on and on!

WALTER   Mock me all you want. I am not going to apologize for its success. It's so easy for the smug wannabe to judge those who actually put themselves on the line and *make* things! You're one to talk, Elliot. What have you done? Huh? Besides squander your life on vitriol. You've stewed in it. Remove the anger and what's left? Nothing. A big, fat void where a life should be!

[ELLIOT *growls in rage and attacks* WALTER, *knocking him to the floor.*]

ELLIOT   Fuckin' sonofabitch . . . !

WALTER   My knee!

[ELLIOT *gets on top of him.*]

ELLIOT   Fuckin' piece a shit . . . !

[*He has his hands around* WALTER's *throat.*]

WALTER   Get off me! Help! Get him the hell of me!

[ANNA *and* NELL *rush in from the kitchen. Pandemonium.*]

ANNA   Oh, my God!

[*Calls.*]

Oh, shit! Elliot! Michael!

[NELL *tries to help.*]

NELL   Get off of him!

[SUSIE *runs downstairs.*]

SUSIE   Uncle Elliot! Stop!

[MICHAEL *runs in from the patio and tries to restrain* ELLIOT.]

MICHAEL   Jesus, Elliot!

ANNA   Are you out of your mind?!

[MICHAEL *pries* ELLIOT *off* WALTER.]

MICHAEL   What the fuck is the matter with you?!

[ELLIOT *runs out of the house while the others tend to* WALTER. NELL *finishes helping him upstairs while* MICHAEL *and* SUSIE *go after* ELLIOT *and* ANNA *returns to the kitchen.*]

End of Scene

Scene 2

[*A few hours later. Late afternoon.* NELL *comes downstairs with her luggage.* SUSIE *enters, sees* NELL, *and decides to stay. She starts to straighten up the room.* NELL *tries to help her.*]

SUSIE   I've got it.

NELL   I can do it.

[*They tidy in silence.*]

It looks like it's gonna rain again.

SUSIE   Are we going to talk about the weather?

NELL   I'm trying to make conversation.

SUSIE   Why bother? You're leaving.

NELL   Not right away. Your father needed to lie down. He was pretty shaken up. Susie, are you going to look at me?

SUSIE   Susan.

NELL   You avert your eyes whenever I look at you. Do you think you can pretend I don't exist? Susie . . .

SUSIE   Susan!

NELL   You want me to treat you like an adult, then act like one!

SUSIE   You're not my mother. . . .

NELL   I'm well aware of that.

[*Pause.*]

SUSIE   Look, I don't mean to be rude . . .

NELL   Oh, no?

SUSIE   Why did you come here?

NELL   To lend your dad moral support.

SUSIE   That thing last night with Michael: Is that how you lend moral support?

[NELL *doesn't know what to say.*]

You still plan on marrying my father?

NELL   Of course.

SUSIE   Why? He's old.

NELL   [*Wearily.*] He's not old.

SUSIE   Why would you want to be married to an old man?

NELL   That's not how I see him.

SUSIE   Maybe not now you don't. One day, tomorrow: A blood clot, a crack in the sidewalk, a knee replacement: He's old.

NELL   Age has nothing to do with it; bad stuff can happen to anyone at any age. Your mother was young, so there goes your theory.

SUSIE   Do you have a "daddy thing"?

NELL   What? No. I don't think so . . . Maybe I do.

[They smile.]

SUSIE   What is *your* daddy like?

NELL   I didn't really know my dad.

SUSIE   Ah ha! Well, there you go. So you want mine.

NELL   I don't want your father. I want Walter Keegan. He'll still be your father.

SUSIE   Did you tell him what happened?

NELL   There was nothing to tell because nothing happened.

SUSIE   It sure *looked* like something happened.

NELL   That's not what it was.

SUSIE   Oh, no? What do *you* call it?

NELL   [Ashamed.] Temporary insanity.

[Pause.]

SUSIE   Yeah.

[A beat.]

I know what Michael does to people.

NELL   What do you mean?

SUSIE   I've loved him my entire life.

NELL   You have?

SUSIE   I can remember seeing Michael's face when I was really, really young—I mean, *really* young—like in my crib—and thinking to myself—before I had words, even: This is a beautiful man. I swear. I remember that.

[A beat.]

NELL   Y'know? You should be grateful I want to marry your father.

SUSIE   Why grateful?

NELL   Because someday he will be old. And he'll need taking care of, and *I'll* be the one doing the heavy lifting, not you.

SUSIE   Why are you signing on for this? I don't get it. What's in it for you? The money? You don't seem like the gold digger type.

NELL   [*Shrugs.*] It must be love.

SUSIE   Why would you want to be a part of this fucked-up family, anyway?

NELL   [*Shrugs.*] *That* I couldn't tell you.

[NELL *laughs.* SUSIE *looks at her.*]

What.

SUSIE   You're so beautiful.

NELL   I'm not.

SUSIE   I can't even hate you for it because your beauty is so indisputable, it would be like hating sunsets. Did you know my mother?

[NELL *shakes her head.*]

Her movies don't do her justice. Her skin, she had such incredible skin. Even when she was dying, her skin was luminous. I had the worst zits from like twelve on, it was like a cruel joke that I should have this gorgeous movie-star mother who was perfection. It just wasn't fair. What must it be like to wake up every morning and see *that* [NELL'*s face.*] in the mirror.

NELL   Are you *asking* me?

SUSIE   Yeah. How does it feel?

NELL   I don't feel beautiful.

SUSIE   I hate when beautiful people say that.

NELL   I don't, I mean it. I *never* felt beautiful. I was never very kind to myself.

[*A beat.*]

I had an eating disorder till I was way in my twenties.

SUSIE   Really? You did?

NELL   Uh-huh. My dark secret. Now you know. Ruined my teeth. See? All new veneers.

SUSIE   [*Elated.*] Wow!

[MICHAEL *enters from the patio.*]

MICHAEL   Hi.

NELL   Hi.

SUSIE   Still no sign of him?

MICHAEL   No.

SUSIE   I couldn't find him either.

MICHAEL   [*To* NELL.] How's Walter?

NELL   Resting. I'm gonna throw this bag in the car.

[NELL *takes her bag and goes.*]

MICHAEL   I was hoping he showed up while I was out looking for him.

SUSIE   No.

MICHAEL   Say good-bye to him for me. Will you let me know he's alright?

SUSIE   Okay.

MICHAEL   Thanks.

[*She starts to go.*]

SUSIE   Well . . . see ya.

MICHAEL   Hey. 'Cmere.

[*He gestures for her to come closer. She does, tentatively. He hugs her, kisses the top of her head.*]

Love ya.

SUSIE   "Love ya" is the coward's way of saying "I love you." Love ya, too. Bye!

[*She heads for the stairs.* NELL *returns.*]

MICHAEL   [*Calls.*] Susie.

[*She stops.*]

Come see my show. Come opening night.

SUSIE   Yeah, sure. If I'm around.

[*She's gone.*]

NELL   I'm sorry I won't get to see you in *The Guardsman.*

MICHAEL   Don't be. Walter's right: Just me seeking absolution.

NELL   I should get him up.

MICHAEL   Nell . . . Listen. I, uh . . .

NELL   You don't have to say anything.

MICHAEL   I'm sorry.

NELL   *I'm* sorry. My mistake. I was curious. I should never have gone near you.

[*She extends her hand.*]

Good-bye, Michael.

[*They shake hands. She starts to go upstairs.*]

I hope you find what you're looking for.

[Anna *enters from the garden with freshly cut flowers and sees them.* Nell *exits.*]

Anna   [*To* Michael.] You're leaving.

Michael   Yes.

Anna   Where will you go?

Michael   My place. I think it's safe for me to move in, finally.

Anna   You're not worried about asphyxiation?

Michael   The air should be clear by now.

Anna   [*Nods, then.*] That's not why you stayed on here, is it.

[*He avoids eye contact.*]

It was her. It was Nell. You stayed to be close to Nell.

[*A beat.*]

You know? When I saw you in the market the other day . . . posing for pictures by the organic fruit . . . I was transported, instantly, back to a happier time. The years, age, death, everything disappeared. I was your Candida again.

Michael   You're still sensational.

Anna   Sweet of you to say. Tell me: Was I really so deluded, to think I might have gotten some comfort from you—

Michael   Anna . . .

Anna   —a little reassurance, from an old friend?

Michael   I . . . didn't understand.

Anna   What's not to understand? I thought it was obvious.

Michael   What can I say? I'm not that smart.

Anna   Hm. Maybe not. Here's a bit of advice, then: When a woman invites you into her home . . . and you don't seduce *her* . . . Don't seduce *another* woman, darling, certainly not under the same roof. It's bad manners— ungallant to say the least.

Michael   I never thought of you like that.

Anna   Never?

Michael   Well, not for a very long time.

Anna   You mean now that my sell-by date has come and gone.

MICHAEL   That's not what I'm saying. I had a young man's crush on you. *I'm* the one who's changed.

ANNA   I could have seduced you all those years ago. But Kathy got you first. I could have gone all *Mildred Pierce* on you. But I still had a modicum of dignity back then. Just a smidge. Now, apparently, not so much.

MICHAEL   I don't know who you think I am.

ANNA   I thought I knew.

MICHAEL   You've bought the press. I'm not some Lothario. I don't sleep with just anyone. I mean . . .

ANNA   Am I just anyone?

MICHAEL   I mean, I'm not cavalier.

ANNA   Oh. I see.

[*A beat.*]

Do you know what it's like being lit on a movie set for hours and hours because your eyes look like shit and no matter what the DP does your eyes *still* look like shit? There's only so much magic lighting can do. Producers pace, and look at their watches, and shake their heads about how much this is costing them, and how beautiful I *used* to be. Do you have any idea what it's like to lose one's powers? Do you?

[*He shakes his head.*]

No. And you never will.

MICHAEL   Well . . .

[*He hoists his bag onto his shoulder.*]

We're both gonna be up here for a while. . . . Once I get settled, how about I cook for *you* for a change?

[*She nods.* MICHAEL *leans in to kiss her cheek. She kisses him full on the mouth.*]

ANNA   Alright, you may go now. Go! Your work here is done.

[ANNA *goes to the kitchen with the flowers.*]

MICHAEL   [*To himself.*] Jesus.

[*He sees* ELLIOT, *soaking wet, enter from the garden.*]

Hey. Where were you?

ELLIOT   Walking.

MICHAEL   Where?

ELLIOT   Around. In the woods.

MICHAEL   You're drenched.

ELLIOT   I needed to think.

MICHAEL   And?

ELLIOT   I had an epiphany.

MICHAEL   Yeah . . . ?

ELLIOT   My mother doesn't love me.

MICHAEL   What kind of shit is that? Of course your mother loves you.

ELLIOT   Why "of course"? You think all women love their children? Medea? Gertrude? Not all women should be mothers. It wasn't a role that came naturally to her. She was miscast. And spent all these years "indicating" like crazy: the least convincing performance of her career.

[A beat.]

Did you know I had a stutter?

MICHAEL   I *didn't* know that.

ELLIOT   I did. Something we don't talk about. I'm a recovering stutterer. Like being an alcoholic: you're never really cured. Always one consonant, one breath away from an avalanche. Whenever I spoke, I'd see Mother, clenched jaw, frozen smile, staring into her salad, or down at her shoes, and imagine her thinking, like a thought-bubble in a comic book: "Get on with it, Elliot, for God's sake, don't humiliate yourself, or more importantly, me." And I'd get so nervous, I'd lose traction and fly off the rails. She set me up! Over and over again! She wanted me to fail!

MICHAEL   No she didn't.

ELLIOT   She does it to this day! Whenever I open my mouth! Listen to me: What a joke I am, huh?

[*Mock tears.*]

"My mother doesn't love me."

MICHAEL   What are we gonna do with you, Elliot?

ELLIOT   You don't have to do anything.

[MICHAEL *hugs him, reacts to his saturated clothing.*]

MICHAEL   It's a good thing we're old friends, you know that?

ELLIOT   Oh, yeah? Why's that?

MICHAEL   Because if I just met you for the first time...? I wouldn't want to have anything to do with you.

ELLIOT   Thanks.

MICHAEL   Take care, buddy.

ELLIOT   You bet!

[MICHAEL *hoists his bag on his shoulder as* NELL *comes downstairs carrying* WALTER'*s bag. They exchange looks.* NELL *waves.* ELLIOT *observes them as* MICHAEL *exits the house. She approaches* ELLIOT.]

NELL   Listen: Elliot . . .

ELLIOT   Do me a favor?

[*She nods.*]

If you're going to cheat on Walter, do it with me?

NELL   *Listen:* No matter how much you try to blame him for everything that's gone wrong in your life . . . Walter did not give Kathy cancer.

ELLIOT   She had a tremendous capacity for happiness, my sister. I marveled at her ability to put up with that man. She elevated him with her love.

NELL   Never mind.

ELLIOT   It kills me to see him landing another one of the world's great women.

[*We hear* WALTER *and* SUSIE *on the stairs.*]

NELL   Good-bye, Elliot.

[NELL *walks away.*]

WALTER   You think you'll make it home before the end of the summer?

SUSIE   At some point I will. . . . I want to see my friends.

WALTER   Nell, honey, you about ready?

NELL   Yup.

SUSIE   [*To* ELLIOT.] There you are. God.

[WALTER *looks at* ELLIOT *leerily.*]

Talk to him.

ELLIOT   No.

[ELLIOT *starts to go;* SUSIE *stops him.*]

SUSIE   Dad?

[*To* ELLIOT.]

Tell him you're sorry.

ELLIOT   I'm not sorry. What am I sorry for?

SUSIE   For behaving obnoxiously. Now tell him.

WALTER   Elliot, there's nothing you could possibly say to me . . .

[SUSIE *pushes* ELLIOT *toward* WALTER.]

ELLIOT   Hey!

[SUSIE *gestures for him to speak.*]

I'm sorry.

SUSIE   [*Prompting.*] I'm sorry I behaved obnoxiously.

ELLIOT   I'm sorry I behaved obnoxiously.

WALTER   You didn't just behave obnoxiously, you had your hands around my throat.

ELLIOT   Fine. Forget it.

WALTER   There is a distinction. Your behaving obnoxiously I'm quite used to; being attacked physically, that's new and, frankly, worrisome. You've always been slightly unhinged. But in a lovably benign sort of way. Now you're fucking out of control.

[*A beat.*]

What's our plan, you and me? Hm? Is this how we're going to live out the rest of our lives? Sniping at each other? Let's not. God help us, but we're family, Elliot, whether we like it or not.

ELLIOT   Kathy was the best thing that ever happened to you.

WALTER   Don't you think I know that?

[ANNA *returns.*]

ANNA   Oh, Walter, must you go?

WALTER   I think so.

ANNA   Everybody's leaving! When will I see you again?

WALTER   You'll come and see us in LA.

[*He hugs her.*]

Good-bye, dear.   Have fun with *Mrs. Warren.* You're going to be fabulous.

SUSIE   [*To* WALTER.] I'll walk you to your . . . Porsche.

[*As* SUSIE *leads* WALTER *out.*]

ANNA   I still want your notes!

WALTER   I'll send them to you!

ANNA   Don't forget me!

WALTER   How could I?

[*They're gone.* NELL *approaches* ANNA.]

NELL   Anna . . . Thank you so much.

ANNA   For what? A fiasco? It couldn't have gone much worse.

NELL   No, I suppose not. Next time we'll all be in better form.

ANNA   I should hope so. Good-bye, dear. Good luck with everything.

NELL   Thanks. You too.

[NELL *glances at* ELLIOT *as she heads out the door.*]

ELLIOT   [*Calls.*] Nell!

[*She stops. A beat.*]

We'll always have Louisville.

[NELL *shakes her head and goes.* ANNA *and* ELLIOT *are alone. Silence.*]

ANNA   Happy now?

ELLIOT   Hm?

ANNA   You got what you wanted. You drove them all away.

ELLIOT   Oh, and you had nothing to do with this farce?

ANNA   Me?! What did *I* do?

ELLIOT   Not only do you let Walter bring his new girlfriend: the only woman I ever loved . . .

ANNA   How was I to know that?

ELLIOT   But Michael?!

ANNA   What *about* Michael?

ELLIOT   *Flinging* yourself at him like that?

ANNA   I don't know what you're talking about. Michael could be my son.

ELLIOT   Exactly. How icky is that? Shame on you. Trying to get a mercy fuck out of Michael.

ANNA   How *dare* you . . . ! What an outrageous thing to say!

ELLIOT   So much for the grieving mother.

ANNA   [*Enraged.*] Are you questioning my grief?! Are you? She was *my child*! She may have been *your* sister but she was *my child*! I will not quantify my suffering because of some primitive notion you have of how I should or should not conduct myself. You don't know what it's like to lose a child. You have no idea. If having Walter and Michael here made me feel closer to Kathy, so be it!

ELLIOT   I wish it had been me, Mother. I so wish it had been me.

ANNA   Oh, for God's sake . . .

ELLIOT   I should have been the one who died. An early death would have lent my life a little dignity, y'know?, a touch of tragedy. It would have been so much better all around.

ANNA   What a childish thing to say.

ELLIOT   Oh, come on, don't pretend you haven't thought it.

[*She turns away. Pause.*]

Look at me, Mama.

[*He waits for her to face him.*]

How did this happen to me? How did I become this . . . sad excuse for a man? I wasted so much time! On what? Auditions! Rehearsals for living, not living. Kathy dies. My magnificent sister. Of lung cancer! Never smoked a day in her life. But I, with my self-destructive habits and . . . *mediocrity*, get to go on breathing? Why? It doesn't make sense.

ANNA   You know, dear, I've often thought you cultivated bad habits just to make yourself more interesting.

ELLIOT   I don't interest you. Do I?

ANNA   I'm not going to play this game.

ELLIOT   [*Prosecutorially.*] Do I interest you. Answer the question.

ANNA   No, my dear. You do not.

ELLIOT   You could at least make a show of protest.

ANNA   You haven't interested me in quite some time.

ELLIOT   Nice.

ANNA   Watching you flail about. How do you think that made me *feel*?

ELLIOT   Made *you* feel?!

ANNA   It was torture—torture!—sitting by helplessly while you failed time and time again.

[*Pause.*]

ELLIOT   All my life . . . I've been the only nobody in the room. I have dropped your name to people I wanted to like me. Directors have cast me in plays hoping *you'd* show up opening night—which, of course, you never did.

ANNA   If I *could* have, of *course* I would have come.

ELLIOT   I had promise. Once.

[*A la Brando.*]

"I coulda been a contenda. I coulda been somebody." Comedy! I did improv at school. But you never came to see me! You were always working.

ANNA   I *was* always working.

ELLIOT   I was good! I was funny! If only you had seen for yourself! But, no, you didn't come, you assumed I'd be bad.

ANNA   I *couldn't* come because I was working.

ELLIOT   Kathy you saw in every damn thing she was in. If she was one of a multitude of *sugarplum fairies*, you were there!

ANNA   Listen to yourself!

ELLIOT   Would it have taken so much to offer me even the slightest bit of encouragement? Would it? You were so . . . withholding, so stingy. As if offering praise meant giving up a vital part of yourself. If only you had told me I was good at something! Instead you told me I was hopeless, there was nothing I did well.

ANNA   I never said you were hopeless!

ELLIOT   You may as well have.

ANNA   I didn't want you to get your hopes up. That's not the same thing.

ELLIOT   How could you deprive your child of hope?!

ANNA   I was protecting you!

ELLIOT   Protecting me?!

ANNA   So you wouldn't be disappointed.

[*Long pause.*]

ELLIOT   It's unnatural. Y'know . . . ? When I was a boy . . . and you'd go off to the theater . . . ? I'd wait up for you to come home, force myself to stay awake till one or two in the morning. My heart would pound when I'd hear your keys jingle and your footsteps in the hall, and pray you'd come in to kiss me. You'd breeze in, in the dark, smelling like night, cold cream on your cheek. I'd lay there pretending to be asleep because I knew that if you found out I waited up, you would stop coming in and that would be that. I spent years at grade school exhausted from lack of sleep—until one night you discovered my gambit and those good-night kisses came to an end. I'm still that boy in the dark, praying for your kiss.

ANNA   Darling, I . . .

[**ELLIOT** *drops to his knees, clutches his mother around her legs.*]

Elliot   Oh, Mama . . .

Anna   [*Trying to walk away.*] What are you doing?

Elliot   Please, Mama, don't walk away!

Anna   Get up! Let go of me!

[*She extricates herself; he remains on the floor. We hear a car on gravel. Susie returns, assesses the situation, but doesn't address it.*]

Are they gone?

Susie   [*Nods.*] All gone.

[*Pause. Thunder.*]

Anna   Is this rain ever going to stop?

Susie   Uncle Elliot?

Elliot   Yeah?

Susie   The man in your play who kills himself . . .

Elliot   Not necessarily.

Susie   Don't be coy; he *is* you.

[*He shrugs.*]

He's you, right? You'd rather be dead? Is that what you're saying?

Elliot   I'm saying . . . I can understand what it must be like to be in so much pain, you'd do whatever it takes to make it stop.

Susie   You really believe that?

[Elliot *nods.*]

[*Emotionally.*]

Why would you say that to me?

Elliot   What?

Susie   I see you killing yourself, slowly. And it's terrible.

Anna   Oh, darling . . .

Susie   Watching you seethe and drink and you're so jealous of other people's happiness. If you're unhappy you don't want anyone else to be happy, either. You lost your faith a long time ago, I know. And when Mom died, it gave you like all the proof you needed that everything was shit. But she would hate to see you like this, Uncle Elliot, she'd hate to see what you're doing to yourself and everybody else. Please. Try to have a little faith. For me. For Mom.

[Susie *joins him on the floor, leaning against the couch.*]

ELLIOT   She was my best friend.

SUSIE   I know. ANNA   Yes, she was.

ELLIOT   Yin to my yang. Gretel to my Hansel. I have nobody now.

ANNA   That's not true. Of course you do.

ELLIOT   Nobody who loves me unconditionally, not like she did. Who do I have?

SUSIE   You have *me* . . . Idiot.

[*A beat.*]

Remember that? When I was little? I called you Uncle Idiot?

ELLIOT   [*Remembering.*] Uncle Idiot. Yes. Who knew how prophetic?

SUSIE   I thought it was the most hilarious thing in the world.

[*He pulls her closer to him and kisses her forehead.* ANNA *gets the photo album; she can't bring herself to open it but hands it over and joins them.* SUSIE *and* ELLIOT *look at pictures.*]

That's this room. How come there's no furniture in it?

ANNA   We hadn't moved in yet. We hadn't even put a bid on it yet. We were looking at the house for the first time. Elliot and Kathy were so excited, they ran through all the rooms and up and down stairs. That clinched it for Leonard and me: We could see ourselves being so happy here.

SUSIE   [*Another photo.*] God, look how cute she was. You know? I kind of looked like that when I was that age.

ANNA   Uh huh. You did.

SUSIE   [*Another photo.*] Why were you dressed like that?

ELLIOT   It was our Christmas play. I was Joseph. See? Your mom was the Virgin Mary.

SUSIE   Who are they?

ELLIOT   Oh, just some cousins who were staying with us. Whoever happened to be visiting got to be donkeys and camels.

SUSIE   Gran, tell about the time Mom and Uncle Elliot surprised you for your birthday.

ANNA   For *my* birthday?

SUSIE   Yeah. Mom told me. You were up here doing a play?

ANNA   What play was I doing?

SUSIE   I don't remember. You were in rehearsal and a call came?

ANNA From whom?

ELLIOT From me.

ANNA Saying what?

ELLIOT "Kathy's scared! Come home right away!"

[*To* SUSIE.]

There was a thunderstorm. She *hated* thunderstorms, your mom.

ANNA And what did I do?

ELLIOT You came home.

ANNA I left rehearsal?!

ELLIOT Uh-huh.

ANNA When have I *ever* left rehearsal?

ELLIOT You did. You were in costume.

ANNA What was I wearing?

[*Thinks, then:*]

Oh! I was doing Nora! I was wearing my dress for the Tarantella! Yes, and I got in the car, raced to the house . . . and ran inside calling, "Kath-yy. . ." And out she popped, from behind the sofa—that little imp—"Surprise!" It was all a ruse! I was furious!

[*She slips down to the floor near* ELLIOT.]

And then came Elliot, holding the saddest, flattest, home-baked birthday cake, candles blazing, and the two of them sang "Happy Birthday" and my anger . . . went away. We blew out the candles and plopped ourselves down, right here, the three of us, and tore into that chocolate cake—with our fingers!—and talked . . . and laughed . . . and ate it all up, we devoured it, till there was nothing left on the plate but crumbs!

[ELLIOT *and* SUSIE *slide closer to* ANNA. *She leans in closer and puts on her glasses to join them in looking at the album as the lights fade completely to black.*]

CURTAIN

End of Play

DINNER WITH THE BOYS

by
Dan Lauria

To Charlie, Dom, Jack & Peter
The best of the best.

Production History

The World Premiere of *Dinner with the Boys* was produced by New Jersey Repertory Co., September 11–October 12, 2014. The cast was as follows:

CHARLIE: Dan Lauria
DOM: Richard Zagalia
BIG ANTHONY JR./THE UNCLE SID: Ray Abruzzo

Directed by Frank Megna

This play was given its first public reading at the Coronet Theatre in Los Angeles with the following actors:

In Order of Appearance:

CHARLIE: Charles Durning
DOM: Dom Deluise
BIG ANTHONY JR.: Peter Falk
THE UNCLE SID: Jack Klugman

. . . to whom this play is dedicated.

Setting

The play takes place in a modest kitchen in the wilds of New Jersey about a two-hour drive from the heart of Brooklyn.

ACT I

Dinner on Leo

[*Lights up: we are in a kitchen. A simple, old-fashioned kitchen; wrought-iron stove with six burners, an old refrigerator (circa 1980s), and a double sink with a dish rack. The sink sits directly behind a wooden kitchen table with four chairs. There is a window over the sink and a kitchen door that opens to the back porch and yard. There are three doors in all; the back entrance leading outside, (sr) an archway leading to a dining/living room, and a door (sl) to a walk-in pantry and cellar entrance (optional). As the lights come up, we find* CHARLIE *sitting at the table peeling potatoes. He obviously hates doing this mindless task. He cuts, stabs, and chops at the innocent inanimate vegetable. He curses his knobbed white defenseless opponent.* DOMINIC *enters carrying a paper bag partially filled with groceries and singing opera.* DOMINIC *puts the groceries down on the counter next to the sink and then takes off his jacket and hangs it on a peg next to the door.* DOMINIC *puts the groceries away and starts to prepare tonight's dinner throughout the first act.*]

CHARLIE   [*Pissed off.*] Well, it's about time.

DOMINIC   I had a little shopping to do.

CHARLIE   You should have called.

DOMINIC   Then I had to do a few things.

CHARLIE   What if *he* called?

DOMINIC   He never calls before six.

CHARLIE   What if he does?

DOMINIC   Between six and eight.

CHARLIE   What do I say? Huh? *What*, do I say?

DOMINIC   Every Sunday.

CHARLIE   [*Sarcastically.*] He's gone to the market?

DOMINIC   Well . . . ?

CHARLIE   And how would that sound?

DOMINIC   That's where I was.

CHARLIE   You should have called.

DOMINIC   Will you stop.

[DOM *starts unpacking.*]

CHARLIE   I thought you got knocked off.

DOMINIC   God forbid.

CHARLIE   Next time you're late; call.

DOMINIC   All right.

CHARLIE   You hear me?

DOMINIC   I hear ya!

CHARLIE   Huh?

DOMINIC   I hear. I hear. Aaah! You started peeling the potatoes.

CHARLIE   Yeah! I'm peeling.

DOMINIC   Peel 'em good 'n' clean.

CHARLIE   I'm peelin', I'm peelin'.

DOMINIC   No fries.

CHARLIE   Whataya mean, "No fries?"

DOMINIC   It's a special dinner tonight.

CHARLIE   Always a special dinner with you.

DOMINIC   Tonight is very special.

CHARLIE   Six months of special dinners. I'm tired of this crap.

DOMINIC   [*Sarcastically.*] Well, aren't we in a good mood.

CHARLIE   Up yours.

DOMINIC   I don't do requests.

CHARLIE   Funny!

DOMINIC   Whataya getting upset about?

CHARLIE   What am I getting upset about? What am I . . . Well, let me see. My stock portfolio has plummeted below expectations. No, no! Actually, my spiritual advisor has informed me that I've missed my last chance to connect with the Great Spirit from beyond, now I'm destined to spend all eternity here in the wilds of New Jersey with you. What am I upset about? What, am I alone here?

DOMINIC   I was only askin'.

CHARLIE   [*Quickly.*] Don't ask.

DOMINIC   Easy, easy. This is no good for your blood pressure, Charlie.

CHARLIE   A lot you care for my blood pressure.

DOMINIC   You won't be able to digest your dinner. Agita!

CHARLIE   I could never digest this whole damning business. I'm up to here with Leo. I can't take it anymore.

DOMINIC   We're almost done, we're at the end.

CHARLIE   How could this have happened to men like us?

DOMINIC   Slice 'em thin and we'll have 'em scalloped.

CHARLIE   Strong, independent men, like us.

DOMINIC   You like scalloped potatoes.

CHARLIE   Huh? What?

DOMINIC   Scalloped potatoes!

CHARLIE   Scalloped potatoes?

DOMINIC   With the onions, like you like.

CHARLIE   Paprika?

DOMINIC   You want paprika?

CHARLIE   Paprika's good.

DOMINIC   You got it. Now slice 'em thin.

CHARLIE   All right. I'll slice 'em thin.

[DOM *begins tonight's dinner by preparing the salad.*]

DOMINIC   I got the vegetables right out of your garden, Charlie. The calcium from the bones crunched up with the fertilizer and shit must be great for the plants. Look at that tomato. Nice, huh!

CHARLIE   Yeah.

DOMINIC   Nice?

CHARLIE   Yeah, nice.

[DOM *sings as* CHARLIE *stares at him,* DOMINIC *smiles.*]

This doesn't bother you, does it?

DOMINIC   What?

CHARLIE   *This!* This whole thing. Big Anthony Jr.? What we're doing here? Leo?

DOMINIC   Hey! Leo was our best friend.

CHARLIE   That's what I'm saying.

DOMINIC   We put our lives on the line for Leo.

CHARLIE   More than our lives.

DOMINIC   More is right. That's why I want this done the right way. Not like some bunch of . . . of . . .

CHARLIE   And this is the right way to you?

DOMINIC   The best I can do.

CHARLIE   Men like us deserve better.

DOMINIC   That's a given.

CHARLIE   I told Big Anthony Jr. that. I said it right to his face.

DOMINIC   You sure did. I was there. Give me the pepper, will ya?

[CHARLIE *hands* DOMINIC *the pepper mill, then goes back to the table, slices potatoes.* DOM *at the counter.*]

CHARLIE   Here.

[*Pepper.*]

I was a made man.

DOMINIC   Top of the line.

Charlie   Over thirty years of faithful service to that family.

Dominic   We started at about the same time. Remember?

Charlie   I remember. Bet your ass I remember. Does Big Anthony Jr. remember? *No!* Am I right or am I right?

Dominic   You're right.

Charlie   Huh?

Dominic   When you're right, you're right.

Charlie   You know I . . . I . . . never mind.

Dominic   What?

Charlie   I shouldn't say this.

Dominic   Say what ya gotta say.

Charlie   Don't take it wrong.

Dominic   You're talkin' to me for God sakes.

Charlie   I coulda been sitting where Big Anthony Jr.'s sittin' right now.

Dominic   If Big Anthony Sr. didn't have a Jr. you would have been sitting in his chair. You or Leo. Not even the Uncle Sid . . .

Charlie   Sid? Those old corp guineas would never let the Uncle Sid take over. *Never!*

Dominic   Bunch a bigoted . . . bums.

Charlie   Still; bad rug and all, you gotta watch out for the Uncle Sid. Big Anthony Jr. may be the muscle and the Uncle Sid the brains, but they're both sick in the head. They have the blood in the mouth, as Leo would say. The *blood!*

Dominic   Charlie, can I ask you something?

Charlie   Spit out what ya gotta ask.

Dominic   I have no right to ask this.

Charlie   Spit.

Dominic   Totally unprofessional on my part.

Charlie   Hey, after what we've been through!

Dominic   There is *one* hit you never told us about and I . . .

Charlie   The Uncle Sid?!

Dominic   You never said what . . .

Charlie   Forget it. No way. No how.

[CHARLIE *places the sliced potatoes on the counter, then washes his hands at the sink.*]

DOMINIC   I know, if ya coulda' said something, you would have told us twenty-five years ago but . . .

CHARLIE   Dom, Some things you just don't talk about.

DOMINIC   I loved the way you'd tell us about the hits over one of my dinners.

CHARLIE   Don't put me on the spot here.

DOMINIC   You never told us what happened after those two pimps from the house on Gates Avenue cut Sid's throat and left him for dead.

CHARLIE   They cut his throat from ear to ear and the snake still didn't die. The Uncle Sid, asked me and Leo to bring the two pimps to him alive. We did that . . . that Leo and I did. That's all I can say. Except the Uncle Sid is a sick, sick, sick man.

DOMINIC   You brought them to Nunzio's Pizzeria over on Atlantic Ave.

CHARLIE   [*Jumps up.*] HOLD IT! Hold it right there. You did not, *not*, hear that from me. No way you *ever* heard that from me.

DOMINIC   Nunzio told me. But he never said *what* you did to those guys.

CHARLIE   That's all he could say, because he wasn't there. Me, Leo, and the Uncle Sid and the two that were never heard from again was the only ones there.

DOMINIC   So what did you do?

CHARLIE   Dominic, I can't. If the Uncle Sid ever . . .

DOMINIC   I give you my word I'll never . . .

CHARLIE   Nooo! Not even for you. The Uncle Sid would . . .

DOMINIC   I thought, now that Leo is . . .

CHARLIE   No.

DOMINIC   [*Sulks.*] Okay. *Fine!* If that's the way you want to be about it.

[DOMINIC *sits at the table and sulks.*]

CHARLIE   Any of the other hits, I'd be glad to tell ya about. Any one of them.

DOMINIC   I know all about the other hits.

CHARLIE   I'd tell you if I could, Dom.

DOMINIC   [*Brokenhearted.*] It's okay. Forget it.

CHARLIE   Aaah! Don't be like that.

DOMINIC   I just thought after all we been through with Leo.

CHARLIE   Dom, please, I . . .

DOMINIC   It's okay.

CHARLIE   Dom!

DOMINIC   No. It's alright.

CHARLIE   Will ya stop.

DOMINIC   [*Almost in tears.*] Fine.

[*There is a pause.*]

CHARLIE   Leo and I brought the two pimps to Nunzio's wrapped up in duct tape. Wrapped up and gaged. The Uncle Sid just got out of the hospital, his neck was still covered up in bandages. Couldn't speak a word. Did you know, at that time, they didn't think he'd ever speak again. There was an eerie, kinda, *silence.* The two about to be dead, they couldn't say anything. Me and Leo didn't know what to expect and the Uncle Sid, quiet as a mouse with this shit-eatin' grin on his face. Now, one of the pimps is quiet 'cause he knows. The other one is crying, like he's praying for something that ain't ever gonna come. The Uncle Sid fires up the pizza oven and he motions for us to throw in the quiet one minus the gag. We did. Dom, I never heard anyone scream like that in my life.

DOMINIC   *God!*

CHARLIE   The Uncle Sid just sat there watching this guy fry like a piece of bacon. Funny thing is, Sid is watching the crier as much as he's watching the fryer. And the crier, after about an hour of watching his buddy burn, falls to the floor in a dead faint. Finally the Uncle Sid motions to Leo to un-gag the crier. Leo does so and guess what.

DOMINIC   What?

CHARLIE   The crier is dead. He didn't faint. He swallowed his own tongue.

DOMINIC   Woof!

[*Puts kitchen towel in mouth.*]

CHARLIE   The Uncle Sid motions to throw him in anyway. We did. We waited for a couple of hours while the Uncle Sid just sat there and watched them burn till there was nothing left but ashes. Just watching. Quiet! You don't mess with the Uncle Sid.

[DOMINIC *puts his hand on* CHARLIE's *shoulder.*]

DOMINIC   Thank you for sharing.

CHARLIE   Now you know.

DOMINIC   Charlie, I can't tell you what it means to me.

CHARLIE   Don't ever say a word.

DOMINIC   It'll always be something that you and I can share together.

CHARLIE   The only hit the Uncle Sid was actually at.

DOMINIC   It'll be our little secret.

[*Pause.*]

Now I know why Nunzio's crust has that unique taste.

CHARLIE   You think?

DOMINIC   The best crust in Brooklyn! You see, Charlie, you see, there is always a bright side to everything that you and Leo ever did.

CHARLIE   The things Leo and I did for that family. I can't begin to tell you.

DOMINIC   You and Leo were the best.

CHARLIE   If it wasn't for us that family would still be selling olive oil on Mott Street.

DOMINIC   They owe you big, Charlie.

CHARLIE   Yeah, and look what I get for thanks.

DOMINIC   They have no sense of appreciation.

CHARLIE   None. They don't know the meaning of the word. Ever since Big Anthony Sr. died, the whole thing has gone to hell.

DOMINIC   In a handbasket.

CHARLIE   There's no respect anymore, *no* honor.

DOMINIC   No class.

CHARLIE   Thirty years, Dom. What do I get, huh? Respect? Gratitude? A little appreciation?

DOMINIC   I know, Charlie.

CHARLIE   What *do* I get!?

DOMINIC   Don't do this to yourself.

CHARLIE   TELL ME!

DOMINIC   Charlie, we screwed up.

CHARLIE   Since when is loyalty a screwup?

DOMINIC   Big Anthony Jr. doesn't see it that way. He only . . .

CHARLIE   What other way is there to see it?

Dominic   You're preaching to the ordained.

Charlie   Leo was our best friend.

Dominic   Tell me something I don't know.

Charlie   Leo was a pro, he would of never talked.

Dominic   I know that.

Charlie   Everybody knew that.

Dominic   Everybody except . . .

Charlie   That bastard.

Dominic   Big Anthony Jr.

Charlie   To hell with 'im. You hear me?

Dominic   Yeah.

Charlie   Huh?

Dominic   I hear you, I hear you.

Charlie   Look, forget all that. Forget the thirty years. Forget the loyalty.

Dominic   That's a lot to forget, Charlie.

Charlie   Forget it, I tell ya.

Dominic   It's forgotten.

Charlie   If Big Anthony Jr. had a heart, he never would of given us the hit on Leo. Am I right or am I right?

Dominic   You're right.

Charlie   Huh?

Dominic   When you're right, you're right.

Charlie   I hate that bastard.

Dominic   Big Anthony Jr.'s heart is whattaya call . . . a . . . a moron ox.

Charlie   [*Pause.*] WHAT!?

Dominic   He ain't got a heart. To him a contract is a contract. Thank God we got a second chance.

[Dom *goes to his work area at the sink and studies a zucchini.* Charlie *sits, as his anger mounts.*]

Charlie   A second chance!? Is that what this is? A man like me, to be punished like this . . . like a schoolboy, a child, an infant.

Dominic   This is a wonderful zucchini.

Charlie   How will I ever face my friends?

DOMINIC   Not like store bought.

CHARLIE   They all knew Leo.

DOMINIC   [*Smelling.*] No wax on it or nothin'.

CHARLIE   They look at me and they'll be seeing him, like he's a part of me or something.

DOMINIC   It smells sweet almost.

CHARLIE   [*About to blow.*] It's wrong, I tell you!

[DOMINIC *takes zucchini over to* CHARLIE.]

DOMINIC   Here, smell this zucchini.

CHARLIE   WRONG!

DOMINIC   Smell.

[DOM *pushes the zucchini into* CHARLIE'S *face.*]

CHARLIE   [*Exploding.*] WHAAAA! What the hell are you sticking in my face?

DOMINIC   This is the freshest zucchini.

CHARLIE   Are you out of your mind?

DOMINIC   Well, you don't have to get nasty.

CHARLIE   I'm talking about our lives here.

DOMINIC   Would you relax for Christ . . .

CHARLIE   Our fall from grace.

DOMINIC   Charlie, please . . . You'll give yourself a heart attack.

CHARLIE   I can't take it anymore.

DOMINIC   Stop this right now!

CHARLIE   I can't take in Leo anymore.

DOMINIC   CHARLIE!

CHARLIE   Hell with Big Anthony Jr. The hell with him. YOU HEAR ME! TO HELL . . .!

[DOMINIC *smacks the ranting* CHARLIE *over the head with the zucchini.* CHARLIE *raises the potato peeler as if to stab* DOMINIC *in the chest.* DOMINIC *just stands there calmly holding the zucchini and looking at* CHARLIE *knowing full well that his best friend could never hurt him.* CHARLIE *slowly lowers the peeler.*]

DOMINIC   What are ya gonna do, peel me to death?

CHARLIE   [*Sits.*] I'm losing it, Dom, losing . . .

DOMINIC   Now, I want you to take a deep breath. Come on. Breathe. In-out-in-out. Now smell the zucchini.

CHARLIE   Nice.

DOMINIC   Isn't it?

CHARLIE   [*Smells.*] Sweet, kinda.

DOMINIC   Isn't it though?

CHARLIE   You have a very nice zucchini, Dom.

DOMINIC   The simple things, Charlie, I'm tellin' ya. You gotta learn to stop and smell the zucchini.

[DOMINIC *picks up broken zucchini as* CHARLIE *rubs his head.*]

CHARLIE   Your zucchini is very hard, Dom.

DOMINIC   I'm sure gonna miss that garden of yours. An accomplishment. You must be very proud.

CHARLIE   I'm sorry. I could no more hurt you than I could Leo.

DOMINIC   I know.

CHARLIE   That's the way it's always been.

DOMINIC   The Three Musketeers. One for all and all for one.

CHARLIE   I gotta talk this out with you.

DOMINIC   I'm all ears.

CHARLIE   We're near the end of Leo.

DOMINIC   Closer than you think.

CHARLIE   You gotta try to understand what I'm saying here.

DOMINIC   I'll try.

CHARLIE   Can you comprehend, can you fathom, what guys like Leo and I had?

DOMINIC   Where was I, Mars?! I was there.

CHARLIE   Yeah, yeah. You were there, but Leo and I were in the know. We had all the answers. Top of the food chain.

DOMINIC   What do you want me to say?

CHARLIE   There's nothing to say.

DOMINIC   I say nothing then.

CHARLIE   We had it all within our grasp. I walked this earth as few men have ever walked this earth.

DOMINIC   Proud!

CHARLIE   Proud, shit! Leo and I walked with strength, with real muscle. They feared us.

DOMINIC   Two truly respected men.

CHARLIE   Respect? I don't know from respect. But I know that we knew. And everyone knew that we knew.

DOMINIC   I never knew.

CHARLIE   Few ever do.

DOMINIC   I never did.

[*Pause.*]

You want eggplant?

CHARLIE   Forget the eggplant.

DOMINIC   Some broccoli rabe, it's all ready.

CHARLIE   Dominic, you . . . you never knew. Did you?

[CHARLIE *stares at the happy-go-lucky* DOMINIC.]

DOMINIC   What?

CHARLIE   What we knew? What we had?

DOMINIC   Hey! I played the hand I was dealt.

CHARLIE   Yeah! Yeeeah, I can see that.

[CHARLIE *shakes his head and goes back to the table.*]

DOMINIC   It shows?

CHARLIE   *Weelll,* what can I say.

DOMINIC   It really shows?

CHARLIE   You were better off without knowing.

DOMINIC   Just a guy on the fringe?

CHARLIE   I wouldn't say that.

DOMINIC   An outsider.

CHARLIE   Never to me and Leo.

DOMINIC   But to the others?

CHARLIE   Never with us.

DOMINIC   But with the others?

CHARLIE   Can I be honest?

DOMINIC   To Big Anthony Jr.?

CHARLIE Especially Big Anthony Jr.

[*A pause as* DOMINIC *takes this in and accepts it.*]

DOMINIC All right. All right, I accept my faith [*Malaprop.*].

[DOMINIC *goes back to work at stove.*]

CHARLIE THAT! *That's* what I'm trying to get at. Do we have to accept faith?

DOMINIC Charlie, "To accept is faith."

CHARLIE Aaaah! You! You are a very perceptive man, Dominic.

DOMINIC I'm just the cook.

CHARLIE No, no, no, you have real insight.

DOMINIC What can I say; it's a gift.

CHARLIE From God?

DOMINIC Perhaps.

CHARLIE How can we know?

DOMINIC We can't.

[*Pause.*]

CHARLIE Dominic, are we being punished?

DOMINIC I would say what Big Anthony Jr.'s doing to us is a punishment. Yes.

CHARLIE I'm not talking Big Anthony Jr. now.

DOMINIC Ouoh! I get ya.

[*To heaven.*]

You think?

CHARLIE [*Sits.*] It's like we are being punished for things that Leo did.

DOMINIC Things that Big Anthony did.

CHARLIE Junior and Senior.

DOMINIC Yeah!

CHARLIE We're being consumed by their sins.

DOMINIC Or vice a versa, in this case.

CHARLIE How's that?

DOMINIC We're consuming more than just food.

CHARLIE [*Shocked.*] You think!?

DOMINIC I'm just the cook. What do I know?

CHARLIE   To know what I have known, to do what I have done, *this* is truly a gift turned into a curse.

DOMINIC   A Trojan horse.

CHARLIE   What horse? I'm not talking horses here now.

DOMINIC   The Greeks, I'm talkin'.

CHARLIE   Diners!?

DOMINIC   Forget diners! Remember that Greek broad.

CHARLIE   Dames! That's another subject.

DOMINIC   Beware of Greeks bearing gifts.

CHARLIE   What are ya talkin'?

DOMINIC   Remember the Trojan horse? The gift that Greek broad gave those other Greeks.

CHARLIE   Ooh! Oooh! The one full of soldiers?

DOMINIC   That's it.

CHARLIE   A bunch of dopes, fallin' for that.

DOMINIC   I mean, come on. *But* you get what I'm saying? Pieces of Leo enter you and destroy somethin'. Somethin' good, somethin' bad, we don't know. But destroy! Just like those Greeks jumpin' outta that horse and destroying the city for that bush.

CHARLIE   Yeah. Yeah! It's the same thing in a different way. So, you get my drift? You feel it too.

[*Pause as* DOM *nods in agreement.*]

I don't think she was Greek though.

DOMINIC   You sure?

CHARLIE   I think she was from Sicily.

DOMINIC   No kiddin'. Siciglian, huh?

CHARLIE   My ex-wife, Amelia, was from Sicily.

DOMINIC   That's what we're talkin' here.

CHARLIE   You lost me.

DOMINIC   Maybe . . . just maybe . . . if she was a Greek she would have stayed.

CHARLIE   You think?

DOMINIC   You can't tell. God works in mysterious ways.

CHARLIE   Dominic, did we just get off the track here, or is this all related?

DOMINIC   Everything. And I mean everything . . . the air you breathe, the video games you play, the food you eat, it's all related, Charlie.

CHARLIE   Leo was married to a Greek.

DOMINIC   [*Point made.*] You see what I'm sayin'?

CHARLIE   He could go no higher in the family because of the Greek wife.

DOMINIC   You see. You see how it's all related. Another gift turned into a curse. Leo's curse has transferred . . . been imposed on us.

CHARLIE   Dominic, you're a very wise man.

DOMINIC   I try.

CHARLIE   You know that tall Italian guy works for Big Anthony Jr.?

DOMINIC   Tall?

CHARLIE   A giant. Italian guy—I think his last name begins with an "S."

DOMINIC   [*Thinks.*] Gerber?

CHARLIE   Nooo! I don't think that's it.

DOMINIC   Anyway.

CHARLIE   Anyway. He's married to a Greek.

DOMINIC   She still with 'im?

CHARLIE   Over twenty somethin' years.

DOMINIC   Well, there you go. Ya shoulda married a Greek.

CHARLIE   [*A revelation.*] THAT'S! *That's* what Leo always said. I'm tellin' ya, Dom, something . . . something has happened *here*.

DOMINIC   Six months of dinners on Leo. That's what's happened.

CHARLIE   No, no, no, it's more than that. For the first time in my life I've realized a truth. A real truth.

DOMINIC   First time?

CHARLIE   The rest is bullshit. All the rest of our lives is bullshit.

DOMINIC   That's a little hard, Charlie.

CHARLIE   Dominic, we are fools. Idiots goin' blindly forth, being led by a Judas goat. We know nothin'. We feel nothin'. We taste nothin'. We smell not—

DOMINIC   [*Upset.*] I take exception. I'm a cook. I grant you Einstein has nothin' to worry from me. I ain't the sharpest coal in the bin. I'm an idiot about a lot of things but not cooking. I draw the line. I taste and I smell!

CHARLIE   Exception noted.

DOMINIC   As long as that's clear.

Charlie   It's clear! It's clear, but it's not what I mean, Dominic. And I can't tell you what I mean because I lack the words. The vocabulary. The verbiage. It's like . . . it's like the garden in my mind has grown since we've been here. It's like an illuminating light that shines forth revealing this, this . . .

Dominic   What?

Charlie   This darkness.

Dominic   A light showing the darkness?

Charlie   Yeah.

Dominic   You lost me.

Charlie   Me too. I got a feelin' I've been lost since the first time Leo asked me to back him up on a hit.

Dominic   A little late, don't you think?

Charlie   I shoulda never asked you to be my backup on the Leo job. I was wrong to do that.

Dominic   Hey! You didn't know it was going to be Leo. Besides that's the only time anyone ever asked me to do somethin' besides cook. I'm grateful. I don't care how this worm turns. I appreciate it.

Charlie   I know you do and there's something wrong with that too. What? I don't know. I don't know the answers to any of these questions. I *do know* the answers are *not* here with Leo.

Dominic   You think too much.

Charlie   You can't think too much.

Dominic   Oh! Yes you can.

Charlie   Dom, let's get the hell out of here.

Dominic   [*Surprised.*] You *are* nuts?!

Charlie   When Big Anthony Jr. calls tonight we don't let on, see. We let him bust our chops like he always does, we laugh when he wants us too, *then* he hangs up and we move on.

Dominic   Move on?!

Charlie   It'll be a week before he even knows we're gone.

Dominic   And no time before he finds us.

Charlie   You don't know that.

Dominic   Oh, yes I do. . . .

Charlie   We can be far gone in a week.

DOMINIC   [*Stirs sauce.*] Not far enough.

CHARLIE   Please, Dom.

DOMINIC   No!

CHARLIE   I'm begging you.

DOMINIC   I said, "No."

CHARLIE   But, Dom . . .

DOMINIC   [*Slams spoon.*] Izzy Schultz.

CHARLIE   Izzy?!

DOMINIC   Yeah, Izzy Schultz.

CHARLIE   Aaaah! You had to bring that up, didn't you?

DOMINIC   Twelve years in the witness protection program.

CHARLIE   Why did I ever open my *big* mouth about Izzy?

DOMINIC   TWELVE YEARS!

CHARLIE   Go on, drag up the past.

DOMINIC   TWELVE YEARS!

CHARLIE   Throw it in my face.

DOMINIC   No one should die like that.

CHARLIE   It wasn't my idea.

DOMINIC   How could you?!

CHARLIE   Leo was against it too.

DOMINIC   Still.

CHARLIE   It was the Uncle Sid's idea.

DOMINIC   . . . And you carried it out.

CHARLIE   "An example," the Uncle Sid says.

DOMINIC   You and Leo acting like a pair of Indians out of an old Randolph Scott movie. For God sakes.

CHARLIE   We was following orders.

DOMINIC   Staking Izzy down in the hot desert sands of Arizona . . .

CHARLIE   Don't remind me.

DOMINIC   . . . pouring honey on his head and watching red ants eat his face off.

CHARLIE   They eat the eyes out first.

DOMINIC   That, *that* is really . . . disgusting.

CHARLIE   [*Not letting go.*] At least he had twelve more years.

DOMINIC   Twelve more years waiting for the red ants. *No thank you!* There ain't no escape and you know it.

CHARLIE   [*Pause.*] Aaagh! I guess you're right.

DOMINIC   I *know*, I'm right.

CHARLIE   Yeah, yeah.

DOMINIC   You *know* I'm right.

CHARLIE   When you're right, you're right.

DOMINIC   God! How could you sit there and watch such a thing.

CHARLIE   We didn't.

DOMINIC   [*Surprised.*] You didn't?

CHARLIE   No.

DOMINIC   [*Shocked.*] You left a mark before he died?

CHARLIE   You could say that.

DOMINIC   I'm surprised. That doesn't sound like you and Leo. Very unprofessional.

CHARLIE   I know. I know. But I couldn't take the screaming anymore. I got sick. I threw up. Leo says, "Let's get the hell outta here." So we jump in the car and Leo accidentally on purpose backs over Izzy's face.

DOMINIC   No kidding?

CHARLIE   It felt like the speed bump in the parking lot at the Whole Foods. Then there was no more screaming.

DOMINIC   Really? Leo did that?

CHARLIE   My hand to God.

DOMINIC   [*Pause.*] Leo . . . was a good driver.

CHARLIE   Yeah, he liked to drive.

DOMINIC   What a guy!

[CHARLIE *and* DOM *reflect.*]

CHARLIE   The best.

DOMINIC   The best.

CHARLIE   You're right, Dom, there ain't no escape. I don't know what I was thinking. I'm sorry.

DOMINIC Too much of the same diet, that's what's wrong with you.

CHARLIE You think?

DOMINIC When we're done here, no red meat for at least a month. I'm tellin' ya for your own good.

CHARLIE Perhaps you're right.

DOMINIC The cook is always right. Now, I don't want to hear any more about it. Relax! Have another wine.

CHARLIE You're right. This thinkin' will drive you nuts. Clouds your mind.

DOMINIC Blow away the clouds. For tonight is a big night and I gotta have you sharp, and thinkin' clearly.

CHARLIE Whatever you say.

DOMINIC Here, taste this sauce.

[DOMINIC *comes to* CHARLIE *with a wooden spoon full of sauce.* DOM *feeds* CHARLIE *like a child.*]

CHARLIE OOH! Now that's good.

DOMINIC I knew you'd like it.

[DOMINIC *wipes* CHARLIE's *chin with dish towel.*]

CHARLIE That's very good. Smells great. Like Leo. Remember?

DOMINIC A dapper guy.

CHARLIE Whenever we went on a hit, Leo would get a shave, a haircut, and a new suit and he'd put on that expensive cologne, that French stuff.

DOMINIC Manicure.

CHARLIE A manicure, yes, yes.

DOMINIC Leo had respect for the about-to-be dead.

CHARLIE The man had class. He had style.

DOMINIC He had heart.

CHARLIE He'd give you the shirt off his back.

DOMINIC Don't even go there. A saint.

CHARLIE The time we whacked Willie the Bug at his place on Sullivan Street?

DOMINIC I remember that.

CHARLIE We tied the Bug to the chair and I held his head while Leo put that long ten penny nail in his ear. Big Anthony Sr. questioned the Bug and every time he got a wrong answer, *wack*, Leo tapped the nail.

DOMINIC   I remember, I went to the kitchen and made us a dinner. Escarole with the tiny white meatballs.

CHARLIE   I love those tiny white meatballs.

DOMINIC   I'll make 'em for you.

CHARLIE   Don't go to any trouble or nothin'.

DOMINIC   What! No trouble; one, two, three.

CHARLIE   That would be good. Where was I?

DOMINIC   Leo tapped in the nail . . .

CHARLIE   Yeah! Once Big Anthony Sr. got what he wanted, he smacked the nail into the Bug's brain and goes to the kitchen to eat your escarole.

DOMINIC   Madonna me! Big Anthony Sr. could eat.

CHARLIE   Yeah! And there's the Bug squirming on the floor. Shaking like a tree in a storm. What does Leo do?

DOMINIC   What?

CHARLIE   He cuts his throat and puts him out of all that pain.

DOMINIC   Whatta guy!

CHARLIE   Leo coulda got himself in trouble with Big Anthony Sr. for that.

DOMINIC   Of course he could.

CHARLIE   Leo had heart, he had compassion.

DOMINIC   That's one way to look at it.

CHARLIE   The time we had to throw that Episcopal minister into the alligator pond at the zoo. What did Leo do?

DOMINIC   What?

CHARLIE   You don't know?

DOMINIC   Only what you told us over dinner.

CHARLIE   Okay, don't ever tell anyone this.

DOMINIC   Like Leo's goin' to care now?

CHARLIE   [*Angered.*] HEY! We're talkin' a professional reputation here, Dom. I wouldn't want anyone to think Leo was soft or nothin'. Ya know what I mean?

DOMINIC   You're right.

CHARLIE   Huh?

DOMINIC   When you're right, you're right.

CHARLIE [*Whispers.*] Leo cut the Reverend's throat before we threw him in with the gators.

DOMINIC Really?

CHARLIE Is that a stand-up guy or what?

[*Pause.*]

Aaah! Dom, I tell ya, those were the good old days.

[CHARLIE *sits at the table with* DOM.]

DOMINIC Charlie, can I say somethin'?

CHARLIE Spit out what ya gotta say.

DOMINIC We're talkin' here, right?

CHARLIE Spit.

DOMINIC You and Leo were always my two best friends and I gotta say it; I miss him not being around.

CHARLIE AH! Don't start now.

DOMINIC [*Sadly.*] I'm just sayin'. In a way, it's kinda nice to know that Leo will always be a part of us.

CHARLIE Come on, this is no time to get all sentimental and stuff.

DOMINIC Actually, it's the perfect time, Charlie. Guess what we're having for dinner tonight. CERVELLO!

CHARLIE Cervello?

DOMINIC The ole Italian sweet bread.

CHARLIE [*Surprised.*] CERVELLO! Tonight?

DOMINIC With onions and herbs in a lobster bisque sauce. Scalloped potatoes and broccoli rabe.

CHARLIE Cervello! Does that mean . . . ?

DOMINIC YES! Our farewell dinner! I called Junior from the grocery store.

CHARLIE [*Panic.*] You called him already?!

DOMINIC Yeah, he should be here any minute.

CHARLIE YOU CALLED BIG ANTHONY JR.?!

DOMINIC Remember what he said? He stood over this table and held Leo's heart in his hand. He took a bite out of it. Then he said, "You wanna live? You eat the rest of the heart first and the brain last. In between, you eat every last bit of this . . . this . . . rat! Call me for the last supper. Maybe I'll let you live." I thought I was gonna puke. Raw like that. Disgusting!

[*Thinks.*]

I could of made a nice cacciatore.

CHARLIE   [*Panic.*] What the hell did you call him for?

DOMINIC   What are you talking about? Those were our instructions.

CHARLIE   You should of told me before you called him.

DOMINIC   I wanted to surprise you.

CHARLIE   [*Furious.*] Well, you sure as hell did.

DOMINIC   I was following orders.

CHARLIE   Following orders, huh?

DOMINIC   That's right. We wouldn't of been in this mess in the first place if you knew how to follow . . .

CHARLIE   Big Anthony Jr. gave me orders for the last supper too, Mr. Know It All.

DOMINIC   What orders?

CHARLIE   [*Pause.*] Never mind.

DOMINIC   What orders, Charlie?

CHARLIE   Shut up! I gotta think.

DOMINIC   Tell me.

CHARLIE   Not now.

DOMINIC   Tell me, Charlie; so help me God . . .

[DOMINIC *stands facing* CHARLIE *with a large meat clever in his hand.* DOMINIC *looks as if he's about to slice* CHARLIE *in half.* CHARLIE *stares him down.*]

CHARLIE   [*Re: knife.*] What's this?

DOMINIC   What orders?

CHARLIE   You couldn't . . .

DOMINIC   Don't bet our lives on it. I can butcher just as good as Leo ever could. Now, for the last time . . .

[*Someone tries to enter, then there is a loud knock at the back door.*]

CHARLIE   Don't open it.

DOMINIC   I'm not afraid of Jr.

[DOM *goes to the door and* CHARLIE *tries to head him off, but* DOM *waves the clever at* CHARLIE, *who backs up quickly.*]

CHARLIE   You should be.

[Dominic *pushes open the door with a force and determination that soon dissipates as he looks into the eyes of* Big Anthony Jr. *For* Anthony, *dressed in a long black cashmere coat, black suit, black hat, is evil itself. A dozen years younger, he commands the fear of the older and more experienced mobsters.*]

Anthony   You gonna have me come in or what?

Dominic   Sure, sure, come in, why don't you?

Charlie   Yeah, we've been expecting you.

[Big Anthony Jr. *walks around the kitchen taking in the aroma of tonight's meal.* Charlie *and* Dom *play the coming scene protecting each other.*]

Anthony   Six months. It's about time you been expecting me.

Dominic   Well, Leo was a big man.

Anthony   [*Laughs.*] Leo was a big man?

Dominic   You know. Big like . . .

Anthony   Oh! Big. Like a big fat disgusting stoolie?

Dominic   Yeah! Somethin' like that.

Anthony   He *used* to be a big man. Now?

Charlie   Now, he's gone.

Anthony   So, this is the last supper, huh?

Charlie   You could put it that way.

Anthony   What am I, an orphan here. Somebody gonna take my coat or what?

Dominic   Charlie, take Big Anthony Jr.'s coat and hat.

[Charlie *starts to remove* Big Anthony's *coat.*]

Charlie   I'll hang it by the door, Boss!

Anthony   You do that.

Dominic   Charlie; get Anthony a glass of wine. While I get things ready.

Anthony   A little wine would be nice. Will you smell this? What a smell! You having fish tonight, Dominic?

Charlie   You know what we're . . .

Anthony   [*At* Charlie.] I'm askin' Dominic. You wanna know what the speciality of the house is, you ask the chef. You don't ask the busboy.

Charlie   [*Quickly.*] Wine.

Anthony   You first, Charlie.

[Charlie *takes a quick sip from the bottle.*]

Now, what's that great smell?

[CHARLIE *begins to set the table for the last supper.*]

DOMINIC   That's lobster bisque sauce, for the cervello.

ANTHONY   Lobster sauce?

DOMINIC   Yeah.

ANTHONY   Cervello?

DOMINIC   Cervello al a Leo on a bed of broccoli, it's tonight's special.

ANTHONY   Tonight's special, huh? You cook like this every night?

CHARLIE   [*Setting table.*] You know how he is.

[*As* ANTHONY *goes to stove to sample the sauce.*]

ANTHONY   Oh yeah! We all know how Dominic can be. You're a very good cook.

[*Tastes.*]

Mmmmmm! A great cook. This is some sauce. My compliments!

[*Toasts* DOMINIC *with wineglass.*]

DOMINIC   Well . . .

[*Blushingly shy.*]

ANTHONY   Well what?

DOMINIC   I don't like to brag or nothin' . . .

ANTHONY   Don't be so modest. Ain't he the best, Charlie? Huh?

CHARLIE   Yeah, for sure, the very best ever cooked for the family. The truth.

ANTHONY   You hear that, Dominic? You hear what your friend Charlie says?

DOMINIC   [*Shyly.*] Well, Charlie's my best friend.

ANTHONY   Not just Charlie. Everybody. The whole gang. Dominic could cook this, Dominic could cook that; DOMINIC, DOMINIC, DOMINIC! If they knew you two were still alive I'd have a mutiny on my hands. I mean it. A real live mutiny.

DOMINIC   Thanks, it's nice to be appreciated.

ANTHONY   When I left today I told the Uncle Sid I was going to visit a couple of ghosts. Ghosts are guys what are dead but don't know it, I says. You know they all think you two are dead. I mean, I couldn't let 'em know you was just bein' punished. I'd look like I'm getting soft or something. *Musciad!* Like I'm not my father's son. Like maybe someone else should be runnin' things. Right? I said; right, Charlie?

CHARLIE   [*Setting table.*] Whatever you say.

ANTHONY   But when they find out what the punishment was, well . . . We'll see what we shall see.

DOMINIC   Ain't they gonna be surprised when we show up again, huh?

ANTHONY   That *would* be a surprise. You get back tomorrow, you gonna cook a special meal for everybody?

DOMINIC   The best meal they ever ate. I'm gonna make: veal Milanese, with a side order of *puttanesta*, and to start off with; an anti-pasti followed by a bowl of escarole. . . .

ANTHONY   *Escarole!*

DOMINIC   Yeah, in a chicken broth.

ANTHONY   With the little white meatballs?

DOMINIC   Sure, *and* with an egg whipped in!

ANTHONY   [*Screams at* CHARLIE.] I LOVE ESCAROLE WITH THE EGG!

DOMINIC   Tomorrow night, as soon as we get back. You'll see. It'll be just like it was before.

CHARLIE   Can only be like before with Dominic's cookin'.

[CHARLIE *serves the scalloped potatoes with mittens on both hands.*]

ANTHONY   Yeah, Dom, they all miss your cookin', Tony, the Mouse, and Vinny, *forgetaboutit!* Every time we go to the East Side for seafood, Vinny starts to cry.

DOMINIC   No kiddin'. For real?

ANTHONY   Would I lie to you?

DOMINIC   Vinny always loved my clam sauce.

ANTHONY   "Nobody can make clam sauce like Dominic. *Nobody!*" Vinny yells it out. The whole restaurant turns and looks at us.

[BIG ANTHONY JR. *imitates Vinny crying at a restaurant.*]

Then you see Vinny's eyes well up with tears. "Poor Dominic wouldn't hurt a fly. Dominic was the best there ever was."

DOMINIC   Vinny said that?

ANTHONY   'Course they're talkin' about the cookin', right? I said, *right?*

DOMINIC   Right.

CHARLIE   Anthony, *please!* Don't do th—

Anthony   Please what? I'm tellin' a truth here. My father always said you was the best, ain't that right, Dom?

Dominic   Big Anthony Sr. was good to me.

Anthony   My father says you're the best. Hey! Who's gonna argue with that, huh? Who? Who?

Charlie   Nobody.

Anthony   Nobody is right. Who's the best baseball player? Babe Ruth? Joe D.? You know why they didn't play hockey? Huh? You know why?

Dominic   Something to do with the wrist?

Anthony   [*Pause. . . . To* Charlie.] You know why they didn't play hockey? Because they don't want to play hockey. Because they are already the best at somethin' else. They don't want to play football or basketball or chess even. They don't want to be killers because they are already the best at what they do. So you don't ask 'em to do somethin' else. If I was the best cook, I'd be the best cook. Know thy station in life. "A rose is a rose is a rose and a rose by any other name is still a stinking flower." *Capisce?!*

Charlie and **Dominic**   *Capisce.*

Anthony   [*To* Dom.] You understand what I'm sayin'?

Dominic   I understand.

Anthony   [*To* Charlie.] You understand?

Charlie   I understand.

Anthony   Good, as long as we all understand.

Dominic   You want we should eat now? 'Cause it's all done and I don't want Leo to get cold.

Anthony   No, no, no, no. I don't want *you two* to eat nothin' here tonight.

Charlie and **Dominic**   You don't? *What?!*

Anthony   [*Calmly.*] No. Not tonight. Tonight, I'm gonna eat. Dominic here is gonna be the chef and you, Charlie, are gonna be the waiter and I'm gonna eat what's left of my enemy. *And then!* Charlie's gonna entertain us.

Charlie   You can't ask me to do this.

Anthony   [*Screams.*] I DON'T ASK NOTHIN'. NOTHIN'! I tell people what to do and they do it or they pay.

[*To* Charlie.]

I tell you to kill a fink, a stoolie, you don't do it, you pay.

Dominic   Leo ain't no stool—

ANTHONY   [*To* DOM *screaming.*] ANOTHER COUNTRY HEARD FROM! Who the hell told you to speak. Huh? You're the cook. So COOK!

CHARLIE   Leo was our best friend.

ANTHONY   [*To* CHARLIE.] SHUT UP! I don't give a damn who Leo was. I said kill the dirty fink and you didn't.

[*Furious.*]

Thank your God, I whacked him before the feds got him to a grand jury or you'd be dead right now; dead, *dead*, DEAD! I don't care how well you knew the old man. I don't give a damn if you gave birth to the old man. You disobeyed me.

[*Composes himself.*]

Now serve up Leo's brains.

[DOMINIC *goes to the counter to prepare salad.*]

DOMINIC   Salad first?

ANTHONY   [*Calmly.*] Why not? This is gonna be a treat. You know why? The blood of my enemy, the heart, the brains of my enemy makes me strong. Makes me feared. Now play waiter.

CHARLIE   Yes, sir!

ANTHONY   You know, Dominic, you should have never left the kitchen. Never left your kingdom. Why the hell Charlie ever wanted you to be his backup on a hit is beyond me. "Give Dominic a chance to make his bones." That's what Charlie said.

[CHARLIE *sets the salad in front of* BIG ANTHONY JR.]

CHARLIE   Salad.

ANTHONY   Charlie, you should of seen your face when I told you the mark was your best friend Leo.

[*Eats.*]

I thought I was looking at a ghost.

[*Mouth full.*]

Oh! This is a great salad. Your own dressing?

DOMINIC   Of course.

ANTHONY   [*To* CHARLIE.] Of course, he says.

CHARLIE   Anthony, we need to talk.

ANTHONY   [*Yells.*] I believe I was talking about salad to the chef here.

DOMINIC   [*Quickly.*] We grow the tomatoes and the cucumbers in the backyard.

ANTHONY   [*Calmly.*] Is that right?

DOMINIC   Yeah. We crushed all of Leo's bones in the mulcher with the leaves and sticks and shit, and used it for fertilizer. Best garden ever.

ANTHONY   [*Mocking.*] Charlie help you with the garden, did he? Planting and hoeing.

DOMINIC   He did most of the work in the garden. Charlie has a green thumb.

ANTHONY   That right, Charlie, a green thumb?

[CHARLIE *raises his mitted thumb.*]

You chop up the body and use the bones of your best friend to grow vegetables?

CHARLIE   Look, Anthony, we've paid for our sins. We devoured our crime against you and the family.

ANTHONY   [*Yells.*] I TELL YOU WHEN THE DEBT IS PAID.

[DOMINIC *goes to the stove and fixes broccoli rabe.*]

DOMINIC   You want broccoli?

ANTHONY   [*Calmly.*] Rabe?

DOMINIC   Rabe—with garlic and olive oil and a little lemon.

ANTHONY   [*To* CHARLIE.] Is he for real or what?

CHARLIE   He's not kidding.

DOMINIC   It's very nice broccoli rabe, it's already made.

ANTHONY   Yeah. Yeah, sure. Why not some broccoli rabe, from the garden?

DOMINIC   Charlie loves the garden.

[CHARLIE *serves up the cervello to* ANTHONY.]

ANTHONY   Pour yourselves a glass and watch how I devour your friend. Then you know what I'm gonna do?

DOMINIC   Take a walk?

ANTHONY   What take a walk?

DOMINIC   A constitution. It's good for the digestion. Charlie and I always take a little walk after.

ANTHONY   Maybe later. First, I'm gonna watch Charlie kill you.

[*Pause as* ANTHONY *starts eating his meal.*]

Dominic   For real?

Charlie   I won't do it, Anthony. I won't.

Anthony   [*Mouth full.*] This is terrific stuff.

Dominic   What's he talkin' about, Charlie?

Charlie   Dominic, that's why I didn't want you to call him. Jr. said when we was through with Leo I had to kill you or he'd feed me to the dogs.

Dominic   He said that?

Anthony   I said sharks.

Charlie   Those were my orders.

[Dominic *thinks for a moment, shrugs his shoulders.*]

Dominic   Well, Charlie, if that's your orders.

Charlie   *What!?*

Dominic   You gotta do what you gotta do.

[*Mouth full,* Anthony *nods with approval at* Dominic.]

Anthony   This guy is beautiful.

Charlie   No way! Besides, as soon as you hit the floor, he'd stick that fork in my head. I know him.

Dominic   He can't kill us both, Charlie.

Charlie   Sure he can.

[*Mouth full,* Anthony *stops eating and looks at* Dominic.]

Dominic   No, he needs one of us to tell of his deeds . . . his masterful way of punishing anyone who would think to disobey. Ain't that right, Boss?

Anthony   [*Smiles.*] Definitely! This is terrific. I can't believe this is Leo. It needs a little something, though, a little . . . You got any red pepper?

Dominic   [*Overlapping.*]. . . .ed pepper. Always with the red pepper. Just like your father. May he rest in peace.

[Dominic *reaches into his apron pocket for the red pepper knowing* Big Anthony Jr. *would ask for it.*]

Charlie   Dom, you sure you understand what's going on here?

Dominic   I understand. Your red pepper.

Anthony   Thank you. Love hot pepper. Go on, Dominic, don't let me stop you. I find your dinner conversation as entertaining as the meal itself.

Dominic   Thank you.

[*To* CHARLIE.]

Jr. here needs someone to spread the word that he's a man to be feared. Like father, like son.

[*Then:*]

Charlie, can I tell you a truth?

CHARLIE   Spit out what you gotta say.

DOMINIC   This is just an observation. I don't want you to get pissed off at me or nothin'.

CHARLIE   Spit.

DOMINIC   Sure?

CHARLIE   *Spit* already.

DOMINIC   That was always your job. Big Anthony Sr. would come up with the punishment, Leo would execute it. You, Charlie . . . you would spread the word. Just like your ancestors, the bards of old Ireland, you kept the family legend alive. I loved listen' to you over one of my dinners.

CHARLIE   Are you kidding me? I was the key. I was the setup.

[ANTHONY *just shrugs his shoulders.*]

ANTHONY   Dom's got a point.

CHARLIE   [*To* ANTHONY.] What the hell are you talkin'?

ANTHONY   [*To* DOMINIC.] Charlie, you just led them to the slaughter. The Judas goat that the lamb followed to his last reward.

CHARLIE   [*Angered.*] That's not the way it was.

DOMINIC   This family was feared by everyone because of you and your stories.

CHARLIE   I was Leo's right hand man.

DOMINIC   You're pissed. I should never say it again, so help me God.

CHARLIE   This is bullshit.

ANTHONY   [*To* CHARLIE.] Know thy station in life.

CHARLIE   [*To* ANTHONY.] That all I was to you? A messenger boy? Someone to spew forth your bile so others would cringe.

ANTHONY   Someone had to do it. These are great scalloped potatoes. What did you do to the onions?

DOMINIC   I lightly fried them in garlic and olive oil and a little honey.

CHARLIE   Paprika.

DOMINIC   . . . and paprika.

ANTHONY   Honey? You believe this guy? I'll be sad when Charlie puts you down.

CHARLIE   Dom, you sure you understand?

DOMINIC   I understand, Charlie, I understand.

[*To* ANTHONY.]

Try a little red pepper on the potatoes. It gives it a hot and sweet taste.

ANTHONY   If it's all right with the chef, I'll just do that. I don't want to insult your cooking, Dominic, but it needs the red pepper.

DOMINIC   Just like your father. See, Charlie, just like Big Anthony Sr., always with the red pepper.

[BIG ANTHONY JR. *puts red pepper on his potatoes.*]

CHARLIE   What's with the red pepper here!

DOMINIC   It's good for the heart and it's good for the love. Huh, Junior? What the old man used to say.

ANTHONY   Yeah, yeah, he always said that. I'm almost done here, Charlie.

CHARLIE   I think you're both nuts!

[BIG ANTHONY JR. *starts to rub his forehead with a napkin and starts to loosen his tie and collar.*]

ANTHONY   Only thing, it makes you hot. Okay, Charlie, let the floor show begin.

CHARLIE   Hell with you, Anthony . . . and the hell with your old man. I'm finished. I'm done. I don't give a damn if you kill me too.

ANTHONY   [*Rises.*] Open a window.

CHARLIE   I AIN'T KILLING DOMINIC!

ANTHONY   [*Rubs throat.*] I said, Open the window.

CHARLIE   Drop dead.

DOMINIC   He will.

[ANTHONY *reaches for* CHARLIE *but then suddenly and violently grabs his own throat and starts to move about the kitchen in a sporadic manner, knocking things every which way.*]

CHARLIE   [*Surprised.*] He's choking.

DOMINIC   Yes! The red pepper is laced with an acid that has a lime base.

[ANTHONY *trashes the dishes in the sink rack and grabs a large knife.*]

CHARLIE   This is beautiful, Dominic. Beautiful!

DOMINIC   Right now the acid is eating through his throat and lungs.

CHARLIE   Die, you bastard.

[BIG ANTHONY JR. *makes one more violent attempt to rise up and attack his killers but falls onto his knees with knife in hand waving it in the air, as he begins to convulse.*]

DOMINIC   I was gonna use strychnine but that would have ruined all the meat.

CHARLIE   How does it feel to die by the hand of your own creation. Die, you bastard, die.

[ANTHONY *continues to shake but not as violently.*]

DOMINIC   He could convulse for hours.

CHARLIE   Good, good! Let him die slow.

DOMINIC   Now, Charlie.

CHARLIE   No, no, I wanna watch.

DOMINIC   Charlie, have we learned nothing from Leo?

CHARLIE   But . . . Aaagh! Do I have to?

DOMINIC   Yes. You must.

[CHARLIE *stares at* DOMINIC *and realizes he's right.*]

CHARLIE   Oooh! I guess you're right.

DOMINIC   Thank you.

CHARLIE   When you're right, you're right.

[CHARLIE *takes the kitchen knife from* BIG ANTHONY JR.]

Let me have that. Thank you.

DOMINIC   Put him over the sink. I don't want blood all over my floor.

[*With one hand full of hair and the other arm around JR.'s midsection,* CHARLIE *spins* ANTHONY *around and lays him over the sink directly behind the table.*]

CHARLIE   Get over the sink, you sick bastard.

DOMINIC   Just like his father with the red pepper. Hot! Hot! Hot! Well, what are ya gonna do? A matter of taste.

[CHARLIE *cuts* BIG ANTHONY JR.'s *throat; blood splashes up on the window over the sink.*]

CHARLIE   He's bleeding like a stuck pig. Dom, help me prop him up here.

DOMINIC   Sure thing.

[Dom *holds* Junior *up by the pants as* Charlie *gets a chair to prop up* Big Anthony Jr. Dom *and* Charlie *talk over* Big Anthony Jr.*'s body.*]

Charlie   Dominic, I'm proud of you. I'll tell ya somethin' else; Leo would have been proud of you too. A masterful job. A piece of art. I . . . I just wish Leo was here to see this. This is something he would have done. It's got his mark.

Dominic   I guess there's a little piece of Leo in all of us.

Charlie   You're a very wise man, Dominic.

Dominic   Thanks, Charlie.

Charlie   You are *very* welcome.

Dominic   No. I mean, *thanks*, Charlie.

Charlie   For what?

Dominic   For believing in me.

Charlie   Aaah! Forget it.

Dominic   For not killin' me.

Charlie   How can you kill a best friend?

Dominic   That's the real question, isn't it?

Charlie   Right now, the question is: What do we do with Big Anthony Jr.?

Dominic   I better clean Big Anthony Jr.'s plate from the table.

[Dominic *starts cleaning off the table.*]

Charlie   Dominic, focus for a second here, I'll get this. What do we do with Big Anthony Jr.'s body? We can't just dump it. They find the body and God knows what could happen.

Dominic   [*Sits.*] Whatta ya mean, find the body?

Charlie   This could start a war between the families.

Dominic   I don't care about that.

Charlie   Dom, they trace the body back to us and we are dead meat. You hear me? Dead meat.

Dominic   We're dead already.

Charlie   Whatta ya talkin'?

Dominic   That's what Big Anthony Jr. said. No one knows we're even alive.

Charlie   Yeah. Yeah, that's right. His ego wouldn't let anyone know we was still breathing. How 'bout that? We ain't even alive.

Dominic   So let's make sure no one ever finds any part of this bum.

CHARLIE   Are you sayin' we . . . ?

DOMINIC   Strip 'em. Bleed 'em. Wash 'em down and I'll butcher him tonight in the basement.

CHARLIE   You think?

DOMINIC   I'm open to suggestions.

CHARLIE   Probably the safest thing.

DOMINIC   Besides, I like it here. Cookin' for us. The house. Your garden.

CHARLIE   Yeah! I got cabbage and squash startin' to come up.

DOMINIC   Yellow squash?

CHARLIE   Yeah. Nice. You'll see.

DOMINIC   Oooh! You won't believe what I'm gonna do with your squash.

CHARLIE   Hey! We gotta do what we gotta do. I'll put his car in the garage and burn his clothes. Then I'll help you downstairs; I'll wrap and pack the freezer while you cut.

DOMINIC   This could take all night. We better eat somethin'.

CHARLIE   Yeah. Maybe you're right. I could use a little somethin' right about now. It's been a tough day.

DOMINIC   We need a little respite.

[DOMINIC *and* CHARLIE *start fixing their plates.*]

CHARLIE   Well, whatta ya think?

DOMINIC   Tomorrow night; Shank Marsala ala Junior with roasted cauliflower and peppers, and with a bowl of Escarole on the side.

CHARLIE   With the little white meatballs?

DOMINIC   With the little white balls.

CHARLIE   I love those balls.

DOMINIC   You got 'em.

CHARLIE   You're beautiful, Dominic. Beautiful. *Salute!*

DOMINIC   *Salute.*

[*They touch glasses and, as our two new killers toast each other, the lights begin to fade.* BIG ANTHONY JR. *falls off the sink.*]

CHARLIE   Pain in the ass.

[Blackout.]

End of Act I

ACT II

Dinner on Big Anthony Jr.

[*Lights slowly up.*]

[*Five months later. The lights slowly come up on* CHARLIE *and* DOMINIC *sitting at the table having just finished dinner. The table is covered with dirty dishes and drained glasses.* DOM *seems a bit sullen and plays with his food,* CHARLIE *with napkin to mouth as the sound effect of a large burp is heard.*]

DOMINIC   In some countries that's the best compliment a cook can get.

CHARLIE   Really?

DOMINIC   A burp.

CHARLIE   Well, it was meant just that way.

DOMINIC   Accepted.

CHARLIE   I love what you do with my squash.

DOMINIC   That is the best yellow squash I ever worked with. I mean it.

CHARLIE   The way you do it in the round dish with the grated cheese and the bread crumbs. It's like pie.

DOMINIC   You really like it?

CHARLIE   I love it.

DOMINIC   It's very simple.

CHARLIE   You're an artist, Dom.

DOMINIC   [*Embarrassed.*] Go on.

CHARLIE   No, I mean it, and the main dish. If I didn't know better I'd say it was *osso buco* right from Luna's down in Little Italy.

DOMINIC   Yeah, it was good. Considering the piece of meat I had to work with.

CHARLIE   Tough, huh?

DOMINIC   Oooff! I beat my meat for an hour and marinated it for two days.

CHARLIE   Two days!

DOMINIC   Two days.

CHARLIE   Well, it was worth the effort. A little more wine?

DOMINIC   Please.

[CHARLIE *pours.*]

Junior is a lot of work. Not like Leo.

CHARLIE   Well, Leo was a soft guy at heart. Beneath that iron exterior . . . mush inside. Junior was a . . . a . . .

DOMINIC   A very hard man.

CHARLIE   No tenderness at all.

DOMINIC   A rhino.

CHARLIE   Inside and out.

DOMINIC   Gamey.

CHARLIE   The hell with 'im.

[*Glass.*]

To Leo.

DOMINIC   I'll drink to that.

[*They drink.*]

There's a couple a pieces of meat left. Finish it off.

CHARLIE   I couldn't.

DOMINIC   One more piece.

CHARLIE   I'm gonna bust.

DOMINIC   Come on.

CHARLIE   Dom, don't do the guinea mother bit on me, please.

DOMINIC   Okay. I'll wrap it up for lunch sandwiches.

CHARLIE   Good plan. I'm done for the night. Besides, I ate twice as much as you. You feeling okay?

DOMINIC   [*Half-hearted.*] Yeah, I'm good.

CHARLIE   You sure?

DOMINIC   Yeah, fine.

[DOMINIC *gets up and starts to clean the table off.*]

CHARLIE   Let me help you with that.

DOMINIC   No, no, no! Just sit there and read me the paper. I'll do this.

[CHARLIE *opens the paper.*]

CHARLIE   Whatta ya want to hear?

DOMINIC   Whatta they got today?

CHARLIE   They got a war in Africa. A war in the Mid East and a revolution in South America?

DOMINIC   Same old, same old. Nothing changes.

CHARLIE   Here's a review for a new video game: The Boy Next Door; twelve ways to mutilate your neighbor.

DOMINIC   Just what we needed.

CHARLIE   Aaah! Page 10. Another kid with a gun shooting up a school; killed four and wounded nine.

DOMINIC   Nine and four! That's terrible.

CHARLIE   I don't get it.

DOMINIC   You and me both, Charlie. You and me both.

CHARLIE   You got a beef with a guy. He's a rat, a stoolie, some kinda scumbag who don't know for what's right. Take 'em out. Kill his ass. That I understand. But blowing away a dozen guys because your feelings is hurt?! Unarmed guys?! Kids for God sakes. I mean, what kinda cowardly bullshit is that? Let me tell ya, Dom, me and Leo did a lot a guys in our time, but I can say here and now, there wasn't a one that didn't have it comin'. Punks, stoolies, guys who welched on their bets, but never without cause, a justifiable cause. You know what I mean?

[DOM *tries to respond.*]

And let me tell you something else, and I'm very proud of this and so was Leo, in all the years we never got the wrong man and we never hurt an innocent bystander. The mark and only the mark. That was our motto.

[*Before* DOM *can respond.*]

And another thing, we never, *never*, in thirty years, never hurt a kid, *never*!

DOMINIC   Or a woman!

CHARLIE   Well.

[CHARLIE *buries his head back in the newspaper.*]

DOMINIC   Charlie?

[*No response.*]

Charlie, you whacked a broad?

CHARLIE   How about a movie tonight?

DOMINIC   You didn't?

CHARLIE   Dom, you know better. Don't ask questions about things you . . .

Dominic   I can't believe that Big Anthony Sr. had you put down a broad.

Charlie   Leave it alone, Dom.

Dominic   Charlie, that's disgusting.

Charlie   It was thirty years ago for God sakes. Let it lay.

Dominic   [*Mocking.*] Big tough guys like you and Leo.

Charlie   Why do I even talk to you!?

[*Justifying.*]

Besides it wasn't a woman, like you're thinkin' a woman.

Dominic   What was it, an alien woman?

Charlie   Remember Ma Greely, the bookie who fixed the fights over in Brooklyn?

Dominic   The dyke who had all the muscle with her wherever she went?

Charlie   Yeah, her. Well, me and Leo didn't look at Ma Greely as a woman. Ma was a loan shark who was tryin' to muscle in where she shouldn't be.

Dominic   That's still no . . .

Charlie   . . . And . . . and . . . she was warned twice by Leo. The second time Big Anthony the Senior was pissed at us for not taking her out like we was told. Gave her two more days. But she couldn't make peace with the man. So we had to go back.

Dominic   What happened?

Charlie   Well, we snatched her away from the muscle. Then I . . .

Dominic   Whoa, whoa! How'd you do that?

Charlie   [*Proudly.*] Aaaah! See now, *that* was my job. I follow Ma and the muscle to d'Torrio's on Myrtle Ave.

Dominic   They have a very nice veal Marsala.

Charlie   Yeah, I like the veal there. So I . . .

Dominic   Their red gravy is a little spicy.

Charlie   Agreed. So I sneak . . .

Dominic   You know who has the best gravy?

Charlie   The best gravy? No. Who?

Dominic   Believe it or not. Vincent's Clam Bar down in Little Italy.

Charlie   Really?

DOMINIC   I swear. Not the mild, not the hot. But Vincent's medium is the best gravy. Solid, never water on the plate.

CHARLIE   That's where they have the shrimp balls.

DOMINIC   I love their balls.

CHARLIE   The best balls I ever eat.

[*Thinking.*]

Where was I . . .

DOMINIC   Ma Greeley, at d'Torrio's.

CHARLIE   I sneak into d'Torrio's through the back way and I'm hiding in a stall in the ladies toilet for two hours.

DOMINIC   Two hours?

CHARLIE   I'm tellin' ya true. Two hours sittin' on the toilet, listen' to the most inane bullshit I ever heard in my life. Another twenty minutes and I would have asked Leo to kill me. Finally, Ma Greely comes in and I know it's her because I hear some other broad say . . .

[*High falsetto voice.*]

"Excuse me, sir, but this is the ladies . . . Oh! Oh! . . . I'm so sorry." Then Ma says . . .

[*Deep voice.*]

"Don't have a kitten, toots, I appreciate the compliment."

DOMINIC   So you knew.

CHARLIE   I knew. I come out with my rod and bar the door. Now I had to get Ma out the ladies room window. Which was a job and a half. Ma and me ain't likely candidates for Jenny Craig after photos. All the while Ma ain't exactly making life easy for me. She is bitching like a nun in a house of lost virtue.

DOMINIC   She could be mean.

CHARLIE   Tell me about it. I'll tell you the truth, Dom, I had to knock her out. Then I ties Ma up and puts her in the trunk of my old Caddy. Now it's four in the morning by time I get Ma to the middle of the Brooklyn Bridge, where Leo already has a rope tied to a beam. Leo puts the noose around Ma's neck. And then Leo . . . now get this . . . he's just been put on the carpet by Big Anthony Sr. himself, remember, he gives Ma one last chance to come up with the vig.

DOMINIC   You're kidding?!

CHARLIE   My hand to God?

DOMINIC   What did Ma say?

CHARLIE   Ma Greely, says nothin' and spits in Leo's face.

DOMINIC   [*Shocked.*] No!

CHARLIE   *One arm!* Leo throws her over the rail and Ma's body just kinda floats through the air. Then suddenly, Ma reaches the end of her rope; and *snap!* The rope takes Ma's head right off.

DOMINIC   *Marone amia. . . .*

[DOM *makes the sign of the cross.*]

CHARLIE   Her body falls into the icy greenish-gray-brown water below and Ma's head just starts swinging. Swinging at the end of a rope hanging from the middle of the Brooklyn Bridge; back and forth, back and forth.

DOMINIC   Like one of those clock things the piano players use when they teach.

CHARLIE   Exactly. Ma was just keeping time. Now, I go to pull up the rope but Leo says: "No. Leave it. Let Ma look over the Brooklyn she loved."

DOMINIC   Leo said that?

CHARLIE   Yeah. So I didn't pull up the rope. We just stood there for a couple of minutes watching the sunrise and Ma Greely's head swinging back and forth, back and forth.

DOMINIC   Leo had a poetic side, didn't he?

CHARLIE   Few people knew that.

DOMINIC   A man of renaissance.

[DOMINIC *goes back to doing the dishes.*]

CHARLIE   Now, how about that movie tonight?

DOMINIC   That might be nice.

CHARLIE   Let me see here.

DOMINIC   No shoot 'em up. I can't stand that gory stuff.

CHARLIE   All special effects; no substance.

DOMINIC   Check the art theater.

CHARLIE   That's forty-five minutes away.

DOMINIC   So we'll take a ride in Big Anthony Jr.'s car. Go shopping at the all-night market on the way back.

CHARLIE   Good plan. Here it is. The Nu-art. Hey, look, Orson Welles.

Dominic Who?

Charlie You know. That fat guy who sold the wine before it's time.

[**Dominic** *looks at the paper.*]

Dominic Oh! Him. He's dead, you know?

Charlie No!

Dominic Long time.

Charlie [*Disappointed.*] Aaaah! That was good wine.

Dominic What's the movie?

Charlie *Touch of Evil.* It says: "A brand-new print, and a interview with Welles in 1974." Whatta ya think?

Dominic [*Unenthusiastically.*] Whatever you say.

Charlie [*Pause.*] Something bothering you, Dom?

Dominic No . . . no, not really.

Charlie [*Putting down paper.*] Come on! What's crawled up your BVDs?

Dominic I don't know how to tell ya.

Charlie Hey, this is Charlie you're talking to; stop the bull and spit it out.

Dominic Well . . .

Charlie Spit.

Dominic It's hard to put into words.

[*Sits.*]

Charlie, do you ever feel that we got something special here? Something we never had before, something guys like us never seem to find in life.

Charlie You mean, like . . . like safety. Like we was in a castle or a fortress?

Dominic No, not that. But that's true too. I never felt so safe as I do here with you, Charlie. I mean that.

Charlie Don't worry! I can take care of any trouble that comes our way.

Dominic I'm sure you could if you had to. I was talking about having "peace."

Charlie Dom, you want piece you got a piece. I'll have a couple a broads out here in two hours. Girls we can trust.

Dominic No, no, no, Charlie. I don't mean that kinda piece. I mean a gentle kinda peace. I mean peace of mind.

Charlie Oh! Peeeace. Like at rest.

DOMINIC   Yeah.

CHARLIE   Like calm. Serenity.

DOMINIC   Yeah. Like that. I mean look at you. Ever since we got rid of Big Anthony Jr. you don't get mad at the little things anymore. It's like we destroyed, like we devoured the evil out of our lives.

CHARLIE   Whatta ya trying to say, Dom?

DOMINIC   I like it here with you, Charlie.

CHARLIE   Well, I like it here with you too.

DOMINIC   Charlie, we're having cervello tomorrow night.

CHARLIE   Yeah! So . . .

[*There's a pause as* CHARLIE *realizes the ramifications of the end of* BIG ANTHONY JR.]

DOMINIC   Yeah.

CHARLIE   One more dinner . . .

DOMINIC   . . . and a good bowel movement . . .

CHARLIE   . . . and no more Big Anthony.

DOMINIC   Junior.

CHARLIE   Junior.

DOMINIC   It's over, Charlie.

CHARLIE   [*Quickly.*] We could go back!

DOMINIC   [*Not happy.*] I knew it.

CHARLIE   We could.

DOMINIC   Charlie, listen to me, please. . . .

CHARLIE   No! No, no, no. You listen, 'cause I got it all worked out.

DOMINIC   Charlie, please. . . .

CHARLIE   We can't kill our best friend. We let him go. Big Anthony Jr. threatens to kill us. We said; "Go ahead." We said; "Go to hell. We don't kill our friends, for nobody." Big Anthony Jr. admires our courage and tells us to leave the state . . . to leave the damn country. So we go to Mexico City.

DOMINIC   I don't cook Mex.

CHARLIE   All right! We go to Toronto.

DOMINIC   Great food there. Ever eat at La Bruchetta's? Benito makes the best dried *proscutte* . . .

CHARLIE   Will you stop with the food already. We go to Canada and we hear that Big Anthony Jr. has been among the missing for the last five–six months. So we have decided to come back and take our rightful place in the family. Huh?

DOMINIC   Charlie, we can't . . .

CHARLIE   Come on! I almost believe it myself.

DOMINIC   That's not gonna work, Charlie.

CHARLIE   Why the hell not?

DOMINIC   Nobody's gonna believe that Big Anthony Jr. let us or anyone else off the snide without punishment and you know it, Charlie. Besides . . .

CHARLIE   All right. All right. Let's tell everyone the truth. We killed the bastard.

DOMINIC   You *are* crazy?

CHARLIE   We lured him up here and I cut his throat and we watched him bleed.

DOMINIC   I knew it. I knew it.

CHARLIE   What? What? You knew what?

DOMINIC   Too much meat and you can't think.

CHARLIE   What's wrong with letting everyone know who the real muscle is around here. Huh?

DOMINIC   And how are we gonna explain all the gaps in time?

CHARLIE   Well, we could . . . we could just say that we . . . we . . .

DOMINIC   Or what happened to big Anthony Jr.'s body?

CHARLIE   Aaaah! We'll think of some . . .

DOMINIC   How about the truth? You got on your knees and begged, pleaded, cried like a baby. And for over thirty years of faithful service to the family you got a second chance provided you eat the body of your best friend, the man we were suppose to kill; your protector . . .

CHARLIE   All right!

DOMINIC   . . . your teacher . . .

CHARLIE   All right. You made your point.

DOMINIC   . . . your mentor, your so called . . .

CHARLIE   [*Angry.*] Alright, already! Shut up, will ya?

DOMINIC   Charlie, please listen . . .

CHARLIE   I said, "Shut up."

DOMINIC   Anything you say.

[*There is a pause as* DOMINIC *goes back to the dishes.*]

CHARLIE   [*Justifying.*] I wouldn't call it begging. It was just the only move to make at the time. You weren't any help as I remember. You just stood there saying nothin'.

DOMINIC   Didn't think it would do any good.

CHARLIE   Well, there you go. We wouldn't be where we are today if I had kept my big mouth shut. Am I right or am I right!?

DOMINIC   You're right, Charlie.

CHARLIE   Huh?

DOMINIC   Oh, when you're right, you're right.

CHARLIE   Okay! Now, you got any bright ideas, because sooner or later they will pronounce Big Anthony Jr. dead, and sooner or later the Uncle Sid will find us. I don't know how but he will and then we *are* toast. We've been here too long, pushed our luck way too far.

[*Pause as* DOM *comes back to the table.*]

DOMINIC   May I speak now, Your Majesty?

CHARLIE   Spit out what ya gotta say.

DOMINIC   I don't want you all pissed off.

CHARLIE   Spit.

DOMINIC   I want you to listen.

CHARLIE   I'm listening.

DOMINIC   Without interruption.

CHARLIE   Spit.

DOMINIC   Because what I have to say . . .

CHARLIE   WILL YOU STOP AND JUST SAY IT!

DOMINIC   I want to stay here.

CHARLIE   I just told you the Uncle Sid . . .

DOMINIC   [*Firmly.*] LET ME FINISH! I know we can't stay here in this house but we can stay here! This town, this area. This *here*!

CHARLIE   What are you talkin'?

DOMINIC   I think between the two of us we could afford our own place.

CHARLIE   [*Sarcastically.*] Your Highness has a place in mind, I presume.

DOMINIC   [*More sarcastically.*] As a matter of fact I do. There's a storefront on Union Street . . .

CHARLIE   A storefront?

DOMINIC   [*Calmly.*] Let me finish. It has a very nice apartment above it. Nothing fancy but nice. More than enough room for us to set up house.

CHARLIE   What about the store?

DOMINIC   I'm coming to that.

[DOMINIC *takes a big breath, and with a broad hand gesture he spells out:*]

Charlie and Dominic's fine northern Italian cuisine.

CHARLIE   What?!

DOMINIC   [*Pleading.*] I don't want to go back, Charlie. I want to stay here with you and open our own place.

CHARLIE   Dom, I don't know nothin' about . . .

DOMINIC   Oh! Oh! Oh! I didn't tell you the best part. There's a large backyard to this building, for your garden. We can grow our own vegetables. Organic. Just think, my pasta primavera with your homegrown vegetables. Boy! That would really pack 'em in. We'll make a killin'.

CHARLIE   Dominic, let's . . . let's just slow down here, for a second.

DOMINIC   [*Worked up.*] I'll be the chef and you greet the costumers and run the restaurant. Be the maître d'.

CHARLIE   The maître d'?!

DOMINIC   I don't know anyone better with people than you.

CHARLIE   A restaurant, huh?

DOMINIC   Yeah. Our restaurant. We could do it, Charlie. The way you can schooze the public with that lovable style of yours.

CHARLIE   Lovable?!

[*Blushing.*]

Lay off the soap, will ya.

DOMINIC   I'm serious. People would come just to hear your stories.

CHARLIE   Well! I'm not bad at organization and I do have to admit I'm pretty good at throwing the bull. Leo use ta say I was a regular raccoon-a-teur.

DOMINIC   Leo said that whenever he was down he'd talk to you and the next thing you know he'd be smiling.

CHARLIE   [*Laughing.*] Oh! Sure. That was easy. Leo was a fun guy, great sense of humor. Hey, Hey!

[*Planning.*]

You know, I did a lot of the bookmaking for Leo. Don't ever say anything but during football season I always ran the betting slips. How 'bout we run the slips from the restaurant?

DOMINIC   If you want.

CHARLIE   Nothing big, mind ya. Just a little action for our regulars. Nothing serious. Hell, in a hick berg like this, even the local cops would be players.

DOMINIC   Sure they would. You'll be running this town in no time.

CHARLIE   Better to be a big fish in a small pond. Am I right?

DOMINIC   Yeah.

CHARLIE   Huh?

DOMINIC   When you're right, you're right.

CHARLIE   Whatta we need to prove to those bums back in the city?

DOMINIC   That's what I'm thinking, Charlie. We don't need to prove nothin'.

CHARLIE   You really want to stay, huh?

DOMINIC   Yes.

CHARLIE   Never go back?

DOMINIC   Never.

CHARLIE   All right, Dom. Let me think on it.

DOMINIC   You think.

[CHARLIE *sits drinking his wine and thinking.*]

CHARLIE   I'd sure like to go back there just to tell them how I cut Big Anthony Jr.'s throat. Let 'em know, you know.

DOMINIC   Charlie, we know. We know the truth.

CHARLIE   Yeah, that's what really counts. Knowing the truth in your own heart. Am I right?

DOMINIC   Definitely.

CHARLIE   [*Sincerely.*] Dominic, Am I right?

DOMINIC   Charlie, you've never been more right in our lives.

CHARLIE   [*Smiles.*] We ain't gonna be missin' very much, that's for sure. What's to see we ain't seen. What's to do we ain't done. And the guys? Not exactly a bunch of enlightened scholars.

DOMINIC   [*Upset.*] Charlie, not for nothing, but I hated being around that bunch of bigots. Prejudice mother . . .

[*Stops.*]

You see, you see how worked up I get just talkin' about them. I almost cursed. They were the lowest of the low.

CHARLIE   Take it easy, Dom, you'll get agita.

DOMINIC   No, Charlie, I spent more time with them then you did. I cooked for that family every night and day. I heard more than anybody. They're all a bunch of bigots. Leo can't go any higher in the family because of the Greek wife, you because you're half a mick. Hell, even *with* the Uncle Sid, for cryin' out loud; he was married to Big Anthony Sr.'s own sister, Angelina, he can only go so far because he's a Heb.

CHARLIE   Believe me, bad rug and all, the Uncle Sid had plenty to say about who got whacked.

DOMINIC   Tell me about it. But behind his back it was; the Jew this and the Jew that. Nobody would say anything to his face, though. They all knew, when he went thumbs-down on somebody that son of a gun was a dead man. A dead man. Like with Leo, no matter what I said in his defense, once the Uncle Sid put his thumb down, it . . . it was over. . . .

[DOM *stops in mid-sentence and stares at* CHARLIE, *who can't believe what he's just heard.*]

CHARLIE   Go on, Dom. You was saying?

DOMINIC   I was just saying that no matter what I said in Leo's defense, the Uncle Sid was—well, he . . .

CHARLIE   You knew, didn't you? You knew they were gonna order me to put down Leo. Didn't you?

DOMINIC   Yes, I knew.

CHARLIE   Well, why the hell didn't you tell me?

DOMINIC   Charlie! Charlie, what difference would it have made? Once that family goes thumbs-down on someone it's over.

CHARLIE   Why did you agree to come along?

DOMINIC   Because I knew you couldn't do it.

CHARLIE   And you could have?

DOMINIC   Yes, Charlie, I could have.

CHARLIE   Then why didn't ya?

DOMINIC   Because you let Leo off the hook before I could get to him. When you took Leo in the alley, I didn't know you was gonna let him go.

CHARLIE   You would have killed Leo?

DOMINIC   Charlie, I loved Leo too, but I would have done what had to be done. For us!

[*The back door to the kitchen bursts open and there stands the* UNCLE SID.]

[*The* UNCLE SID *is a man in his late seventies who is dressed in a style reminiscent of dapper days gone by.* SID'S *ill-fitting toupee sits atop of the brains of the infamous crime family.*]

CHARLIE   GOD!

DOMINIC   The Uncle Sid!

SID   [*Surprised.*] I don't believe my eyes.

DOMINIC   Well, this is a surprise, Sid.

SID   I mean, what I tell you, it *is* a surprise. It's like walking into an old horror movie. You're both dead.

CHARLIE   [*Trying to laugh.*] We ain't dead, Sid.

SID   [*Smiles.*] We'll see.

DOMINIC   Well, well, we never expected to see the Uncle Sid up here in the country.

SID   You weren't expecting me?

CHARLIE   We weren't expecting nobody.

SID   Nobody? Not even Big Anthony Jr.?

DOMINIC   We definitely weren't expecting . . .

CHARLIE   Shut up, Dom.

SID   So, no one is expecting, that's good.

DOMINIC   Let me get you a glass of wine.

SID   Wine? Ah! No. No wine.

CHARLIE   Let me hang up your coat.

SID   Sure. Sure. Hang the coat.

DOMINIC   Sit, sit; let me get you something.

SID   Don't trouble yourself, Dom.

[SID *sits: as* CHARLIE *hangs his coat.*]

DOMINIC   [*Goes to fridge.*] Sid, believe me, it's no trouble.

CHARLIE   You know how he is, Sid.

SID   Good ole Dominic always with the food.

DOMINIC   Whatta ya have? I got everything.

SID   Cup coffee, piece cheesecake? If you got?

DOMINIC   I got. I got.

[*As the scene goes on* DOMINIC *takes a cheesecake from the refrigerator and cuts a piece with a large knife.*]

SID   Dominic, I gotta tell you, the boys really miss your cooking. I swear you're a legend since your death.

CHARLIE   Dom ain't exactly dead.

SID   We'll see. Death is a funny thing.

CHARLIE   Funny?

SID   Depending from which side of the grave you're looking.

CHARLIE   I guess if you see it that way.

SID   Believe me, that's the only way to see it. From this side of whatever.

DOMINIC   Here you go, Sid; cheesecake, coffee coming up. Just made a fresh pot.

[CHARLIE *serves the cake, as* DOM *gets the coffee.*]

SID   So. Where's Big Anthony Jr.?

[SID *takes a bite of the cheesecake.*]

CHARLIE   [*Like he didn't hear.*] What?

SID   [*Mouth full.*] I said; "Where's Junior?"

CHARLIE   Well, you see, Sid, it's like this . . .

SID   This is some good cheesecake, Dom.

DOMINIC   From scratch.

SID   From scratch? What's that I taste?

DOMINIC   Orange rinds.

SID   No kidding? Dom, let me tell you, everyone is skinny now you're dead.

CHARLIE   Sid; Dom ain't dead, I ain't dead.

SID   We'll see. *So,* where's Junior?

CHARLIE   Who?

SID   Whatta ya deaf all of a sudden, Charlie? Where's Junior?

CHARLIE   We have no idea where he is.

DOMINIC   [*To* CHARLIE.] We don't?

SID   [*To* DOM.] You don't?

DOMINIC   [*To* SID.] We don't.

SID   [*To* CHARLIE.] You don't.

CHARLIE   We don't. Ain't seen him since he put down Leo.

DOMINIC   That's when he brought us here.

SID   This is funny. 'Cause I coulda swore that was his Caddie we saw as we came up the driveway.

CHARLIE   [*To* DOM.] His car!?

DOMINIC   [*To* SID.] Yeah, yeah. He left us his car.

CHARLIE   [*To* SID.] Yeah. He couldn't leave us way out here in the country without a car.

SID   He left you his car? Six months after Leo goes down, Junior drives up here, give you his car? *Strange!*

DOMINIC   You said; "We." You got some of the boys with you, Sid?

SID   [*Thinking to himself.*] Why would he leave you his . . . ?

DOMINIC   Who you got with you, Sid?

SID   Huh? What? Oh, I got two young ones. Remember Vinny's son Paulie? He's been driving me as of late.

[DOM *and* CHARLIE *go to the windows and look out.*]

DOMINIC   Little Paulie, no fooling. I use to watch him when he was a kid. I'd have him cook with me in the kitchen when Vinny was on a job.

SID   That's him all right.

DOMINIC   Little Paulie, whatta ya know.

CHARLIE   [*Looking out.*] Who's the other guy? I don't recognize him.

SID   He's a new guy right off the boat. Suppose to be top a the line. He'll get a chance to prove himself tonight.

CHARLIE   He going on a hit tonight, Sid?

SID   Yeah. We're still trying to find a replacement for Leo and you since you been dead.

Charlie   I ain't dead, Sid.

Sid   We'll see.

Dominic   [*Quickly.*] Who's the mark, Sid? Who's the kid gonna hit?

Sid   You shouldn't be asking that, Dom.

Dominic   I'm sorry, Sid, it's been a while.

Sid   Well, I guess it couldn't hurt, since you're both dead.

Charlie   Stop it, Sid.

Sid   Paulie. We're hitting Paulie.

Dominic   [*Shocked.*] NO!

Charlie   The kid? Vinny's kid?!

Sid   What can I say?

Dominic   [*Goes to window.*] I don't believe it.

Sid   Believe it, believe it. I mean what I say, it breaks my heart. What are ya gonna do?

Charlie   Why Sid? Why the kid?

[**Dominic** *starts to heat up some food.*]

Sid   This is an interesting thing. 'Cause every year Junior asked little Paulie, "You want work? We got work for you." Every year from little Paulie it's; "No, thank you." I think to myself, that's fine, that's good, better a nice clean-cut kid like this stays away from *mishegas*. Junior felt the same way. I mean what I say; the only reason Junior kept asking was a respect thing for Vinny.

Charlie   Does Vinny know?

Sid   He'll find out soon enough.

[*To* Dom.]

Whatta ya doing there, Dom?

Dominic   I'm serving up a last meal for the kid, if you don't mind.

Sid   Sure, sure, you do that, you make a meal for the executioner too. Make something special.

[*Drinks.*]

Dominic   It'll be special, don't you worry.

Charlie   It's always special around here.

Sid   Good coffee, a real body to it.

Charlie   Yeah, yeah. You were saying, Sid?

SID   Huh? Ah! Yes. Little Paulie comes to us during his summer break from college. He says he wants to work for the family. We say, "Why not? You're already *mishpocheh*." But you know Junior. He says sure and then he has me go up to the college and see what was what with Vinny's kid. Why the sudden change of heart?

CHARLIE   Big Anthony Jr. never trusted nobody.

SID   Our business, it's better you don't.

DOMINIC   Too much red pepper.

SID   What do I find? That little *pisher*, little Paulie, has been writing a book on the family.

CHARLIE   College kids! Not a cerebellum to the carload.

SID   Talk about *chutzpah*! All these years of sitting around Dominic's kitchen listening to the stories, plus what his old man tells him, he thinks he's Ernie Hemingway. Some smart professor realizes the stories are too good to be not true. One thing leads to another, this and that and the other thing, we find out that little Paulie has been working for the Feds for over a year.

CHARLIE   Over a year?

SID   Over a year!

CHARLIE   Over . . . . . .hen he's the one. I told you and Big Anthony Jr. that it wasn't Leo. Leo would have died before he sang.

SID   It's not just a boat that loose lips sink. You, like a *yenta*, also told a lot of stories around Dom's table to little Paulie. A lot of stories, a lot of details, made us think that the Feds knew too much about Leo's business. Junior figures it's you or Leo and then he figures you ain't got the nerve to work with the Feds, so it must be Leo.

CHARLIE   What are you saying!?

SID   Or maybe he was always figuring to get rid of both of you from the beginning. Who could tell what was going on in that mind of his. *Meshugah!*

DOMINIC   Junior should have never underestimated Charlie.

SID   Or you Dominic, huh? Hey! Mistakes happen; what can I say?

CHARLIE   What can you say?!

DOMINIC   That's enough, Charlie. We'll take it up with Big Anthony Jr., if we ever see him again.

SID   Nobody seen him in five months. Said something about going to see a couple of ghosts.

DOMINIC   Their last meal is ready.

SID   Bring with my compliments. And, Dom, you understand it's not going to do any good to say anything.

DOMINIC   Sure, I understand. I'll take care of the boys. You, Charlie, cut the Uncle Sid another piece of cake.

[DOM *waves the big knife behind* SID's *back as he motions for* CHARLIE *to kill the* UNCLE SID.]

SID   I couldn't, Dom.

DOMINIC   Oh, go on. It's homemade, what can it hurt?

[DOM *places the large knife in front of* CHARLIE *as he starts to exit with a tray, on which are two full plates and two beers.*]

CHARLIE   Dom, maybe . . .

DOMINIC   I'll be right back, Charlie.

CHARLIE   I know but . . .

DOMINIC   Just open the door for me and take good care of the Uncle Sid.

[DOM *exits.* CHARLIE *with knife in hand stands behind the* UNCLE SID *and stares.*]

SID   Not even a sliver, Charlie.

CHARLIE   Wha?

SID   No more cheesecake.

CHARLIE   Oh! Yeah. No cake. Sure.

SID   Seriously, I think all Dom wants is the whole world to eat and be happy. That's why, he was a great cook. Too bad he died.

CHARLIE   I ain't gonna say it again, Sid.

[*SID calmly rises and goes for more coffee.*]

SID   I'll pour another cup coffee myself, if you don't mind. How long you know me, Charlie, thirty-five years?

CHARLIE   Something like that.

SID   Then you know with me everything has to be neat and just so. Like our books. Every set of books is kept just right. We got books for the Feds, we got books for the State, we even got books for the City. Then we have books for ourselves. In that, we're a lot like Hollywood. We want to show a profit, we show a profit. We don't want to show a profit, we don't show a profit. My job is to make sure everything is just the way it's suppose to be.

CHARLIE   What's your point, Sid?

SID   Things ain't the way they're suppose to be.

CHARLIE   Why's that?

SID   Well, you take this place. Used to belong to my sister-in-law, Carmela. Every year I pay the bills on this piece of property. Taxes, water, power. Shit like that. The gardener who use to come around twice a month. You know the gardener don't come around anymore?

CHARLIE   We take care of the place.

SID   I know that now. *Now* that is clear. Before today I wasn't sure what was what because I see the water bill is larger, the electric bill is larger, and the gardener is less. I thought maybe some young punks are drugging the house. I figure Paulie and the new kid come up with me and throw them a beating and that's that. But instead what do I find? I find two dead men screwing up my books.

CHARLIE   Sid, you better . . .

[DOM *enters the kitchen to see* CHARLIE *facing* SID *with the large knife in hand as* SID *just stands there calmly drinking his coffee.*]

DOMINIC   [*Causally.*] Boy, you should see those two kids eat. It's like they never been feed. What's going on, Charlie?

CHARLIE   The Uncle Sid was just saying how he found us through the books. Water bills, electric bills; stuff like that.

DOMINIC   You was always very smart, Sid. The smartest of the bunch.

SID   Smart enough to take over now that Junior is gone. Gone, somewhere. Someplace. Somehow. I just want to make sure he's gone for good.

[*A car horn starts to blow causing everyone to jump up, the horn is loud and constant.*]

CHARLIE   Holy Mother of !!!!!

SID   What the hell . . . ?

DOMINIC   The kids must be finished with their dinner.

SID   What the hell are they blowing that horn for?

DOMINIC   I told them to blow me for seconds.

[DOM *grabs the skillet off the stove and exits to remove the pressure of the dead body on the horn.*]

SID   [*Talking over the horn.*] I know how much Paulie loves Dom's cooking but this is . . . I mean what I say when I tell you, I'm gonna have a serious talk with him about this horn business before the new kid puts him down. No respect, these kids. No manners.

[*Horn stops. SID yells.*]

THANK GOD!

[*Then.*]

I thought I was gonna *plotz*.

CHARLIE [*Yells.*] YOU WAS SAYING!?

SID What's with the yelling?

CHARLIE You was saying?

SID [*Pointedly.*] Huh? Oh! Junior has been missing for five months. We gotta assume he has gone to Hoffa land. So, the Uncle Sid is running the show now and that's how I want to keep it. I don't need any storytellers givin' the family false hope.

[DOM *enters out of breath carrying empty frying pan.* CHARLIE *runs to the door and sees the bodyguard coming and locks the door.*]

DOMINIC They liked it.

SID What happened with you?

DOMINIC Just horsing around with the kids.

CHARLIE You sure they had enough, Dom?

DOMINIC Well, sorta. That new kid is a horse. But I think he's resting now. Yeah!

CHARLIE Maybe you should serve some more?

SID Enough with the food already.

[*Just then a shadow of a man clutching his throat appears at the back door and forcefully bangs on the door frame, then slowly falls down.* DOM *and* CHARLIE *jump to their feet and go to the door,* DOM *with frying pan in hand.*]

DOMINIC and **CHARLIE** Whatever you say, Sid!

SID [*Startled.*] What the hell was . . . ?

DOMINIC I'll get it. I'll get it. They're just returning the plates.

[DOM *tries to open the door but the fallen body is blocking it and he can't get the door to open.*]

I told him to knock on the door for seconds.

[DOM *is breaking his back trying to open the door as* CHARLIE *tries to help.*]

SID You told him, knock the door down?

DOMINIC   It's the new kid . . . it's a Sicilian thing.

CHARLIE   [*At door.*] You want a hand with this stuck door, Dom?

DOMINIC   How many times have I told you to fix this damn . . . your mother's ass.

[DOM *and* CHARLIE *finally push the body far enough back to open the door so* DOM *can slip by.*]

CHARLIE   [*Turning to* SID.] You want to know what happened to Big Anthony Jr.? I killed him.

SID   What the hell was that all about?

[*When* SID *turns we can see* DOM *through the kitchen window swinging the frying pan on the fallen killer that was pounding on the door.*]

CHARLIE   Sid, did you hear me? I killed Big Anthony Jr. I cut his throat right over the sink . . . this table.

[*Pointing* SID *downstage.*]

SID   Charlie, please, this is the Uncle Sid you're talking to.

CHARLIE   You don't believe me?

SID   Boychick, you never killed anyone in your life. You ain't got it in you.

CHARLIE   Whatta ya talkin' about. Leo and me put down dozens a guys.

SID   Leo put down dozens, then you come back and play the court jester for the family.

CHARLIE   You calling me a clown, Sid?

SID   If the shoe fits, Charlie, if the shoe fits.

[DOM *comes back through the door carrying a bloody frying pan.* DOM *is breathing heavy.* SID *is standing by the entrance to the living room.*]

DOMINIC   Well, they're finished now.

SID   Again I ask! What's with you?

DOMINIC   Oh! You know how those kids love to horse around.

CHARLIE   [*Softly.*] I ain't no clown!

SID   You didn't say anything, Dom?

DOMINIC   [*Catching his breath.*] Me. Never. I ain't said squat in over thirty years.

SID   'Cause it ain't good for dead men to talk too much.

CHARLIE   [*Screams.*] WE AIN'T DEAD!

[CHARLIE *plunges the knife into* SID'*s chest and pushes* SID *into the living room offstage right. We hear* CHARLIE *sticking* SID'*s body over and over again with the knife. Blood flies into the kitchen as* CHARLIE *screams offstage.*]

I was not a clown. I was the setup. I was the brains. You miserable bastard. All you ever did was put your thumb down. We did it. Me and Leo. NOW! You are a dead man, YOU!

[CHARLIE, *exhausted, comes back in the kitchen and sits looking at the knife with* SID'*s wig on it.*]

We are not dead!

SID   [*Offstage.*] We'll see.

[CHARLIE *looks at the wig as if it said something, then flings it in* SID'*s direction.* DOM *slowly walks to the living-room entrance and looks offstage at* SID'*s mutilated body.*]

DOMINIC   My God!

[*Pause.*]

Did you have to do that on the new *white* rug?

CHARLIE   [*Looking at knife.*] I killed him.

DOMINIC   You know that rug is ruined.

CHARLIE   I killed him. ME! Not anyone else.

DOMINIC   You can't get blood out of a white rug. I could soak it in club soda and carpet cleaner for a year and you'd still see the blood stain.

CHARLIE   What are ya talkin' . . . ?

DOMINIC   The rug . . . The rug!

CHARLIE   The rug?!

DOMINIC   You ruined the new rug.

CHARLIE   Forget the rug. I killed a man.

DOMINIC   On my new rug.

CHARLIE   I killed the Uncle Sid.

DOMINIC   Charlie, that rug is worth a hell of a lot . . .

CHARLIE   [*Yells.*] Will you shut up about the Go damn rug, Dominic. Will you just shut the hell up for two minutes and let me have a moment here. I'm having a moment here. I want to enjoy it.

DOMINIC   All right, Charlie, all right. Enjoy.

CHARLIE   GET ME SOME COFFEE!

DOMINIC   Charlie, you don't have to get nasty.

CHARLIE   Get the coffee, Dom.

DOMINIC   Sure. Anything you say.

[DOM *goes and pours a cup of coffee as* CHARLIE *sits at the table looking at the knife.*]

CHARLIE   We played our cards just right. Those bums had no idea who they were dealing with.

DOMINIC   Charlie, can I say something?

CHARLIE   Spit!

DOMINIC   We have a lot of work to do. The Uncle Sid, little Paulie, and that new kid is a moose. I put enough juice in his gravy to kill ten guys and he still made it to the door. I mean, Poor Little Paulie, his head went right down on the car horn but the other one, MENGIA! We have to wash, cut, and package three of them

CHARLIE   We ain't cutting up the Uncle Sid.

DOMINIC   You're probably right. At his age I doubt if I can make a decent meal with that old meat. To stringy. Besides, Sid knew, I don't cook kosher. *But* with the two boys we should be able to stock up the restaurant freezer.

CHARLIE   There ain't gonna be no restaurant.

DOMINIC   Whatta ya talkin', Charlie?

CHARLIE   Not here anyway.

DOMINIC   But, Charlie, you said before . . .

CHARLIE   That was before, Dom. Before I took care of the Uncle Sid. Before I realized what is now in our grasp.

DOMINIC   But, Charlie, the restaurant?

CHARLIE   Will you stop cryin' about the restaurant. You'll have a joint, back in the city. Back in the heart of all our action, the book, the broads, the loans, it can all be run from your restaurant. They wanna do business in our territory, they'll have to come to Charlie's place. Yeah! We'll call it Charlie's.

DOMINIC   [*Sadly.*] Charlie's?

CHARLIE   First thing we do is go back to Big Anthony Jr.'s office and throw Sid's mutilated body on the desk. Then I tell all the boys, I tell them all, how you and me, how we baited Junior and the Uncle Sid. We waited up here for them to come to us and when they did I killed them.

DOMINIC   But, Charlie, I . . .

CHARLIE   They don't have to know that Big Anthony Jr. was pretty much dead before I cut his throat. All they have to know is that I cut his throat. Ain't that right, Dom?

[CHARLIE *stands, faces* DOM *with the bloody knife.*]

DOMINIC   Sure. But . . .

CHARLIE   You'll do that for me, won't ya?

DOMINIC   Anything you say.

CHARLIE   You'll keep your yap shut.

DOMINIC   When have I ever opened my mouth?

CHARLIE   'Cause you know as well as me; you can't have two head cooks in the same kitchen. Am I right?

DOMINIC   Yeah, right?

CHARLIE   Huh?

DOMINIC   When you're right, you're right. Look, why don't we have coffee and decide what to do with the two boys outside?

CHARLIE   Good plan.

[DOM *goes to pour two mugs of coffee.*]

DOMINIC   You want a little something in your coffee? Some anisette or some of the Irish?

CHARLIE   Sure. Sure, why not? We should celebrate. Make it the Irish. Yeah, we'll have a toast. A toast to these fallen rats.

[DOM *reaches into a cabinet above the stove and pulls out a bottle and pours a shot into* CHARLIE'*s mug.*]

DOMINIC   You know that in some countries they eat rat. In one place I hear it's a delicacy.

CHARLIE   Well, there you go, Dom. That's what New Jersey has been for us. Just a foreign country where we had to eat the local food. A little respite.

[DOM *brings over the two mugs of coffee.*]

DOMINIC   Here's your coffee, Charlie.

CHARLIE   You know, Dom, the more I think about it the more I think we should tell them the truth about Big Anthony Jr. We ate the bastard.

DOMINIC   Drink your coffee, Charlie.

CHARLIE   What did Junior say: "The blood of my enemy, the flesh . . ." Something!

DOMINIC   Junior should have never asked us to kill Leo.

CHARLIE   Yeah, Leo. Guess, we don't have to say anything about Leo.

DOMINIC   That might not be in good taste.

CHARLIE   Then again, maybe it would be good to let everyone know that Leo is a part of me. They feared Leo, and you are what you consume.

DOMINIC   I've come to realize that.

CHARLIE   Maybe we should just tell the truth.

DOMINIC   Always best to tell the truth.

CHARLIE   The truth is Leo was my best friend and you don't kill your best friend.

DOMINIC   That is a truth, isn't it, Charlie?

CHARLIE   No greater truth has man. A true friend is the greatest gift of all.

DOMINIC   Where would we be without a friend?

CHARLIE   Alone! That's where you'd be. *Alone!*

[CHARLIE *goes to drink his coffee.*]

DOMINIC   DON'T!

[DOMINIC *covers the cup in* CHARLIE's *hand.*]

CHARLIE   What the hell . . . !?

[*Shocked.*]

You were going to kill me. ME!

DOMINIC   I'm so sorry.

CHARLIE   How could you?

DOMINIC   I *couldn't*! I could never hurt you. Do what you gotta do, Charlie. Kill me if you must, I'm not going back.

[DOMINIC *hands* CHARLIE *the knife he used to kill the* UNCLE SID *and cut the cheesecake.* DOM *closes his eyes and sticks out his chest.* CHARLIE *lowers the knife.*]

CHARLIE   What do ya mean, "kill you"?

DOMINIC   Charlie, you got the blood in the mouth. That sweet and bitter taste. Just like those bums back in the city. I could never be like them again, not after living here with you. Cooking for you. Watching your garden grow.

[*pause.*]

I'll get you a fresh cup of coffee while you make up your mind to kill me or not. You want cheesecake?

CHARLIE   Forget the cheesecake. You gonna stay here by yourself?

[DOM *goes for one fresh cup of coffee.*]

DOMINIC   I'll get the restaurant going, don't you worry about me. I'll make do.

CHARLIE   [*Shocked.*] You'd go into business without me?

DOMINIC   You'll be too busy being a big shot to care about our, *excuse me, my* restaurant.

CHARLIE   Fine, that's the way *you* want it.

DOMINIC   [*Stamps his foot.*] No, that's the way you want it. Kill me to death, or *not*! I'm staying.

CHARLIE   Will ya stop with the killing talk!

DOMINIC   I'm staying dead or alive.

CHARLIE   You're such a drama queen.

DOMINIC   Don't make fun of my feelings, Charlie. I'm hurt.

CHARLIE   Well, get over it 'cause I'm going.

DOMINIC   GO! Go, see if I care.

[DOM *cries as* CHARLIE *goes to the door and stops.*]

CHARLIE   Gonna run the book by yourself too?

DOMINIC   That's your thing, not mine. I'll just cook. Somehow, I'll survive.

CHARLIE   It'll be hard to make a go of it without the book to hedge the cost.

DOMINIC   A lot you care.

[CHARLIE *at the door watches* DOM *sniffling.*]

CHARLIE   Dom?

DOMINIC   What?

CHARLIE   Are we having our first fight?

DOMINIC   You think?

CHARLIE   I'd say trying to poison me to death was a sure sign of a disagreement.

DOMINIC   I'm really sorry about that, Charlie. I apologize.

CHARLIE   Aaaagh! Forget it.

DOMINIC   But I'm still staying.

CHARLIE   I guess I could stick around until we, *excuse me*, until *you* got going.

Dominic I wouldn't want to keep you from your criminal empire.

Charlie You're like a Turner Classic movie, when you get like this.

Dominic *Little Caesar.*

Charlie Oh, stop with the soap opera. I'm gonna check on my garden before I . . . before . . .

Dominic Before you what?

[**Charlie** *opens the door and it bangs against the dead body of the* **Uncle Sid**'s *giant bodyguard.*]

Charlie Holy mother of . . . !

Dominic What?

Charlie You weren't kidding. This guys is a freakin' moose.

Dominic I told ya. I told you. Between him and little Paulie we should be able to get a three-month head start on all our meat entrees.

Charlie Well, there is no way I'm going to let you carry him to the basement by yourself. Not with your back.

Dominic I'll manage somehow.

Charlie The last thing I need on my back is your conscience. I'll help you wrap and pack the freezer.

Dominic Thank you, Charlie, I appreciate *that* much.

Charlie I guess . . . I guess I could stick around until we get Dominic & Charlie's off the ground.

Dominic Dom & Charl . . . you mean that, Charlie?

Charlie Sure.

Dominic Oh, Charlie.

Charlie Anything for a pal.

Dominic You've made me so happy.

Charlie Besides, I have onions and carrots coming up.

Dominic Oh, Charlie, what I can do with your onions.

[**Dominic** *starts to dance the mambo.*]

Charlie Okay. Okay, Carmen Miranda, I'm in, I'm in.

Dominic I could never of done it without ya.

Charlie Yeah, yeah, now get off the soapbox and let's get to work on that moose outside the door.

DOMINIC   No, no. Let's have desert first. Cut two pieces of cheesecake.

[CHARLIE *picks up the knife with* SID's *blood on it and wipes it off on his pant leg.* CHARLIE *cuts two pieces of cheesecake while* DOM *puts out a new cup of coffee.*]

CHARLIE   Good plan. Dom, I'm sorry about the white rug.

DOMINIC   What's the diff? We'll be moving soon.

CHARLIE   I just got carried away.

DOMINIC   You were magnificent.

CHARLIE   It had to be done.

DOMINIC   A real warrior. Like on the video games.

CHARLIE   It was the Uncle Sid or us.

DOMINIC   Leo would have been proud of you.

CHARLIE   Yeah. Yeah, Leo would of been proud of both of us.

[CHARLIE *places two pieces of cheese cake on table.*]

DOMINIC   Well, we can say we was taught by the best.

CHARLIE   [*Eating.*] Oh, Oh! Oh! Dom, this is one hell of a cheesecake.

DOMINIC   Oh, go on.

CHARLIE   No, I mean it. I can taste the uh, the uh . . .

DOMINIC   The orange rinds?

CHARLIE   The orange . . . Yeah!

DOMINIC   Little Paulie loved my cheesecake with the orange. I wish he was still with us.

CHARLIE   Yeah! Shame about little Paulie. You'll have to do something special with him.

DOMINIC   Millanese ala little Paulie in a white wine and lemon sauce. With a side order of spaghetti with white clam sauce.

CHARLIE   An Italian surf and turf. Sounds delicious.

DOMINIC   I think Vinny would appreciate it.

CHARLIE   I'm sure.

[*Raises glass.*]

Sempre Duro.

[*Fingers touch.*]

[*The lights begin to slowly fade as the music rises.*]

DOMINIC   *Sempre Duro.* I was thinking, Charlie, when the freezer gets low we could always con one of the other guys up here.

CHARLIE   They'll probably come up on their own.

DOMINIC   You think?

CHARLIE   Don't worry about a thing. We'll be ready for 'em.

[*Eats.*]

DOMINIC   Sure we will, I got a poison for every occasion. I'd like that *sfacimm'* {AU: What's this word?} Harry the horse to come up. I always hated that sadistic pain in the ass.

CHARLIE   [*Laughing.*] How about Tiny Randuzzi?

DOMINIC   [*Laughs.*] We could fill the freezer for a year with Tiny Randuzzi.

CHARLIE   Don't worry, Dom, if they don't come—

[*Both actors look to the audience.*]

there are a few around here I wouldn't mind getting rid of.

The End

[*Blackout.*]

MALA HIERBA

by
Tanya Saracho

Production History

Mala Hierba was originally produced by Second Stage Uptown at the McGinn/ Cazale Thaeatre

First preview: July 14, 2014
Opening night: July 28, 2014
Closing: August 9, 2014
Directed by Jerry Ruiz

Cast

MARI: Roberta Colindrez
YUYA: Sandra Marquez
LILIANA: Marta Milans
FABIOLA: Ana Noguiera

Creative Team

Scenic Design by Raul Abrego
Costume Design by Carisa Kelly
Lighting Design by Jen Schriever
Sound Design by Jill BC DuBoff
Fight Choreography by Thomas Schall
Production Stage Manager: Lori Ann Zepp
Stage Manager: Alisa Zeljeznjak

Tanya Saracho was born in Sinaloa, México. She's a playwright, actor, theater director, and TV writer (HBO's *Looking* and *Girls*), and is currently writing for *How To Get Away With Murder*. Produced at: Oregon Shakespeare Festival, the Goodman Theater, Steppenwolf Theater, Teatro Vista, Teatro Luna, Fountain Theater, Clubbed Thumb, NEXT Theater, and 16th Street Theater. Plays include: *The Tenth Muse, Song for the Disappeared, Enfrascada; El Nogalar* (inspired by *The Cherry Orchard*); an adaptation of *The House on Mango Street* for Steppenwolf; *Our Lady of the Underpass; Kita y Fernanda*, and *Quita Mitos*. In development with: HBO, Goodman Theater, Steppenwolf Theatre, Two Rivers Theatre, Denver Theater Center, and South Coast Rep.

Characters

LILIANA: Late twenties. Wife of border magnate. Sports the prerequisite dyed-blonde hair that a proper upper class, border wife sports. She was born in Mexico to a proper family but these days, only the name remains. Lili's always decked out. Always dressed to the nines. Even when playing tennis, she's impeccable. And underneath all that bling and pomp is her youth. It's in there somewhere. All her life she's been an object of desire because she's got that thing that only a few people have—that sparkle. The kind of charm that can't be taught.

MARITZA: Same age as Liliana more or less. Mari is a visual artist based in Chicago, with South Texas roots. Some might call her a "boi" or a "stud" and she wouldn't mind it. She has a few tattoos she loves, some she regrets. She's done the dread thing, but now is sporting something more hip. More gender neutral. Black used to be her favorite color, but now she's not minding rocking the retro gear she grew up with. She's an artist and is well respected in her community, some might call her well known. She loves fiercely and is fiercely loyal. This is the friend you want for life.

YUYA: Older than Liliana by at least twelve or fifteen years, but perhaps older. Yuya raised Liliana and her siblings and had served that household until she imported herself to Liliana's new household after she married. She's usually smarter than anyone in the room, and she always knows what the heck's going on. She knows her place but hides her resentment well. It is what it is.

FABIOLA: The twenty-five-year-old only daughter of Alberto Cantu, Liliana's husband. Fabi lives in Houston. Has always had everything. If you asked her, she'd consider herself liberal and progressive but it all depends on your definition. She's been working on her degree for seven years, going on eight now, and she's so over it. It's a requirement really. To get a big chunk of change from her dad. Hey, they made a deal.

Place

Sharyland, Texas, in the Rio Grande Valley

Time

The span of one week, late this spring

A Note About the *

Every * cues the following line of dialogue to an overlapping effect.
Please follow.
ALSO: [This denotes the translated Spanish.] Not meant to be spoken.

Scene 1

[*Thursday morning: The Cantu's master bedroom. This is a decadent room, with a big wooden bed and matching bedroom furniture; 1000-thread-count sheets, that sort of thing. The best that money can buy and also the tackiest money can buy. Alright, not tacky but these people have had Versace furniture back when it was in style, know what I mean? It's just too much, too fabulous, this house could definitely be on MTV's Cribs. Lots of crème colors and lots of wood. Gilded things. It's morning. The bed is unmade, and it's seen some major: the sheets are all rumpled and disheveled and there are belts everywhere. Like seven of them, strewn across the floor and the bed. Two are fastened to the bed as restraints. Fastened to the posts.* LILIANA *is getting dressed as* YUYA *enters.*]

YUYA   A mira pues, I thought you were still in there showering.

LILIANA   Come help me with this.

[YUYA *helps zip her up.*]

YUYA   Que purty, this color. Is this from the big box that came yesterday?

LILIANA   Yes. All the other dresses are disgusting, though. Will you send them all back?

YUYA   Tu y tus Internet addictions. Yeah, I'll send them back. No pero, it does look purty on you, this color.

[LILIANA *goes to sit by the vanity and absentmindedly picks up a belt from the bench and hands it to* YUYA. *The belt is nothing, just a belt.* YUYA *picks up and puts away belts during the next exchange.*]

LILIANA   I also got it in rosita and lilac but both made me look too . . . Texan.

YUYA   Oooh, lilac would look purty with your green eyes.

LILIANA   Maybe I'll keep that one.

[*A crash is heard in the garden. Your general metal-chairs-on-table crash.*]

LILIANA   Puta madre, Yuya! All morning these men have been* with the banging and the—

YUYA   They're just unloading the chairs and the tables. I just went to supervise. It's fine.*

Que quieres que te diga, it's going to be noisy like that.

LILIANA   Pero que relajo se traen!

YUYA   It's looking real good down there, though. You'll see right now when you go down.

LILIANA   It better look amazing. It better look like a pinche editorial in a pinche magazine with all the money I'm spending.

YUYA   It will, todo mundo will be talking about it. You'll see.

LILIANA   Oh, God, I hope so.

YUYA   This room es todo un desmother. I'm going to change these sheets, okay? Should I put on the satin ones that he likes?

LILIANA   Ay, no, Yuya. Those make me feel so *Scarface.*

YUYA   The peach ones then.

LILIANA   Which peach? Oh, the crème? Si, pon esas, Yuya. [Yes, put those on, Yuya.]

[YUYA *goes about redressing the bed.*]

YUYA   Adivina [guess] who came last night?

LILIANA   Porfavor, crees que no me di cuenta? [Please, you think I didn't notice?] The whole neighborhood heard her come in in the middle of the night. Driving in like a manica, stomping around like a pinche elephant.

YUYA   Es una malcriada. [She is a brat.]

LILIANA   I don't want to say anything because you know, because I feel bad for her, raised by mother after mother.

YUYA   Please. I have kids, okay? And they only turned out to be good kids because I gave them sus buenos guamazos [beat them upside the head] if they ever got sassy with me. Which is exactly what this girl was missing. With kids you can't be afraid to make a fist.

LILIANA   No, if I ever have kids, I'm never going to hit them. If I ever have kids voy a razonar con ellos. [I am going to reason with them.]

YUYA   Yeah, razonar like this with them.

[*Makes a bitch-slap movement.*]

No te digo [I'm telling you] that's the only way. If not you'll turn out big brats like this one.

LILIANA   Me da lastima. [I feel bad for her.]

YUYA   You feel bad for that brat?

LILIANA   A little.

[YUYA *continues making the bed.*]

YUYA   She didn't never go to sleep. Se fue [she went] straight to the study to the computer, she was still up when I get up this morning y viene y me dice en [and she comes and tells me in the] la kitchen, "I want eggs benedict. But with fresh mozarella instead of ham. Make it." Asi nomas [just like that], "make it." And she never says my name neither, siempre se le olvida. [She always forgets it.] How long have I worked here and she don't remember my name? Every dog's name she remembers, pero el mio ni maiz paloma. [But mine, she doesn't remember.]

LILIANA   You know what a big fuss they made when I brought you asi que dale las gracias [so just be grateful] that she even talks to you. Just don't . . .

YUYA   Oh, I know. I know. Please, you know that I know how to act. Twelve years working for your family, I know how to act.

LILIANA   I know, just . . . please, porque va con el cuento con Alberto [because she'll got tattle tell to Alberto].

YUYA   [To herself.] "Eggs Benedict" . . . Pinche huerca.

LILIANA   [About earrings.] The gold or the silver?

YUYA   Gold. Aunque the silver looks good too.

LILIANA   I have a million things to do before tomorrow. We have to call the bakery and order a whole new cake. Alberto changed his mind about the red velvet, now he wants tres leches for the party cake. But he still wants it to be five tiers. I can't tell him tres leches doesn't hold up in tiers. It would be mush.

YUYA   Just get him a tres leches para el solito y dale a [just for him and give] everybody else red velvet.

LILIANA   Oh, because it's as simple as that, verda? You know how he is. He'll check and then, well, we don't want him to get how he gets at his own birthday party. The bakery is going to have to work it out. And I'm sorry that they have a day to make a whole new cake. Pero a ver como le hacen. That is not my problem. Por eso se les paga lo que se les paga, verdad? [That's why we pay them what we pay them, right?]

[Beat.]

Santo Dios, que desmadre. [Dear God, what a mess.] If his fifty-fifth birthday is this much trouble, I don't want to know what will happen when he turns sixty. Me va a dar un infarto. [I'm going to have a heart attack.]

YUYA   We'll see if you're around for that.

[A dirty look from LILIANA.]

Digo, si Dios nos da vida. [I mean, God willing.] You never know what will happen.

LILIANA   No te pases conmigo, cabrona. [Don't be disrespectful with me.] You think I don't know what you mean? What people say? I know I'm married to Henry the Eight. {Eighth?}

[*She throws a brush at* YUYA.]

COMO ME VAS A DECIR ESO? [How are you going to say something like that to me?!]

[*Consciously quieting down.*]

I don't need this shit from you, Yuya! Five years I've lived tip-toeing around this pinche family and I don't need you for eggshells right now. Not you too, pinche cabrona [bitch].

YUYA   I'm sorry. I didn't mean it like that—

LILIANA   Claro que [of course] you meant it like that. Vibora. [Viper.]

YUYA   Disculpame. [Forgive me.] I wasn't—

LILIANA   [*Throwing another brush at her.*] Con esa pinche lengua de vibora! [With that fucking viper tongue.] You viper!

[FABIOLA *enters without knocking.*]

FABIOLA   Anybody know if there's an art supply store in this hicksville? I want to paint.

LILIANA   Fabiola! Hola muneca! Llegaste bien? [*Hi. Did you get here okay?*]

[*The two kiss on the cheek and* FABIOLA *throws herself on the freshly made bed.*]

FABIOLA   Yeah, sorry I didn't call you guys. I got here like at 6 actually, but I grabbed dinner with some friends. Did you know there's a P.F. Chang's here now?* Finally, something other than fucking taquerias and Whataburgers. And then we went to this wannabe beer garden place. I'm like, alright, McAllen, don't try so hard. But then it was like 2 a.m. and I was like, fuck, I guess I better get home.

LILIANA   Yes, since last year . . . Yuya, eso es todo. Gracias. [Yuya, that is all. Thank you.]

[YUYA *exits.*]

How was the drive?

FABIOLA   What do you mean how was the drive? It was a drive. What am I going to tell you? I drove, I stopped to pee, I ate Cheetos in the car.

[*A beat.*]

Can we please talk about the fucking madness going on downstairs? All those men everywhere. I could barely come up the driveway.

LILIANA   They're setting up for your dad's party.

FABIOLA   Obviously. But do they have to be in everybody's way?* Hey, what are you wearing tomorrow. What are you wearing to Dad's thing?

LILIANA   I'm sorry about this, Fabi.

LILIANA   [*She takes a quick beat.*] Ah, I have a couple of options. . . .

FABIOLA   Can I see?

LILIANA   I don't . . . do I have them all here? Let me see.

[*Goes into the closet.*]

FABIOLA   I didn't bring anything that I like and forget trying to find something here. Porfavor. I'll end up with a cowboy hat or something . . . and ropers.

LILIANA   [*Emerging from closet with two dress bags.*] I was thinking this red one, because it's going to be hot. I don't want to, you know, I don't want to sweat, so no sleeves. But really I think I'm going to wear this white one because I love the—

FABIOLA   Oh, my God. No, you're going to let me wear the white one. Where did you get this?!

LILIANA   I ordered it.

FABIOLA   Where from?

LILIANA   Online.

FABIOLA   From where? I love it!

[*She takes off her clothes to try it on.* LILIANA *gives a quick sigh, she obviously wanted to wear that one.*]

LILIANA   I don't even remember. You know how you get to shopping online and you have like a thousand opened tabs and you just click buy and . . . yeah, I don't remember.

FABIOLA   Shuddup, this fits me like a glove. Look at this. Do you have gold shoes?

LILIANA   Aaah, I think so.

FABIOLA   Oh, I really like how it looks. You don't mind, do you?

LILIANA   No, como crees. [No, of course not.]

FABIOLA   You sure?

LILIANA   Please, no. I was going to wear this red one anyway.

FABIOLA   Okay, great, so I got the dress, now for the shoes.

LILIANA   Yeah, let me show you what I got. . . .

FABIOLA   Hey, so you got a new car. Huh?

LILIANA   [*Slight "oh no" beat. She knows what's coming.*] . . . Yeah. You saw it.

FABIOLA   How can one miss it? It's like taking up two spaces in the garage.

LILIANA   Yeah, it's a little ridiculous, isn't it?

FABIOLA   I love it.

[*Pause.*]

LILIANA   Yeah, I love it too.

FABIOLA   Yeah.

[*Pause.*]

LILIANA   While you're down, if you want to you can drive it.

FABIOLA   Could I?

LILIANA   Of course. It's such a smooth ride.

FABIOLA   I know. I drove it out to get a shake last night.

LILIANA   You what?

FABIOLA   I was dying for a shake, like dying—I'm probably getting my period—and the keys were right there. So I was like, let me check it out. And you're so right, it's like butter. I feel so tall in it. I don't know how easy it can be to have something like that in Houston, like so big, you know? But it's like butter. The seats. Ah, so comfy. And I like all the stuff on the dash.

LILIANA   Yeah, it's like you're driving a spaceship, isn't it?

FABIOLA   I want it.

LILIANA   I have no doubt that—Alberto wouldn't even blink if you asked him for one. How long are you down for? We can go to the dealership together—

FABIOLA   I like that one.

[*Pause.*]

I like, totally fell in love with it. The color.

LILIANA   . . . Ah, my little truck . . .

FABIOLA   Not so little. Your little . . . big truck.

[*Pause.* LILIANA's *trying to deal with the knot in her throat.*]

LILIANA   [Ah, man, this hurts.] No.

[*Beat.*]

Your big truck.

FABIOLA What? No way.

LILIANA Yes, please. Your truck.

FABIOLA Are you serious?

LILIANA Fabi. Of course. You're the one that's up there in Houston—

FABIOLA Like for real, for real? You'll give me your car? Title transfer and everything?

LILIANA Claro. No se diga mas. I didn't buy it, right?* You're the one up there working so hard. And studying so hard, you know? Of course. Come on.

FABIOLA Nope. But your good taste did choose it.

FABIOLA Why are you the best? You are my favorite of my dad's wives, you know that? Totally mean it.

LILIANA Oh, that means so much to me, Fabi. De verdad. [For real.]

FABIOLA I'm super serious. You know I didn't get along with that gringa he fucking brought back from Arizona.* Ugh. Arizona is the new Alabama, it's a fucking toothless hicksville.

LILIANA Oh, I know. No, yeah, I know.

FABIOLA Nasty fucking gringa with no class.

LILIANA I know.

FABIOLA I mean it. You're like . . . you're almost like a sister to me, but like not.

[She pulls out the keys from the pocket of her sweatpants on the bed.]

So, all mine?

LILIANA Well, we just have to run it by Alberto.

FABIOLA Oh, I know you'll convince him. You're the best!

[Big hug.]

Oh, and the best taste in clothes. Hands down.

[About the dress.]

Thank you, mil! It looks good, no?

LILIANA Way better than it would've looked on me.

FABIOLA Shuddup, don't say that. I'll give it back to you tomorrow. Okay, I'm going to go get a raspa. That's the one thing I crave from here. In

Houston the closest thing we get to it is a slushy but I tell people, I don't want a fucking neon red slushy that taste likes sugary ass, I want a fucking raspa like with the shaved fucking ice from the valley. That's what I want. If I could learn to shave ice myself, I'd totally eat that for breakfast, lunch, and dinner.

[*Beat.*]

Oh, guess who I ran into this morning? Same bright idea, I guess, we were both getting a shake. Maritza Perez. Do you remember her?

LILIANA   Mari Perez?

FABIOLA   Yes! Oh my God, she looks amazing. She was a sore thumb standing there with all her, like . . . I don't know. Gear. She's like all emo or something. Anyway, apparently she was living in Detroit.

LILIANA   Chicago.

FABIOLA   Yeah. Chicago and she's visiting because, actually, I don't know. She told me but I wasn't paying too much attention. Anyway, she's here for a little while. So I invited her to Dad's thing tomorrow.

LILIANA   You what!

FABIOLA   She's your friend, right?

LILIANA   I haven't talked to her in like decades.

FABIOLA   Oh, she told me she saw you at some wedding? Or a funeral?

LILIANA   I mean, sure. She, she knew my brother and she came down for the memorial, but I'm sorry I didn't really talk to her, I literally passed her in the hallway . . . I didn't really talk to her. . . .

FABIOLA   Well, now you get a chance to catch up.

[*About the dress.*]

Hey, thanks again. It fits like a glove.

[*Exiting.*]

You know what? I'm going to do something nice for you 'cuz you've been so badass with me. What flavor raspa do you want?

LILIANA   I don't really . . .

FABIOLA   Vanilla! I'm going to get you vanilla. So I can have a taste.

[*Exits.* LILIANA *sits down on the bed, the air has been popped out of her chest. Lights go down.*]

End of Scene

Scene 2

[*Friday night: The master bedroom. We hear the dull sound of a party down below. Clinking and music and the occasional cackle, etc. You know, party shit.* LILIANA *enters in her red dress. She looks amazing in it; she's a little sweaty, though. She digs in a vanity drawer for a packet (not bottle) of pills from Mexico. Tafil to be exact. She pops one in her mouth and chases it with the glass of malbec she's brought with her. A little while before* YUYA *enters with a similar pack.*]

YUYA   I couldn't find* your purse.

LILIANA   I found some.

YUYA   Me encontre este paquete [I found this package] in the kitchen. You had another stash behind the diet pills.

LILIANA   Ah, thank God I have foresight. Should I take two? No porque luego [No, because then] I'll fall asleep or something. I don't know what to do? I want to take the whole freaking box. He hates the band. He hates it.

YUYA   He's over that. He forgot about it as soon as he yelled at you.

LILIANA   I hope so. I hope he forgot. Osea ojala because during the toast all I kept thinking is, chingada madre [fucking shit] he's going to start yelling as soon as he sees we couldn't make a five-tier tres leches.

YUYA   It's just cake.

LILIANA   Como que [What do you mean] it's just cake? It's not just cake.

YUYA   The governor loved the red velvet. Les dimos tres pieces. [We gave him three pieces.]

LILIANA   I know. It's the only thing that saved me. Did you see his son? He looks like a movie star now. There was a time, long time ago, there was a time I thought we'd end up married.

YUYA   Nombre [*no way*], you don't want to move back to Mexico and be a governor's wife. They're killing governors right now. La mafia is making a video game of beheading them for points.

LILIANA   Ay, Yuya! Porque me traumas? [Oh, Yuya! Why do you traumatize me?]

YUYA   Me? The news trauma! They traumatize you every day at 6 o'clock. People don't even know if what they're watching is the news or some video game con good graphics. Blood everywhere.

[*Beat.*]

He did get so handsome, though. He got tall. Maybe he won't get into politics like his dad.

LILIANA   Please, they're all politicians. His entire family. There's no way. Let's stop talking about him. If Alberto notices the little looks he's been giving me, no para que quieres. . . . Do I look okay?

YUYA   He was watching you like this.

LILIANA   He was, wasn't he? I'm not just imagining. Good. Oh, but his wife es una mustia [mousy little thing]. Did you see her? No hips. No boobs. Dark. Ugh. De donde saco a esa indita? [Where did she find that little Indian?]

YUYA   I didn't believe it was his wife at first.

LILIANA   I know! Yo aqui como que "Hola! Mucho gusto." Guacala. [Me right here like, "Nice to meet you. Hi." Gross.]

YUYA   At least the one thing you can say is that you're always the prettiest one everywhere you go.

LILIANA   [*Still messing with her hair.*] At least we can say that.

[*Beat.*]

You like my hair like this? Should I wear it down?

YUYA   No, he told you to wear it up. Luego se enoja. [Then he'll get mad.]

LILIANA   That's true. But I always feel so old with it up.

YUYA   You don't look old. Se te ve bien. [It looks good on you.]

LILIANA   I know, but it makes me feel like I'm thirty-eight or something. Over the hill.

[*A knock on the door.*]

Si? Adelante. [Yes? Come in.]

[MARITZA *enters the threshold, not the bedroom yet, but her presence is like hot vapor in the room.* LILIANA *jolts up.*]

LILIANA   Yuya, ve a ver si se ofrece algo abajo. Andale ve. [YUYA, *go see if someone needs something downstairs. Go.*]

[*Pause.*]

MARITZA   Hey, Yuya. How you been?

YUYA   [*Ignoring* MARITZA, *to* LILIANA.] I think maybe you should go downstairs and see if Alberto wants to dance now. Andaba diciendo before that he wanted to dance.

LILIANA   Yuya, go downstairs, I said.

YUYA   I think maybe you should come too.

LILIANA   No te lo vuelvo a repetir! [I'm not going to say it again.] Go check on the guests! Go!

[YUYA *exits glaring at* MARITZA.]

MARITZA   Bye, Yuya. Nice seeing you too.

[*Very pregnant pause. Like nine months pregnant.*]

LILIANA   Hi.

MARITZA   Hi.

[*Pause.*]

Great party.

LILIANA   Thank you. Been planning it half the year. Did you see who we got to play?

MARITZA   I know. Fancy.

LILIANA   Alberto hated them in person. They sound different in person.

MARITZA   I thought they sounded good. Speakers were a little loud, though.

LILIANA   I don't think anyone noticed that. I mean, you know about that sort of thing, but I don't think . . . people seemed to be enjoying themselves.

MARITZA   They always do at these things, no? All the decadent food and endless drinks.

LILIANA   Let's hope so.

[*Pause.*]

MARITZA   You look amazing.

LILIANA   Thank you. Thanks.

MARITZA   You really do.

LILIANA   Thanks. You look . . . I like your blazer. It's like '80s, right?

MARITZA   I guess.

LILIANA   Aren't you hot in that? It's too hot for a blazer. No te estas asando? [Aren't you melting/cooking in it?]

MARITZA   Alberto's wearing a blazer.

LILIANA   I'm sure he's cooking in it. I'm sure all the men are cooking in their blazers. That's why it's good to be a woman in weather like this, because we can wear things like this and not cook in blazers.

MARITZA   Well, if he can cook in his blazer, I'll cook in my blazer.

LILIANA   I should have gotten giant fans to put everywhere, or cooling stations.

[A pivot.]

MARITZA   I've been here a week.

LILIANA   Maybe we should go downstairs. Everyone will wonder where I went.

MARITZA   A week, Liliana.

LILIANA   Want to try a fun drink? They designed it just for the party. It's like a Mai Tai but better.

MARITZA   I've been sitting on my ass for a whole fucking week asking myself, "Did that phone call really happen?"

LILIANA   I want to go downstairs.

MARITZA   Sitting there at my cousin's, who is too polite to ask, "What the fuck are you doing down here?" and me sitting there wondering the same fucking thing.

LILIANA   Que malhablada eres, eh. [What a potty mouth you have, eh.]

MARITZA   [*Quickly.*] What? See, don't start doing that.

LILIANA   Shut up, I hate it when you act like you don't understand. You speak Spanish.

MARITZA   Since when do I speak Spanish? You won't ever fucking believe that I don't.

LILIANA   Well, why don't you? It's never made sense to me. Your last name is, what it is. Your parents speak it. You look like you do. I mean, it just makes no sense to me.

[*Quick beat.*]

Can we please go downstairs?

MARITZA   What am I doing here, Liliana?

LILIANA   I don't know, to be honest. I didn't invite you, not to be rude, but I didn't invite you. So . . . I don't really know what you're doing here.

MARITZA   Oh, really? You didn't invite me?

LILIANA   Not to the party. No.

MARITZA   Shut the fuck up! What am I doing in Texas?

LILIANA   Could we talk tomorrow? Wait, no because . . . Could we talk on Monday? I'll meet you at your cousin's on Monday.

MARITZA   You want to wait to fucking talk until Monday?!* I'm supposed to just sit on my ass waiting for you until Monday, when I've been down here for a fucking week with you avoiding my phone calls, just sitting on my ass.

LILIANA   Shhhh . . . shhh . . . calmadita calmadita . . . please, Mari. Please.

[*She goes to lock the door.*]

Shhhh.

MARITZA   I'm not your fucking puppet, Liliana.

LILIANA   Porfavor no levantes la voz. [Please don't raise your voice.] Someone will hear you. This is not how I wanted this to go.* I promise you this is not how I wanted this to go.

MARITZA   And how exactly did you want this to go when I get a phone call in the middle of the night where you sound as if the sky is fucking falling falling . . .

LILIANA   No seas exagerada. You take everything so seriously. Sometimes I take an Ambien* and I just get—

MARITZA   Jesus fucking Christ. Are you serious right now?

LILIANA   Listen. Let's go downstairs. Let's just make the best of it and enjoy the party, vale?

MARITZA   This is you on the phone, "Please come down, Mari. You're the only person I can turn to, Mari. Please, please, Mari." You said that—among other things. So my stupid ass gets on the first plane, which is not cheap, Liliana. I get on the first plane because I think, "Fuck, Liliana's about to die or something," and here I am—almost a fucking week because for whatever reason you're now avoiding me and have locked yourself up in your fucking, in your fucking narco compound—do you know how enraging that is?* You ignoring my texts and my Facebooks and my fucking e-mails?!

LILIANA   Please, please keep your voice down. I'm sorry. You're right. I shouldn't have called you like that in the middle of the . . . I'm sorry. I promise you, everything is fine. I don't know what I was talking about. Just, just ignore everything I said, okay?

[*A knock at the door.*]

Oh, fuck me. Quien? [Who is it?]

FABIOLA   [*Offstage.*] Lili, these shoes suck. I need to look for new ones.

LILIANA   What? Ah, yeah, hold on.

[*To* MARITZA.]

Just . . . please. Yes, you're right, I owe you an explanation. Tomorrow. Or ah, Monday. I promise.

MARITZA   Fucking puppet master.

[LILIANA *unlocks the door and opens it.* FABIOLA *is a little drunk.*]

FABIOLA   Where the hell did you get these shoes from? They are cheap as hell. The strap is slicing my heel. Only cheap shoes do that. Oh, hey. What are you guys doing in here? What you don't want to be downstairs* dancing to that god-awful . . .

LILIANA   I was looking for a headache . . . for an aspirin for Mari, only stronger and we were, you know, catching up.

FABIOLA   Were you?

[*Taking out some coke.*]

That's nice. It's good to catch up with friends.

[*To* MARI.]

You want a bump?

[*Pause.*]

MARITZA   Sure.

LILIANA   What? Mari, don't. Oh, God.

[*Goes into the closet.*]

I'll look for some shoes for you. I'll see if I have some shoes.

FABIOLA   Nice hair on her, huh? Hello, prom 1997. Why does she do her hair like that? She tries so hard. Poor thing.

[*Bump.*]

Oh, my God. It's so fucking hot out there.

[*Bump.*]

Let me see your ink.

[*MARI shows* FABIOLA *her tattoo. MARI bumps.*]

FABIOLA   I like that. I like the style 'cuz it's not too obvious, you know? But it's still a flower. What kind of flower is that?

MARITZA   It's a lily.

FABIOLA   Right. I want like a big arm-sleeve tattoo one day. Like from here to here.

MARITZA   Really?

FABIOLA   Not really. But wouldn't that be cool?

Maritza   Are you the tattoo kind?

Fabiola   Are you kidding? Look at this.

[*She lifts her dress and pulls down her panties.*]

It means "bullshit" in Chinese. Or like the equivalent.

Maritza   Nice.

[**Liliana** *enters to* **Fabiola** *pulling down her panties. She enters with tons of shoes. She spills them on the table.*]

Liliana   Fabiola, que haces?

Maritza   She's showing me her bullshit. Or the equivalent.

[**Fabiola**'s *delighted with MARI.*]

Liliana   I brought everything out, everything I think that goes with that dress. I mean, you could do color if you wanted because it's white.

Fabiola   Maybe I'll just go barefoot. What do you think?

Maritza   Do it.

Fabiola   I need a fucking pedicure, though.

Maritza   Nah.

Fabiola   Yeah? Barefoot?

[*Bump.*]

So where did you find that design?

Maritza   [*Re: tattoo.*] What? This?

Fabiola   Yeah, who drew it? I might want a flower like that. Like right here.

Maritza   I drew it.

Fabiola   You drew that? That's like really good.

Maritza   Well, thank you.

Liliana   Maritza is actually an amazing artist, I mean, do you still do your art thing?

Maritza   Unfortunately. Yeah. I never learned to do something respectable with my life.

Liliana   She's being modest but she's actually kind of famous, right?

Maritza   I wouldn't use the term famous.

Fabiola   Shuddup, are you serious?

Maritza   Your stepmother here is being kind. I have a gallery. And yeah, some people like my work. But I wouldn't say that makes me famous.

FABIOLA   Shuddup, that's amazing. Dude, I paint. I do.

MARITZA   Oh, yeah?

LILIANA   She makes these like, huge canvas things with—

FABIOLA   Shuddup. I love it. Okay, you have to take a look at my stuff.

MARITZA   Sure.

FABIOLA   Lili, who knew that you had cool friends! Like, who knew?

[*Offering coke.*]

Lili?

LILIANA   I don't . . . no thanks.

FABIOLA   Oh, right. Pills are your thing.

LILIANA   De que hablas? [What are you talking about?]

FABIOLA   I don't blame you, to deal with my dad you need like an IV of Xanax to like drag around with you. My dad, as soon as you start to be emotional about anything—shit you could be watching *Oprah* or like a Disney movie with puppies and who doesn't cry at that, you know? But you start crying and it annoys my dad so much that he'll literally pop a pill in your mouth. I mean, like he'll take out a pill, pull down your jaw, and pop the fucking Tafil in your mouth. All those pills right there? Reynosa. They're all from Mex. He doesn't need a prescription. He's got everyone sedated with those fucking pills, right, Lili?

LILIANA   Everybody takes those. I only take it here and there when I'm stressed. Tafil is for children anyway, I just take the child dose.

FABIOLA   Pop two in your mouth: grown-up dose. Pop three:

[*Snores.*]

This party sucks. The music is atrocious. I told my dad that that band was shit.

LILIANA   Did you?

FABIOLA   It's shit. Mari, let's go do something. You seem like a fun girl. Let's go look for trouble in this shit hole of a town. What do you think?

MARITZA   [*Pause.*] Okay. I'm down.

FABIOLA   Awesome.

LILIANA   I don't know if you should. . . . Mari and I were catching up since . . . she's leaving tomorrow.

FABIOLA   Are you leaving tomorrow?

MARITZA   Maybe.

FABIOLA   Ah, well, if you're leaving, then we should definitely go party, you know?

MARITZA   Like I said . . . I'm down.

LILIANA   But we didn't get to catch up. We were . . . we didn't get to catch up and I haven't talked to you in so long and we were catching up.

MARITZA   Maybe I'll stay till Monday then. We can catch up later.

LILIANA   Why don't we catch up now?

FABIOLA   [*Laughing.*]Sounds like the two of you are saying you want some ketchup. Like for fries.

[*Laughing.*]

Come on, let's peace out. Liliana, tell Papi I had to go. That I just had to go because this music, it's making my ears bleed. Okay?

LILIANA   He's going to be angry.

FABIOLA   Well, make sure he's not. You're so good at calming him down.

[*To* MARITZA.]

I've never seen anyone calm him down the way she does. I don't know what she does. You got like fairy dust. Okay, let's go. Ciao ciao.

[*She exits.* MARITZA *lingers.*]

Maritza!

MARITZA   Monday.

[LILIANA *looks like a wet dog or something. No air in her chest again. A moment.*]

End of Scene

Scene 3

[*Friday into Saturday: The back deck of the Cantu's huge patio. There are beautiful equipales with the family crest and lots of fabulous patio décor. It's like tacky but fabulous, you know? Firstly with a touch of Northern Mexico, including some Tapatio pieces (like the equipales and some big talavera vases) but also with a little Southwest/American comfort thrown in there, like stuff from the Sharper Image. There's one of those electronic, self-contained fire pits and the wavy light from the pool reflects onto the deck, giving it a sort of glow.* LILIANA *is sitting in the dark, although it's not that dark since the pool is lit and the Texas moon is smiling. She's eating a bowl of Fritos with lime juice and salsa Tabasco. She licks her fingers every so often. Maybe she uses an exprimidor de limones to put more lime on the Fritos. She's got the cordless house phone and*] *her cell phone and checks it a couple of times. It's like 3 or 4 a.m., dude, it's mad late. She should be in bed.* YUYA *enters after a while.*]

YUYA   That's gonna put a big hole in your stomach.

LILIANA   This is my second bowl.

YUYA   Shoot, I'm going to have to roll you up the stairs.

LILIANA   Shut up, Yuya. Fuck, why don't I smoke? If I smoked I'd be super-skinny.

YUYA   Maybe you should take it up. No porque luego the man upstairs, he wouldn't like the smell.

LILIANA   Verda? My hair would reek. Okay, we need a better plan to make this little belly be flat again. It needs to go down like this, not stick out like that. Guacala, I'm so gross.

YUYA   I didn't want to say it, but you are getting a little wide right here in the middle.

LILIANA   Shut up, don't say that to me, Yuya. Are you serious?

YUYA   Have I ever lied to you?

[*Freaked-out pause.*]

LILIANA   Oh, my God, you're right. I think I'm growing some back fat. Do you see? I'm getting back fat and love handles. Que trauma.

YUYA   The best was when you used to throw up, that's when you look the best.

LILIANA   Yeah, I looked so good then. You could see my bones right here. But my breath smelled<emspace>so bad and you know . . . I kept getting dizzy everywhere.

YUYA   Plus your hair . . .

LILIANA   Oh, I know. I thought I was in that movie *The Craft* all of a sudden. Like that girl washing her hair in the school shower and she's like washing it and it's coming off all over her hands. Callate, no me lo recuerdes. [Shut up, don't remind me of it.] Imagine if I lost my hair? I'd be so ugly.

[YUYA *nods in agreement. A quick moment.*]

Maybe we need to go back to Monterey for those injections again because that totally worked. I was so skinny with the injections because I couldn't keep anything down. But we need to find a doctor who doesn't make me break out into hives. I don't know what was in that stuff, but the last time we went—

YUYA   Uy, you looked like the swamp thing.

LILIANA   I did. Shut up, Yuya. Stop stressing me out.

[*Eats more Fritos.*]

Ya ves como me tienes? [You see how you have me?] Here I am eating trash. But why does it have to be so fucking good?

YUYA   You gonna rot your guts.

LILIANA   Good, maybe I'll get an ulcer and not get hungry.

YUYA   Luego [then] you're gonna be complaining in the morning que acid reflux this and que acid reflux that.

LILIANA   What are you talking about, it is morning. It's going to be light out in a couple of hours.

[*Beat.*]

Ah, I hate it when Fabiola's here. I fucking hate it when she comes down. Right when we got Alberto calm and . . . you know, appeased and mansito, aqui vienes esta pinche huerca . . . [tame, here comes this fucking . . .]

[*Beat.*]

I'm going to have to give her the car, you know? Hija de su puta madre [Motherfucker]. I'm going to have to give her my fucking truck.

YUYA   I don't know. Her daddy no esta muy happy with her [is not very happy with her].

LILIANA   Oh, please. He always does whatever she wants in the end. Always gets her way. Nadamas saca la mano. [She just sticks out her hand.]

[*Stretching out her hand.*]

"Please, Papi. Papito porfavor." [Daddy, please.]

[*Beat.*]

Wait.

[*Goes to look through the glass door.*]

Imaginate si nos cacha Alberto. Porfavor Diosito que no se despierte. [Imagine if Alberto catches us. Please, God, don't let him wake up.] We're all fucked if he wakes up and sees his Porsche missing. How did she find the keys? I don't even know where he keeps the fucking keys. Me lleva . . . [Fuck me . . .]

YUYA   Para que te preocupas por ella? [Why do you worry about her?]

LILIANA   Como que porque me preocupo? [What do you mean why do I worry?]

YUYA   I don't understand why you're sitting out here todo worried about her.

LILIANA   She's got his car, Yuya. Estas mensa? [Are you stupid?] She's got his car.

YUYA   Alla ella, that's her problem.

LILIANA   [*Raising her voice, then catching herself.*] It's everybody's problem. He wakes up and notices that she's gone with his brand-new—I mean, the man hasn't even gotten to drive it, we went around the neighborhood for ten minutes.

YUYA   He took you to the beach in it.

LILIANA   Well, yes, he took me to the beach in it. Still.

YUYA   You're not mad because she took his car, tu 'tas enchilada 'cuz she went off with Maritza to who knows where.

LILIANA   Yuya.

YUYA   Am I saying the truth here?

LILIANA   Mejor te callas, Yuya.

YUYA   You are out here in the middle of the night waiting because you can't stand that* your little friend there . . .

LILIANA   I'm going to throw this bottle at you,* let it splatter, and hit you with hot sauce in the eye!

YUYA   Andale. [Go on.] Throw it and wake him up.

[LILIANA *puts the bottle down. Glares at* YUYA. *Silence.*]

You think I say this to make you mad or something.

LILIANA   I know you say it to make me mad.

YUYA   Lili, if he ever gets wind of—

[*In a flash* LILIANA *has gotten up and is holding* YUYA *by the face. Tight. One hand on her throat maybe. This shuts* YUYA *up. For a moment.*]

LILIANA   Shut up! Cierras el hocico or do I shut it for you?!

[*Pause.*]

YUYA   He'll kill you.

LILIANA   I know he will.

[*Pause.*]

YUYA   You think I don't have feelings and that I don't feel anything and that when we clean you up in the morning from, from whatever he does to you at night—

LILIANA   Te estas pasando, Yuya. [You're crossing the line, Yuya.]

YUYA   Hey, I've been married too.

LILIANA   I doubt your husband had my husband's appetite, I doubt it very much.

YUYA   I know. Por eso digo [that's why I'm saying] that I'm not just saying this to be some jerk or something. Lili, you're like my daughter. To me you're like a daughter.

LILIANA   I know.

YUYA   You know that's the truth. And my job is to take care of you. When I saw her here, in your house. It's just bad business* to have her here.

LILIANA   Just stop talking, Yuya.

YUYA   I knew there would be trouble. There can be trouble if you don't just send her away. You need to send her away.

LILIANA   I tried.

YUYA   No. You can't half-ass try. You gotta send her away.

LILIANA   Oh, like I have any power over whether she comes or goes. She doesn't listen to me. Nobody listens to me.

[*Sound of garage door.*]

The door—the garage door.

[YUYA *gets up to go see.*]

Wait, don't go. Wait until she goes upstairs or she goes to get online. I just want to make sure the car is in the garage.

YUYA   She probably left wrappers and things y sabra Dios que tanto [and God knows what]. I'm going to have to go in there and clean it up.

LILIANA   Yeah, we clean it up when she goes to—

YUYA   The keys. We need the keys from her. Si no la jodimos. [If not we're fucked.]

[*Suddenly* FABIOLA *bursts out onto the deck, as she's taking off her top. She's followed by* MARITZA.]

FABIOLA   . . . because they don't fucking trust me with house keys like if I'm nine years old! It's like gestapo nation up in here.

[*Re: shirt.*]

Help me take this off.

[MARITZA *helps her with the shirt.*]

MARITZA   Fabi, I think you should call it a night.

FABIOLA   No, come on, the pool it's heated. We'll swim and it'll be so perfect.

[*She notices the other women.*]

Oh, my God, what are you two doing here. Like little gargoyles.

[*To* YUYA.]

Oh, yes, perfect, you! Hey! Will you make us some—

[*To* MARITZA.]

Do you want tuna fish? I am like feelin' for some tuna fish with lots and lots of mayo right now. Like a vat of mayo. Do you want some?

[*To* YUYA.]

Will you go make us some. Like right now.

[YUYA *gets up to go.*]

YUYA   Do I bring you something to drink?

FABIOLA   Yes, you bring us something to drink. What are we going to eat the sandwiches with nothing to drink? Mari, what do you want to drink?

MARITZA   I'm good. I don't need anything.

FABIOLA   Oooh, freshly squeezed lemonade. With like the whole thing of sugar, pour the whole jar of sugar in there. Con Topochico. Go.

[YUYA *exits.*]

Let's jump in now because we die if we eat and then swim. Isn't that what they say? That you'll get like a cramp in your stomach and die.

MARITZA   Maybe we should chill for a little bit.

FABIOLA   Fuck that, I thought we were going to jump in.

LILIANA   Fabi, maybe you shouldn't. Your dad can wake up.

FABIOLA   Fuck him. He didn't even pay attention to me at the fucking . . . Did you see how he's treating me?

LILIANA   Que esperabas? It really hurt him when you left in the middle of his party.

FABIOLA   I came down for him, didn't I? I was there at the fucking party. Oh, God, he's such a fucking . . .

[*About the Fritos.*]

What the hell is this?

MARITZA   It's Fritos with lime and hot sauce.

FABIOLA   That's disgusting.

MARITZA   It's actually really, really good.

FABIOLA   No way. Let me taste.

[*Eats.*]

This is like . . . gross good.

MARITZA   I think, um . . . we have a little situation with the car.

LILIANA   What do you mean with the car?

MARITZA   I think, you're going to have to call a tow truck. But maybe not.

FABIOLA   Oh, it's not even that serious, I just didn't want to figure it out this late—

LILIANA   Where's the car?

MARITZA   That's why I gave her a ride. . .

LILIANA   Where's the car.

MARITZA   It's at the bar.

FABIOLA   We left it in the parking lot.

LILIANA   What happened to it?

FABIOLA   The freaking tree. There shouldn't be trees in parking lots, it's so fucking stupid. You put a tree in the middle of a parking lot, you're going to run into it when you're backing up. It's like simple geometry.

MARITZA   The headlight got a little beat up—

LILIANA   Backing up?

MARITZA   Sort of. I mean, the left brake light too.

LILIANA   Dios mio, que va a decir tu Papa?

FABIOLA   Fuck him. It's a fucking car. A fucking obvious ass Porsche, hello. Can you get any more obvious than that. My dad is so fucking obvious about everything. This fucking house, his fucking cars, his little wives—no offense, Lili, you know I adore you, but he's such a fucking douche. You know what's a good classy fucking car? A Bugatti. That's a real fucking car. Have you seen those cars? Have you seen them?

MARITZA   No.

FABIOLA   You would die.

MARITZA   [*To* LILIANA.] I can take it to my cousin's in the morning.

LILIANA   Could you take it to him right now?

MARITZA   I can't wake him up right now.

LILIANA   Could you take it first thing? Alberto leaves for Guadalajara for the whole weekend and he won't be back until Tuesday and if we are lucky he won't notice when Chuy drives him to the airport in the morning.

FABIOLA   You know what? Let's go wake Papi. Papi! I'm going to wake him and tell him that I took it and I rammed it into a tree. Papi! I don't care. Papi!

LILIANA   We don't want to do that, Fabi. De verdad. [Seriously.] We have three days to make it right, y que suerte porque si se entera tu papa que andabas— [and we're lucky because if your dad finds out that you were—]

FABIOLA   I don't care. You think I care? Tell him. I'll tell him as soon as he wakes up.

LILIANA   Fabi!

FABIOLA   Are we going to jump into the pool here?

MARITZA   Not right now, Fabi.

FABIOLA   My buzz is like . . .

[*Makes womp-womp sound.*]

How long does it take to make tuna sandwiches for God's sake?

[*Beat.*]

Lili, I love that color on your nails. You're cool, you know that? I like you. Mari, Lili is my favorite of my dad's wives.

MARITZA   Yeah, you said that.

FABIOLA   He's had some bad fucking bad taste, straight up. There's no one like my mom, man. No one like my mom. No offense, Lili. You're like awesome. But some of these . . . ugh. I hate white people. There. I said it. I hate white people. I would never date a white guy. I mean a white Mexican, sure. But like, a white American? Yuck. Would you date a gringo, Mari? A gringa.

MARITZA   I date all kinds. I take people as they come.

FABIOLA   Yeah, I do too. I mean, yeah. I don't really hate white people. Come on, I live in Houston. How would I hate white people?

[*Beat.*]

I want to visit you in Chicago.

[*Oh, man, sloppy drunk now.*]

I like you, Mari. I like you a lot. I'm coming to Chicago. I'm so coming to see you for sure.

MARITZA   Yeah?

FABIOLA   Yeah.

LILIANA   It's very cold in Chicago. It's like subzero in the summer.

MARITZA   Is that why you've never been to Chicago? Because of the temperature? I mean, you've never been to Chicago, have you?

LILIANA   Why would I go to Chicago? There's nothing in Chicago for me. There's nothing . . . what's there in Chicago. I rather go to like, New York, if I'm going to go somewhere freezing cold.

MARITZA   New York is not as cold as Chicago.

LILIANA   Exactly.

FABIOLA   [About Fritos plate.] I want to like, lick this plate.

MARITZA   Told you it was good.

FABIOLA   Fuck Yuya. Why is she taking so long? Am I going to have to carry these sandwiches out myself?

[Exits.]

LILIANA   You want to go follow your girlfriend over there?

[MARITZA smiles big.]

All of a sudden you're BFFs, the two of you? What you could possibly have in common with that girl—

MARITZA   She's actually not bad once you get her to calm the fuck down. She has a lot of potential.

LILIANA   Oh, she has a lot of potential? She has a lot of potential.

MARITZA   Why are you getting all worked up?

LILIANA   I'm not getting all worked up.

MARITZA   I think you're tweaking* out a little bit.

LILIANA   Ugh, I'm going to . . . I'm going to take this bowl and bust open your head right now. I want to fucking beat you over the head with this.

[MARITZA smiles super big.]

Stop smiling. Stop it. I hate you.

MARITZA   No you don't.

LILIANA   [Diffused. A beat.] I do. Te deteste.

[Beat.]

Pinche Mari. How bad is the car?

MARITZA   I mean I'm not going to lie, it's not like he won't notice if you don't get it fixed. There's a big hole in the headlight and the brake light is dangling.

LILIANA   What the hell was she doing? Why was she driving? Why did you let her drive?

MARITZA   Hey, I brought her back in one piece, okay? But I'm not her babysitter. You can't babysit that.

LILIANA   Mari?

MARITZA   Yeah?

LILIANA   I think you should go.

MARITZA   Yeah, I think I should go too. We don't want old boy coming down in his bathrobe finding me here. I think Fabi's okay and she's in your capable hands now. Going to peace out now.

[*Starting to leave.*]

Lovely seeing you—

LILIANA   No, I mean you should go. Go back home.

MARITZA   You know that's not going to happen until we talk. I've sat around all week waiting for a word from you.

LILIANA   There's nothing to talk about. Everything's actually fine.

MARITZA   I'm not leaving until we have a proper talk. And I promise you, this will be the last time we talk, Liliana.* The last time. Because I'm not doing this shit again!

LILIANA   God. Not here, please. Shhhhh. Keep your voice down, Maritza. Please . . .

[*Silence.* MARITZA *stares at* LILIANA. *For like a long time. After awhile* YUYA *enters with the tuna sandwiches and the keys to the Porsche.*]

YUYA   She passed out.

[*Holding out the keys.*]

Are you all still eating the sandwiches?

LILIANA   Nobody's eating sandwiches, Yuya! Here give me these.

[*Grabs keys from* YUYA.]

Mari, I'll meet you super early at your cousin's right after Alberto leaves. His flight leaves at 8 so he'll be leaving around 7, 6:30. I'll text you when I'm on my way.

MARITZA   I might forget to have my phone on.

LILIANA   Don't joke with me right now, Maritza.

MARITZA   Come on. When have I failed you?

[*Pause.*]

YUYA [*Picking up* FABIOLA's *T-shirt from the ground.*] I think we should move this girl upstairs before she drools or guacareas en el [barfs on the] sofa.

LILIANA Yeah, you go take her upstairs, Yuya. I'm walking Mari out.

[YUYA *exits with a glare at* MARITZA.]

MARITZA When have I failed you?

[LILIANA *grazes* MARITZA's *cheek tenderly as they exit.*]

End of Scene

Scene 4

[*Sunday afternoon: A motel room.* MARITZA *has just helped* LILIANA *onto the dresser as the lights are coming up.* LILI's *only wearing a bedsheet around her.* MARITZA's *in front of her, in a tank top and boy shorts.*]

MARITZA [*Re: sheet.*] More over the shoulder.

LILIANA Like this?

MARITZA Yeah. Now just stand there for me.

[LILIANA *stands in her pose, then feels silly.*]

LILIANA [*She starts getting off the dresser.*] Mari, me siento ridicula. [Mari, I feel ridiculous.]

MARITZA No, come on, babe. Just stand for me.

[*She's all hands with* LILIANA *and turns her around.*]

Let me see your back.

LILIANA Are you arresting me?

MARITZA No, I'm imagining you with wings.

[*She runs her hands all over* LILIANA, *then she pulls off the sheet.*]

LILIANA Hey!

MARITZA Lilith sprouted these amazing wings and dragon talons. All my new pieces are of wings and talons.

LILIANA I don't want dragon talons.

MARITZA Oh, but you do. Lilith was a badass with fucking dragon wings. She'd terrorize men in their sleep and incite nocturnal emissions from them.

LILIANA Her superpower was making guys have wet dreams?

MARITZA   Yeah. And also killing babies. A hundred babies a day.* So some people think of her more as a demon.

LILIANA   What. Well, yeah. If she went around killing babies.

MARITZA   It's complicated. She only killed the babies because God sent his angels to kill her babies for leaving Adam.

LILIANA   I never heard any of this.

MARITZA   Before Eve, God made Lilith.*

[Beat.]

And God made her equal to Adam in every way. But Adam was kind of an asshole who got it in his head that she should lie beneath him and let him fuck her.

LILIANA   Is this in the Bible? He liked to do it missionary style. Nothing wrong with that.

MARITZA   No, he didn't want her on top. As in, he wanted her to know that she was beneath him and less than him, so she was like "fuck that" and she uttered the hidden, unutterable name of God. And, poof, she went off flying and wouldn't come back. No matter how many angels God sent for her. She was like "fuck that, I will not lie under that douche bag."

LILIANA   Adam has always sounded very boring to me. Like wouldn't be a very good dancer.

MARITZA   He didn't have to try too hard, did he? Everything was handed to him. He was a daddy's boy. Why would Lilith want to stay with him?

LILIANA   Well, he did come from a good family.

MARITZA   Adam was a pussy. He goes and whines to Daddy about the wife situation, so God—being the enabler that he is—gives Adam Eve. Made from his rib and willing to be his little wifey and lie beneath him and have dinner for him on the table when he got home from doing nothing.

LILIANA   Poor Eve. Second wives always have it the worst.

[Beat.]

Are we going to order room service?

MARITZA   There's no room service in motels, baby girl. I can go run and get you something.

LILIANA   Whataburger. Toasted bun.

MARITZA   You want Whataburger?

LILIANA   Yes. But in a little bit.

[*They stare at each other a bit.*]

So this is what you're making your art about? I mean, like your paintings.

MARITZA   Not just paintings. But yeah. Lilith is what I'm taking a look at next. Not just in paintings, though. I'm starting to work with other materials.

LILIANA   Maritza. You're so smart. You're the smartest person I know.

MARITZA   I'm not smart.

LILIANA   [*Getting down from the dresser and onto the bed.*] No, you are*. You teach me things.

MARITZA   Whoa. Easy.

LILIANA   Can I like, make a hole on your head and put a straw in and suck out your smarts?

MARITZA   Ouch. That would hurt my head.

LILIANA   I mean, I'd leave you a little bit so you could finish your art stuff.

MARITZA   Well, thank you.

[LILIANA *sucks on her ear playfully.*]

LILIANA   Here, give me some smarts, right now.*

[*Nuzzling her ear.*]

. . . Come on, don't be stingy.

MARITZA   That's creepy, Lili. That's so creepy.

[*This whole thing builds into a pretty sweet but hot make-out session. I mean, you let this go on for a while, okay? They end up tangled,* MARITZA *on top of* LILIANA.]

Run away with me.

LILIANA   Bite my toe. Here . . . bite my toe—

MARITZA   I'm dead serious.

LILIANA   Me too. Bite it.

MARITZA   I can't just leave you down here this time. I think you're going to go putrid here.

LILIANA   Wilting flower. Me voy a churir.

MARITZA   I'm serious.

LILIANA   Wait, Changuita [little monkey], Alberto is out of town. We have a whole day left. Ah, do you know what it's been here with you for two whole fucking days? I got freakin' bed sores and I love them. When do we just get to lie around and . . . Mari, please. Not yet. This is the best two days I've had in five years. Please, could we wait?

MARITZA   Why wait? I mean, let's just fast-forward to the end right now*. Let's spare us the—

LILIANA   [Starts tugging on MARI's jeans, trying to prevent her.] No no no no . . . what are you doing . . . nonono.

[She's got the jeans.]

Not yet. Please. Why do you want to put these on? Why are you trying to leave me?

MARITZA   Give me back my pants, Liliana.

LILIANA   Why are you being like this? Que mala eres? [You are so bad.]

MARITZA   Oh, I'm being bad?

LILIANA   See? You do understand Spanish. Cuando te conviene verdad . . . [Only when it's convenient, right . . .]

MARITZA   [Trying to get her jeans back.] Give me back my pants. . . .

[LILIANA sticks her fingers in her panties and MARITZA stops. LILI then sticks her wet fingers in MARI's mouth.]

Mala hierba [bad seed/weed]. See how bad you are?

LILIANA   Don't call me that. I hate it.

MARITZA   My mom was right. You're a bad seed.

[LILIANA wraps herself in the sheet again.]

LILIANA   Don't call me that. Why doesn't your mom like me? I hate that she never liked me.

MARITZA   Well, what do you think? Her daughter never moved on, walking around this world with a wire still stuck in your socket*, even 1,000 miles away.

LILIANA   The way you say things . . .

MARITZA   It's true. I've been on pause for what? Seventeen years?

LILIANA   I don't want to talk about all this.

MARITZA   No, of course not.

LILIANA   Pinche choro mareador . . . [Fucking broken record . . .]

MARITZA   Fuck you*, I don't know what that means.

LILIANA   You always kill it. You kill the mood*. We're sitting here super nice talking about baby killers and the missionary position and you just have to go a tirarme tu pinche rollo que marea [with the same old fucking dizzying song].

MARITZA   What is this to you? Wait, answer that. Why do I ask this every time? I ask this every fucking time and your answer breaks my heart every fucking time.

LILIANA   What do you want me to do?

MARITZA   You know what I want you to do.

LILIANA   You think this, between these four walls, you think this is real?

MARITZA   Do I think it's real or do I think it's sustainable?

LILIANA   What?

MARITZA   Do I think you'd come out of this room holding my hand? No.

LILIANA   [*Overlapping.*] Oh, my God, Maritza. Claro que no! [Of course not!]

MARITZA   But do I think this is real? Do I think you've been in love with me since we were thirteen? Do I think I've been the *one* for you no matter what dudes have come in and out of your life? And do I think that you're too chicken shit to do anything about it 'cuz you're too fucking hooked on being a fucking rich girl? Do I think that? Sure.

[*Silence.*]

LILIANA   Here are your jeans. Here. We should go, both of us.

[LILIANA *starts to look for her dress. She finds it and puts it on. Finds her panties and puts those on too, now she looks for her shoes.* MARITZA *watches her do all this. Doesn't put on her jeans.*]

I can give you cash for . . . I can't use my card but I can give you cash.

[*They stare at each other.*]

Mari, you think I'm here . . . you think this doesn't cost me. You think it's just nothing. That you're nothing to me. To me you're actually . . .

[*Beat.*]

But everything costs. This is something I realized very early on. Everything has a price. And these two days with you, they're going to cost me big. But I don't care, I'll pay. Because it was so worth it.

MARITZA   What the fuck are you talking about?

[*A moment.*]

LILIANA   He is a monster. He likes choking. He likes belts.* He likes sticking things in places where they shouldn't be stuck. He's not a human to me sometimes. When he's grunting on top of me, or when he's ripping out my ass with no warning—because with Alberto, the more I scream the hotter he gets. But only if I mean it. No faking that shit . . .

Maritza   Wait, what? Lili . . .

Liliana   And that's the price. I pay for everything I own, Maritza. Everything I have. That car out there? Oh, I paid for that. With interest!

Maritza   I think . . . you need . . . to stop telling me this or I'm going to go and kill this motherfucker.

Liliana   No. Just . . . please, stop being in a fucking Antonio Banderas movie! Just. Stop. If you say something. If you do something, what will happen? He tosses me and my father's medical bills don't get paid. My mother loses her house, her health insurance too. My little sister has to come back from college and what? Wait tables? And me. I mean, what would happen to me? I have nothing. All I have is him.

[*Beat.*]

We should go.

Maritza   You can't keep paying for your sister's tuition with your body.

Liliana   Okay, now you're calling me a hooker.

Maritza   You're calling you a hooker.

Liliana   It's so easy for you. You're free up there—

Maritza   This is free?

Liliana   You're up there, doing what you love. You can see who you want. You can go where you please. I got a family to feed, plus I'm not going to stand here and tell you that every thing's all bad. Que hipócrita sería. [I'd be a hypocrite.] So before you give me those googly ass eyes, don't think that I got it so bad. Let's go, I want to go.

Maritza   Why did you call me down here?

Liliana   Because I'm a fucking idiot.

Maritza   No, it's because you want to be with me. That's the truth of it.

Liliana   God, don't you know that that is the only thing I think of sometimes. Forgetting everything and running to you? Not having to worry about my dad, my mom, my sister. Everybody.

Maritza   Alright then. This time we make it happen. This time you come with me.

Liliana   In what world are you living, Maritza?

MARITZA He's out of town, we can do it before he comes back. We borrow a car from my cousin and we drive all the way up to Chicago.

LILIANA He'll find me, Mari.

MARITZA That's why we dismantle that narco truck of yours. Trade it with my cousin for parts so he can give us some hooptie that will take us north. It's not hard, Lili. He won't be able to track us. You just leave that iPhone here and take only what you need.

LILIANA What do you mean only what I need?

MARITZA Okay, you take whatever you want. Whatever we can fit in the backseat and in the trunk. Nothing electronic, though, okay? No iPad. No laptop. No . . . whatever else you got. Just you and your drawers* and your face paint and your fancy shoes. But come on, not all of them, okay? And we go, Liliana. We just start it. Take the video out of pause and finally press play. Like it was meant to be.

LILIANA Mari.

MARITZA This is a long time coming. Every so often we keep getting pulled back for a reason.

LILIANA I know.

MARITZA That's why you called me, Lili. And we are going to be fucked up unless we finally do this, we're never going to be whole. We'll walk around with big gaping holes for the rest of our lives.

[*Beat.*]

Please, baby, you have to leave with me.

LILIANA . . . [*She kisses* MARITZA.]

MARITZA Tonight.

[*A pause while she waits for an answer.*]

Lili?

[*Then* LILIANA *kisses her back forcefully: It's a yes.*]

End of Scene

Scene 5

[*Sunday evening: The master bedroom.* LILIANA *is packing. She does a little mad dance of "should I take this? No. Yes, I need it" with almost everything she considers. After a while we hear a knock.*]

LILIANA I'm taking a nap!

[*More knocking.*]

Quien es?!

YUYA   [*Offstage.*] Soy yo.

LILIANA   I'm taking a nap te digo. I'm napping! Go away.

YUYA   [*Offstage.*] Open the door.

LILIANA   Yuya, respeta! I'm napping! Go away.

[*Some furious knocking.*]

YUYA   [*Offstage.*] Open the door!

LILIANA   Vete muchisimo a chingar a tu madre! Que no te digo que estoy tomandome . . .

[YUYA *has opened the door with her key. Fucking* YUYA.]

LILIANA   Fucking Yuya. I fucking hate you.

YUYA   Que haces?

LILIANA   Te odio, me oyes? I fucking detest you.

YUYA   What are you doing? What are you doing?

LILIANA   What does it look like I'm doing? Close the fucking door at least.

[*As she says this and* YUYA *goes to close the door*, FABIOLA *enters the room in a freaking tornado of tears and* Housewives of the Rio Grande Valley *drama-rama.*]

FABIOLA   . . . Aaaggrr . . . he's a fucking asshole! Mydad'samotherfuckingasshole! Oh, my God! I can't stand him! I can't fucking stand him. I want him to fucking fall off a cliff.

[*Some crying. It's deep for* FABIOLA *right now.*]

I'm like completely . . . He's totally cut me off!

[*She holds out five credit cards. Gold, platinum . . .BLACK.*]

He cancelled them all! My Saks card, my Macy's card. He cancelled . . . HE CANCELLED MY NORDSTROM'S CARD FOR FUCK'S SAKE. What am I going to have to shop at fucking Old Navy now?!

[*Slight breakdown.*]

My gas card. He cancelled my motherfucking gas card! You know what that means, right? That I can't fucking go anywhere. That means I'm trapped here.

YUYA   [*To herself.*] Ay no, Dios mio.

FABIOLA   What the fuck am I supposed to do with my motherfucking life right now?!

Liliana   What happened? Your dad's in Guadalajara. He's not even . . . calm down, Fabi. Calmadita . . . when did you talk to him?* Is he here?

Fabiola   Yeah, on the phone just now. And now he hung up on me and won't answer.

Liliana   Fabi, is he here?

Fabiola   I want to kill myself right now.

Liliana   Fabi, what happened?

Fabiola   He saw that I wasn't going to school.

Liliana   He what?

Fabiola   I haven't . . . I'm not in school right now. I just needed some time to figure some stuff out. . . . Hey, I don't need the righteous shit right now, okay? I don't need judgment right now, Liliana.

Liliana   You haven't been going to school?

Fabiola   No. But that's only because I didn't enroll, okay? And the thing he doesn't see is that I made that decision with like a clear adult mind. It wasn't like my first two years where I had to drop out of classes because I wasn't going, you know? Because I overslept or because, well, most of my professors were total douche bags. They didn't know what the hell they were talking about. Whatever. That's not even the . . . But why can't he see that this time, I made a conscious, responsible decision. To actually not waste money and time and whatever aggravation. I consciously didn't enroll this semester. Alright, I didn't enroll this whole year. Okay? I didn't enroll this year and well . . . He got all—Oh, God, he scared the fuck out of me. He was like King Kong. You know how he gets like King Kong.

Liliana   Yes.

Fabiola   Yeah, but see he never gets like that with me.

Liliana   I know.

Fabiola   And he just . . . took it all away. He's never done that, Liliana. I'm like really scared right now because he's never done that. Even when I went to rehab for the . . . I mean he was like more caring than he was mad. Oh, my God, I'm going to kill myself. That's what I'm going to tell him. That I'm going to kill myself.* See how he'd like his only daughter to . . .

Liliana   Shh. Calm down, calm down, Fabi.

Fabiola   Don't fucking tell me to calm down! Are you listening to me?!

Liliana   Yes, I am listening to you.

Fabiola   You have to talk to him.

[*Beat.*]

Liliana. You have to talk to him for me.

Liliana   . . . Ah, I think this is between you and him. Yo no me quiero meter.

Fabiola   You have to help me!* I mean, what am I going to do? Live here like a prisoner? Like a slave? Just because he got into a mood?

Liliana   Fabi, I don't want to get in the middle of . . .

Fabiola   I need some cash.

Liliana   If I take cash out right now, Fabi . . .

Fabiola   That's true. Who's to say he didn't cancel your shit too, right?

Liliana   He wouldn't cancel my . . .

Yuya   You should check anyway.

Liliana   Shh. Cierra el pico.

Liliana   I can't help you with actual money, Fabiola. I don't think he'd be very happy about that.

Fabiola   Right. But if you . . .

[*She heads to the jewelry boxes. Plural. There are a few.*]

gave me one of your little danglies here to sell, he wouldn't ever notice. Because why would he notice?* Or no, the really fancy stuff is in your closet, I know because I looked once. You have like fucking Cartier and Harry Winston shit. Oh, you have the Tiffany brooch he gave you the first year! The one with the big ruby.

[*She has gone in the closet and hasn't stopped talking.*]

Liliana   What! What are you . . .

Fabiola   [*Offstage.*] It's in all these drawers right here, I've seen them. I just need one of these and . . . Oh, my God. Is this a Chopard watch? Yes. Look at this thing! Why don't you ever wear this? Fuck me. David Yurman bracelets are worth nothing right? They won't give me shit for these. Where are your earrings?

[*The following four lines overlap with* Fabiola's *closet monologue.*]

Yuya   You're just going to let her?

Liliana   What do you want me to do?

Yuya   You can't just let her.

Liliana   What do you want me to do? Little fucking bitch.

Yuya   You're going to let her clean you out like that?

[FABIOLA *emerges with a ton of things and the brooch.*]

FABIOLA Found the brooch. This thing's huge and tacky. You don't want to wear this.

LILIANA Fabi, mivida, could you sit down so we can . . .

FABIOLA Do you have earrings?

LILIANA . . . You can't take those things.

FABIOLA He's not even going to notice.

LILIANA No, you can't take those things because they're mine.

FABIOLA Liliana, I like you but I don't want to say something offensive to you, okay?

[*Moves to go.*]

LILIANA You're not going anywhere with those. Those are my things.

FABIOLA Excuse me, but nothing in this house is yours, okay? You're here on lease. Don't start getting any ideas and DON'T start getting comfortable, honey.* You got a shelf life of about . . .

LILIANA [*She snatches the shit.* FABIOLA *puts up a little fight but loses.*] Well, *honey*, until he sends me away, these are my things. And you're a spoiled little bitch to come in here and think you can just take my stuff. Do you hear that? Who raised you?

FABIOLA Are you serious right now?

LILIANA Dead serious. Who fucking raised you? Wolves?

[*Pause.*]

FABIOLA I'm calling my father and telling him exactly what kind of a gold digger he brought into our house.

LILIANA Do it. Maybe he'll answer the phone.

FABIOLA Fuck you.

LILIANA Come on. Call him. Oh, wait. Did he cut off your phone too?

FABIOLA Fuck you, you tacky bitch.

[*Storming off, she bumps into* YUYA.]

Get out of my fucking way, you fucking idiot!

[*She exits. Good riddance. Door slam.* YUYA *and* LILIANA *are a little stunned. A moment. Oh, shit.*]

YUYA Si se contenta con su Papa—It won't be pretty if she gets her daddy's ear again.

LILIANA   I *know!* Don't you know I know that blood is blood. It doesn't matter, though. That doesn't matter anymore.

[*She starts to pull herself together and resumes the packing.*]

I don't give a fuck. Fuck that little bratty bitch. And fuck Alberto. I don't care anymore. What can he do to me now, huh?

[YUYA *is staring at* LILIANA. *It's unnerving.*]

WHAT? What is this face? What!

YUYA   How many years and I've kept my mouth shut? Not one word. And don't think I don't know the cochinadas you do with her. Doing disgusting things with your bodies—the two of you. Sucias.

LILIANA   Callate pendeja.

YUYA   Liliana, you know you can't leave with her. What, you would leave your father, the way he is right now? So sick?* You would leave your pobre mamacita? That poor woman. You think you get to run off with that puta in your happily ever after and not think about anyone but yourself? Mi'ja, what will happen to your family then? You know Alberto will cut them all off.

LILIANA   *Shut up.

YUYA   Callate Yuya.

LILIANA   Shutthefuckup! Shut the fuck up hija de tu puta madre! Shutthefuckup . . . shut up, Yuya. . . .

[*She has rushed to* YUYA *in a fury. She is beating her back, her arms.* YUYA *cowers and covers her face, and takes the blows.* LILIANA *lets it all go. They both end up on the floor. The hitting becomes an embrace of sorts.*]

Don't say these things to me, Yuya.

YUYA   You can't go anywhere. Too many of us depend on you. Who knows how long this guy will keep you around, but in the meantime, you have to be a smart girl y aprovechar.

[*Quick beat.*]

Man, if I had your possibilities, I would not be fucking this up. I'd be saving every penny I could. Hiding shit. Stashing it away. You need to get smarter about this, Lili. And then, when it's done, then maybe you can think of . . . maybe you can think of whatever cochinadas you want to think about. When you've squeezed everything you can out of this whole thing. Es un investment. Are you listening to me?

[*Takes* LILIANA's *face, still both on the floor.*]

This is all an investment. But you gotta buck up. Be a mujercita. You think I don't want to go off, galavanting and . . . I don't know. You think I like being for your every whim? I didn't say when I was a baby girl, a mira, that's what I want to do with my life. Live at the whims of those who have more. But I got people who are counting on me and I'm the only thing they got. And your papi and your mami, tu hermana Cecilia, you're the only thing they got. It's not about you, it's about them. So buck up.

[*She untangles herself and stands up.*]

You listening? You're gonna have to buck the fuck up.

[*She exits.*]

End of Scene

Scene 6

[*Late Sunday: Outskirts of McAllen. One of those side roads off of another side road made of dirt.* MARITZA *is sitting on a rock, the headlights from an old car are her only light source. She's pacing. Making plans. Awhile before we hear the crackle of tires on the dirt.* LILIANA *gets out of her Expedition and* MARITZA *is activated; she's a galvanized girl right now. She's on go.*]

MARITZA See? I told you that it would take no time at all. Nolana and then to the highway.* It's actually easy to get to, right?

LILIANA Yeah, no . . . it wasn't hard.

MARITZA The iPhone. You left that iPhone at home, right? They can track it.

[LILIANA *nods.*]

And the GPS. You didn't use the GPS, right? I mean, you kind of didn't need it the way I told you to come.

LILIANA No, I didn't use the GPS.

MARITZA Good. That's good, baby.

LILIANA I hate that thing anyway. That woman always sounds like she's mocking me. "Turn left here." Fuck you! *You* turn left here.

MARITZA Is this bag all you got?* We should switch out your bags and put them in my car.

LILIANA What? No, of course not. Do you expect me to shove the contents of my entire—This is a purse! This is a purse, Maritza. It's kind of big for a purse, but whatever. You could fit a head in there.

MARITZA   Yes. I'm sorry, this is a purse.

[*She holds* LILIANA *by the arms. She stares deep into her. Checks her to see if she's alright. Kisses her maybe.* LILIANA *lets her.*]

Hey.

[*Pause.*]

Hey.

[*Beat.*]

How are you doing, baby?

LILIANA   I think I have to pee.

MARITZA   There's a gas station. We can stop there* before . . .

LILIANA   Do you live in a two flat?

MARITZA   Do I what?

LILIANA   Do you live in a two flat. And what *is* a two flat, for that matter? I've heard people in big cities say they live on two flats, and actually to me that sounds very uncomfortable.

MARITZA   What, like a condo? Like a split home?

LILIANA   What's a split home?! A split home sounds even worse than a two flat. I don't . . . Maritza, do you split your home?

MARITZA   Are you asking if I have a roommate? I don't have a roommate.

LILIANA   What kind of a house do you have?

MARITZA   I don't have a house. You know that. People in Chicago don't have houses, Lili. Well, not like the houses you're used to. I have an apartment. And not like the apartment where your sister lives that is basically a townhome. Okay. Liliana, what's with the questions?

LILIANA   So nobody has a house in the entire city of Chicago?

MARITZA   Some people do.

LILIANA   Some? Which people? How do people have kids?! Where do people put their kids?

MARITZA   Where do people put their kids?

LILIANA   O sea, I find it hard to believe that a family with three kids lives in an apartment. That's something I find very hard to understand.

MARITZA   [*Really trying hard not to lose her patience.*] Well, yes, actually, families with three kids do live in apartments but also people who need more room move to the suburbs. If space happens to be an issue.

LILIANA   Would we live in the suburbs if we needed more room?

MARITZA   No, I'd rather stab myself in the eye than live in the suburbs! Where the fuck is all this coming from? Why would we need more room? What, are we thinking of having kids now? Is that what we're doing?

LILIANA   Well, are we? Those are questions, right?

[*Beat.*]

In your life, do you ever want kids, Maritza?

MARITZA   Um, you know what I want? I want to get going. I want to get on the road, put some distance between McAllen and us and when we get to like, I don't know, Austin or Dallas, then I can talk about kids, or getting a pet or whatever else you want.* Right now I want to get on the road.

LILIANA   [*Overlapping.*] Kid are not pets.

MARITZA   I know kids are not pets.

LILIANA   You don't want kids either, do you? Alberto doesn't want kids. That was one of his conditions. I want kids. I want kids really bad. What's the point if there are no kids, you know? What's the point? God, I've never said that out loud.

MARITZA   All of this. I mean, all of it, baby, we will sit down and talk about. I want to spend days and days just talking about this kind of shit. Imagining this life and that life. I can't fucking wait. But right now, I want you in that truck, I want to drop it off where my cousin told me to drop it off and I want to get the fuck out of the valley. Now can you please get your ass in that truck? Liliana.

[LILIANA'*s like on another planet.*]

LILIANA   It was like a diamond heist getting out of the house. You know what you forgot to think about? The cameras. We have a million cameras. But don't worry, I thought of the cameras. I thought about everything. I said, I'll pack my life in those suitcases and think about everything. The cold. The stairs. What kind of shoes will be good for the subway, because you're making me go on the subway, right?* That's the kind of thing I'm signing up for. Hey, I like the subway. I've been on the Underground. I rode around in that.

MARITZA   The El. Yeah, you're going to have to take the El, Liliana. It's not a fucking tragedy that your ass will have to get on the bus once in a while.

LILIANA   Wait, what? What did you say? It's not a fucking tragedy? To you maybe it's not a fucking tragedy but what am I going to do up there? Nunca he conocido a un negro, Maritza! I've never in my life had a conversation with a black person? What will I say?

MARITZA   Alright, you know what—

LILIANA   I won't know what to say to them.

MARITZA   Alright, you're going to have to not say racist shit like* that when we're up there, Liliana. We're going to have to retrain that fucking xenophobic mind of yours.

LILIANA   Why is that racist? It's true!

[*Beat.*]

Retrain? Like I'm a doggie?

MARITZA   I didn't mean like a dog.* Come on, Liliana. Jesus, come on.

LILIANA   Because I'm a little animalito to be trained? Because I'm a little idiot who didn't go to college to learn words like xenophobic. For your information, I know what xenophobic means. Para que lo sepas. Everybody always thinking I'm so stupid.

MARITZA   Who's thinking you're stupid? Baby, I don't think you're stupid. Lili, please. You're picking a fight right now.* You're afraid of this trip and you're picking a . . .

LILIANA   Don't tell me what I'm doing! Plus we're not just taking a trip, Maritza. Para ti esta facilito, no?* I'm about to flip myself upside down, but to you it's just a trip.

MARITZA   Alright, you're right. Not just a trip.

LILIANA   This is the—no*, listen to me. Callate! Listen to me. Logistics. you and I didn't talk about the logistics. What's so bad that I want to talk about the pinche logistics, huh? What's so wrong with that?

MARITZA   But, baby . . . We have to . . . What logistics?

[*An "oh fuck" beat.*]

Liliana. Do you have bags in that truck?

[*Beat.*]

Are there suitcases in that truck? Are you coming with me, Liliana?

LILIANA   My father. In all of this never have you mentioned what we're going to do about my father. My sister. How come you haven't brought that up? You haven't talked about anything but Chicago, but here. The life I'm leaving here, you haven't mentioned that once. What the fuck am I going to do about . . . I don't know, my friends. I'm leaving all my friends!

MARITZA   Those people aren't your friends, Lili.

LILIANA   I know you don't think so but I do have friends, Mari. I have good friends here.

MARITZA   Fake ass people that greet you with a kiss on the cheek and a stab in the back.

LILIANA   What do you know about my life?

MARITZA   What?

LILIANA   What do you know about my life anymore? En serio. What do you know about what my life is now?

MARITZA   You're serious?

LILIANA   Look, I have a life here.* Que a ti no te guste es otra cosa. [That you don't like it is another matter altogether.] But I like a lot of my life here and that's what you will never understand. I like walking into a restaurant and seeing people gasp. I like to hear them whispering. Them whispering in that good way.

MARITZA   Wait, what are we talking about right now? What are you saying? They're not whispering in the good way. They are measuring you up and down, Liliana.

LILIANA   What! I like that. You don't get that I like that. I like being recognized. I like it when Alberto and I make our appearance. I know that's stupid to you, pero a mi me gusta que me envidien. [I like to be envied.] For so long I had nothing. Nothing, Maritza. And now look at me. Oh, you don't get it. You don't get that it's not all so bad. That man saved our life. What would we have done? My family would be on the street. I'd be working at Sally's Beauty Supply or something. On welfare . . . who knows. I don't want to think about it.

MARITZA   What are you saying right now, Lili?

LILIANA   Nothing. I'm not saying anything. Just that it's kind of hard to be told your life is shit. My whole life is not shit. I'm not . . . shit . . .

[*She breaks down. Like falls to the ground and shit.* MARITZA *is on her, kissing her, trying to hold her.* LILIANA *pulls away but* MARITZA's *clasp is strong.* LILIANA *finally gives in.*]

MARITZA   I'm sorry if I made this sound easy. Shhh. It's not easy. Oh, you're shaking. Nonono, no shaking, Mama. You don't have to be scared anymore.

[*Kisses.*]

It's all done. Tonight, that's all over and done with. In a day we'll be in St. Louis at my brother's and then, two days, tops, we'll be in the Chi. Just you and me in Chicago. You know the first thing I'm gonna do for you when we get home? I'm going to run you a bath. You loved baths, right? Well, I have a big old bath tub.

LILIANA   I'll turn into a raisin.

MARITZA   Yeah, a big old sexy fucking raisin. And then, when you've gotten your fill of baths and sleeping and whatever the fuck. Then you go do you. You go do what you got to do for you. I mean, what you were always meant to do before the money problems and this motherfucker got ahold of You. You can just be you.

LILIANA   Who the fuck is that?

MARITZA   No. I know you. You're in there, you're somewhere in there under all this shit on your face, under this weave.

LILIANA   It's not a weave. Son extensiones. [They're extensions.]

MARITZA   Denial.

LILIANA   Hey, this is Indian hair. It cost me 1,200 dollars.

MARITZA   Oh, is that right? Well, let's me and you and your Indian weave get out of here so we can get going. Plus your skirt's going to get dirty sitting there on the ground like that.

LILIANA   The ground is so dry here. You know, you never think about that . . . You never touch the ground. So rocky . . .

MARITZA   You don't care if you get all dirty?

LILIANA   I never just sit like this.

MARITZA   I know. You're going to rip your tight ass skirt. You okay?

LILIANA   [Nods.] Look at this big old rock . . .

[She's been fingering a rock, she picks it up, it's heavy in her hand.]

MARITZA   You know, I like you a little dirty. When you're just you. When you don't give a fuck. I like it when you get whispies like this, these little strands. I like it when they fly away. When your makeup rubs off, when I see your real lips without all the sticky shit.

LILIANA   Eres una pinche hippie. [You're a fucking hippie.]

MARITZA   I like the color of your lips. They don't make that color in a lipstick. I love your lips.

[Kisses and kisses and maybe, if it's not too much, more kisses. They're both tangled on the ground. A long pause as they size each other up. MARI stands up. LILIANA *is going to do something, there's a moment, a good moment there and then* LILIANA'S *iPhone rings.* MARI'S *mood changes. She sees that it's not her phone.*]

That's not my phone.

[*Beat.*]

Why is your iPhone ringing?

LILIANA   I thought I left it at home.

MARITZA   Did you?

LILIANA   Es Alberto.

MARITZA   I told you to not bring that shit with you.

LILIANA   What am I going to do? Not have a phone?

MARITZA   You're not thinking of answering that shit, are you?

LILIANA   I have to answer it, Maritza.

MARITZA   Don't fucking—

LILIANA   [**Answers that shit.**] Bueno? Hola mi amor. Que paso mi rey? [Hello? Hi, sweetheart. What's going on, dear?] Already? I thought you were coming back on Tuesday—you're here now?

[*To* MARITZA.]

Fuck he's here.

[*To* ALBERTO.]

Si mi amor. [Yes, of course.]

MARITZA   Oh, God, I'm gonna hurl . . . you had to bring your fucking piece of shit iPhone.

LILIANA   Como? Eh, si no . . . esque ando aqui con una amiga. [Excuse me? Eh, yes no . . . I'm here with a friend.

[*Beat.*]

Just a friend. We're just having coffee.

[*Beat.*]

Si—Si, Nadamas termino aqui y voy directito para la casa— [Yes—yes, as soon as I finish here and I'll head straight home.]

[MARI *yanks the phone from* LILIANA *and hangs up.*]

MARITZA! Me va a matar. [He's going to kill me.] You can't just hang up on him. Give me the phone. Maritza. Give me the phone.

[*The following is a messy game of "keep away,"* MARITZA *gets a little rough at pushing* LILIANA *away, but* LILIANA *keeps hurling herself at her trying to get the damn iPhone.*]

MARITZA   Do you even have bags in the car?

LILIANA   Of course I have bags in the car. I HAVE TWO FUCKING BAGS IN THAT TRUCK WHICH NOW HOLD EVERYTHING I HAVE IN THE WORLD.

[MARITZA's *holding the phone above her head,* LILIANA *lunges for it again.*]

Puta madre, dame el pinche telefono! [*Fucking shit, give me the motherfucking phone!*] I have to call him back!

MARITZA   Fuck you, you mala hierba.

LILIANA   [*She's a hot mess for real now.*] Please, Mari.

MARITZA   Fuck you and your tears, fucking actress. You had me do this whole fucking thing—

LILIANA   We'll talk in two seconds, just please . . . Mari, let me call him back. I'm not doing this to be . . . you are not understanding, he'll be so pissed. He'll get like a maniac.* OhGodOhGod. He probably came back early to deal with fucking Fabi. Maritza, please!

[*She's bawling by now.*]

Mari, please...

MARITZA   You were never coming to Chicago. Why would you bring this phone? GOD! And I'm a fucking dumb ass who runs around making this whole elaborate plan—Fuck . . . My mom always warns me too. "Es mala hierba. She'll break your heart or worse."

LILIANA   Mari, please . . .* you don't know what will happen. . . .

MARITZA   She kept telling me. "She's bad news."

[*The phone rings again. They freeze.*]

LILIANA   Maritza, he will kill us!*

[*Dives for the phone.*]

Dame el telefono porfavor. [*Give me the phone, please.*]

MARITZA   Get the fuck away from me. . . .

[*They start being a little too rough with each other over this fucking phone.*]

LILIANA   I'M NOT PLAYING, I NEED TO ANSWER! DAME EL PINCHE TELEFONO— [*Give me the fucking phone—*]

MARITZA You know what? You're right, somebody should answer this motherfucking phone.

LILIANA Maritza . . .

MARITZA [*Answers it.*] Hello?

LILIANA NO!

[*The following is even messier.* LILIANA *lunges for the phone as* MARI *tries to remain on it. They struggle.* MARI *drops the phone and dives to get it. She gives* LILIANA *a giant kick that sends her flying to the ground.* LILIANA *almost hits her head against that big ass rock she was playing with. Ugh. Why are they being a Latina lesbian stereotype right now?* MARITZA *puts the stupid phone to her ear and speaks.*]

MARITZA Hey . . . hey, sorry about that. Sorry, my man. What's up, Alberto? How are things, my friend? Hey, I meant to tell you, nice party the other night. Loved the band. Classy stuff.

[*Beat.*]

Ah, funny you should ask that, funny story. You see, I'm a friend of your wife's. Actually, very good friend, you stupid fuck! Let me tell you a little fucking story about destiny and about . . .

[LILIANA'*s gotten up in a flash, and in her panic, she's picked up that rock she was playing with earlier. That fucking thing is heavy as hell but before she has a chance to think, she rushes to* MARITZA *and raises it over her head to hit* MARI *in the back of the head! But right before we see the blow.*]

[*Blackout.*]

Oh, shit.

End of Scene

Scene 7

[*Sunday night:* LILIANA, *face scrubbed clean and wearing a messy ponytail, stands like a statue staring into the eerie light of the pool. From inside the house you can hear* ALBERTO *shouting something and* FABIOLA *replying with loud whimpers. We can't really understand what the fight is about, but we can tell someone is very angry. After a bit* YUYA *enters. She lights a cigarette and takes a drag. After a beat she notices* LILIANA *standing by the pool.*]

YUYA No asustes. [Don't scare people.]

[*Beat.*]

I knew you'd come back.

LILIANA   [*Still looking at the pool.*] I came back.

YUYA   I know. That's good. That's real good, Lili.

LILIANA   I came back.

[*A pause. We can hear the fight going on inside.*]

YUYA   Don't even think about going in there. Es Armaggedon up in there. Book of Revelations. Pinche huerca's in there pleading her case.

LILIANA   He'll get over it.

YUYA   I don't know if her tears will work this time, I watched him go in el study; red steam was coming out de sus ears.

[*Beat.*]

Whatsu matter? You sad?

LILIANA   Am I sad . . . ?

YUYA   Yo sabia que you'd come back. You did the right thing, mi'ja.

[*Pause. Some more shouting from inside.*]

What happened to your face?

LILIANA   [*Suddenly a slight worry.*] Why, do I have something on my face?

YUYA   Well, no tienes makeup on.

LILIANA   Oh.

[*Beat.*]

I had to scrub it all off.

YUYA   Why are you all . . . looking like that? With your hair like that? Ah, ya se. A last hurrah before you sent her off? Ey, whatever you had to do. S'long as you got rid of her. However you had to say your good-byes. Because, chulita, you got some shit to worry about in that house.

[*Beat.*]

Wait. You sent her away, right? Liliana, did you send her away?

LILIANA   She's gone.

YUYA   A que bueno.

LILIANA   And I came back.

[*Beat.*]

Because this is what I chose, right?

YUYA   Si, mi'ja.

LILIANA   [*Finally animating.*] Yuya, do you know the story of Lilith?

YUYA   De who?

LILIANA   She was a wife first and then, because she didn't do what she was told, she became a demon. But I know she was no demon. It's just what people say. People like to say awful things. People call you things, when you're little, they say things because maybe your dad doesn't have money and he owes people and you show up with torn shoes and all the girls in school, they . . . they say mean things. They say mean things about your family. They call you names. But you're not a mala hierba. You're not. You're not a demon.

[*Beat.*]

Poor Lilith. She had to grow those talons to claw her way out. I understand her.

YUYA   Te estas freakiando, Lily? You want me to get you a Tafil to calm down?

LILIANA   I'm no demon, Yuya.

YUYA   Stop saying demon, it's freaking me out. You want a pill?

LILIANA   Tell me I'm no demon.

[*Beat.*]

YUYA   Ey. Whatever you got going on, todo tus feelings, you gotta know it's worth it because this whole thing? All this? It takes work. And you puttin' in the work, mi'ja. You're good at this. At this wife thing.

LILIANA   Yes, I am. I can be Eve and lie beneath him.

YUYA   Yeah, you do what you got to do. Convince him now for a baby and you will be golden.

LILIANA   You think he would let me keep a baby this time?

YUYA   There are ways. But you have to do something with that face and just put yourself together.

LILIANA   I want babies, Yuya. Lots of them.

[*Abruptly and out of freakin' nowhere,* FABIOLA *and her puffy, wet face enter through the patio doors.*]

FABIOLA   Great. Fucking great.

[*She starts to go back inside.*]

Is there nowhere to go in this fucking house!

LILIANA   Fabi, wait.

FABIOLA   What. Seriously, what. I really don't feel like fighting with you right now.

LILIANA   I don't want to fight with you either.

FABIOLA   Oh, please.

LILIANA   I don't.

FABIOLA   Listen, you win it all, okay? You win.

LILIANA   You think somebody wins here? Nobody ever wins.

FABIOLA   All I know is that ever since you came to our house Dad has been completely different. He would have never, I mean never screamed at me like he just screamed at me. You totally turned him against me.

LILIANA   You think I did that?

FABIOLA   Of course.

[*Beat.*]

Not that you give a fuck, but he's the only person I have left in the world. You swooped in here and poisoned him. He wants nothing to do with me. He just told me. You don't know what that feels like. To have absolutely no one.

[*A silence while* FABIOLA *cries.* LILIANA *slowly gets up.* YUYA's *just in the corner observing.*]

LILIANA   What did he say to you? What exactly did he say to you?

FABIOLA   What didn't he say to me . . .

LILIANA   What was the last thing he said? Does he want you to leave? Is he going to help you anymore?

FABIOLA   You—know—what—Liliana . . . !

LILIANA   I'm trying to help you.

[*Beat.*]

What did he say?

FABIOLA   That I'm out of chances.

LILIANA   You're not out of chances.

[*Beat.*]

Are you hungry?

FABIOLA   What?

[*It's as if* LILIANA's *wings expand throughout the following . . .*]

LILIANA   Fabi, you're going to go inside with Yuya. She's going to make you dinner, because I'm almost positive you haven't eaten. Yuya, you're going to make her dinner. Whatever she wants. You figure it out. And I'm going to go, I'm going to go talk to your dad. And then you're going to talk to him again. And apologize. Without all this. Like a grownup. And tomorrow you're going to go back up to Houston. With his support. And you're going to go back to school, and stay out of trouble. You will stay out of trouble, okay. And you and me, Fabi, you and me we are going to have an understanding.

[*Beat.*]

Do we have an understanding?

FABIOLA   What?

LILIANA   Do we have an understanding?

FABIOLA   I don't even know what you're . . .

[*Beat.*]

Yeah. We have an understanding.

[LILIANA *takes out a makeup compact from her purse.*]

LILIANA   Good. Yuya. Take her inside and make her some dinner.

[*She starts applying makeup.*]

Go on. Anda, ve con Yuya. I'll be in to talk to your dad in just a minute. Don't you worry about a thing.

YUYA   [*To* FABIOLA.] Do you want your eggs Benedict?

FABIOLA   What? No. Just . . . whatever. Just make me whatever. Thank you.

YUYA   Buena pues.

[She goes inside and FABIOLA follows.]

LILIANA   [*Stopping her.*] Fabiola. We're not going to worry about a thing.

[*They exit.*]

[LILIANA *slowly applies blush. This is a meticulous ritual. Something happens to her before our eyes. A hardening? Carefully, she takes out a blood red lipstick from her purse and applies it like a neurosurgeon. She stares into the compact as if she's lost something. Nope. It's all still there. But better. Her attention turns to the bag. She contemplates it for a moment, then she grabs it and stands up. She heads towards the patio doors and right before she's going to go inside,* LILIANA *pulls down her gorgeous hair from that ponytail and fluffs it up. In she goes. Mala hierba.*]

FIN

OUR LADY OF KIBEHO

by

Katori Hall

Production History

World Premiere produced by Signature Theatre, New York City
James Houghton, Founding Artistic Director
Erika Mallin, Executive Director
November 16, 2014

Cast

ALPHONSINE MUMUREKE: Nneka Okafor
ANATHALIE MUKAMAZIMPAKA: Mandi Masden
MARIE-CLARE MUKANGANGO: Joaquina Kalukango
STUDENTS: Jade Eshete, Danaya Esperanza, Stacey Sargeant, Angel
    Uwamahoro
SISTER EVANGELIQUE: Starla Benford
FATHER TUYISHIME: Owiso Odera
NKANGO: Bowman Wright
BISHOP GAHAMANYI: Brent Jennings
EMMANUEL: Niles Fitch
VILLAGERS: Kambi Gathesha, Irungu Mutu, Jade Eshete, Danaya
    Esperanza, Stacey Sargeant, Angel Uwamahoro
FATHER FLAVIA: T. Ryder Smith
A REPORTER: Stacey Sargeant

Creative Team

Scenic Design: Rachel Hauck
Costume Design: Emily Rebholz
Lighting Design: Ben Stanton
Sound Design: Matt Tierney
Projection Design: Peter Nigrini
Original Music and Music Direction: Michael McElroy
Special Effects Design: Greg Meeh
Aerial Effects Design: Paul Rubin
Fight Direction: Rick Sordelet
Dialect Coach: Dawn-Elin Fraser
Props and Set Dressing: Faye Armon-Troncoso
Production Stage Manager: Winnie Lok, Michael McGoff
Casting: Telsey + Company, Karyn Casl, CSA

Katori Hall is a writer/performer hailing from Memphis, Tennessee. Hall's plays include: *The Mountaintop* (2010 Olivier Award for Best New Play), which ran on Broadway in 2011 starring Angela Bassett and Samuel L. Jackson (for the past two theatrical seasons, the play has been one of the most produced plays in America), *Hurt Village* (2011 Susan Smith Blackburn Prize), *Children of Killers, Hoodoo Love, Remembrance, Saturday Night/ Sunday Morning, WHADDABLOODCLOT!!!, Our Lady of Kibeho, Pussy Valley,* and *The Blood Quilt.* Her plays have been presented on six continents, and she is currently under commission to write a new play for the UK's National Theatre.

Her additional awards include the Lark Play Development Center Playwrights of New York (PoNY) Fellowship, the ARENA Stage American Voices New Play Residency, the Kate Neal Kinley Fellowship, two Lecomte du Nouy Prizes from Lincoln Center, the Fellowship of Southern Writers Bryan Family Award in Drama, a NYFA Fellowship, the Lorraine Hansberry Playwriting Award, the Columbia University John Jay Award for Distinguished Professional Achievement, the Otto Rene Castillo Award for Political Theatre, and the Otis Guernsey New Voices Playwriting Award.

She was a participant of the Sundance Screenwriter's Lab, where her play *Hurt Village* was developed into a film, and also Sundance's inaugural Episodic Story Lab, where she developed her television show *The Dial.* She is currently developing a show with John Wells Productions based on Stephen L. Carter's NY Times bestseller, *The Emperor of Ocean Park.*

Hall's journalism has appeared in the *New York Times,* the *Boston Globe,* UK's the *Guardian, Essence,* and the *Commercial Appeal,* including contributing reporting for Newsweek.

The Mountaintop and Katori Hall: Plays One are published by Methuen Drama. Hall is an alumna of the Lark Playwrights' Workshop, where she developed *The Mountaintop* and *Our Lady of Kibeho,* and a graduate of Columbia University, the American Repertory Theater at Harvard University, and the Juilliard School.

She is a proud member of the Ron Brown Scholar Program, the Coca-Cola Scholar Program, and the Fellowship of Southern Writers. She is currently a member of the Residency Five at Signature Theatre Company in New York City. Katori will make her directing debut with a film adaptation of *Hurt Village,* which received its world premiere at Signature in 2012.

Characters

The Trinity

ALPHONSINE MUMUREKE: Sixteen-year-old Rwandese girl, cultural name means "Leave her alone, she speaks the truth"

ANATHALIE MUKAMAZIMPAKA: Seventeen-year-old Rwandese girl, cultural name means "One who settles arguments and brings peace"

MARIE-CLARE MUKANGANGO: Twenty-one–year-old Rwandese young woman, cultural name means "Woman"

The Church

FATHER TUYISHIME: head priest at the school

SISTER EVANGELIQUE: the head nun of the school

BISHOP GAHAMANYI: the town bishop, head of the Butare Diocese

FATHER FLAVIA: Italian, an investigative priest from the Holy See, the "miracles office" at the Vatican

NKANGO: Anathalie's father, a farmer

The Chorus

EMMANUEL: young boy who is cured of AIDS

GIRLS 1–4: classmates at Kibeho College

VILLAGERS 1–3: Kibeho villagers

Setting

Kibeho College, an all-girl Catholic school in Kibeho, Rwanda. 1981–1982

Notes

Rwandese accents—they would probably be speaking French and Kinyarwanda to each other, but for an English-speaking audience, a French-based Rwanda accent is ideal.

/ denotes overlapping dialogue.

-- denotes continuous dialogue

— denotes interrupted dialogue

Prayer to Our Lady of Kibeho

Blessed Virgin Mary, Mother of the Word, Mother of all those who believe
in Him, and who keep Him in their life;
We look upon you in contemplation.
We believe that you are with us, like a mother in the midst of Her children,
even though we do not see you with our eyes.

You, who are the infallible pathway to Jesus the Saviour. We bless you for all
the favors you gratify our life, especially since you humbled yourself
And chose to appear miraculously in Kibeho at the very time our world
needed it most.

Grant us always light and strength, so that we may worthily keep in us
Your message of conversion and repentance
In order to live in accordance with your Son's Gospel.
Teach us how to pray truly, and love one another as He loved us, so that, as
you willed, we may always be beautiful flowers
That produce nice flavor to everyone and everywhere.

Virgin Mary, Our Lady of Sorrows, grant us to value the cross in our life,
So that we may complete in our own bodies All that has still to be
undergone by Christ for the sake of his mystic Body, the Church.
And when we come to the end of our pilgrimage on earth, let us live with
you for all eternity, in the heavenly Kingdom.

Amen

Inspired by true events . . .

ACT I

Scene 1

[*Kibeho, Rwanda. 1981. Lush hills can be seen rolling in the distance. Passion fruit and bananas hang from towering trees. Fact: it is the most beautiful place in the world. Even God goes on vacation here. The sounds of girls singing a hymn in an exquisite four-part harmony in Kinyarwanda can be heard echoing through the corridors.* ALPHONSINE, *a teenage girl, sits outside an open door. She is conservatively dressed with her hands folded in her lap looking down. She has no shoes. Her slender thigh pulses up and down, making her foot pat the concrete floor. She is nervous. The* CHOIR *can be heard beneath the following exchange.*]

SISTER EVANGELIQUE   She is a liar! Just a / liar!

FATHER TUYISHIME   Sister Evangelique!

Sister Evangelique   I don't know who this little snot thinks / she is!

Father Tuyishime   Sister, why do you have to speak such nastiness?

Sister Evangelique   I wouldn't have to say such things if she wasn't such a liar.

Father Tuyishime   What if she is telling the truth?

Sister Evangelique   Do you believe in tall tales now?

Father Tuyishime   No, of course not, / Sister!

Sister Evangelique   She could not have seen what she said she saw. She is just trying to frighten the other girls. Keep them from sleeping at night.

Father Tuyishime   It *is* a good story.

Sister Evangelique   It is blasphemy!

Father Tuyishime   Sister!

Sister Evangelique   She must be punished! We let her get away with this, the whole school will crumble under the weight of blasphemy, / ANARCHY!!

Father Tuyishime   Sister.

Sister Evangelique   She will cause the other girls to begin lying, too!

Father Tuyishime   Sister!

Sister Evangelique   If she thinks this is the way to get an A in catechism, well—

Father Tuyishime   SISTER!

[*Beat.*]

Did you punish her yet?

[*The singing stops. Beat.*]

Sister Evangelique   Just. A little. Bit.

Father Tuyishime   Sister . . .

Sister Evangelique   I leave the rest to you.

[*Beat.*]

Father Tuyishime   [*Offstage*] Alphonsine!

[Alphonsine *grips the side of the chair. She does not get up.*]

Father Tuyishime   [*Offstage*] ALPHONSINE!

[Sister Evangelique, *a tall brown woman dressed in all of her blessed nunnery, steps out of the office.*]

Sister Evangelique   Do you hear Father Tuyishime, my child? Or have you been struck deaf and dumb again?

Alphonsine   Yes.—I—I—I mean, no . . . Yes, I hear—I heard him, Sister.

Sister Evangelique   Hmmmm. Well, you better go get your licks then.

[Father Tuyishime *walks out and leans against the door. He is a handsome man. Charming and young. The Sister waits.*]

Father Tuyishime   You can come in, Alphonsine.

[Alphonsine *stands up softly. She passes* Sister Evangelique, *who gives her a stern look. The Sister waits. Beat.*]

The other girls might need your . . . loving presence, Sister Evangelique.

Sister Evangelique   [*Sincerely.*] You think I have a loving presence?

[*Beat.*]

Father Tuyishime   Please, Sister.

Sister Evangelique   Fine. Shall I come by later? To help you with the—

Father Tuyishime   I can fill the jerricans myself, Sister.

Sister Evangelique   Well . . . I guess my work here is done.

Father Tuyishime   Yes. Sister. It is.

[*The Sister walks away leaving the two alone. A picture of Jesus floats above their heads. The Father looks to it for some strength. Beat. The Father turns to* Alphonsine. *He sighs heavily. He opens a file on his desk.*]

Alphonsine Mumureke . . . Tutsi . . .

[*He looks at her features. Nods to himself. Closes the file. Beat.*]

Would you like a sip of water?

Alphonsine   Please don't send me home. My mother would be / so disappointed.

Father Tuyishime   First. Let us get you some water.

[*He walks to a jerrican and pours* Alphonsine *a cup. She gulps it down. He pours her another. She bangs it back gladly. She finishes.*]

Alphonsine   Thank you.

Father Tuyishime   Must be parched. Tongue must be toasted from all those tall tales you have been telling.

Alphonsine   No. I am. Just. Hot.

Father Tuyishime   Amen.

[*He takes off his collar and places it on the desk.* ALPHONSINE'*s eyes bug out and she bursts into laughter.*]

Shhhhh! Don't tell.

[ALPHONSINE *laughs louder. Her smile is like the sun rising above the hills in the distance.*]

Tutsi you are indeed. Tutsi women always have the prettiest smiles.

[ALPHONSINE *stops smiling and looks down.*]

I'm sorry if that makes you uncomfortable.

[ALPHONSINE'*s thigh begins to pulse nervously.*]

I did not mean it. Like that. I mean—I am one who cannot tell a lie.

ALPHONSINE   As well as I.

[*Beat.*]

FATHER TUYISHIME   So I must "punish" you somehow. What do you think your "punishment" should be?

ALPHONSINE   I can help you here in the office.

FATHER TUYISHIME   [*Smiling.*] Oh, that would be a punishment, eh?

ALPHONSINE   Yes. No . . .

[*Giggling.*]

Maybe.

FATHER TUYISHIME   It would. I wake up in a such a foul mood most mornings. Wooo, watch out!

[ALPHONSINE *laughs again, bringing more of the sun into the tiny cramped office.*]

ALPHONSINE   You are a very honest man.

FATHER TUYISHIME   I try to be, Alphonsine. Are you honest?

ALPHONSINE   Yes. I try to be.

FATHER TUYISHIME   So are you telling the truth? About what you saw?

ALPHONSINE   Yes.

FATHER TUYISHIME   Alphonsine, I think you imagined / that.

ALPHONSINE   No, no! I saw. I saw! Almost like I could touch Her, smell Her.

FATHER TUYISHIME   Well, maybe you were just . . . hot. Hallucinating!

ALPHONSINE   No, Father, I was not hallucinating--

FATHER TUYISHIME   With so many of you all, packed like tea leaves in a box. No air to circulate in those dormitories. I have to tell Sister Evangelique to leave the door open—

ALPHONSINE   —She was real. No, you're not listening to me. I promise you, I swear to you that I saw Her. I saw Her. I saw Her. NO! I SAW HER!

[*The Father is taken aback by her ferocity.* ALPHONSINE *clamps her hand over her mouth.*]

ALPHONSINE   I am / sorry.

FATHER TUYISHIME   It is alright.

ALPHONSINE   I am soo, soo sorry.

FATHER TUYISHIME   It is alright.

ALPHONSINE   I was not *hot.* I am not lying. I promise. I only speak the truth.

[*Beat.*]

So what is my punishment for this?

FATHER TUYISHIME   Ehhh, you will have to . . . ehhh . . . empty the dormitory buckets at night. . . .

ALPHONSINE   Anything else?

FATHER TUYISHIME   And sweep the halls in the morning. . . .

ALPHONSINE   Anything else?

FATHER TUYISHIME   . . .

ALPHONSINE   *Anything else,* Father Tuyishime?

[*She holds her hands out, expecting the licks of the ruler. Beat. He puts his hand over her hand and pushes it down. She looks up in surprise.*]

FATHER TUYISHIME   Report to my office. Every morning. 7 o'clock. Sharp.

[ALPHONSINE *rises from her chair. She begins to walk out of the cramped office.*]

One more thing, Alphonsine.

ALPHONSINE   Yes, Father.

FATHER TUYISHIME   What did She look like?

ALPHONSINE   Look like?

FATHER TUYISHIME   Was She *muzungu?*

[*He points to the picture of the white Jesus on the wall looking down at them. With the bluest of eyes and the blondest of hair . . .* ALPHONSINE *takes a pause, as if she is in a trance.*]

ALPHONSINE She was not white or black. She was just . . . beautiful.

FATHER TUYISHIME Like you?

[*The sweet sounds of the choir start back up.* ALPHONSINE *blushes.*]

ALPHONSINE No. Much more beautiful than me.

FATHER TUYISHIME [*To himself.*] Hmph.

[*To her.*]

Hurry on. You will be late for rehearsal.

[ALPHONSINE *walks out.* FATHER TUYISHIME *looks after her.*]

Scene 2

[*Lights shift.* ALPHONSINE *joins the group of girls at choir rehearsal outside in the courtyard.* MARIE-CLARE *is utterly bored out of her friggin' mind and she keeps on getting the harmony wrong.* ANATHALIE *sings sweetly. But then it starts raining.*]

SISTER EVANGELIQUE See, God is crying because you all sound so horrible. We are done for today.

[*The girls giggle as they run away from the rain. Everyone makes sure to steer clear of* ALPHONSINE. MARIE-CLARE *points at* ALPHONSINE'S *messy hair, which makes* ANATHALIE *giggle. They giggle together.*]

SISTER EVANGELIQUE Marie-Clare! Can I speak with you a moment?

ANATHALIE Ooooo!

MARIE-CLARE Hush it. Meet me in the back by the banana beer / trough.

ANATHALIE Shhhhh! I know! I know . . .

[ANATHALIE *giggles and walks away.* MARIE-CLARE *walks up to* SISTER EVANGELIQUE. *They stand beneath a partition keeping them from the rain.*]

MARIE-CLARE Sister, I promise that I will have the harmonies memorized by tomorrow.

SISTER EVANGELIQUE Oh, will you?

MARIE-CLARE I just have a horrible time remembering.

SISTER EVANGELIQUE Perhaps it is because you are getting so old.

MARIE-CLARE But I am only twenty-one, Sister.

SISTER EVANGELIQUE In Kibeho, that means you practically have one foot in the grave.

[*Silence.* MARIE-CLARE *is not amused.*]

Excuse me, Marie, I am not myself lately. These recent happenings have put me on edge.

MARIE-CLARE   They have put me on edge as well.

SISTER EVANGELIQUE   Have they?

MARIE-CLARE   Yes, Sister.

SISTER EVANGELIQUE   What do you think of them?

MARIE-CLARE   What is there to think of them?

SISTER EVANGELIQUE   Do you believe this fool?

MARIE-CLARE   Ennnh, my father once said, "The village fool sometimes speaks the truth."

SISTER EVANGELIQUE   Did he really?

MARIE-CLARE   Yes.

SISTER EVANGELIQUE   I've never heard of such a saying.

[*Slight disgust.*]

Must be Tutsi.

[MARIE-CLARE *stiffens.*]

MARIE-CLARE   No, it is from our people.

SISTER EVANGELIQUE   Hmph.

[*Pause.*]

So you believe her?

MARIE-CLARE   No. I did not say that. I have my own mind.

SISTER EVANGELIQUE   And what does your own mind say?

MARIE-CLARE   She just wants attention.

SISTER EVANGELIQUE   Well, she certainly knows how to get it.

[*Under her breath.*]

She has Father Tuyishime's full attention now. She will be working in his office. As punishment.

MARIE-CLARE   That's all she gets for punishment?

SISTER EVANGELIQUE   Does she need more?

MARIE-CLARE   If *I* were the head nun, I would have given her twenty licks with the ruler, made her clean the latrines, and wash everyone's knickers for the entire month. If I can speak my mind openly--

SISTER EVANGELIQUE   [*Trying to interrupt.*] Go ahead.

MARIE-CLARE [*Continuing.*]--and honestly, I would have made her do all of that and then some. I would have been smacked clear across the face for such blasphemy, probably even expelled! It's disturbing to think she could actually get away with, get AWAY with / it all.

SISTER EVANGELIQUE She hasn't gotten away with anything. Rather she won't.

MARIE-CLARE I could run this place much better than you—

[SISTER EVANGELIQUE *yanks her up hard.*]

SISTER EVANGELIQUE Until you are across the river, beware how you insult the mother alligator.

[*Beat.*]

MARIE-CLARE Sorry. Sister.

[SISTER EVANGELIQUE *lets her down gently.*]

SISTER EVANGELIQUE The next time she goes into another one of her little trances, you pinch her. You pinch her hard.

MARIE-CLARE I don't want to touch her when she goes there. Her eyes . . . gone. No life. Almost like she's sleeping with her eyes / wide open.

SISTER EVANGELIQUE Watch her. In the dorms. You are the eldest of the girls. I am going to need you to take control of things.

MARIE-CLARE Control of things?

SISTER EVANGELIQUE Yes, my darling Marie-Clare. Control.

MARIE-CLARE I can do that.

[SISTER EVANGELIQUE *looks into* MARIE-CLARE*'s face as if looking into a mirror.*]

SISTER EVANGELIQUE I know.

[MARIE-CLARE *smiles.*]

Go along, now. Don't you have some songs to be learning?

Scene 3

[*The thunder rolls and lights shift. The sun has broken through the clouds.* ALPHONSINE *is taking the books from* FATHER TUYISHIME*'s office and dusting them.*]

[ANATHALIE *comes up behind her and watches her through thick glasses.*]

ANATHALIE How long are you on punishment?

ALPHONSINE   He say a week.

ANATHALIE   Ahhhh, that means you get to go to confession!

ALPHONSINE   There is nothing to confess.

ANATHALIE   Is it weird that I love to go to confession?

ALPHONSINE   Perhaps it's that you have an unclean heart.

ANATHALIE   [*Offended.*] I am a virgin, Alphonsine. All virgins have unclean hearts.

[ALPHONSINE *continues to dust.*]

[*Pushing up her glasses.*]

I'd love to be on punishment for Father Tuyishime.

ALPHONSINE   Anathalie!

ANATHALIE   Wha? He's extraordinarily cute. Too bad he can't get married.

[ALPHONSINE *laughs, bringing more sunlight to drive away the storm.*]

ALPHONSINE   You better get away, before she comes.

ANATHALIE   Ah-ah! Marie-Clare doesn't rule me.

ALPHONSINE   Are you sure about that?

ANATHALIE   She is a lion all roar and menace, but you? You are a flea. Quiet. Little. Almost invisible.

ALPHONSINE   Well, a flea can bother a lion, but a lion cannot bother a flea.

ANATHALIE   Too smart for your own good.

ALPHONSINE   And too dumb for yours.

ANATHALIE   You are the one who goes deaf and dumb, pretending that you are gone. But we know. We know you are just acting. You just want attention. You silly, silly girl. You just want people to see you.

ALPHONSINE   See me? No, I want you to see Her, Anathalie. Oh, I wish you could see what I see. Know what I know. Know Her! She wants to embrace us with the greatest love. Her arms are so wide that they wrap around the world twice over. She loves us more than our parents. She loves us even though we live in sin. She wants us to pray, Anathalie. Pray! It is the only way to stop the pain. The only way. She showed me how this world could be.

ANATHALIE   She did? What did She show you?

ALPHONSINE   I don't know if I can tell you.

ANATHALIE   Come on! How did the world look?

[*Beat.*]

ALPHONSINE   More beautiful than this land of a thousand hills, my friend. Rwanda has nothing on where She would take us. It is a land where mountains float. Where one is never hungry. It is a land where sickness is no more. Darkness is no more. Fear is no more. Hate does not hide itself in the cracks of men's hearts. It is a land of love. Everywhere love.

ANATHALIE   Sounds like heaven alright, but don't we have to die to get there?

ALPHONSINE   No, Anathalie, no! She said, we can have it. Here on earth. We just have to pray. Repent. Purge your unclean virgin heart, Anathalie. Pray with me. So you can see it, too. . . .

[ALPHONSINE's *hand is stretching to* ANATHALIE's. ANATHALIE *steps closer and begins to reach out her hand, but—*]

ANATHALIE   I wouldn't want to see that.

ALPHONSINE   Why?

ANATHALIE   Because I don't think the world could ever be that beautiful.

[MARIE-CLARE *enters with her gang of girls trailing.* ANATHALIE *quickly brings her hand up to push up her glasses.* MARIE-CLARE *pushes* ALPHONSINE, *who was already on her knees, making her fall spread eagle onto the ground.*]

ANATHALIE   Marie-Clare!

[*Drunken giggles.*]

MARIE-CLARE   What?

ANATHALIE   Leave her alone.

ALPHONSINE   You all reek of banana beer.

THE GIRLS   So!

GIRL #1   I think I'm going to be sick.

MARIE-CLARE   Such a light-weight. Anathalie, I thought I told you to meet us by the banana beer trough?

ANATHALIE   [*Looking at* ALPHONSINE.] I was. I was going to, but—

GIRL #1   Alphonsine, where did Father Tuyishime give you licks?

MARIE-CLARE   On the bottom?

ANATHALIE   Marie-Clare!

MARIE-CLARE   What? Bad girls usually get it on the bottom. Where did he put your welts? Let me see. Let me see!

[MARIE-CLARE *goes to lift* ALPHONSINE's *skirt. Balling up her fist—*]

ALPHONSINE   Do that again and I will slap you so hard your descendants will feel the sting!

THE GIRLS   Whoa. . . .

MARIE-CLARE   So the Virgin Mary visits mean old nasty girls like you?

GIRL #1   A Tutsi on top of that.

ALPHONSINE   I'm not lying.

GIRL #2   Tutsis lie.

ALPHONSINE   We do not.

GIRL #1   That's what my ma said.

ALPHONSINE   Well, maybe your ma is proof that Hutus lie.

GIRL #3   Why don't I see Her, huh? Why doesn't She speak to me?

ALPHONSINE   I do not know. How I wish She would.

ANATHALIE   But wouldn't it be something? If Alphonsine wasn't lying? Our Lady. Here. In Kibeho . . .

MARIE-CLARE   The day Our Lady visits Kibeho is the day the Pope comes to Africa.

ANATHALIE   Stranger things have happened.

MARIE-CLARE   Wha, Anathalie? Do you believe this liar? This blasphemer. This WITCH!

[MARIE-CLARE *pushes* ALPHONSINE *again.*]

ANATHALIE   Marie-Clare, stop it.

MARIE-CLARE   Whose side are you on, Anathalie? You must walk on the side of the righteous! She is a witch.

THE GIRLS   [*In unison.*] A witch!

MARIE-CLARE   We all know you come from the village of Zaza.

GIRL #1   Those people are fools. They worship statues and drink the blood of babies.

GIRL #3   I heard they cut out the hearts of chickens and dance with them above their heads.

MARIE-CLARE   They are heathens!

THE GIRLS   Heathens!

ANATHALIE   Marie-Clare. I said / stop it! Leave her alone. You all stop!

MARIE-CLARE   You are a witch! A witch!

THE GIRLS   [*In unison.*] A witch! A witch!

MARIE-CLARE   What, you want to protect the little witch from Zaza?

[MARIE-CLARE *snatches* ANATHALIE'*s glasses off of her face.*]

ANATHALIE   Give my spectacles back, Marie Clare.

GIRL #1   You blind fool.

[MARIE-CLARE *tosses them to the other girl.*]

GIRL #2   Here give them to me!

ANATHALIE   Stop it! Stop it! I can't see!

MARIE-CLARE   You believe what she says, huh?

ANATHALIE   Give them back!

[*Forgotten on the ground,* ALPHONSINE *slowly rises up until she is on her knees. We see that she is staring into the distance. Her back arches and the winds begin to change. The pages of the books she was dusting begin to rustle like the leaves on a tree.*]

MARIE-CLARE   Look! Look! She's doing it again.

GIRL #1   She's possessed.

GIRL #3   Look at that evil in her eye.

[ALPHONSINE *looks utterly at peace. Exuberant even. Stars stream from her eyes. She is somewhere else. . . .*]

GIRL #1   Don't go near her!

MARIE-CLARE   Pinch her.

ANATHALIE   Marie-Clare! Stop being mean!

MARIE-CLARE   [*Ignoring her.*] Go *pinch* her.

GIRL #1   Eh-eh! She's not going to possess me.

GIRL #2   I told you! I told you! She's a witch!

GIRL #3   I think she's just possessed.

MARIE-CLARE   I said pinch her.

THE GIRLS   EH-EH!!

MARIE-CLARE   Fine, I'll do it.

[MARIE-CLARE *goes up to her and pinches her. Pinches her hard.* ALPHONSINE *does not move; she luxuriates.*]

ANATHALIE   Leave her alone!

MARIE-CLARE   You won't move, enh? You won't move?

[*To the other girls.*]

Let's play a little game.

[MARIE-CLARE *takes her rosary off. She goes to the far corner of the corridor. She throws her rosary. It hits* ALPHONSINE *in her head, who doesn't flinch. She is in another world.*]

MARIE-CLARE   Damn it!

ANATHALIE   Marie-Clare! I'm going to tell Sister Evangelique.

MARIE-CLARE   Don't be such a snitch!

GIRL #1   Ooooo, I wanna try!

GIRL #2   Me, too!

[*They take their rosaries off and they play their ad hoc game—similar to horse shoes or a game one plays at the carnival.*]

THE GIRLS   Ring around the rosary . . . Ring around the rosary!

GIRL #4   [*Sings in Kinyarwanda.*] Eii ooooooo Eii oooooooo Eii oooooooo!

[*They continue to hit her in her head. But* ALPHONSINE *is gone. Not hearing the yells of the girls. She begins to speak to someone high, high above their heads.*]

ALPHONSINE   I have been. I've been praying my rosary every night.

MARIE-CLARE   What is she saying? What are you saying, devil girl?

GIRL #1   [*Simultaneously.*] Don't get too close. She's gonna bite you.

GIRL #3   [*Simultaneously.*] Yaaaay! I scored.

ALPHONSINE   Are you sure? / They make fun of me all the time. It is getting hard.

MARIE-CLARE   Point one for you! Come, Anathalie, join us.

[ANATHALIE *does not move.*]

MARIE-CLARE   I said Anathalie join us.

[MARIE-CLARE *slaps* ANATHALIE. ANATHALIE, *buckling beneath the peer pressure, reluctantly takes off her rosary.*]

MARIE-CLARE   Throw it! Throw it!

[*Tears stream down* ALPHONSINE'S *cheeks. She is looking at the Virgin Mary.*]

[ANATHALIE *tries to throw it around* ALPHONSINE'S *neck, but it hits the floor.*]

MARIE-CLARE   You throw like my grandmother.

ANATHALIE   Well, I wouldn't have to throw like your grandmother if I could see! Give me back my specs—

MARIE-CLARE   Not until you do it again. Again!

THE GIRLS   Do it again! Do it again!

[ANATHALIE *takes another throw, but* ALPHONSINE'S *hand rises and she catches the rosary with her hand.*]

THE GIRLS   Ooooooo!

MARIE-CLARE   See, she's lying! She's lying!

[ANATHALIE *is staring at her.*]

ANATHALIE   Give it back! Give it back!

MARIE-CLARE   [*Simultaneously.*] Give it back to her. Give it back!

[ALPHONSINE *refuses or rather she is lost. . . .*]

ANATHALIE   Give it back! Give it— [*Gasp.*]

[*Suddenly* ANATHALIE *is struck by something. Her back arches and she bends backwards onto the ground as if she is a prima ballerina.*]

THE GIRLS   Give it back! Give it back!

[ANATHALIE *falls onto her knees. She begins to look at the same direction as* ALPHONSINE.]

GIRL #1   Look! Look at Anathalie. Look at her. . . .

[*A warm light begins to dance across* ALPHONSINE'S *and* ANATHALIE'S *faces. It's as if the sun is reflecting on water, and playing peek-a-boo with their lips. An intense joy ripples through their bodies.* ANATHALIE *is staring up at something floating high above their heads. Tears begin to stream from her eyes. She is somewhere else. . . .*]

MARIE-CLARE   Anathalie . . . Anathalie? Wha-What's going on? What's happening? Anathalie, Anathalie! Come back! Come back. Come back. Come . . . back. . . .

Scene 4

[FATHER TUYISHIME'S *office.*]

[ANATHALIE *and* ALPHONSINE *are sitting with bags packed.* SISTER EVANGELIQUE *is looking over them . . . pleased.*]

SISTER EVANGELIQUE   Soon these shenanigans will all be over.

ANATHALIE   Why did you bring him here?

SISTER EVANGELIQUE   Someone needs to knock some sense into you.

[FATHER TUYISHIME *comes in followed by* NKANGO, ANATHALIE'S *father, a big hefty farmer.*]

FATHER TUYISHIME   I'm glad that you could come on such short notice, Nkango.

NKANGO   Anything that concerns my child is my business. Where is she?

SISTER EVANGELIQUE   Over here.

NKANGO   So this is how you treat my hard work, Anathalie? You go and get yourself in trouble.

ANATHALIE   Papa, please understand.

[*His hand goes to his belt.*]

NKANGO   Excuse me, are you speaking?

ANATHALIE   No, Papa, / I'm not.

ALPHONSINE   Shhhh, / Anathalie.

[*To* ALPHONSINE.]

ANATHALIE   Wha?

NKANGO   Is this the one you're in cahoots with?

ANATHALIE   Papa, I'm not in cahoots with / anyone.

ALPHONSINE   SHHHHH, Anathalie!

[NKANGO *begins to take off that belt.*]

NKANGO   We said go to school and this is what you go and do? Follow some heathen right out of an education.

[*Pointing to* ALPHONSINE.]

What are you going to do with her?

SISTER EVANGELIQUE   She is an orphan. No father.

NKANGO   What a shame. She needs someone to beat her good for this foolishness.

FATHER TUYISHIME   Nkango, there is no need—

NKANGO   You might be a Father, Father Tuyishime, but you are not the father to Anathalie Mukamazimpaka. Come on, Anathalie, get your things. I am taking you out of this school for good.

ANATHALIE   No, Papa, please. I promise. I promise I won't speak to her again. I promise!

FATHER TUYISHIME   Nkango, I'm sure Anathalie is very sorry for her actions. For lying—

NKANGO   She'd better be. Come on.

[ANATHALIE *doesn't move. She continues to hold on to* ALPHONSINE.]

You don't want to listen?

[*He quickly begins to remove his belt.*]

FATHER TUYISHIME   Maybe we can come to some kind of agreement.

SISTER EVANGELIQUE   Agreement?

NKANGO   No, she's coming home. I don't know why you have not expelled her.

SISTER EVANGELIQUE   That is what I said.

NKANGO   Come, Anathalie.

FATHER TUYISHIME   Perhaps because it is imperative that she learn from these mistakes, she can . . . confess.

NKANGO   [*Sarcastically.*] And how many Hail Marys will get her out of this?

SISTER EVANGELIQUE   A hundred and twenty-three.

FATHER TUYISHIME   Sister Evangelique!

ANATHALIE   I will do them. I will do them. Whatever I need to do, Papa. But please just let me stay in school. Hail Mary, full of grace. The Lord is / with thee. Blessed are thou among women . . .

[*Continuing beneath the following exchange.*]

FATHER TUYISHIME   See, she has already started. A hundred twenty-two more to go—

NKANGO   No, she must get out of here.

FATHER TUYISHIME   But she needs her schooling.

[**NKANGO** *slaps his belt against the desk. It makes everyone jump. Silence.*]

NKANGO   I am but a lowly farmer, Father. We are all just farmers. If the village thinks I have a daughter who is a witch, who will buy my banana, huh? Who will buy my cassava, huh? Who will buy? The entire village would rather go hungry than eat the ground nuts of a man who has fathered a witch. I cannot have it. She will come back to the field where she will not catch this-this-uh, virus. You are infecting my daughter.

FATHER TUYISHIME   I am not a mosquito.

NKANGO   Well, I much rather her die of malaria than of lies. I should have never let you come. This was nonsense anyhow and all of this is proving me right. Your mother was always wrong. Book-learning makes a girl go crazy. Come now, Anathalie, before I have to come and get you.

[*But* **ANATHALIE** *is gazing off.*]

ANATHALIE   [*Pointing.*] But, Father, *She* wants me to stay.

NKANGO   Anathalie, get your things NOW! I don't care what your little friend says—

ANATHALIE   N-N-N-N-No, not Alphonsine. *Her* . . .

[ANATHALIE *points to an empty space.*]

NKANGO   Anathalie, don't make me come and GET YOU!

[*The hefty farmer punches the wall. It splinters. Everyone except for* ANATHALIE *jumps. . . .*]

ANATHALIE   But, Papa, look! Look how She floats . . .

[ANATHALIE's *eyes start rolling into the back of her head.* SISTER EVANGELIQUE *bolts from her chair.*]

SISTER EVANGELIQUE   Ah-ah. Not again.

[ANATHALIE *falls down on her knees and there is the most angelic expression on her face. She laughs. Giggles. Coos. Laughs. Giggles. Coos. Like a baby staring up at her mother.*]

ALPHONSINE   It's spreading. Just like She said it would. . . .

NKANGO   She? Who is She? / Wha . . .

FATHER TUYISHIME   What does She look like, Anathalie?

ANATHALIE   So beautiful words cannot describe—

FATHER TUYISHIME   What is She wearing?

ANATHALIE   A long veil. White. Glowing. Like the stars on a clear night—

FATHER TUYISHIME   And Her skin?

ANATHALIE   Smooth. No marks. Like no one I have ever seen—

NKANGO   My God, Father! Why are you egging this nonsense on? / Jesus Christ!

FATHER TUYISHIME   SHHH, Nkango! And Her eyes—

[NKANGO *goes to pick up the tiny* ANATHALIE. *He grabs her and—*]

NKANGO   Eh-eh!

[*She does not budge. He tries to pull on her again, but the hefty farmer's strength cannot pick up his slim daughter. He hems and haws, but she is like a tree trunk rooted to the floor. He tries to lift her again. But can't. . . .*]

Will somebody help me?

[SISTER EVANGELIQUE *jumps up to help. But she, too, cannot lift her.*]

SISTER EVANGELIQUE   She must have a belly full of stones.

[*These adults grunt and twist, but she is like Mount Kilimanjaro. Immovable. She giggles. Coos. Laughs and coos some more. Finally, spent from their lifting, they watch* ANATHALIE, *whose tongue is like a television changing channels. She speaks French. Then Kinyarwanda. She speaks in many, many tongues. The tongues of the universe.*]

NKANGO   What are you saying, my child? Father, Father! What is going on?

FATHER TUYISHIME   [*Ignoring him.*] Alphonsine, what is she saying?

ALPHONSINE   She needs the people of the village to listen. She needs them to hear the message.

NKANGO   No, she needs to come home. She's sick.

ALPHONSINE   She needs to be heard. It is the only way. This is Mama Mary's decree. . . .

FATHER TUYISHIME   What is Anathalie seeing now?

ALPHONSINE   She is seeing the goodness . . . The beauty . . .The light . . .

FATHER TUYISHIME   What light, Alphonsine?

[*Just then* ALPHONSINE *drifts off and they are looking at the same space. Both of the girls cooing like little babies.*]

NKANGO   My child! My poor child! She has been struck dumb. She is dumb. My child.

[ANATHALIE's *father holds her, softly. Suddenly the young women draw in seven quick breaths. As if they are gasping for air underwater.*]

Anathalie, Anathalie . . .

[*They take in one big breath and both* ANATHALIE *and* ALPHONSINE *collapse to the floor.*]

NKANGO   Is she . . .

SISTER EVANGELIQUE   Are they?

[*Lights shift.*]

Scene 5

[*A candlelit room.*]

[ALPHONSINE *and* ANATHALIE *are lying side by side in two beds.* SISTER EVANGELIQUE *looks over* ALPHONSINE. *She does the sign of the cross over her. Puts a dab of holy water over her head. She turns her back to* ALPHONSINE *to the bed* ANATHALIE *is lying in. She pulls out her pocket watch. She checks the time. She is about to put the watch back into her pocket until she gets an idea.*]

SISTER EVANGELIQUE *stares at* ANATHALIE, *who lies there stiff as a board.*
The Sister puts the pocket watch beneath her nose. She waits for the fog, but—]

SISTER EVANGELIQUE   No breath.

[SISTER EVANGELIQUE *lifts her arm. Checks it.*]

Barely a pulse?

[*Behind* SISTER EVANGELIQUE, ALPHONSINE *slowly rises, not making a sound.*
The candlelight pushes her shadow around the room. SISTER EVANGELIQUE
puts her ear to ANATHALIE'*s chest. She waits and waits and waits. She*
hears . . . nothing. Concerned, SISTER EVANGELIQUE *takes* ANATHALIE'*s face*
lovingly into her hands. She makes the sign of the cross and—]

ALPHONSINE   Don't worry. She will not succumb.

[SISTER EVANGELIQUE *practically jumps out of her skin and lunges at*
ALPHONSINE *in the darkness!*]

SISTER EVANGELIQUE   [*Simultaneously.*] Jesus!

ALPHONSINE   [*Simultaneously.*] Oh.

SISTER EVANGELIQUE   Jesus!

ALPHONSINE   Didn't mean to scare you.

SISTER EVANGELIQUE   I thought you were asleep.

ALPHONSINE   Seems like you are hell-bent on making that permanent.

[*Beat.* SISTER EVANGELIQUE'*s eyes bore holes through* ALPHONSINE. *Not*
caring, ALPHONSINE *stretches as if she's had the best nap in her life. She takes*
her time. An extensive yawn that lasts eons. Finally, she swings her leg around
the side of the bed. She smiles at SISTER EVANGELIQUE. *Beat.*]

SISTER EVANGELIQUE   Oh, so you think this is funny?

ALPHONSINE   I am not laughing, Sister.

SISTER EVANGELIQUE   Well, get that silly little smirk off your face, before I
slap it off.

ALPHONSINE   I cannot help but have a bit of Easter in my heart. I shall
come back to Earth now and be in despair like all you others.

[ALPHONSINE *mocks the Sister's deep frown lines.* SISTER EVANGELIQUE *is not*
pleased. Then ALPHONSINE *bursts into laughter.*]

Oh, Sister. Frowns make a woman look so ugly. Always remember a
Rwandan woman's beauty is in her—

[SISTER EVANGELIQUE *sharply smacks* ALPHONSINE. *Weak from her trip to*
the other side, ALPHONSINE *falls onto the bed.*]

SISTER EVANGELIQUE   How dare you? How. Dare. You? You little ingrate, you little

[*Searching for the word.*]

. . . witch! Yes . . . Is that what you are? A witch. A shitty little witch? I think so.

I think that's exactly what you are. I know you. I know your kind. You shake hands with the devil and use the same hand to make the sign of the cross. You've been conjuring your little spells and everyone is falling beneath the spell you are casting. The Father and now ANATHALIE. But I will cast you out. I will cast you OUT!

[ALPHONSINE *has brought her gaze back to* SISTER EVANGELIQUE's. ALPHONSINE, *though she is smaller and more slight than the Sister, seems to grow taller and wider. Her presence expanding. Swallowing up all the space in the tiny room. The Sister begins to shake in fear. Actually. Visibly quake. There is a fire in* ALPHONSINE's *eyes that has not been there before. A blinding light. . . .*]

ALPHONSINE   You do not scare me anymore.

[SISTER EVANGELIQUE *takes a step back. She turns her head away. She gathers herself. The shaking soon subsides.* ALPHONSINE *turns sweet.*]

ALPHONSINE   She will be heard. Whether you like it or not.

SISTER EVANGELIQUE   Is that so?

ALPHONSINE   Yes.

[*Beat.* SISTER EVANGELIQUE's *glare melts. Asking from the deep end of her heart:*]

SISTER EVANGELIQUE   Why can you hear Her, and I cannot?

ALPHONSINE   You can hear Her through me. If you are ready to listen. . . . Are you ready?

[*Silence from* SISTER EVANGELIQUE.]

May I go now?

SISTER EVANGELIQUE   [*Breathless.*] Please.

[ALPHONSINE *hops off the bed. She does the sign of the cross over* ANATHALIE. *She looks at her friend and smiles. Satisfied.*]

ALPHONSINE   She'll be coming out of it soon. Very soon.

[ALPHONSINE *exits. Incredulous,* SISTER EVANGELIQUE *stares after her.*]

[*Lights shift.*]

Scene 6

[*Day. The Father's office.* FATHER TUYISHIME *has a visitor,* BISHOP GAHAMANYI. *They are very relaxed. In man mode, cracking up.*]

BISHOP GAHAMANYI   And Mama Rusibanga chased Dada Rusibanga down the hill with her hoe. I tell you it was a sight to see.

FATHER TUYISHIME   [*Wiping tears from his eyes.*] I wish I could have been there.

BISHOP GAHAMANYI   [*Shaking his fist?*] Dada Rusibanga should have given Mama a piece of his mind.

FATHER TUYISHIME   [*Laughing uncomfortably.*] Well . . . he was supposed to be turning the field, not playing futbol.

BISHOP GAHAMANYI   It was Saturday!

FATHER TUYISHIME   Still he should have—

BISHOP GAHAMANYI   [*Interrupting.*] Eh-Eh! Two lions cannot rule one valley.

SISTER EVANGELIQUE   Your Excellency, that is very true.

[*The men stop and turn and look at the door.* SISTER EVANGELIQUE *genuflects upon seeing the Bishop.*]

BISHOP GAHAMANYI   Sister Evangelique, so you agree with me?

SISTER EVANGELIQUE   To a certain extent.

BISHOP GAHAMANYI   Good. Good.

[*Uncomfortable silence.*]

FATHER TUYISHIME   Are the girls—

SISTER EVANGELIQUE   Fine. They are both fine.

BISHOP GAHAMANYI   Young girls will do anything for attention these days.

FATHER TUYISHIME   [*Smiling.*] Indeed, they will.

BISHOP GAHAMANYI   Sometimes I don't mind it. We all need to be listened to—be heard. But this might all be going a bit too far—

SISTER EVANGELIQUE   Yes, usually all one needs is a pretty face and nice waist to get your attention. Your Excellency, sooooo nice of you to bless us with your presence today. Last time we saw each other, I think it was dry season.

[*The men stop smiling.* FATHER TUYISHIME *shoots* SISTER EVANGELIQUE *a "shut the fuck up" glare.*]

BISHOP GAHAMANYI [*Tightly smiling at the Sister's audacity.*] It is true that I don't get a chance to come to Kibeho very often.

FATHER TUYISHIME Well, those seven hills can be as big as mountains. Whew!

BISHOP GAHAMANYI Eh-Eh! Did I tell you Dada Rusibanga banged me in the knee at the last futbol game?

FATHER TUYISHIME Sorry, sorry.

SISTER EVANGELIQUE I suppose if you are out of shape with a flabby stomach and a banged-up knee, yes, those hills can be hard. But most of my girls can run up them with jerricans full of water balanced on their heads. All of this, of course, before they get their lesson at 7:30 in the morning.

[BISHOP *ain't got time to play with no* SISTER EVANGELIQUE, *so:*]

BISHOP GAHAMANYI Well, I'm here at 6:30 this morning because there is a rustle down in the valley. It's making the banana trees shake with a whisper that might soon grow into an uncontrollable roar.

FATHER TUYISHIME I am trying my best to control it, Your Excellency.

SISTER EVANGELIQUE You are?

FATHER TUYISHIME Yes . . . I am.

BISHOP GAHAMANYI Well, one of the girls' fathers has been spreading rumors about how he saw his daughter . . . ehhhh . . . catch the spirit so to speak. That his daughter is a prophet?

SISTER EVANGELIQUE I bet his bananas are selling like Primus beers now.

BISHOP GAHAMANYI This is not a time for joking, Sister. There's worse news.

FATHER TUYISHIME Worse news?

BISHOP GAHAMANYI A reporter from Radio Rwanda wants to interview me about these two girls. Radio Rwanda.

[*Pause.*]

Have they been punished?

SISTER EVANGELIQUE [*Simultaneously.*] No.

FATHER TUYISHIME [*Simultaneously.*] Yes.

BISHOP GAHAMANYI Well, which one is it?

SISTER EVANGELIQUE [*Simultaneously.*] [*Lying.*] Yes.

FATHER TUYISHIME [*Simultaneously.*] [*Admitting.*] No.

Well, no and yes.

BISHOP GAHAMANYI   No and yes?

SISTER EVANGELIQUE   [*Simultaneously.*] Yes and No.

FATHER TUYISHIME   [*Simultaneously.*] No and Yes.

BISHOP GAHAMANYI   You know how our village folk can be. They believe. They believe so easily. It warms my heart that they believe. It makes our jobs easier for us, eh?

FATHER TUYISHIME   Yes, Your Excellency.

BISHOP GAHAMANYI   Yes. The village folk will believe anything you tell them. But we cannot, we absolutely cannot have them believing in this.

FATHER TUYISHIME   But you didn't see it. Them. The girls.

BISHOP GAHAMANYI   I don't need to see in order to—

[*Pause. Wait a minute. . . .*]

Don't tell me you believe these shenanigans, Father?

[*Pause. The Father and Sister look at each other.*]

SISTER EVANGELIQUE   Someone from the diocese needs to investigate these girls. Give them psychological evaluations. For young girls to do this they are not right in the head.

BISHOP GAHAMANYI   There are no psychologists here in Rwanda—

SISTER EVANGELIQUE   Well, we should fly one in! Eh-if I were the head of the diocese, I would order an investigation so fast that it would have started yesterday.

BISHOP GAHAMANYI   But you are not the head of the diocese, neither will you ever be, *Sister* Evangelique. As I said, I know what young girls will do to get attention. To get the Father's attention. Isn't that right, Father?

[*The Bishop hits the Father in the arm.*]

FATHER TUYISHIME   [*Blushing.*] Oh, stop it.

BISHOP GAHAMANYI   It is only natural. I understand. I understand it all. Look at him. That skin. Those chestnut eyes.

SISTER EVANGELIQUE   Yes, yes, yes. I know. I see them every day.

BISHOP GAHAMANYI   Well, then you know. Maybe if you meted out some well-needed discipline more often, Sister Evangelique, maybe this situation would be under control.

SISTER EVANGELIQUE   Are you blaming / me?

BISHOP GAHAMANYI   [*Overlapping.*] You must lead by example, Sister. You are like their mother. Please, act like one. Let them know that these lies will only lead them down the path of perdition. It cannot be tolerated.

SISTER EVANGELIQUE   But—

BISHOP GAHAMANYI   Father Tuyishime needs your help. I know how you women can be, coddling them, letting them get away with things, but--

SISTER EVANGELIQUE   [*Interrupting.*] Me?

BISHOP GAHAMANYI   [*Continuing.*]--with Father Tuyishime's recent appointment as head chaplain, he cannot deal with these shenanigans. It is your responsibility now.

SISTER EVANGELIQUE   Now? It has always been mine.

BISHOP GAHAMANYI   Sister, please. The diocese is none too happy with the recent happenings of bullshit.

SISTER EVANGELIQUE   And neither am I.

BISHOP GAHAMANYI   But it seems like you're allowing these girls to run amok and take control of the school.

SISTER EVANGELIQUE   Perhaps if *he* were not goading them on.

FATHER TUYISHIME   Sister Evangelique, I have not been goading them on!

SISTER EVANGELIQUE   You have too!

BISHOP GAHAMANYI   [*To* FATHER TUYISHIME.] You've been goading them on?

SISTER EVANGELIQUE   [*Simultaneously.*] Yes.

FATHER TUYISHIME   [*Simultaneously.*] No!

SISTER EVANGELIQUE   He has! Asking them what She looks like, what kind of veil She has on.

FATHER TUYISHIME   Sister!

SISTER EVANGELIQUE   Yes, it's been you the whole time.

BISHOP GAHAMANYI   I don't care who is goading who and what and where and why. Get it under control or I will SHUT. IT. DOWN. This school will be closed. Do you understand me? Do you both understand me?

SISTER EVANGELIQUE   [*Simultaneously.*] [*A whisper.*] Yes.

FATHER TUYISHIME   [*Simultaneously.*] [*A whisper.*] Yes.

BISHOP GAHAMANYI   Finally, something you both can agree on.

[*The Bishop walks out of the door with a wobbly knee. The Sister glares at the Father.*]

SISTER EVANGELIQUE   Your Excellency, next time you choose to grace us with your lovely presence it will all be settled. Kibeho will soon be quiet.

BISHOP GAHAMANYI   Good. Because the roar in the valley is getting rather loud.

Scene 7

[*Nighttime. All is quiet.* SISTER EVANGELIQUE *is walking the corridor with a candle in one hand and her rosary in the other.*]

SISTER EVANGELIQUE   Hail Mary, full of grace, the Lord is with thee; blessed are thou among women, and blessed is the fruit—

[*She stops. She tries again.*]

Hail Mary, full of grace, the Lord is with thee; blessed are thou among women—

[*She stops. She brings her rosary and puts it on her lap. She cannot pray her rosary. She begins to cry.*]

[*The door to the girls' dormitory opens.* SISTER EVANGELIQUE *hurriedly wipes away her tears. A figure appears in the shadows.*]

Who's there?

[*The figure does not answer.*]

I said who's there?

MARIE-CLARE   It is me.

[MARIE-CLARE *in bare feet walks into the corridor.*]

SISTER EVANGELIQUE   Why are you not asleep?

MARIE-CLARE   I need to use the latrines.

SISTER EVANGELIQUE   There are buckets in the dormitory.

MARIE-CLARE   I need my privacy.

SISTER EVANGELIQUE   Don't we all.

[*They stare at each other.* SISTER EVANGELIQUE *gestures for* MARIE-CLARE *to go ahead. But she doesn't.*]

MARIE-CLARE   You are upset.

SISTER EVANGELIQUE   No. Dear child, why would you—

MARIE-CLARE   Your eyes are blood red.

SISTER EVANGELIQUE   It is just the dust. The red Rwandan dust. Go on. Go ahead.

[*Silence.*]

You don't need to use the latrines, do you?

MARIE-CLARE   No, Sister.

[MARIE-CLARE *takes* SISTER EVANGELIQUE's *hand into her own.*]

SISTER EVANGELIQUE   If only those silly girls knew the consequence of their actions. Bishop Gahamanyi wants to close down Kibeho College because of them.

MARIE-CLARE   No!

SISTER EVANGELIQUE   Yes! Yes, all because of their little stunts.

MARIE-CLARE   He cannot close the school just because of a few spoiled ground nuts. They cannot stop all of us from going to school. They cannot.

SISTER EVANGELIQUE   But they are, Marie. Unless they stop, they will ruin the dreams of every young girl sleeping in that dormitory. And every mother's, too. I have watched many young girls plucking potatoes from their field, fetching water from the well with many a baby on their back. I have seen many young girls start life with bright eyes only to have them swollen shut by the hand of a man. If only they knew that there was much more to life than being a man's wife. My mother carried me on her back. Never learned to read. Never learned much. Well. I promised myself that I would never be like my mother. Fetching water, sewing, babies . . .

MARIE-CLARE   That will not be me, either.

SISTER EVANGELIQUE   No, Marie-Clare. Not you. That will not be your life. You are too feisty for that. A man would kill you with that mouth of yours.

[SISTER EVANGELIQUE *pinches* MARIE-CLARE *on her cheek.*]

You should go into the nunnery. You'd be a good nun.

MARIE-CLARE   Like you?

SISTER EVANGELIQUE   Like me.

[*They sit in silence drinking in the darkness.*]

Next time they want to play their little games. You burn them.

[*She smiles to herself.*]

That should awaken them from their spell.

MARIE-CLARE   Burn them?

SISTER EVANGELIQUE   Yes, you have my permission. Truth and morning become light with time.

[*She blows out the candle.*]

[*Lights shift.*]

Scene 8

[*Day.* MARIE-CLARE *and her mean-girls are holding court outside in their "cafeteria"—a tree.*]

GIRL #1   Today's eggs are soooo horrible.

GIRL #2   I miss my mama's *bitoki*.

MARIE-CLARE   You may not have to miss it for long.

GIRL #2   I will surely be missing it. Holiday isn't for another . . . wha? . . . three months until Easter. . . .

GIRL #3   Ugh.

MARIE-CLARE   Well, those little witches keep on spinning their tales, we'll have a holiday sooner than later.

THE GIRLS   What do you mean?

MARIE-CLARE   The Diocese is going to close Kibeho College.

THE GIRLS   Nooooo!

MARIE-CLARE   Yes!

GIRL #1   But I like it here.

MARIE-CLARE   I thought you hated the eggs.

GIRL #1   I rather eat these runny eggs than cook a batch for my ugly brothers any day.

GIRL #2   You ever thought it was true?

MARIE-CLARE   Of course not!

GIRL #3   But it's Anathalie. If it was just weirdo Alphonsine, maybe not, but Anathalie, too? Anathalie prays her rosary seven times a day.

MARIE-CLARE   So?

GIRL #2   She's the most devout of us all. . . .

GIRL #1   If I had her ugly Tutsi teeth I'd be praying the rosary a million times a day.

GIRL #3   Eh-Eh! She Hutu.

GIRL #1   [*Jeering.*] Well, she must be mixed then.

GIRL #2   It's Alphonsine who started it all. Tutsi Lying Through Her Teeth Alphonsine. My mother was right. They are all liars. They think the whole world revolves around them. They don't care what they do to hurt other people—

GIRL #3   Yeah . . . they are . . . selfish!

GIRL #1   So selfish!

GIRL #3   Yeah . . . that's what my da-da said. They think they are better than everyone.

GIRL #1   Smarter.

GIRL #2   Taller!

GIRL #1   Wiser!

GIRL #2   Prettier.

[GIRL #1 *and* GIRL #3, *sucking their teeth, looking at* GIRL #2.]

GIRL #2   Well . . . they are.

GIRL #1   No, they're not.

GIRL #2   Eh-eh! My da-da said that Tutsi women always have such a pretty face.

GIRL #3   Well, Marie-Clare has a pretty face.

[*The girls look at* MARIE-CLARE's *face.*]

MARIE-CLARE   What are you saying?

THE GIRLS   [*Very quickly.*] Nothing.

MARIE-CLARE   Go get me another plate of eggs. NOOOOWWW!

[*The worker bees hurriedly fly away to bring back honey for their queen.* MARIE-CLARE *pushes away the food. Actually, she is not very hungry. She eyes* ALPHONSINE *eating her breakfast quietly beneath another tree.* MARIE-CLARE *walks over to her.* ALPHONSINE *does not look up.*]

ALPHONSINE   You can have my eggs if you want.

MARIE-CLARE   Where is Anathalie?

ALPHONSINE   Resting. The first few trips are always very tiring. But she will get used to them—

MARIE-CLARE   You know not what you do.

ALPHONSINE   I am a human being. We never know what we are doing.

MARIE-CLARE   I hate you and all your "mysterious" talk. You're not so mysterious, Alphonsine. I know you. I know your kind.

Alphonsine   I bet you do.

Marie-Clare   If I was your father, I'd beat you black and blue—eh-eh, wait, you don't have a father. I heard he divorced your mama and left you to fend for yourselves. Must have been a rotten household. She didn't know how to take care of a man. Maybe that's what you are after. A father. A Father Tuyishime.

Alphonsine   I do not need a father—

Marie-Clare   You crave his attention, don't you?

Alphonsine   His attention is not the one I crave.

Marie-Clare   Whose attention *do* you crave?

Alphonsine   Yours, Marie Clare. Do I have it? *

[*Beat.*]

Marie-Clare   You just want everyone to hate you.

Alphonsine   [*She shrugs.*] The speaker of truth has no friends.

Marie-Clare   And the teller of lies is an unfortunate fool. You are hell-bent on dying. If the people from the village hear about this . . . well . . . *en, henh* . . .

Alphonsine   [*Chuckles to herself.*] I have already been made aware of this. She has told me that and it is fine. I am fine with it. With it all. Truth is not afraid of the machete.

Marie-Clare   So . . . You want to die?

Alphonsine   If you had seen the world She's shown me. That could be ours? Well . . . you would die for it, too, Marie-Clare.

Marie-Clare   No, I will live out my days and grow old here. In Kibeho. A nun.

Alphonsine   You? A nun?

Marie-Clare   Yes, I'd make a good one.

Alphonsine   That you would.

Marie-Clare   Shut up! I've been called!

[Marie-Clare *goes to strike* Alphonsine, *who does not move, does not flinch.*] You are not afraid of me? Why?

Alphonsine   [*She looks at her softly.*] 'Cause we are sisters of the same tribe.

[Marie-Clare *stands stunned. Caught. Does she know?*]

Marie-Clare   I am not and will never be your sister.

[Alphonsine *looks after* Marie-Clare *as she stomps away.*]

Scene 9

[*Confession. Dusk makes the light flowing through the stained-glass window dance across the red dirt floor.* FATHER TUYISHIME *is in the confession booth nodding off, slightly snoring.* ALPHONSINE *enters.*]

ALPHONSINE   Father . . . Father . . . FATHER.

[*He wakes up with a jolt.*]

ALPHONSINE   Father—

FATHER TUYISHIME   Alphonsine?

ALPHONSINE   Yes, Father, it's me.

FATHER TUYISHIME   Oh, sorry, sorry, my dear child. This coffin has become a bit warm.

ALPHONSINE   Don't worry. All the girls say this is the best place for a nap. All warm and cozy.

[*He laughs then takes a deep breath. He stares at her through the scrim.*]

ALPHONSINE   Yes, Father?

FATHER TUYISHIME   Nothing.

ALPHONSINE   I thought you were staring at me because I have not been to confession in so long. How long has it been?

FATHER TUYISHIME   About . . . one month, six days, give or take, more or less, around thereabouts. You've been / busy.

ALPHONSINE   Oh, that long.

FATHER TUYISHIME   Yes, that long.

ALPHONSINE   I'm sorry.

FATHER TUYISHIME   As I've said, you've been busy. . . . What is on your heart today, child?

ALPHONSINE   I have much I must / confess.

FATHER TUYISHIME   Mmmm.

ALPHONSINE   Much I need to say.

FATHER TUYISHIME   Mmmmmmmmm.

ALPHONSINE   Much I need to release.

FATHER TUYISHIME   What has made your heart so heavy, dear child?

ALPHONSINE   I am trying to understand this, Father. This mantle that has been placed upon my head. I don't understand it, Father.

Father Tuyishime　Neither do I.

Alphonsine　I am just a dirt-poor girl with no shoes, no friends, no father who has not read every word in that Bible, and yet She chose me.

Father Tuyishime　There are things beyond our control, my dear child.

Alphonsine　Why did She choose me? I mean, why didn't She choose, Sister Evangelique?

Father Tuyishime　We all know why She didn't choose Sister Evangelique.

Alphonsine　But at least I feel as though people would have listened to her. She is a grown up. She's . . . loud . . .

Father Tuyishime　It is much better to be burned by the sun than by a raging fire, Alphonsine.

Alphonsine　She tells me things, Father. She wants me to do things. Things a girl is not supposed to do. Things I do not know how to do.

Father Tuyishime　What does She tell you Alphonsine?

Alphonsine　I don't know if I can say.

Father Tuyishime　Alphonsine, let your tongue confess.

[*Beat.*]

Alphonsine　Do you know the President?

Father Tuyishime　President Habyarimana?

Alphonsine　Yes. Do you know him?

Father Tuyishime　No, I don't know him. I know of him.

Alphonsine　Of him?

Father Tuyishime　Yes, like every other Rwandan I suppose.

Alphonsine　Well, She needs me to give him a message.

Father Tuyishime　A message? To the President?

Alphonsine　Yes, I need to give him a message. She says it's important.

Father Tuyishime　The Virgin Mary has a message for the President of Rwanda?

Alphonsine　I know it sounds weird, but—

Father Tuyishime　Maybe this booth is indeed a bit too hot. Would you like to step out for a moment, catch a whiff of sanity, and then we could / continue?

Alphonsine　You think I'm lying, again.

FATHER TUYISHIME   No, I don't think you're lying. I think you are . . . crazy.

ALPHONSINE   Father, please—

FATHER TUYISHIME   Really, Alphonsine, this is all getting to be a bit—

ALPHONSINE   She says it's urgent and that if I need to, I should walk from Kibeho to Kigali to get it to him.

FATHER TUYISHIME   That's a pretty far walk for a young lady with no shoes.

ALPHONSINE   He must know—

FATHER TUYISHIME   Know what, Alphonsine?

ALPHONSINE   That there is evil lurking in men's hearts. More evil than he has ever known. It is close to him.

FATHER TUYISHIME   Alphonsine, this is preposterous.

ALPHONSINE   He must purge it. Purge the madness from men's hearts. Purge it from his own. She says I must get to Kigali and tell him this.

FATHER TUYISHIME   But as you say, you're but a dirt-poor girl, a Tutsi no less. Do you think a man of his stature would listen to you?

ALPHONSINE   *You* listen to me.

FATHER TUYISHIME   That is my job.

ALPHONSINE   Is that not his, to listen to his people?

FATHER TUYISHIME   Depends if it is a message he wants to listen to.

ALPHONSINE   But he's the President, he must listen to everything.

FATHER TUYISHIME   Which means he tends to listen to nothing at all.

ALPHONSINE   Then he is a fool.

FATHER TUYISHIME   I concur.

ALPHONSINE   She needs him to pray, like She needs *you* to pray.

[ALPHONSINE *clamps her hand over her mouth.*]

FATHER TUYISHIME   Like what, dear child, what?

ALPHONSINE   You have not prayed for yourself in eight years, eight months, and two days. Ever since—

FATHER TUYISHIME   How do you know that, Alphonsine?

[*Silence.*]

HOW DO YOU KNOW?

ALPHONSINE   She told me.

[ALPHONSINE *reaches her hand across the divide.* FATHER TUYISHIME *does not touch her.*]

ALPHONSINE   I'm sorry for your sorrow.

FATHER TUYISHIME   Has it been that long since . . .

ALPHONSINE   Our Lady says your mother was beautiful.

FATHER TUYISHIME   Oh, Alphonsine, she was. Mama used to wear purple flowers in her hair. She would never let me have all the porridge in the pot. She would say, "Always leave something at the bottom for the ancestors." Such a giving woman, beautiful woman. Slaughtered. Like a goat. 1973. Eight years ago, when your president, President Habyarimana, overthrew President Kayibanda. When the world changed. . . .

ALPHONSINE   Was your mama like me?

FATHER TUYISHIME   Yes, she was Tutsi like you.

ALPHONSINE   Have you cried lately, Father Tuyishime?

FATHER TUYISHIME   No, Alphonsine . . . I cannot cry. . . .

ALPHONSINE   Well . . . a man's tears fall into his stomach.

FATHER TUYISHIME   Ah, so that is why I'm always sooo full.

ALPHONSINE   You must get out of this coffin. Come into the sunlight.

FATHER TUYISHIME   Alphonsine, your laughter is all the sunlight I need.

[*She laughs.*]

ALPHONSINE   Come outside. The Son awaits you.

[*Lights shift.*]

Scene 10

[*Soon after.*]

[SISTER EVANGELIQUE *goes to the well to fill her jerrican with water.* EMMANUEL, *a young boy, has a baby tied to his back. He has on ragged clothing. No shoes.*]

SISTER EVANGELIQUE   You do not belong here. Get off the premises. No vagabonds allowed.

EMMANUEL   How come you're here?

SISTER EVANGELIQUE   *Sa,* you little runt!

EMMANUEL   Sorry. Sorry.

SISTER EVANGELIQUE   No begging. This is a school, not a bank. We have no francs for you.

EMMANUEL   Please, Sister. My little sister and I have the "sickness."

SISTER EVANGELIQUE   The "sickness," eh?

EMMANUEL   My parents. Both died of the "sickness."

SISTER EVANGELIQUE   [*Softening.*] Eeehhhhhh.

[*She looks around, then digs into her pocket and presents some coins.*]

EMMANUEL   This is all you have?

SISTER EVANGELIQUE   Sisterhood doesn't pay very much.

[*The sounds of singing can be heard coming in the distance.*]

SISTER EVANGELIQUE   What? What is that sound?

EMMANUEL   Sounds sweet, doesn't it?

SISTER EVANGELIQUE   I've never heard that song before. . . .

EMMANUEL   The village made it up. For the girls.

SISTER EVANGELIQUE   For the girls?

EMMANUEL   The girls who have favor with the Virgin.

SISTER EVANGELIQUE   Who told you that?

EMMANUEL   The village is vibrating with the good news. Isn't it good news? Mama Mary. Here. In Kibeho? We've come to see the miracle.

SISTER EVANGELIQUE   There are no miracles here.

[*There is singing coming far from the hills in Kinyarwanda.*]

EMMANUEL   We've all come to see the girls who see.

[*The singing is growing louder and louder and louder.*]

EMMANUEL   Is that one of them?

SISTER EVANGELIQUE   Yes . . .

[*He looks to* ALPHONSINE, *who is standing beneath a tree. She waves to him.*]

EMMANUEL   Look at that light around her.

SISTER EVANGELIQUE   Yes, there is a light.

EMMANUEL   Look at her glowing. Just look at her.

[ALPHONSINE *actually does begin to glow. It begins to blind her.*]

[*The tree that* ALPHONSINE *was standing beneath begins to move and sway as if a great wind is moving in, but* ALPHONSINE *stands there unmoved.*]

EMMANUEL   I need to touch her.

[*Her light grows brighter.*]

SISTER EVANGELIQUE   I . . . I . . . cannot see. . . my eyes are burning. . . .

[*The sound coming up the hill sounds beautiful, rising like a wave coming to break over the school. ALPHONSINE is bathed in a beautiful light. She looks upward.*]

VILLAGER 1   Where are they?

VILLAGER 2 (A BLIND MAN)   My feet hurt.

VILLAGER 3   Quit complaining.

VILLAGER 1   The girls better be here.

VILLAGER 2 (A BLIND MAN)   These girls are just lying.

VILLAGER 3   I should have left you home in bed. This man of mine. Always so negative.

VILLAGER 2 (A BLIND MAN)   Woman, just hold my hand.

VILLAGER 3   You are!

VILLAGER 2 (A BLIND MAN)   I'm here just in case.

VILLAGER 1   Just in case?

VILLAGER 2 (A BLIND MAN)   Just in case this is real—

EMMANUEL   I want to touch her. She's glowing.

SISTER EVANGELIQUE   Don't! Don't go over there! She might burn you!

[*The singing is getting louder and louder.*]

VILLAGER 1   Who is that girl talking to?

VILLAGER 3   Where?

VILLAGER 1   See her! See her over there!

EMMANUEL   Look at that light around her. I need to touch her. Me and my baby sister. We got the "sickness."

[*The singing gets louder and louder. A crowd is coming closer.*]

EMMANUEL   Please let me touch your light.

[*The noon sun, hanging high in the sky, begins to dance across the aqua blue of the day. ALPHONSINE raises her hands to the sun. It splits in half and starts dancing around her fingertips. Rainbows stream from her fingertips. The crowd has stopped singing, stunned into silence. Another sun pops out from behind the first. And it, too, splits in half, it is a sky with four suns spinning round and round. A sky with four suns has the light of four universes, but the light is not blinding; it's warm. A cloud parts and there is a face. A slight face. Something. Lips moving. EMMANUEL starts crying.*]

EMMANUEL   See it! In the sky!

[*The cloud suddenly begins to swirl like a tornado. The winds start blowing again.*]

SISTER EVANGELIQUE   Where?

EMMANUEL   In the sky! Mama Mary's in the sky!

[*There is a swirl of clouds. A faint figure can be seen. But as soon as it appears it is disappeared by the sky.*]

Scene 11

[*Night. The girls dorm.* SISTER EVANGELIQUE *is walking past. The girls are all abuzz discussing what happened just hours before.*]

SISTER EVANGELIQUE   If you do not go to bed now every bottom in here will be feeling the licks of Father Tuyishime's cane.

[*The girls look at each other in even more excitement.*]

GIRL #3   But Sister Evangelique—

SISTER EVANGELIQUE   But nothing. Finish up. Then Go. To. BED.

GIRL #3   But we just can't get it out of our minds.

GIRL #4   Speak for yourself. . . .

[GIRL #3 *imitating the sun.*]

GIRL #3   The sun danced with us. It split in half again and again and then it danced with us. Sister, didn't you see it?

[*Tots lying.*]

SISTER EVANGELIQUE   See what?

GIRL #4   I didn't see it either.

GIRL #3   It is because you are a heathen.

GIRL #4   Are you calling Sister Evangelique a heathen, too?

[SISTER EVANGELIQUE *gives* GIRL #3 *the I'm-a-beat-yo-ass-right-now look.*]

GIRL #3   [*Stammering.*] No-no-no-no-that-that is not what I meant.

SISTER EVANGELIQUE   Everyone, finish your wash up. Then get to bed. I don't want to say it again

[*Just then* ALPHONSINE *and* ANATHALIE *enter with the other girls. Everyone ignores* SISTER EVANGELIQUE. *They are drying their hair off, fresh from their showers. The other girls tend to them. Taking away their towels , their basins, their soaps.* SISTER EVANGELIQUE *glowers then goes. . . .*]

GIRL #1   Oh. My. Goodness. You made the sun spin.

GIRL #3   You are so cool. *Kwela!*

GIRL #1   I mean, WOW! You made the sun spin.

GIRL #2   That was just—WHOA.

ALPHONSINE   I did not make the sun spin. It was She.

GIRL #1   Whatever you did, it was the most amazing thing ever. Oh, my God.

GIRL #2   Ah-ah! You are breaking a commandment—

GIRL #1   Eeeeh.

[GIRL #1 *makes the sign of the cross and starts doing a Hail Mary.*]

GIRL #2   Tell us, tell us what She said again.

THE GIRLS   Yes, tell us! Tell us!

ANATHALIE   She says that young women must be chaste in spirit and chaste of heart.

GIRL #1   I don't know how much longer I can stay chaste with Father Tuyishime around.

GIRL #2   Me neither. . . .

[*The girls do a little handshake.*]

ANATHALIE   She says that we should not use our bodies as instruments of pleasure. True love comes from God. Instead of being at the service of God, we have been at the service of men, but we must make of our bodies instruments destined to the glory of God.

GIRL #3   Speak plainly, Anathalie.

ANATHALIE   Keep your legs closed!

THE GIRLS   Oooohhh!

[MARIE-CLARE *walks in with a soccer ball. She is athletic and lithe, kicking the ball with her slender leg. She catches it on the back of her head.*]

MARIE-CLARE   Anyone want to play futbol with me?

GIRL #1   You know Sister Evangelique doesn't like it when we play inside.

GIRL #2   Yes, Marie-Clare.

MARIE-CLARE   What, you two don't want to play with me / now?

GIRL #2   [*Ignoring her.*] And then She said we should be pious, right?

ANATHALIE   She says we must be pious.

MARIE-CLARE   No one wants to play a quick game?

THE GIRLS   NOOO!

GIRL #3   Marie-Clare, did you see Alphonsine make the sun spin?

Marie-Clare   I heard about it.

Girl #3   [*Sighing.*] It was soooooooooo amazing.

Girl #4   Ah-ah! I don't believe it.

Marie-Clare   Me neither. It is rainy season, ya know.

Girl #4   For true!

Marie-Clare   For true!

[**Marie-Clare** *kicks the ball around. She sees the entire dorm kowtowing to her enemies. She sets up the ball as if she's about to kick it into play. She sends it flying right into the crowd of girls. It hits somebody—probably* **Anathalie**—*in the head.*]

Girl #2   Marie-Clare!

Marie-Clare   Ooops!

[**Marie-Clare** *and GIRL #4 laugh.*]

[**Marie-Clare** *retrieves the ball from the corner and comes back to the middle of the dorm, bouncing it on her foot and then bouncing it on her knee.*]

Girl #1   Why do you play around so much?

Alphonsine   Are you okay, Anathalie?

[**Anathalie** *picks up her glasses that have fallen off.*]

Anathalie   Marie-Clare, you do not have to resort to such nastiness. I am still your friend—

Marie-Clare   Friend? No friend of mine would link arms with the likes of her. What, you could not stand for Alphonsine to have all the attention?

Anathalie   No, Marie-Clare, I think that is you.

Marie-Clare   Ah! Attention garnered in the wake of lying is attention I do not need. You are insane, following this knappy-headed heathen through the gates of hell. You both are going to rot for these lies.

Anathalie   You just go ahead and sit high and mighty on your pedestal of judgment, Marie-Clare. You may be my best friend, but Mother Mary is not a friend worth losing for a nonbeliever.

Marie-Clare   Nonbeliever?

[**Marie-Clare** *comes up to* **Anathalie** *to rough her up, but* **Anathalie** *this time decides to fight back. The girls are utterly shocked at* **Anathalie**'s *ferocity. Almost like she's become a new woman.*]

Anathalie   Look, Marie-Clare, I'm tired of your shit!

THE GIRLS   Ooooooooo! She said shit! Shit! She's tired of your shit!

ALPHONSINE   Anathalie, do not be pulled into her despair.

ANATHALIE   As long as she doesn't pull another one of her pranks out of her dirty knickers.

MARIE-CLARE   [*Gasping.*] I do not have dirty knickers.

ANATHALIE   That's right, you don't have any!

THE GIRLS   Ooooooooooooo!

[*An embarrassed* MARIE-CLARE, *feeling her power dwindling, takes aim and sends the ball flying into the group of girls yet again.* SISTER EVANGELIQUE *appears at the door of the girls' dormitory.*]

SISTER EVANGELIQUE   That is enough, Marie-Clare! What did I tell you about playing with that ball in here!

[*All the girls scatter-scatter and run to their beds.*]

Lights out! And put that damn ball up before I burn it!

[SISTER EVANGELIQUE *slams the door. And the girls giggle and giggle. They are giggling.*]

[SISTER EVANGELIQUE *offstage.*]

What. Did. I. Say?

[*Silence.*]

[MARIE-CLARE *once again throws her ball at the girls, but the ball becomes frozen in air as if caught by an invisible hand.*]

[ANATHALIE *and* ALPHONSINE'*s beds are bathed in the most gorgeous light, like a supernova, like the light of every star God ever made. Their bodies writhe as they are bathed in the brilliance.*]

GIRL #1   Oh, my God!

GIRL #2   What is going on?

GIRL #3   They are doing it again!

MARIE-CLARE   I'm so sick and tired of this!

[MARIE-CLARE *pushes a girl off of the bed.*]

Hand me that candle!

GIRL #4   Where?

MARIE-CLARE   Right there! Right there!

[*The girl runs and retrieves the candle.*]

GIRL #1   Marie-Clare! Why are you doing this? Why?

[MARIE-CLARE *takes the candle and places it beneath* ALPHONSINE's *right arm. Smoke emits as fire meets flesh, but* ALPHONSINE *is so entranced she doesn't feel the burn. . . .*]

MARIE-CLARE   What in the hell's name . . .

ALPHONSINE   [*To the Virgin Mary.*] I'm being burned?

[ALPHONSINE *moves her left arm out of the way. MARIE- CLARE stands there stunned as* ALPHONSINE *refuses to move her right arm—the one that is being burned.*]

[ALPHONSINE *finally removes the other arm.* MARIE-CLARE *drops the candle in fear.*]

MARIE-CLARE   Sister Evangelique! Sister Evangelique, they are doing it again.

GIRL #1   Oh, my God!! Look at their eyes. They are rolling into the back of their heads.

GIRL #3   It is a possession!

GIRL #4   I want to go home! This school is overrun by demons. I want to go home, I need to go home, I want to go home—

ALPHONSINE   I care not about this world. I only want to speak your truth.

MARIE-CLARE   Sister Evangelique!

GIRL #3   Oh, my God! Look at their eyes.

MARIE-CLARE   Sister Evangelique!

[SISTER EVANGELIQUE *bursts in.*]

SISTER EVANGELIQUE   What did I tell all of you? Go. To—

MARIE-CLARE   Sister Evangelique, look at them!

ALPHONSINE and **ANATHALIE**   She says we must pray.

[*Those girls who believe get their rosaries out and begin to pray. . . .*]

THE GIRLS   Our Father which are / in heaven . . .

GIRL #3   I'm scared. I'm scared. / They're scaring me.

GIRL #1   Shhh and just pray. Do as she says!

ALPHONSINE and **ANATHALIE**   We must pray.

MARIE-CLARE   Sister Evangelique! Look at them.

SISTER EVANGELIQUE   No no no no no no no, my dear children. Do not be fooled.

[*The dormitory is filled with prayer.*]

ALPHONSINE and **ANATHALIE**   She says we must pray for the sins of man.

[*A soft voice comes riding in on the wind. Buttery and sweet. It slides through the chaos like smoke and embraces the biggest unbeliever of them all. . . .*]

MARIE-CLARE   What who is this?

[**MARIE-CLARE** *looks to* ANATHALIE *and* ALPHONSINE.]

Anathalie! Alphonsine! You are playing tricks on me! You are playing tricks.

[*But they are too busy looking up into the sky. Their mouths are not moving.*]

[**MARIE-CLARE** *buckles over as if she's about to vomit.*]

MARIE-CLARE   I am feeling faint—

SISTER EVANGELIQUE   Marie-Clare—

[**MARIE-CLARE** *turns around and takes a swing. She almost punches* SISTER EVANGELIQUE *straight in the jaw.* SISTER EVANGELIQUE *lurches back.*]

SISTER EVANGELIQUE   Marie-Clare!

MARIE-CLARE   Stop calling my name! Stop calling my name!

[*She continues to swing.*]

No, I'm not. I'm NOT!!

[**MARIE-CLARE** *frantically looks about the room.*]

MARIE-CLARE   [*Under her breath.*] I'm . . . I'm going crazy. I'm going crazy. Noooo. This is all a dream a dream a dream a dream a dream a dream a dream a dream a dream

[*Screaming at the top of her lungs.*]

GET OUT OF ME! GET OUT OF MY HEAD! I AM NOT CRAZY. I AM NOT CRAZY. NOT LIKE THEM. NOT LIKE THEM. PLEASE, GOD! I DON'T WANT TO BE LIKE THEM. NOT LIKE THEM!

[*She starts beating herself in the head. Punching at the air, trying to knock Our Lady out. Our Lady slaps her in the face.* MARIE-CLARE *doubles over. She lands on the bed.*]

MARIE-CLARE   [*Orgasmic.*] It feels like butter melting in my belly.

[**MARIE-CLARE** *is taken over by the rapture. Her toes curl and her body shakes and quakes.*]

SISTER EVANGELIQUE   You are having a seizure! She is having a seizure! Father Tuyishime! Help! Help!

[**SISTER EVANGELIQUE** *runs out into the hallway.*]

MARIE-CLARE   What is this? What is happening to me?

[*She continues to quake. And pulse. Then suddenly:*]

[ALPHONSINE *and* ANATHALIE *rise into the air! The girls start screaming at the two flying above their heads!*]

MARIE-CLARE   [*Moaning.*] Yessssss—I can feel you.

[SISTER EVANGELIQUE *runs back in from the hallway. She screams!*]

MARIE-CLARE   Yesssss—I can touch you.

[MARIE-CLARE *reaches her hands out!*]

[SISTER EVANGELIQUE *stands stunned at the scene. . . .*]

SISTER EVANGELIQUE   Marie-Clare! You, too?

MARIE-CLARE   YES!

[MARIE-CLARE *looks up and she is bathed in Our Lady's light. Her body slackens. And she is hoisted far above the heads of everyone, joining* ANATHALIE *and* ALPHONSINE *in the sky.*]

[*The Trinity is now complete.*]

[*The girls are screaming. They are scrambling. But someone or something has locked the door. They cannot get out. There is nowhere to run. Nowhere to hide.*]

[*Three big bangs occur. The bed* ALPHONSINE *floats above breaks in half. The bed* ANATHALIE *floats above breaks in half. The bed* MARIE-CLARE *floats upon breaks in half.*]

[*Blackout.*]

End of Act One

ACT II

Scene 1

[*Six months later.*]

[FATHER TUYISHIME'*s office.*]

[FATHER TUYISHIME *sits at his desk.* FATHER FLAVIA, *an Italian priest, sits opposite. A group of girls are outside the door whispering.*]

THE GIRLS   [*Sotto voce.*] It's Jesus! Jesus . . . Come here. Look! It's Jesus! Jesus!

FATHER TUYISHIME   Father Flavia, I'm so glad you could make it.

THE GIRLS   [*Getting louder.*] It's Jesus! It's Jesus! *Muzungu! Muzungu* Jesus!

FATHER TUYISHIME   *Sa!*

[FATHER TUYISHIME *shoos them away. The girls run, but their excited whispers can still be heard down the corridor.*]

[*Sotto voce.*]

THE GIRLS   It's Jesus! It's Jesus!

FATHER FLAVIA   They are very excitable.

FATHER TUYISHIME   They act like they've never seen a white man before. Forgive them, please.

FATHER FLAVIA   They are forgiven.

FATHER TUYISHIME   Would you like some water?

FATHER FLAVIA   Would love.

FATHER TUYISHIME   It's not holy, but it'll have to do.

[FATHER TUYISHIME *fills a can of water.* FATHER FLAVIA *accepts, but does not drink. Beat. Looking deep into the cup, inspecting it. . . .*]

FATHER FLAVIA   If only I could turn water into wine.

[*He knocks it back.*]

FATHER TUYISHIME   Father Flavia, I hope the trip has not been too rough for you.

FATHER FLAVIA   Ah, the plane ride was fine. Rome to Addis Ababa then Kigali. But the road to Kibeho . . .

[*Laughing.*]

FATHER TUYISHIME   . . . is not a road.

[*Fanning himself.*]

FATHER FLAVIA   It is a bumpy spiral staircase up a very huge hill.

FATHER TUYISHIME   A hill that stops at Heaven's doorstep.

[FATHER TUYISHIME *points out the window.*]

Look at that view. They call it the Switzerland of Africa.

FATHER FLAVIA   Who says that?

FATHER TUYISHIME   There is a saying in our country, Rwanda is so beautiful that even God goes on vacation here.

FATHER FLAVIA   He might vacation in Rwanda; but always remember He lives in Rome.

FATHER TUYISHIME   I see . . . We are glad that someone from the Vatican has taken the time to grace Kibeho with a papal presence.

FATHER FLAVIA   Eh, well, the Pope was too busy so . . .

[*They burst into laughter.*]

FATHER TUYISHIME   It is a joy to see these young women confirmed. Validated—

FATHER FLAVIA   Validated?

FATHER TUYISHIME   Why, yes, is not your role here but to validate?

FATHER FLAVIA   I am only here to be the Church's eyes and ears. I could never validate, just gather the evidence.

FATHER TUYISHIME   Surely we must be valid enough if you've come this far. We must be important if you are here to be the Church's eyes and ears as you say.

FATHER FLAVIA   Surely you are not so naïve as to think that. The validations of apparitions must carry with them the weight of remarkable evidence, and three broken beds in a girls' dormitory in Rwanda does not remarkable evidence make.

FATHER TUYISHIME   So you are not here to prove them right but rather to prove them wrong?

FATHER FLAVIA   I should have been a lawyer.

FATHER TUYISHIME   But it happened.

FATHER FLAVIA   Were you there? Were you a witness?

FATHER TUYISHIME   No, but were you there when Jesus was crucified?

FATHER FLAVIA   I'm not that old, Father.

FATHER TUYISHIME   Well, some things do not need to be seen in order to be believed.

[SISTER EVANGELIQUE *appears at the door.*]

SISTER EVANGELIQUE   And yet some do. I had to see for myself if the Son had come down from Heaven.

[*Chuckling to herself.*]

Jesus, indeed.

[*The two men look towards the door to see* SISTER EVANGELIQUE *towering.*]

FATHER TUYISHIME   Rumors spread fast here.

SISTER EVANGELIQUE   If only I could say the same for truth.

FATHER TUYISHIME   Father Flavia is on special assignment from the Holy See.

SISTER EVANGELIQUE   First time I am hearing about this special visit from our friends at the Vatican. Wish the deputy head nun would have been informed of such a special visitor to Kibeho College.

[FATHER FLAVIA *holds out his hand to* SISTER EVANGELIQUE.]

FATHER FLAVIA   And you must be that deputy head nun.

SISTER EVANGELIQUE   Let us not concern ourselves with such silly little titles, just call me Sister Evangelique. I am just glad that per my suggestion someone is here to investigate these girls.

FATHER FLAVIA   What do you think of these . . . occurrences?

[SISTER EVANGELIQUE *looks to* FATHER TUYISHIME *for approval to speak. He gives it.*]

SISTER EVANGELIQUE   Me? I am not of the same mind as my superior here.

FATHER FLAVIA   [*To* FATHER TUYISHIME.] So you believe the visions are real?

FATHER TUYISHIME   I don't know if I believe they are real . . . I just . . . I just hope they are.

FATHER FLAVIA   Hoping and believing are two different things, Father Tuyishime.

FATHER TUYISHIME   Cannot have belief without hope that what you are believing is true.

FATHER FLAVIA   [*Smiling.*] I'll drink to that. When was the last "vision" as you call it?

FATHER TUYISHIME   The Virgin Mary has been coming frequently, visiting with the girls since the dorm incident six months ago. But that incident was perhaps the most expressive of them. The girls flew into the sky like crested cranes. After which their beds rose and buckled mid-flight. Sister Evangelique saw it even though she will not admit. . . .

SISTER EVANGELIQUE   'Til this day I know not the heathens who hoisted them into the sky.

FATHER FLAVIA   So you were the only witness?

FATHER TUYISHIME   Other girls saw it, too—

[*With a wave of her hand.*]

SISTER EVANGELIQUE   They were suffering from hysteria.

FATHER FLAVIA   As young girls are wont to do.

FATHER TUYISHIME   [*To* SISTER EVANGELIQUE.] And what about you? Where you suffering from hysteria?

SISTER EVANGELIQUE   I was suffering from trickery. If I could go back to that night and smoke out the culprit who helped them work their magic trick, I would.

FATHER TUYISHIME   I know your girls are strong and all, lifting and balancing jerricans atop their heads for hours at a time, but certainly they cannot have lifted themselves and their beds with their minds.

SISTER EVANGELIQUE   Would you rather they have been possessed by the devil? If they are not lying, which let us hope to God they are, then surely it was the devil himself that entered those girls.

FATHER FLAVIA   [*Agreeing.*] Truth be told, it sounds more like a possession.

FATHER TUYISHIME   I have performed an exorcism before. This was no such thing. The room smelled like jasmine on a misty morning for weeks. In fact, the girls have turned the dormitory into a chapel, eh—a shrine! Stacked the broken beds and surrounded it with fruits for the Virgin to eat. No, no, no . . . The devil did not enter these gates of Kibeho.

SISTER EVANGELIQUE   But you were not there. *I* was there. Me. And what I saw were three girls shaking hands with the devil. Father Flavia, I hope you find what you have come here for, which are three lying little blaspheming snots—

FATHER TUYISHIME   Sister—

SISTER EVANGELIQUE   Excuse me, I must go pray. You will find me in the chapel if you need me.

[SISTER EVANGELIQUE *swiftly excuses herself.*]

FATHER FLAVIA   Oh my. She would fit in splendidly at the Holy See.

FATHER TUYISHIME   Yes, her habit is steeped in the perfume of skepticism.

FATHER FLAVIA   Smells divine.

FATHER TUYISHIME   No, what is divine is that there have been continuing occurrences . . . miracles happening.

FATHER FLAVIA   Miracles? Here?

FATHER TUYISHIME   Yes, there seems to be such a thing. The girls say *Nyina wa Jambo* wants them—

FATHER FLAVIA   Nina-who-wha?

FATHER TUYISHIME   [*Enunciating loudly and slowly.*] *Nyina wa Jambo.* That is what the girls say She calls herself. "Mother of the Word."

FATHER FLAVIA   So the Virgin Mary speaks—

FATHER TUYISHIME   Kinyarwanda.

FATHER FLAVIA   Well, she certainly knows how to get to all of her children.

FATHER TUYISHIME   Indeed. In fact, She wants the girls to start having weekly presentations with the people of the village. Spread her message "like seeds on a flower bed," She says.

[*Beat.* FATHER FLAVIA *takes this all in.*]

FATHER FLAVIA   Do you know what a precession is, Father?

FATHER TUYISHIME   When someone dies we have one.

FATHER FLAVIA   No, Father, that is a procession, I said *pre*cession.

FATHER TUYISHIME   Is this something I should know about?

FATHER FLAVIA   The world is round, correct?

FATHER TUYISHIME   That is what I've been told.

FATHER FLAVIA   The world revolves on an axis and every 25,800 years supposedly the earth wobbles on its axis. It's called precession. When it happens the constellations in the night sky change. The North Star is no longer the North Star. True north points to some other star. We are due for another wobble in about, oh, 18,274 years.

FATHER TUYISHIME   I do not understand why this is of importance to the girls, / Father Flavia.

FATHER FLAVIA   Do you believe in God, Father Tuyishime?

[*Pause.*]

FATHER TUYISHIME   Of course. Don't you?

FATHER FLAVIA   Of course, of course . . . but sometimes I wonder if God made the stars or if the stars made Him.

FATHER TUYISHIME   Are you a man of the cloth or a scientist?

FATHER FLAVIA   [*Smiling.*] Both. I have traveled all over the world to suss out the truth of these happenings. Our Lady has shown Her face in Portugal. In Italy, quite naturally; even in the mountains of India; but never, ever in the jungles of Africa.

FATHER TUYISHIME   Well, this is not a jungle, Father.

FATHER FLAVIA   I beg your pardon, Father?

FATHER TUYISHIME   Rwanda is not the jungle.

FATHER FLAVIA   Could have fooled me. We are about to embark on a long journey, my dear friend. Confirmations are indeed a long and arduous process. . . . Where can I wash my hands? I hope you don't mind, but I would like to start these tests as soon as possible.

FATHER TUYISHIME   Tests, what kinds of tests?

FATHER FLAVIA   Liturgical, psychological, medical—that is all. It is what we at the Holy See require for the Congregation's archive. Minimum. Where are the girls?

FATHER TUYISHIME   Follow me.

[FATHER FLAVIA *stands up from his chair.* FATHER TUYISHIME *begins to lead him out of the office, but then he stops* FATHER FLAVIA.]

I must warn you. She said something to them. To one girl especially. She has a message. A message for the president.

FATHER FLAVIA   A message for the President? Of Rwanda? Does she have a message for the Pope as well?

FATHER TUYISHIME   Well, actually –

[FATHER TUYISHIME *passes him a sheet of paper.* FATHER FLAVIA *reads it.*]

FATHER FLAVIA   Oh my.

FATHER TUYISHIME   Of course she'd like to tell you herself.

FATHER FLAVIA   Of course, of course . . . let's see if the world is indeed wobbling.

Scene 2

[*The girls sit in the courtyard cafeteria, eating lunch.* ALPHONSINE, ANATHALIE, *and now* MARIE-CLARE *sit at a table all their own. The other girls look at them in awe.*]

MARIE-CLARE   I hope Father Tuyishime's sermon is better than last week.

ANATHALIE   His face is sermon enough. Takes me to heaven for the hour. His tongue just ruins it.

MARIE-CLARE   Anathalie, you are going to hell. Straight to hell.

ANATHALIE   [*With a smirk on her lips.*] Well, see you there.

[GIRL #1 *walks up to the Trinity.*]

GIRL #1   Marie-Clare, can you bless my rosary?

MARIE-CLARE   Of course, dear child.

[MARIE-CLARE *commences to blessing. . . .*]

[*Suddenly* FATHER TUYISHIME *and* FATHER FLAVIA *come into the courtyard.*]

THE GIRLS   [*Giggling sotto voce.*] Jesus. It's Jesus. . . .

MARIE-CLARE   Well, if it isn't the *muzungu*. . . .

ANATHALIE   She said the trials will come.

ALPHONSINE   Well, let them start. This is all par for the course.

ANATHALIE   I'm ready, Alphonsine, but something tells me he may grade more harshly than even Sister Evangelique—

FATHER TUYISHIME   And there they are. The fighter, Marie-Clare Mukangango. Name means "Woman." To her right Anathalie Mukamazimpaka—

FATHER FLAVIA   Mukamizima—whaaaa?

FATHER TUYISHIME   Mukamazimpaka--means "One who brings peace," and the first one, the genesis, Alphonsine Mumureke, "Leave her alone, she speaks the truth."

[*Looking at them is like staring directly at the sun and not being blinded.* FATHER FLAVIA *cannot break his gaze.*]

FATHER FLAVIA   A trinity. Gotta love God. Always works in threes.

FATHER TUYISHIME   That is what the villagers have begun to call them! They have been slaughtering goats daily for the girls. Please, come and have some.

FATHER FLAVIA   Would love.

[FATHER FLAVIA *walks past the schoolgirls, who part to make way for the white man.*]

[*Flirting.*]

THE GIRLS   Jesus. Hey, Jesus!

FATHER TUYISHIME   [*To the other girls in Kinyarwanda.*] *Ni kangaha ngomba kubabgira!* (How many times do I have to tell you!)

[*To the* TRINITY.]

Girls, please meet—

THE TRINITY   Father Flavia.

FATHER FLAVIA   Well, the wind certainly has wings here.

FATHER TUYISHIME   He's here to--

THE TRINITY   We know.

ALPHONSINE   *She* has told us.

FATHER FLAVIA   *She?* Father, can I speak with the girls, privately?

[*They look around to see everyone staring.*]

FATHER TUYISHIME   There are no walls here.

FATHER FLAVIA   I just think it would be better, if I got acquainted with the girls. A bit. By myself.

FATHER TUYISHIME   Surely, anything you need to ask can be—

ALPHONSINE   Father Tuyishime, it is fine.

[*Pause.*]

FATHER TUYISHIME   Fine, but please make it quick. The girls have Mass soon.

[**FATHER TUYISHIME** *haltingly walks away and joins* SISTER EVANGELIQUE *standing on the other side of the courtyard.*]

MARIE-CLARE   [*To* FLAVIA.] Please ask as many questions you want.

ANATHALIE   We can answer a million if need be. Anything to miss Ma—

ALPHONSINE   Anathalie!

FATHER FLAVIA   [*Surprised.*] Mmph. How splendid that I can understand you. Your French is magnifique.

MARIE-CLARE   [*In Kinyarwanda.*] *Icayawe cyumvikana nk' ingurube ibyara.* (Unfortunately, yours sounds like a pig giving birth.)

FATHER FLAVIA   What did she say?

ALPHONSINE   Only that we all should be thankful for your compliment.

FATHER FLAVIA   [*Mmmmhmmm.*] May I sit?

MARIE-CLARE   [*All smiles now.*] Well, what are you two waiting for? Make room for the man. Anathalie, Alphonsine.

[**MARIE-CLARE**, *forever the queen bee, swats at them to make room. She instantly turns into the cultural ambassador of the group.*]

MARIE-CLARE   We heard that you have come here to test us.

ANATHALIE   Marie-Clare, you really do not have any manners about yourself?

FATHER FLAVIA   You indeed do get right to the point.

MARIE-CLARE   Well, the day after tomorrow belongs to the fool. Mother Mary told us you were coming.

FATHER FLAVIA   Did *She?* And what else did *She* say?

[*The girls giggle amongst themselves.*]

MARIE-CLARE   [*Coy.*] Wouldn't you like to know. What questions can we answer for you?

[*Taking out his pad of paper.*]

FATHER FLAVIA   The Holy See requires that a visionary's spiritual knowledge be in compliance with Church doctrine.

[**ALPHONSINE** *looks to her counterparts to translate.*]

MARIE-CLARE   Alphonsine, what he means is that he wants to know if we are good little Catholic schoolgirls. Isn't that right, Father Flavia?

FATHER FLAVIA   Indeed.

[*He brings out his notebook.*]

FATHER FLAVIA   Where is Mary buried?

MARIE-CLARE   She was not buried. She was assumed, body and soul into heaven.

FATHER FLAVIA   Good. Anathalie, is God the Holy Spirit?

ANATHALIE   Yes, Father.

FATHER FLAVIA   The Son?

ANATHALIE   Yes.

FATHER FLAVIA   Is the Father the Son?

ANATHALIE   No, Father.

FATHER FLAVIA   Alphonsine. . . . Alphonsine.

ALPHONSINE   Yes. Yes . . . My answer is yes.

FATHER FLAVIA   But I haven't even asked the question yet?

MARIE-CLARE   [*Barking in Kinyarwanda.*] *Alphonsine gichuchu itonde.* (Alphonsine, you idiot. Get it together.)

ALPHONSINE   [*In Kinyarwanda.*] *Mbabarira. Mbabarira.* (Sorry. Sorry.)
[*In English.*]
What is the question?

FATHER FLAVIA   Are God, the Son, and the Holy Spirit one?
[*Pause.*]

ALPHONSINE   Nooooo.

MARIE-CLARE   [*In Kinyarwanda.*] *Alphonsine, igisubizo ni yego.* (Alphonsine, the answer is yes.)

ALPHONSINE [*In Kinyarwanda.*] *Iki? Uyu muzungu ari kun vanga.* (What? This white man is confusing me.)

MARIE-CLARE [*In Kinyarwanda.*] *Nibyo agomba gukora, ushaka kuba umu visioneri cyangwa?* (That is what he's supposed to do. Do you want to be a visionary or not?)

ALPHONSINE [*In Kinyarwanda.*] *Simbi shaka nkawe.* (I don't want it as bad as you do.)

ANATHALIE [*In Kinyarwanda.*] *Mwebi muziba nonaha!* (Shut up, both you, right now!)

[MARIE-CLARE *jeers towards* ANATHALIE. *She then sharply turns to* FATHER FLAVIA.]

MARIE-CLARE Knowing the answers to your little questions is not what makes us visionaries. It is She. We do not need your approval.

FATHER FLAVIA If you want to be a visionary, my approval is what you need most.

MARIE-CLARE These other girls might joke that you are Jesus, but you are not Him, so do no walk around as such.

FATHER FLAVIA Indeed that is very true, Marie. But I can't help but wonder why Mother Mary would pick young girls who do not know simple basic liturgy. Furthermore, why She would choose someone with such a nasty disposition. . . .

MARIE-CLARE Well, God works in mysterious ways.

ALPHONSINE Please give me another question. Let me answer another—

[FATHER FLAVIA *slaps his notebook closed.*]

FATHER FLAVIA No, no, no, we are done . . . for now. . . .

[FATHER FLAVIA *gets up just as the bell rings. The bell rings.* FATHER FLAVIA *walks away.*]

SISTER EVANGELIQUE Everyone, time to head to the chapel. Now.

ANATHALIE Why did you have to chase the *muzungu* away? Now we have to go to Mass.

MARIE-CLARE I wouldn't have had to, if Alphonsine didn't have the brain of a gecko.

ALPHONSINE Sorry, sorry . . .

ANATHALIE Oh well, if I fall asleep no one will know.

[*Indicating her glasses.*]

That's the great thing about these thick things, don't you think so, Alphonsine? Alphonsine . . .

[*But* ALPHONSINE *is oblivious, looking far into the distance as the winds begin to blow.*]

[*A warmth fills the space, like dinner rolls baking in an oven.*]

MARIE-CLARE   She's here. *Nyina wa Jambo—*

[*The Trinity are suddenly brought to their knees staring in the same direction as before. High above their heads.*]

[*A mad hush envelopes the air. All the other girls grow quiet and surround them.*]

GIRL #2   Look how they stare at the sun as if they are staring into darkness.

GIRL #3   Move over. I want to be closer.

[*They are steadfast and rapt, their unblinking eyes seared to a vision upward.* MARIE-CLARE *in trance mode is pitch perfect. They sing in melodic harmony.*]

THE TRINITY
[*In Kinyarwanda.*]

Mariya mubyeyi mwiza w' amahoro. Ni wow'abakristu bose bakunda
(Mary, Mother of Peace. It is you who all Christians cherish)

Tu rakwambaza mutoni w'imana du haki rw'iteka kuri Yezu
(We pray to you, mother of God, intercede for us before Jesus)

[*More and more girls place their rosary into* MARIE-CLARE's *hands until she has a mountain dangling from her arms.*]

[FATHER FLAVIA *slowly walks up to* ALPHONSINE *staring at the heavens.*]

FATHER TUYISHIME   Finally, these girls will be confirmed.

SISTER EVANGELIQUE   Enh-henh.

[FATHER FLAVIA *stands in front of* ALPHONSINE *for a beat.*]

[*He then pulls out a long needle from his robe. It catches the light of the sun.*]

FATHER TUYISHIME   Wait, what are you doing? What are you doing?

[FATHER FLAVIA *quickly plunges the needle into* ALPHONSINE's *eye!*]

FATHER TUYISHIME   Stop it!

[FATHER FLAVIA *pulls it out.* ALPHONSINE *just keeps looking up into the sky.* FATHER TUYISHIME *runs and grabs* FATHER FLAVIA.]

FATHER FLAVIA   Let go of me.

FATHER TUYISHIME   What do you think you're doing? You cannot hurt these girls.

FATHER FLAVIA   I am not hurting them, I am testing them.

FATHER TUYISHIME   You are torturing them!

FATHER FLAVIA   Sister Evangelique, I need your help. If Father Tuyishime won't help me, surely you will? Hold her still, please.

SISTER EVANGELIQUE   Certainly.

[SISTER EVANGELIQUE *doesn't even have to think about it. She's over there beside him in a hurry.*]

FATHER TUYISHIME   [*To* SISTER EVANGELIQUE.] Don't. Don't do this.

FATHER FLAVIA   Hold her tightly.

[FATHER TUYISHIME *grabs* SISTER EVANGELIQUE.]

FATHER TUYISHIME   Must you be a persecutor as well?

SISTER EVANGELIQUE   They must be outed. They must be outed at once.

[SISTER EVANGELIQUE *yanks herself from* FATHER TUYISHIME's *grip.* FATHER FLAVIA *is now in front of* ALPHONSINE, *posed to plunge the needle through her sternum. She takes her place behind* ALPHONSINE.]

FATHER TUYISHIME   You can plainly see that she is lost. Alphonsine is lost in the rapture—

FATHER FLAVIA   The Congregation for the Doctrine of the Faith demands this for consideration. They must pass the medical tests.

FATHER TUYISHIME   This is what the Vatican calls a medical test?

FATHER FLAVIA   This is only the beginning.

FATHER TUYISHIME   This is BARBARIC!

FATHER FLAVIA   Those who see Her, I mean really see Her can't feel a thing. You can twist their heads to the point where they are looking backwards, or try to rip their legs from their sockets and still, still they can't feel a—

[FATHER TUYISHIME *grabs the needle from* FATHER FLAVIA, *who has its point poised to plunge into her sternum.*]

FATHER TUYISHIME   GIVE ME THIS!

BISHOP GAHAMANYI   [*Interrupting.*] Father Tuyishime, let Father Flavia do what he has come here to do.

[*They look to see that the bishop has found his way up the hill. He looks over the proceedings with a somber look.*]

These girls have to prove themselves. Let them. Let them in the eyes of God.

[*Beat.* FATHER TUYISHIME *can do nothing.* FATHER FLAVIA *nods, then plunges the needle deep into* ALPHONSINE's *sternum, which trickles blood like the body of Christ on a cross. She should be in terrible pain. But she does not move.*]

[*She does not flinch, for she is swept up in the rapture. The girls continue to sing as blood runs a river into the brown ground.*]

Scene 3

[FATHER TUYISHIME's *office.*]

[*En media res—*]

BISHOP GAHAMANYI   But, Father Tuyishime—

FATHER TUYISHIME   That's enough for his evidence—

FATHER FLAVIA   I need more—

FATHER TUYISHIME   That is enough—

FATHER FLAVIA   The medical commission will need a full vetting of medical and psychological history. For all I know, these girls have a high tolerance for pain.

FATHER TUYISHIME   A high tolerance for pain? Contrary to popular belief we Africans are, too, made of blood and bone. Indeed if we stay in the sun too long, we faint.

FATHER FLAVIA   Hmph.

FATHER TUYISHIME   We bleed when you slice our dark flesh. And that is what you did. You sliced into dark innocent flesh. We are on a hill, but this is not Calvary, Father.

FATHER FLAVIA   Your Excellency, please, make him listen.

FATHER TUYISHIME   I am the head of this school. Kibeho College is *my* hill. My responsibility.

BISHOP GAHAMANYI   No one is claiming the contrary, Father Tuyishime—

FATHER TUYISHIME   You no longer have my permission to continue with these tests.

FATHER FLAVIA   I do not need your permission.

FATHER TUYISHIME   Oh, yes, you do.

BISHOP GAHAMANYI   Father Tuyi—

FATHER FLAVIA   I do not need your permission as I have been sent by the Pope, let me repeat, the *Pope*, to be the eyes and ears of the Church. The

Church to which you supposedly vowed a lifetime of obedience and supplication. Now, if you do not let me do my job, then I will leave. I will pack my bags and—

BISHOP GAHAMANYI   Father Flavia, please let us not get ahead of ourselves—

FATHER TUYISHIME   We have to protect these girls. We can not let blood pool in these halls just to prove a point.

BISHOP GAHAMANYI   But you do admit that it is a point that needs to be proven by any means necessary.

FATHER TUYISHIME   By any means necessary? Tsk!

BISHOP GAHAMANYI   We are embarking on a confirmation process. Apparitions require great evidence.

FATHER TUYISHIME   You saw how the girls bled with no feeling. You saw everything. That is enough.

FATHER FLAVIA   That is not enough.

FATHER TUYISHIME   Well, what about the beds?

[*FATHER FLAVIA snorts his disapproval.*]

FATHER FLAVIA   This guy.

FATHER TUYISHIME   You need to leave. You need to leave the premises at once.

BISHOP GAHAMANYI   Father Tuyishime—

FATHER TUYISHIME   I am the head of the school. I demand that he leaves.

FATHER FLAVIA   You have a weak stomach for faith, I see. If you have seen the things I've seen. Seen the lengths parishioners will go to manipulate the Church for their own benefit. Belief in the impossible trumps even the power of believing in God, which is in itself quite impossible. If what they are claiming is indeed happening here, if God has touched their hem, they will be cloaked in the sun, which on this earth, would make. Them. God. They have to earn that cloak, my dear boy. *That* power must be earned.

(*No, he didn't. Mmm, yes he did.*)

[*The Fathers have reached an impasse.*]

BISHOP GAHAMANYI   Sister Evangelique. . . . Sister Evangelique. . . .

[*Though she was listening in the corridor, she pretends that she was far away.*]

SISTER EVANGELIQUE   Yes, Your Excellency, sorry, I was down the hallway. Far, far down the hallway—

BISHOP GAHAMANYI Can you please show Father Flavia to the visitors' quarters? Father Flavia, perhaps you would like to take a nap before supper?

[BISHOP GAHAMANYI *says this more like a command than anything else.*]

FATHER FLAVIA Yes, I would like that very much, Your Excellency.

[FATHER FLAVIA *genuflects, then follows* SISTER EVANGELIQUE *out.* BISHOP GAHAMANYI *turns his attention back to* FATHER TUYISHIME.]

BISHOP GAHAMANYI When two elephants fight, it is the grass that suffers.

FATHER TUYISHIME Who is the head of this school?

BISHOP GAHAMANYI Who is, or who should be?

FATHER TUYISHIME Either.

BISHOP GAHAMANYI Sister Evangelique.

FATHER TUYISHIME Really?

BISHOP GAHAMANYI Yes, she should. But you, dear Father Tuyishime, were chosen for a reason. You are Tutsi, correct?

[*Uncomfortable beat.*]

FATHER TUYISHIME Yes. Yes, I am.

BISHOP GAHAMANYI As has every King of our land been Tutsi.

FATHER TUYISHIME We are a royal tribe.

BISHOP GAHAMANYI Correction, we are a *chosen* tribe.

FATHER TUYISHIME I would say by Belgian corroboration.

BISHOP GAHAMANYI Corroboration indeed, but support nonetheless. You are chosen. You, Father Tuyishime, have been chosen . . . by me.

FATHER TUYISHIME Am I but a figurehead?

BISHOP GAHAMANYI You are truly a figure, but being a head? I'm not so sure. There is always someone above the head, above the tree, and dare I say above the sky. You must remember butter cannot fight against the sun. I understand your concern. I truly do, but if we do not allow him the space and time for an investigation we will regret it. Horribly.

FATHER TUYISHIME And why is that?

[*Pause.*]

BISHOP GAHAMANYI Since this all started happening there have been seven youths who claim to have visions of the Virgin Mary.

FATHER TUYISHIME Seven?

BISHOP GAHAMANYI   Seven so-called visionaries. You remember that boy, Emmanuel, who had the sickness? Claimed that he was cured that day the sun danced? Well, now Emmanuel is saying he saw Jesus in a corn field. Can you believe? Jesus. In a corn field?

FATHER TUYISHIME   Who is to say this boy did not in fact see what he said he saw?

BISHOP GAHAMANYI   Jesus? In a corn field?

FATHER TUYISHIME   Seems like the perfect place—

BISHOP GAHAMANYI   Said he had hair of knotty ropes that fell around his shoulders like a lion. And that he was a tall, wiry man wrapped in a *kitenge*. A *kitenge*? Well, Emmanuel was soon stripped naked in the streets, his clothes shredded like banana leaves before a feast. They say he has gone mad staring at the sun looking for this Jesus. He and the others are all just crazy children who have caught the religious fever, but these girls, *these* girls could make the sun shine forever on this small little village no one knows about, cares about.

FATHER TUYISHIME   This is a change of heart from your previous position.

BISHOP GAHAMANYI   Do you know how many people visited Fatima after those three little children saw the Virgin Mary?

FATHER TUYISHIME   No, but—

BISHOP GAHAMANYI   A million a year. Can you imagine a million a year descending upon Kibeho? The villagers could sell rosaries, shirts, tapes of the girls' lovely messages—

FATHER TUYISHIME   Our faith cannot be commodified, Bishop.

BISHOP GAHAMANYI   I'm not talking about commodification, I'm talking about confirmation. These girls are our only chance, and we need to help them any way we can. They are already passing the medical tests, but the liturgical ones, EN-HENH . . .

FATHER TUYISHIME   Alphonsine gets nervous sometimes—

[BISHOP GAHAMANYI *leans in. Pulls out a paper from his robe and sets it on* FATHER TUYISHIME's *desk.*]

BISHOP GAHAMANYI   Well, sometimes even us chosen ones need some help. Make sure Alphonsine knows these answers backwards and forward. She must pass the next test—

FATHER TUYISHIME   If she gets everything right, he will be suspicious.

BISHOP GAHAMANYI   Say the Virgin Mary told her the answers.

FATHER TUYISHIME   That would be cheating.

BISHOP GAHAMANYI   It would be studying.

FATHER TUYISHIME   So you want me to lie?

BISHOP GAHAMANYI   I want you to help, goddamn it! I have seen Alphonsine's grades. You would think that a Tutsi woman would have passed on better smarts to her child. You'd think she was Hutu with how stupid—

FATHER TUYISHIME   [Barking.] BISHOP GAHAMANYI,

[*Softening.*]

Your Excellency,

[*Even softer.*]

please.

[*Beat.*]

BISHOP GAHAMANYI   This will be good for Kibeho. Good for the future of Rwanda.

FATHER TUYISHIME   The future of Rwanda?

BISHOP GAHAMANYI   If these girls are confirmed, and they will be confirmed, Father Tuyishime, with or without your help, they will make a name for Rwanda, a name for this village. In the future I see a shrine, taller than any tree with a steeple that scratches the belly of the clouds . . . we shall call it Our Lady of Kibeho, a church surrounded by millions, *millions* dancing with love.

FATHER TUYISHIME   Is that what you see, Bishop?

BISHOP GAHAMANYI   Why yes, my dear son, don't you?

[*Beat.*]

We descend from kings, Father. We are the chosen. . . . As it goes for these girls. These girls . . . are meant to be confirmed. Let them be.

FATHER TUYISHIME   I understand, Your Excellency.

BISHOP GAHAMANYI   I knew you would. Well, I have to get home in time for supper. She's making G-nut sauce tonight.

[BISHOP GAHAMANYI *starts wobbling out of the door.*]

FATHER TUYISHIME   Let me help you down the hill. I see, your knee's still paining you.

BISHOP GAHAMANYI   Oh, I'm fine. I've been moving up and down a bit better. The wife makes a tea-leaf bandage for it every night. Made the swelling go down.

FATHER TUYISHIME   Your Excellency, I've been meaning to ask . . . Your wife?

[*The Bishop winks at the Father.*]

BISHOP GAHAMANYI   Only in Rwanda can a bishop take a wife.

[*They do their man-mode crack-up thing, but then they are interrupted by the sound of a wave of voices cresting over the hill. Dusk is turning into night. Along the horizon gas lanterns light the way for a group of villagers. It seems like the space where the skies meet the earth are dotted with hundreds and hundreds making their way to the high point on the hill.*]

FATHER TUYISHIME   My God . . .

BISHOP GAHAMANYI   See, Father Tuyishime. Looks like the people have chosen them, too.

Scene 4

[*Nighttime.*]

[FATHER TUYISHIME's *office.*]

[FATHER TUYISHIME *and* ALPHONSINE *are studying by candlelight.*]

FATHER TUYISHIME   Is the Eucharist Christ's body and blood?

ALPHONSINE   No. It is not his flesh—

FATHER TUYISHIME   Alphonsine!

ALPHONSINE   The answer is yes?!?!!

FATHER TUYISHIME   Yesssss . . .

ALPHONSINE   But, Father, we are not cannibals.

FATHER TUYISHIME   Catholics are. The answer is yes.

ALPHONSINE   The wafer turns into the body of Christ? Eh-eh, I don't believe.

FATHER TUYISHIME   You must. "Unless you eat the flesh of the Son of man and drink his blood, you have no life in you; he who eats my flesh and drinks my blood has eternal life, and I will raise him up at the last day."

ALPHONSINE   Who makes such rules?

FATHER TUYISHIME   Jesus.

[ALPHONSINE *slams her hands on the desk.*]

ALPHONSINE   Sorry, Father, I am just not good at this—

FATHER TUYISHIME   Calm down—

ALPHONSINE   I am never going to get this right. I am going to look stupid in front of Father Flavia, yet again.

FATHER TUYISHIME   No, you won't. I'll make sure you won't.

ALPHONSINE   I mean, how am I supposed to know all of this? I haven't read the Bible. In its entirety. . . .

FATHER TUYISHIME   [*So disappointed.*] Oh, Alphonsine . . . neither have I. [*They both break into laughter.*]

ALPHONSINE   Father!

FATHER TUYISHIME   I know.

ALPHONSINE   How can you call yourself a priest?

FATHER TUYISHIME   I have the collar. Isn't that enough for you, Mademoiselle Alphonsine?

ALPHONSINE   To tell you the truth. I'm not that big of a fan of the Old Testament. The New Testament has a bit more . . . action.

FATHER TUYISHIME   What about the tale of Sodom and Gomorrah?

ALPHONSINE   Ah-ah

FATHER TUYISHIME   Samson and Delilah?

ALPHONSINE   Ah-ah.

FATHER TUYISHIME   Ruth?

ALPHONSINE   Boring.

FATHER TUYISHIME   Fine. What about Cain and Abel? That's one of my favorites. . . . "And the Lord said to Cain . . . 'What have you done? Your brother's blood cries out to Me from the ground! So now you are cursed from the ground that opened its mouth to receive your brother's blood you have shed.'"

ALPHONSINE   I don't like that story.

FATHER TUYISHIME   Why not?

ALPHONSINE   Cain just gets away with it.

FATHER TUYISHIME   No, he was left to wander the world without home. Without family. With an aching heart.

ALPHONSINE   No, he gets to walk around with his life. It's not fair. It is not fair.

FATHER TUYISHIME   [*More to himself.*] God never is.

[*Beat.*]

ALPHONSINE   Should we be doing this, Father? Should you be helping me?

FATHER TUYISHIME   No.

ALPHONSINE   You are too sweet to me. Too sweet.

[*She perches herself elegantly on his desk.* FATHER TUYISHIME *indicates her bandages.*]

FATHER TUYISHIME   Are you alright?

ALPHONSINE   Yes.

FATHER TUYISHIME   He did not have to do that to you girls.

ALPHONSINE   It is fine. We know that we are to be tested. She has prepared us for it all.

[FATHER TUYISHIME *nods.*]

FATHER TUYISHIME   Did Sister change your bandages?

ALPHONSINE   No, I did not need her to.

[FATHER TUYISHIME *knows what that means.*]

FATHER TUYISHIME   Here, let me look.

[*He touches* ALPHONSINE'*s sternum.*]

ALPHONSINE   Tsssssss!

FATHER TUYISHIME   Sorry, sorry. It must hurt.

ALPHONSINE   Yes.

[*He goes into his desk drawer and pulls out some more bandages. He pours some water from the jerrican into a bowl on his desk.*]

[*He slowly peels the bandage from her sternum. He wipes the coagulated blood away from her chest. It hurts. She flinches in pain.*]

FATHER TUYISHIME   Sorry. Sorry.

[*She lets him treat her.*]

ALPHONSINE   You still haven't prayed.

FATHER TUYISHIME   How do you know?

ALPHONSINE   She told me.

FATHER TUYISHIME   She tells you a lot.

ALPHONSINE   She only tells me what I need to know.

FATHER TUYISHIME   Sometimes that is all we need.

[*He has bandaged her. They stare into each other's faces.*]

ALPHONSINE   Father.

FATHER TUYISHIME   Yes, Alphonsine—

[ALPHONSINE *leans in to kiss the Father.* FATHER TUYISHIME *sits there still, his lips entertaining the possibility of her touch. But just as* ALPHONSINE *leans in he abruptly pushes her away.*]

FATHER TUYISHIME   Alphonsine!

[ALPHONSINE *reacts in pain.*]

Are you alright? Did I hurt you?

ALPHONSINE   I'm sorry, Father Tuyishime. I'm sorry.

FATHER TUYISHIME   What were you doing, Alphonsine?

ALPHONSINE   I do not know, Father.

FATHER TUYISHIME   [*Simultaneously.*] Why did you do that?

ALPHONSINE   [*Simultaneously.*] I do not know, Father. Please forgive me.

FATHER TUYISHIME   Alphonsine—

ALPHONSINE   I want it to stop. I thought that maybe if I did something wrong, then maybe, She would stop. She would stop talking to me. Stop making me feel . . . feel like . . . the way you make me feel sometimes.

FATHER TUYISHIME   And what is that, Alphonsine?

ALPHONSINE   Loved.

FATHER TUYISHIME   Alphonsine. I can't imagine the burden that you must have to bear right now. The emotions that you are dealing with. I do not envy you. But always remember that God does not give us more than we can bear.

ALPHONSINE   Yes, He does. You know He does.

FATHER TUYISHIME   I wish I could help you somehow. Carry your boulder for a day, Alphonsine. But you are stronger than me. You could carry two boulders if necessary. Some of us are made for this life.

ALPHONSINE   Why me?

FATHER TUYISHIME   Why not, you, Alphonsine?

ALPHONSINE   But I am so dumb, Father. I do not know all the answers.

FATHER TUYISHIME   But you know all the questions and you will spend a lifetime asking them.

ALPHONSINE   I do not want to be like you. I want my prayers to be answered.

FATHER TUYISHIME   Well, you must keep asking the questions. I stopped a long time ago.

Scene 5

[*The girls' dormitory.*]

[*The Trinity's three broken beds lay carefully in the corner, cracked and caving in on their sides. The other young girls have surrounded the beds with wildflowers gathered from the countryside, fruits for the Virgin Mary to eat. Candles stand scintillating around the shrine. Some girls tending to it. Others praying in front.*]

[*The entire space is abuzz with excitement. A radio balances on* GIRL #2's *lap.*]

GIRL #1   Do you have some varnish?

GIRL #3   Do you have some water and flour? I need to press my uniform.

GIRL #2   Get off of my bed. You are wrinkling my sheets.

GIRL #1   You are in bed anyway, why does it matter?

GIRL #4   I have some.

[GIRL #4 *passes over the nail polish.*]

GIRL #2   Pink will look good with your skin.

GIRL #1   It's not for me. It's for the Virgin Mary.

GIRL #4   *Ewe!* Give it back. If She's so beautiful she doesn't need my help.

GIRL #3   Shhh! *Ziba!* All of you.

RADIO RWANDA   Thousands are making the pilgrimage tomorrow to see the girls, dubbed the Trinity . . .

MARIE-CLARE   [*In faux shock.*] I will not be equated with God, the Son, and the Holy Spirit.

ANATHALIE   Oh, take your protest out there to the crowds.

MARIE-CLARE   [*Simultaneously.*] You woman! *Wa mugore weh!*

ALPHONSINE   [*Simultaneously.*] Shhhhh!

RADIO RWANDA   In preparation for the Feast of the Assumption, parish priests from southwestern Gikongoro to the capital of Kigali have been sharing tapes of the girls' messages.

[*The voice of* MARIE-CLARE *streams through the radio. It is sweeter. Distant. A different timbre.*]

MARIE-CLARE   [*In a trance.*] "In every garden there will be dry flowers, flowers that are slightly wilted, and flowers that are in full bloom. People are like flowers. Some are good, some are bad, but most are in the in between—

GIRL #1   Can you believe that's you?

[*The girls scream and clap as if the girls are playing a new song.*]

MARIE-CLARE   Shhhhhhh!! I can't hear myself.

[*In a trance.*]

--Wilting. Almost dying. And almost living. But each and every person, no matter where they are in the garden, is deserving of our water, our love.

ANATHALIE   Why does Marie-Clare always gets the good messages?

[*In a trance.*]

Some say it's a waste to water a dying flower. But, as we know, life can be resurrected and continue on. My beautiful little flowers. Our love is never wasted. Never wasted on kindness . . .

ALPHONSINE   It doesn't matter. The only thing that matters is that it is spreading. Spreading like She said it would.

GIRL #1   What time is She coming tomorrow?

ALPHONSINE   We will gather with the villagers and She will come when She wants.

ANATHALIE   [*Under her breath.*] No, tell them 10, so they will be there by noon.

ALPHONSINE   10. I meant 10 a.m. sharp! Do not be late or you will miss your blessing.

GIRL #4   Tomorrow is for the fool.

GIRL #1   Such a bitter nut.

GIRL #2   [*Shaking head.*] Shame, she is still the only one left.

GIRL #4   No, Sister Evangelique still has some sense about her. The only one sane in this place . . .

GIRL #1   So how do you explain the Virgin Mary speaking to Marie-Clare now? How do you explain?

GIRL #4   Maybe old gal wanted to stay around here in school because she couldn't find anyone to marry her.

THE GIRLS   Ehhhhh . . .

MARIE-CLARE   Watch the ground you tread upon, my dear girl.

GIRL #4   What, will you demand that the earth open up and swallow me whole?

[MARIE-CLARE *starts inching towards* GIRL #4.]

MARIE-CLARE   I am warning you.

GIRL #4   Or what? What, Marie-Clare? What will you do? Where is She? Where is your Virgin Mary now? Eh? Where was She when my mother was riddled with bullets? Her body left on the side of the road? Where was She? Where was her Son? Where was everybody? Everybody? Where were they? WHERE WERE THEY?

[*All the girls are stunned by* GIRL #4's *admission. Even the girl herself is stunned by what has fallen from her mouth. Silence descends upon the girls.*]

MARIE-CLARE   If you would just allow me to pray for you, maybe the pain will—

[MARIE-CLARE *reaches out to* GIRL #4, *who snatches her hand away.*]

GIRL #4   I do not need your prayer, Marie-Clare. Where is She?

[GIRL #4 *runs out of the dormitory in the tears.*]

ANATHALIE   She is right, Marie-Clare. You are not Jesus.

MARIE-CLARE   Believe me. I know that I am not a healer. If I were, I wouldn't be walking around looking like somebody's pincushion.

[*Indicating her bandages.*]

Poked and prodded and prodded and poked every time we have a vision? *Tsk.* But, there is pleasure in the pain of proving. . . .

[MARIE-CLARE *begins to climb into bed.*]

ANATHALIE   Oh, "bad girl, gone good." *Ziba.* . . .

MARIE-CLARE   Eh-eh, these months have transformed me. I have repented just like Mama Mary told me to do. She does not ask us to be perfect, but she does ask us to be devout. . . .

[ALPHONSINE *laughs, annoying* MARIE-CLARE.]

We are temples, Alphonsine. Soil the palace gates and She may refuse to come back.

ANATHALIE   What in the world are you talking about, Marie-Clare?

MARIE-CLARE   I have seen her. Sneaking, Alphonsine. You do not belong to Man. You belong to God.

ALPHONSINE   You have not seen me do anything.

MARIE-CLARE   Don't make me say—

[ALPHONSINE, *embarrassed by* MARIE-CLARE's *warning, jumps onto her like a lioness.*]

ALPHONSINE   You are lying!

[*This time* ALPHONSINE *is getting the better of her.*]

MARIE-CLARE   I am not! YOU KNOW I'M NOT!

ALPHONSINE   You are! YOU ARE!

[ANATHALIE *tries to break them apart.*]

ANATHALIE   We cannot let it come to this. Listen to me! Listen!

THE GIRLS   Sister Evangelique! Sister Evangelique!

ANATHALIE   Mama Mary will be so disappointed in us.

[SISTER EVANGELIQUE *runs in with a vengeance.*]

SISTER EVANGELIQUE   Do you all want to cry?

GIRL #1   Sister Evangelique, they are fighting. They are fighting again.

[ANATHALIE *cannot pull them apart.*]

ANATHALIE   Stop it, both of you! Stop it—

GIRL #1   Marie-Clare, calm down! Calm down!

GIRL #4   Sister Evangelique, do you want me to go get Father Tuyishime?

SISTER EVANGELIQUE   Yes, dear child—

[*Suddenly* ANATHALIE *sinks to her knees in convulsions.* ALPHONSINE *and* MARIE-CLARE *turn to the fallen* ANATHALIE. *She has been possessed by Our Lady. She has begun to speak in tongues.*]

On second thought, go get Father Flavia down the hall as well.

[*Vines start growing along the walls. Flowers start blooming out of the cracks and crevices of the dorm. . . .*]

GIRL #3   Oh my!

SISTER EVANGELIQUE   Wha-what-what is this--happening--here--what--is, my--my--goodness.

GIRL #1   She is watering us. Just like She said She would.

GIRL #2   Her little flowers.

GIRL #3   Look! Look!

[*All of the girls stare are in awe of the jungle growing inside of their dorm.*]

[GIRL #4 *re-enters with* FATHER TUYISHIME.]

GIRL #4   I found--BABAWE. . . .

[GIRL #4 *is taken by what is growing at her feet.*]

FATHER TUYISHIME   The girls are--goodness.

SISTER EVANGELIQUE   The room. The room smells like—

FATHER TUYISHIME   Jasmine and hugs.

GIRL #4 She is here. . . .

[*Girl #4, the last convert, falls on her face in supplication.* FATHER FLAVIA, *out of breath, comes into the door.*]

FATHER FLAVIA Do not be persuaded. This is possession. A sweet possession. . . .

[*He takes a step towards* ANATHALIE *with his tools poised to prod.* ANATHALIE *looks at him with enormous serenity. When she opens her mouth, perfect Italian flows out.*]

ANATHALIE (*Our Lady*) [*In perfect Italian.*] *Luis, ci incontriamo di nuovo.* (Luis, so we meet again.)

FATHER FLAVIA Where is that coming from?

ANATHALIE (*Our Lady*) [*In perfect Italian.*] *Qui. Luis! Proprio. Qui.* (Here. Luis! Right. Here.)

SISTER EVANGELIQUE What is she saying? Girl, what are you saying?

ANATHALIE (*Our Lady*) [*In perfect Italian.*] *Digli a quella sgualdrina di chiudersi la bocca. Ho avuto abbastanza dei suoi modi conniventi.* (Tell that wench to shut her mouth. I've about had enough of her conniving ways.)

FATHER FLAVIA [*In perfect Italian.*] *Madre Maria?* (Mother Mary?)

ANATHALIE (*Our Lady*) [*In perfect Italian.*] *Che? Tu non mi conosci? Non puoi credere che le mie parole cadono fuori dalla bocca di una ragazzina nera? Le sue labbra me vanno bene.* (What, you don't recognize me? You don't believe my words would fall out of the lips of a little black girl? Her lips suit me well.)

FATHER FLAVIA [*In perfect Italian.*] *Sono stordito, sono impietrito.* (I am stunned, I am stunned speechless.)

ANATHALIE (*Our Lady*) [*In perfect Italian.*] *Sì, ti vedo con la bocca spalancata. "Faccia di pesce" Luis. Ti ricordi quando ti chiamavano così alla scuola?* (Yes, I see you with your mouth standing agape. Fish-faced Luis. Remember that's what they used to call you in primary?)

FATHER FLAVIA [*In perfect Italian.*] *Come tu puòi--* (How do you--)

ANATHALIE (*Our Lady*) [*In perfect Italian.*] *Conosco tutt'i miei figli. Specialmente quelli che camminano nella fede con me. Mi piace dire "mio piccolo fiore."* (I know all about my children. Especially the ones that walk in faith with me. My little flowers, as I like to say.)

[FATHER FLAVIA'*s feet are consumed by flowers and vines.*]

FATHER FLAVIA [*In perfect Italian.*] *Ma perché qui? Perché Ruanda, Madre Maria?* (But why here? Why Rwanda, Mother Mary?)

ANATHALIE (*Our Lady*)   [*In perfect Italian.*] *Non ti sei lamentato quando ti ho volato in Brasile, ti dico che!* (You weren't complaining when I flew you to Brazil, I tell you that!)

FATHER FLAVIA   [*In perfect Italian.*] *Perdonami, perdonami.* (Forgive me. Forgive me.)

ANATHALIE (*Our Lady*)   [*In perfect Italian.*] *Luis, cio un messaggio molto più grande di Ruanda. È per il mondo intero. C'è una malattia nel cuore degli uomini. E anche nelle ragazzine. Lo conoscono bene. Anche tu lo conosci bene.* . . . (Luis, I have a message that is bigger than Rwanda. It is meant for the entire world. There is a sickness in the hearts of men. And these girls. They know it well. You know it well, too. . . .)

FATHER FLAVIA   [*In perfect Italian.*] *Ma che mi stai dicendo?* (What do you mean?)

ANATHALIE (*Our Lady*)   [*In perfect Italian.*] *Lo so cosa ti e successo, Luis. Perdona, Luis, non sei solo nella pancia della balena.* (I know what happened to you, Luis. Forgive him, Luis, you are not alone in the belly of the whale.)

[FATHER FLAVIA *falls to his knees with tears in his eyes. The others stand back and see that little room has become the most perfect garden.*]

ANATHALIE (*Our Lady*)   [*In perfect Italian.*] *Luis, ho bisogno di passare questo messaggio ai miei piccoli fiori. I miei piccoli fiori, io dico* . . . (Luis, I need you to pass along this message to my little flowers. My little flowers, I say . . .)

MARIE-CLARE   Beloved Mother Mary, whose heart suffered beyond bearing because of us, teach us to suffer with you and with love, and to accept all the suffering God deems it necessary to send our way. Let us suffer--

[MARIE-CLARE *during the ecstasy has fallen to her knees. She raises her rosary. It glows and changes colors.*]

Scene 6

[FATHER TUYISHIME'S *office.*]

[FATHER TUYISHIME *and* SISTER EVANGELIQUE *are staring at a visibly shaken* FATHER FLAVIA.]

FATHER TUYISHIME   Are you alright, Father Flavia?

FATHER FLAVIA   Are you? Do you have something to drink, Father?

FATHER TUYISHIME   Give him some water—

FATHER FLAVIA   Do you happen to have something . . . a wee bit stronger.

FATHER TUYISHIME   Urgwagwa.

FATHER FLAVIA   What is that?

FATHER TUYISHIME   Banana beer.

FATHER FLAVIA   I'll take it.

[FATHER TUYISHIME *takes a bottle out of his desk drawer. He unscrews it and* FATHER FLAVIA *takes a swig, then two, then three.*]

I have seen some rather complex hoaxes. Traveled all around the world. I have seen many, many things, Father, but this, this one is a striking, striking hoax!

FATHER TUYISHIME   Flowers grow fast in Rwanda, but not that fast, Father.

FATHER FLAVIA   Well, maybe it was mass hallucination. We wanted to see something there. We wanted to see--garden. We wanted it to be real.

[*More to himself.*]

Yes, it had to be a hallucination that we all saw.

FATHER TUYISHIME   Why can't you see the miracle that is staring you in the face!

FATHER FLAVIA   Because those girls have been primed.

FATHER TUYISHIME   Primed. Primed to do what?

FATHER FLAVIA   They know things that they are not supposed to know. Especially the Anathalie girl. She knew about . . . about . . .

SISTER EVANGELIQUE   What did she know?

[FATHER FLAVIA *takes another swig.*]

FATHER FLAVIA   Who taught them Italian?

SISTER EVANGELIQUE   The girls speak French and Kinyarwanda. That's it.

FATHER FLAVIA   So no one knows Italian? They've had absolutely, no access to the language?

SISTER EVANGELIQUE   If only the Italians would have colonized us instead of the Belgians.

FATHER TUYISHIME   What did Anathalie say to you? What did she say to you to make you so . . . so . . .

FATHER FLAVIA   The rosary. That Marie-Clare prayed. It's a special one. It originated in the Middle Ages by the Friar Servants of Mary, a sect based in England. It's called The Rosary of the Seven Sorrows.

FATHER TUYISHIME   Seven Sorrows? Never heard of it.

FATHER FLAVIA   Are you sure?

FATHER TUYISHIME   If you are insinuating that we taught these girls these things—

[FATHER FLAVIA *looks to* SISTER EVANGELIQUE.]

FATHER FLAVIA   I'm assuming you do not know either.

SISTER EVANGELIQUE   How I wish I did, so I could wipe that smirk off of your lips.

FATHER FLAVIA   Sorry. Sorry. I know. You couldn't have. There's no way the girls would have known it. It died out centuries ago.

FATHER TUYISHIME   So now do you believe?

FATHER FLAVIA   It doesn't matter if I believe, Father Tuyishime. They in the Vatican have to believe—

FATHER TUYISHIME   But do you believe?

FATHER FLAVIA   It's my job not to—

FATHER TUYISHIME   But do you believe?

[FATHER FLAVIA *looks at* FATHER TUYISHIME. *He will not answer this question, though his eyes say otherwise. . . .*]

FATHER FLAVIA   The girls say Our Lady has something to share tomorrow, during the Assumption. A secret to tell the villagers. If they are devout, if these girls are truly seeing Her, then they will know the true secrets of the Church only those She chooses can know.

FATHER TUYISHIME   And then they will be confirmed?

FATHER FLAVIA   Then they will be considered.

[FATHER FLAVIA *looks back at the photos on the desk.*]

FATHER TUYISHIME   Well, that's all we can ask for.

FATHER FLAVIA   Good night, Father.

[FATHER FLAVIA *looks at* FATHER TUYISHIME. *A beat of understanding passes between them.*]

[SISTER EVANGELIQUE *stands at the door with a flashlight in hand. He looks at her standing in the darkness. He walks slowly to the door. He turns back.*]

FATHER FLAVIA   Can I have the, uh—

[FATHER TUYISHIME *hands him the bottle of the banana beer.*]

SISTER EVANGELIQUE   I will walk you to your room. I know the darkness of these halls well.

[FATHER FLAVIA *nods a thanks and walks out before her.*]

Scene 7

[*Moments later.* Sister Evangelique *walks through the halls doing her usual patrolling.* Marie-Clare *comes out of the dormitory. She walks right up to* Sister Evangelique, *who does not acknowledge her presence.*]

Marie-Clare   Why are you still not speaking to me? After all that has happened?

[Sister Evangelique *begins to walk away.*]

Answer me.

Sister Evangelique   You must think you are hanging in the sky with the sweetest bananas if you think I am supposed to answer to you. Be careful, my dear Marie-Clare. All fruit must fall to the ground.

Marie-Clare   Sooner, if there is someone there to cut them down.

Sister Evangelique   [*Eyes welling at the admission.*] I could kill you. Kill you for being so blessed. By Her presence. By Her light. By Her . . . But now I know . . . I am not worthy of God's grace, for evil thoughts have taken over my mind like vicious vines, breaking through the bricks of my faith. I cannot see the goodness, the garden—

Marie-Clare   Tonight, you saw it tonight.

Sister Evangelique   Yes, I saw it with my eyes, but my heart? I am spiritually blind, my heart dumb. How could I have been so wrong? The same hands I lifted up in prayer are the same hands I used to nail you all to a cross. How easily in the name of God we are turned into monsters. Marie-Clare, can you forgive me? Can you all forgive me—

Marie-Clare   Of course—

Sister Evangelique   But will He? Can my God forgive me? Will He hear my wretched prayers?

Marie-Clare   Only if you ask for His mercy . . .

[Marie-Clare *goes to her knees and tries to bring* Sister Evangelique *down to her knees in prayer.* Sister Evangelique *pulls her hands back.*]

Sister Evangelique   No, I am not worthy. These hands are better for plucking the petals than tilling the soil. . . .

[*A door opens.* Anathalie *steps outside the dormitory with a candle.*]

Anathalie   Marie-Clare. Marie-Clare, are you out here?

Marie-Clare   Yes, Anathalie. I am. I was just going on a short call.

Anathalie   Long call seems more like it. . . . Come back to bed. We must rest; we have a big day tomorrow.

[Marie-Clare *softly walks away.*]

Sister Evangelique   At least I can rejoice that the Virgin Mary does not only favor the Tutsi. She has chosen another Hutu to spread her message. At least I can share in that victory.

[Marie-Clare *stops and turns back to* Sister Evangelique.]

Marie-Clare   She speaks to us all, Sister. Those who are Hutus, like you . . . and those who are Tutsi . . . like me.

[Sister Evangelique *stands stunned.*]

Sister Evangelique   You?

Marie-Clare   Good night. As you have said before, truth and the morning become light with time.

Scene 8

[*The sun pokes its head out from the bottom of the seventh hill. Climbing ever upwards to find its rightful place in the morning sky.*]

[*Thousands of villagers blow out their candles. The murmur is infectious.*]

[*A* Villager *has made a T-shirt with pictures of the girls' faces and is selling cassettes.*]

Villager 1   Trinity tapes. Get your Trinity tapes.

Villager 2   How much?

Villager 1   Two thousand francs, but if you buy two, I'll let you have them both for three thousand.

Villager 2   Give me three.

[Anathalie *stands on her tiptoes looking out into the crowd from the dormitory window.*]

Anathalie   They are too, too early.

Marie-Clare   You said 10.

Anathalie   And it is 7!

Alphonsine   I suppose they want to get a good seat.

Anathalie   I wonder if my papa is out there.

Alphonsine   I'm sure he wouldn't miss this for the world.

[Marie-Clare *swoops in and takes a comb out of her pocket and starts fluffing the girls' afros.*]

ANATHALIE   Ouch!

MARIE-CLARE   If you combed your hair more often it wouldn't hurt!

ALPHONSINE   [*Laughing.*] You two.

[*She fluffs up* ALPHONSINE's *afro, too.*]

MARIE-CLARE   There. We don't want them to think they are raising a group of jungle bunnies up here now, do we.

ANATHALIE   Who cares what they think?

MARIE-CLARE   Eh-eh! I do. Do you see all those cameras out there? You don't want to go down in history as the knappy-headed trinity now do you?

[MARIE-CLARE *looks over her sisters. She settles on* ALPHONSINE. *Beat.*]

MARIE-CLARE   Here, put these shoes on, Alphonsine.

ALPHONSINE   But they are yours.

MARIE-CLARE   Giving to your sister who has given you much is not giving but paying.

[ALPHONSINE *brings the pair of shoes to her chest. Her eyes well with tears.*]

ALPHONSINE   Thank you.

MARIE-CLARE   [*Snapping.*] They are meant to be worn on your feet, not your chest. Hurry, hurry. Finish getting ready. Today is a big day.

[*The courtyard. A reporter stands with a crew in front of the makeshift stage.*]

REPORTER   We are here at Kibeho College, where the three girls, known through the village as the Trinity, say that the Virgin Mary is set to visit this morning. As many as 20,000 have climbed the seven hills up to Kibeho to celebrate the Assumption of Mary.

[*To a villager.*]

And where have you come from?

VILLAGER 1   All the way from Nyamata in the east.

REPORTER   Do you believe?

VILLAGER 1   Ennnnnnnh. If She comes, I will believe. If She does not come, I think these young girls will have a problem on their hands.

VILLAGER 2 (FORMER BLIND MAN)   Well, I believe. I was here that day the sun danced.

REPORTER   You saw the sun dance?

VILLAGER 2 (FORMER BLIND MAN)   I had been blind to my wife for years. But that day Mama Mary ripped me from the darkness and brought me into the light. I saw Her face and then my wife's. . . . Thank God a woman is more than her breasts.

VILLAGER 3   Don't listen to him. He's out of his mind. Just like that little boy over there.

VILLAGER 1   Oh, shame. He was cured of the sickness! Now he has gone crazy.

[LITTLE EMMANUEL, *who had been healed from AIDS, stands disheveled, with barely any clothes on, and welts all over his body. His eyes roll into the back of his head as he repeats his mantra.*]

EMMANUEL   [*In Kinyarwanda.*] *Inzuzi ziza tembgamo amarago.* . . . *Inzuzi ziza tembgamo amarago.* . . . *Inzuzi ziza tembgamo amarago.* . . . (The rivers will run red with blood . . . the rivers will run red with blood. The rivers will run red with blood.)

VILLAGER 1   *Iyoooo, urababje disi.* (Look at him, poor thing.)

EMMANUEL   [*In Kinyarwanda.*] *Imperuka, turi kuba mu'mperuka.* (The end of days are near. They are near. . . .)

VILLAGER 3   Shut up, you fool! You know not what you say.

EMMANUEL   [*In Kinyarwanda.*] *Abahungu baza fata kungupu babo ababyeyl bazi' cya abana babo mzuzi oh inzuzi, imperuka turi kuba mumperuka.* (Brothers will rape their sisters. Mothers will kill their sons. The river. Oh the river. The end of days. We are living in the end of days. . . .)

[EMMANUEL *is pushed aside as the crowd surges to make way for--*]

VILLAGER 1   There is the father of the seer Anathalie!

[NKANGO, *who once wore garments holey from working in the fields, now wears a sorta new Chicago Bulls T-shirt and sneakers bought straight from the market.*]

REPORTER   [*Barking in Kinyarwanda to one of the pilgrims.*] *Igirayo. Igirayo!* (Get out of my way. Get out of my way!)

[*Back to her BBC lilt.*]

Is it true you are the one whose daughter has favor with the Virgin?

NKANGO   Indeed it is me.

REPORTER   How does it feel to know your daughter Anathalie is a visionary?

NKANGO   It is not a surprise to me. Something told me that when she went to Kibeho College she was destined for greatness. That is why her mother and I worked so hard in the fields. To give her the good Catholic education that has led to this opportunity. Like I said, no surprise. She is a good girl.

REPORTER   The passion fruit must not fall too far from the tree?

NKANGO   No-no-no, I'm but a small man. A small man.

[*Other villagers are taking pictures with* NKANGO.]

VILLAGER 1   Nkango! Nkango! Can you get Anathalie to bless my rosary?

NKANGO   Sure, sure, sure.

VILLAGER 2 (FORMER BLIND MAN)   Mine, too!

[*And* NKANGO *is swept away by the singing, surging crowd.*]

REPORTER   And there you have it. The village is awaiting. Waving their rosaries, praying, singing. You hear it? The crowd is calling for them. Waiting on the girls who call the Virgin Mary Nyina wa Jambo, Mother of the Word. Stay tuned. Reporting August 15, 1982, for the BBC.

[*Lights shift.*]

[*The dormitory. The noise of the crowd wafts in through the open windows.*]

[*Before the glistening shrine the girls stand in front of* FATHER FLAVIA *in prayer. Poised. Pressed. He does the sign over them.* FATHER FLAVIA *looks out of the window.*]

FATHER FLAVIA   You girls draw a bigger crowd than The Supremes.

THE TRINITY   Who?

FATHER FLAVIA   You don't know about The Supremes? My goodness, what are they teaching you at this school?

[FATHER TUYISHIME *joins them.*]

FATHER TUYISHIME   Are you all ready?

[*The girls stay put.*]

FATHER FLAVIA   I will be there--

FATHER TUYISHIME   Doing your usual torturing?

FATHER FLAVIA   No, Father, there is no need. But they at the Vatican will need me to record the proceedings. Make sure the young girls are in line with doctrine.

FATHER TUYISHIME   Very well. After you, ladies.

[*The threesome walk from the dormitory into the courtyard, where they are met with love and adoration from a crowd serenading them. Bowing down to them.*]

VILLAGER 1   Trinity tapes. Get your Trinity tapes!

VILLAGER 2 (FORMER BLIND MAN)   Let me touch your robes.

VILLAGER 1   Trinity Tapes. Get them now.

VILLAGER 3   Please pray for me.

NKANGO   Anathalie, your papa is here! Your mother is here, too, over there! Over there!

VILLAGER 1   Two for one. Get your Trinity tapes right here.

EMMANUEL   [In Kinyarwanda.] Imperuka, turi kuba imperuka. (The end of days is near. . . . The end of days is near. . . .)

[The girls pass EMMANUEL and he touches their clothing. A shiver passes through them. The sky begins to darken. . . .]

[The three girls go step by step, climbing the makeshift podium in the middle of the courtyard. They join BISHOP GAHAMANYI, who stands before the microphone in a blinding white robe.]

BISHOP GAHAMANYI   Parishioners, welcome! We know that you have come from near and far—some very far—

[Indicating FATHER FLAVIA.]

to be part of this momentous day. This is the first time we are celebrating our annual Assumption of Mary feast here on the school grounds. As many of you know, there have been rumblings of Our Lady's presence here in Kibeho. Well, I'd like to be the first to—

VILLAGER 2 (FORMER BLIND MAN)   Where are the visionaries?!!?

VILLAGER 3   [So friggin' embarrassed.] Sweetie, please!

VILLAGER 1   [In Kinyarwanda.] Nta muntu ushakakureba Bishop. (Nobody want to see Bishop.)

VILLAGER 2 (FORMER BLIND MAN)   I want to hear the visionaries.

BISHOP GAHAMANYI   Please, be patient. Our Lady I'm sure would be saddened by your blatant disrespect of—

VILLAGER 2 (FORMER BLIND MAN)   Give them the microphone!

VILLAGER 3   Sweetie, PLEASE!

VILLAGER 2 (FORMER BLIND MAN)   I want to hear the one from the radio. The one from the radio, I say!

BISHOP GAHAMANYI   Fine. Fine . . .

[In Kinyarwanda, under his breath.]

Aba baturage! (I tell you, these village folk!)

[Indicating MARIE-CLARE.]

Marie-Clare.

[BISHOP GAHAMANYI *shuffles off.* MARIE-CLARE *steps up to the microphone.*]

MARIE-CLARE   Thank you all for coming. We are happy that despite the heavy clouds you are here to listen, to receive Our Lady's message. It says a lot about your commitment to the teachings of the Church. About your commitment to the Word. The words of Nyina wa Jambo.

ANATHALIE   In order for you to hear them. We must prepare the grounds for her. She only comes when there is kindness.

ALPHONSINE   Join us. Join us in prayer. Lift your hands to the sky.

[*They look up and the sky has shifted from being sunlit to hanging heavy with darkened clouds.*]

[*The girls begin singing a hymn for Mother Mary and the ENTIRE village joins them. The voice of the girls merge into the villagers, creating a sweet fusion. The air vibrates as thousands of voices are lifted into the sky.*]

[*Under her breath.*]

ANATHALIE   Where is She?

MARIE-CLARE   [*Under her breath.*] She is coming. She is coming.

[FATHER FLAVIA *is near the platform recording. The sky is darkening more.*]

VILLAGER 1   We want Mother Mary! Where is Mother Mary?

MARIE-CLARE   Why is it taking Her so long?

VILLAGER 2 (FORMER BLIND MAN)   Look in the sky.

[*Clouds are swirling. Faster and faster.*]

ALPHONSINE   Keep singing. Everyone keep singing.

[*Finally there is a rustle on the wind. . . .*]

[*The sky changes. It now seems as though the brightest sun is in the sky, but there is rain. The heavens open up. . . . She is here. . . .*]

[*They stare above the crowd's heads. Lovingly transfixed . . .*]

[*The crowd surges forward, shaking the platform, but the girls stand unmoved.*]

[*But suddenly, a gush of tears start flowing from the girls' faces.*]

ANATHALIE   Mama Mary, why are you crying?

ALPHONSINE   She's crying.

MARIE-CLARE   Please don't cry.

ANATHALIE   Please.

ALPHONSINE   Mama Mary, what is it?

MARIE-CLARE   But you must.

ANATHALIE   You must.

ALPHONSINE   Show us.

ALPHONSINE and MARIE-CLARE   Show us!

ANATHALIE   Please show us why you are crying.

VILLAGER 1   What are the girls saying?

VILLAGER 2 (FORMER BLIND MAN)   Press closer. Closer.

[*The crowd surges, trying to hear what the Virgin Mary has to say.*]

[*But suddenly the girls start shaking, convulsing, quivering. Shaking.*]

[BISHOP GAHAMANYI, *who is sitting beside the other clergy, suddenly stands.*]

BISHOP GAHAMANYI   What, what is going on?

[*The girls begin to vomit.*]

BISHOP GAHAMANYI   What is She showing them? What is She--

THE TRINITY   The hills of Rwanda will run red with blood. The hills of Rwanda Will Run Red With Blood. THE HILLS OF RWANDA WILL RUN RED WITH BLOOD. THE HILLS OF RWANDA WILL RUN RED.

[*Lights shift. Time is stretched and echoey in this space.*]

[*In the black, there are moans and screams. The crackle of burning of fire. The electric slice of a machete being drug across asphalt. Echoes. A light pulses and we see shards of a vision. Visions of the unthinkable. The unseeable. The unvoiceable.* MARIE-CLARE *is running, running, running, running, red ribbons streaming from her feet. Until she is felled.*]

SISTER EVANGELIQUE   [*Voice-over.*] Marie-Clare, speak to me, sweet child.

NKANGO   [*Voice-over.*] Anathalie, please wake up. She is dead!

SISTER EVANGELIQUE   She is not dead. This has happened before. She can't be--

NKANGO   [*Voice-over.*] Then what is she? What has She done to my daughter?

ALPHONSINE   [*Voice-over.*] [*Whispering.*] The end of days are near.

MARIE-CLARE   [*Voice-over. Whispering.*] The end of days are here.

SISTER EVANGELIQUE   [*Voice-over.*] The fever. The fever is spreading to the other girls.

[*Lights shift.*]

Scene 9

[FATHER TUYISHIME's *office.*]

[MARIE-CLARE *sits staring into space, rocking herself.* ANATHALIE's *body lays across the desk.* ALPHONSINE *is in the same hot chair she started in at the beginning of the play.*]

SISTER EVANGELIQUE   Marie-Clare, speak to me!

[*Aloud but more to herself.*]

I have never seen her so still. So quiet.

FATHER TUYISHIME   She's been that way since the vision. Struck dumb.

SISTER EVANGELIQUE   Eh! She is struck dumb and all the girls are struck with a fever. There aren't enough buckets. It's a mess. I tell you, a mess. These poor girls.

FATHER TUYISHIME   Why did you all say those things, Alphonsine?

ALPHONSINE   She showed us. Showed us what they needed to see.

SISTER EVANGELIQUE   They were mumbling utter nonsense. Utter nonsense, I say.

[FATHER FLAVIA *stands over* ANATHALIE.]

FATHER FLAVIA   Ten hours and still no pulse.

SISTER EVANGELIQUE   No breath.

FATHER FLAVIA   What she saw must have frightened her.

FATHER TUYISHIME   Well, it absolutely frightened me.

BISHOP GAHAMANYI   The other girls seem to be suffering from some mass hysteria.

FATHER TUYISHIME   What about the other villagers?

BISHOP GAHAMANYI   They heard it. Heard it all.

FATHER TUYISHIME   Tell them the girls made it up.

FATHER FLAVIA   Made it up?

FATHER TUYISHIME   Yes, Father Flavia. They have made this nonsense up. Or they have gone crazy. Just like that little boy Emmanuel.

FATHER FLAVIA   But why would they lie?

[FATHER FLAVIA *plays the tape. The girls' disembodied voices fill the room.*]

THE TRINITY   "The hills of Rwanda will be littered with graves. The rivers will run red with the blood of babies. Sons will slaughter their fathers, husbands will rape their wives, babies will have their brains dashed out by mothers. We are in the end days. . . ."

FATHER TUYISHIME   Turn it off.

FATHER FLAVIA   Listen . . .

FATHER TUYISHIME   I said turn. It. Off.

TRINITY   [*Voice-over.*] "Sorrow will sink Rwanda and the passion fruit that grows from our trees will bleed with the blood of the fallen. The hills of Rwanda will run red blood. THE HILLS OF RWANDA WILL RUN RED WITH BLOOD. THE HILLS OF RWANDA WILL RUN RED WITH--"

[FATHER TUYISHIME *takes the radio and throws it against the wall. It smashes into a million little pieces.*]

FATHER TUYISHIME   This is not real. They made it up.

FATHER FLAVIA   We need you to settle yourself--

FATHER TUYISHIME   They have made it up.

[FATHER TUYISHIME *shakes the motionless* ANATHALIE.]

FATHER TUYISHIME   Tell them that you made, that you ALL made it up--

[BISHOP GAHAMANYI *tries to grab* FATHER TUYISHIME.]

FATHER TUYISHIME   Tell them that you are lying.

BISHOP GAHAMANYI   Father Tuyishime--

FATHER TUYISHIME   Please, Alphonsine.

FATHER FLAVIA   If you believed the initial visions why can't you believe this one?

[FATHER TUYISHIME *turns around to* FATHER FLAVIA.]

FATHER TUYISHIME   You SHUT UP! YOU SHUT UP!

BISHOP GAHAMANYI   Calm down, Father.

FATHER TUYISHIME   No, there is not evil here in Rwanda. THIS is where God goes on vacation. THIS is the land of love, of milk and honey. Where I was born--

FATHER FLAVIA   Calm down, Father--

FATHER TUYISHIME   Fix them! We have to fix them! Stop them for seeing these--these--these horrible things--

FATHER FLAVIA   This is something we can't fix, Father--

FATHER TUYISHIME   Cure them! Things need to go back to normal, before, before--

FATHER FLAVIA   Before what?

FATHER TUYISHIME   --They are disrupting the order of things. Making everyone afraid--

FATHER FLAVIA   They should be--

FATHER TUYISHIME   --Getting things out of order here--

FATHER FLAVIA   --But, Father--

FATHER TUYISHIME   --The world is buckling, buckling beneath my--

FATHER FLAVIA   But why wouldn't {**you?**} want to hear what Mother Mary has to say?

FATHER TUYISHIME   BECAUSE I DON'T WANT TO BELIEVE, FATHER! I DON'T WANT TO BELIEVE THIS!

[FATHER TUYISHIME *has covered his eyes like a little boy hiding from the boogeyman. . . .*]

FATHER TUYISHIME   The world. The world is wobbling.

[FATHER TUYISHIME *crouches down on the floor of his office torn asunder.*]

MARIE-CLARE   I saw a girl. Running down a hill. She had legs so long they could take her into tomorrow. She had feet so quick they could cut down blades of grass. She ran up those seven hills of Kibeho to the tippy top, to heaven's doorstep. She knocked hoping that God would let her in, but she could not knock fast enough. It came down. A slice. Her head rolled down those seven hills in search of a grave.

ALPHONSINE   It is a sign.

MARIE-CLARE   It was not a sign; it was me.

SISTER EVANGELIQUE   Where is God? Where is God here?

ALPHONSINE   God has nothing to do with this. Only man. She says we need to--

BISHOP GAHAMANYI   Enough of this nonsense. ENOUGH. It is only hell that they are talking about. And we all know that exists.

FATHER FLAVIA   But they are talking very specifically about a hell on Earth--

BISHOP GAHAMANYI   The world is always ending. Has been ending for years--

FATHER FLAVIA   Not like this. There is something dangerously specific about this vision, and if I were you I'd listen.

BISHOP GAHAMANYI   Is it so easy to believe visions of violence when they fall from African lips--

FATHER FLAVIA   No, Your Excellency, it is easy only when they fall from a visionary's lips, which these three girls undoubtedly are.

[*Beat.*]

FATHER TUYISHIME   So they will be confirmed?

FATHER FLAVIA   They have passed every test. Every physical test. Every mental test. Every psychological evaluation--everything they have said has been in line with doctrine. From the light to the dark. . . .

[FATHER FLAVIA *gathers the tape from the broken recorder.* FATHER FLAVIA's *silence says it all.*]

BISHOP GAHAMANYI   [*Switching gears one last time.*] But, Father Flavia, this is not the kind of vision that engenders the increase of faith.

FATHER FLAVIA   It is the kind of vision that produces fear, which, knowing the God I know, is a good thing.

[*All the bishop can do is watch as* FATHER FLAVIA *seals the tape in a velvet pouch and leaves.* BISHOP GAHAMANYI *stands there staring into the void.*]

FATHER TUYISHIME   Well, Your Excellency, you got what you wanted.

BISHOP GAHAMANYI   Indeed. God help us. God help us all.

Scene 10

[*Next day.*]

[FATHER FLAVIA *walks down the corridor with his bags packed. He passes the girls' dorm. Since the night, the lush garden has turned to a rotting brown. The flowers are wilted from their spring, and now leaves plunge from the vines, committing a million little suicides onto the floor.*]

[FATHER FLAVIA *puts his bags down and walks up to the death and destruction.*]

FATHER TUYISHIME   What will your final report be?

[FATHER FLAVIA *whirls around to find* FATHER TUYISHIME *has snuck up behind him.*]

FATHER FLAVIA   Whew! You scared me.

FATHER TUYISHIME   I said, "What will your final report be?"

FATHER FLAVIA   It sometimes takes a hundred years for the Church to approve apparitions.

FATHER TUYISHIME   Well, hopefully, we have that long.

FATHER FLAVIA   But it only took the Fatima visions thirteen years to be approved. So you never know. . . .

[*More to himself.*]

FATHER TUYISHIME   Thirteen years. . . .

FATHER FLAVIA   That particular "trinity" were mere children when they saw Her in 1917. Lucia, the eldest, said that Mother Mary had given her three secrets. The first secret was that there was a hell. The second was that World War II would come. But she held on to the third secret for twenty-three years until one day in 1944 at the height of the very war She predicted, Lucia wrote it down on one sheet of paper. That sheet traveled by train from Portugal to Rome and was locked away in a special vault in the Vatican. Every Pope who has read it has refused to let the secret be known to the public.

FATHER TUYISHIME   Do you know the secret?

FATHER FLAVIA   Of course, of course.

FATHER TUYISHIME   And did it come to fruition?

FATHER FLAVIA   Remember that letter for the Pope you gave me?

[**FATHER FLAVIA** *gives* **FATHER TUYISHIME** *the piece of paper he gave him earlier in the second act.*]

FATHER TUYISHIME   Alphonsine's?

[**FATHER TUYISHIME** *looks at the paper.*]

FATHER FLAVIA   She even makes a circle over her i's. Just like Lucia. . . .

[**FATHER FLAVIA** *returns* **ALPHONSINE**'s *letter gingerly into his inner breast pocket.*]

FATHER TUYISHIME   I am leaving my post here, Father Flavia. The Bishop says that my appointment was a mistake.

FATHER FLAVIA   Perhaps it was.

FATHER TUYISHIME   Perhaps. Where are you off to next?

FATHER FLAVIA   A place called Medjugorje.

FATHER TUYISHIME   Medju-ju-who-who-wha-wha?

FATHER FLAVIA   Father, you can say Mukamzimpaka but you can't say Medjugorje?

FATHER TUYISHIME   Never heard of it.

FATHER FLAVIA   It's in Yugoslavia.

FATHER TUYISHIME   Whew! Our Lady has been busy this year.

FATHER FLAVIA   Or maybe it is the Devil?

FATHER TUYISHIME   Well, He is often busy, as well.

FATHER FLAVIA   And you? Where are you going?

FATHER TUYISHIME   Where a lot of us are going--

FATHER FLAVIA   "Us"?

FATHER TUYISHIME   Us Tutsis. We are heading to Uganda. It is not where God goes on vacation. But it will have to do.

[FATHER FLAVIA *sadly understands.*]

FATHER FLAVIA   Good day, Father.

[FATHER FLAVIA *takes his bags and starts his way down the hill.*]

Scene 11

[FATHER TUYISHIME *walks back to his office to find* ALPHONSINE *waiting for him. The sounds of the girls singing can be heard outside.*]

FATHER TUYISHIME   You are not on punishment.

ALPHONSINE   I know.

FATHER TUYISHIME   Then what are you doing here so early in the morning?

ALPHONSINE   I thought I would help you clean.

[*She is sweeping the bits of broken radio into the trash bin.*]

It seems we made a mess of your office last night.

FATHER TUYISHIME   Indeed.

[*She begins to pick up books that are scattered on the floor. She tries to put one of the books away high on the shelf. She cannot reach it.*]

FATHER TUYISHIME   Here, let me help you.

[*He takes the book from* ALPHONSINE *and looks deeply into her smile. He breaks their gaze and looks down at the book. He blinks and opens it, inside is a worn rosary.*]

ALPHONSINE   Your mama's.

FATHER TUYISHIME   I've been looking for it.

ALPHONSINE   Well, now it is found. You prayed last night. She told me.

FATHER TUYISHIME   My goodness, She tells you everything.

ALPHONSINE   Well, She has become my best friend.

FATHER TUYISHIME   I'm still trying Her out.

ALPHONSINE   Please, keep praying. She needs you to do this.

FATHER TUYISHIME   I know.

ALPHONSINE And please, please stay. The girls don't want you to leave.

FATHER TUYISHIME The gods I think have decided for me, my dear Alphonsine.

ALPHONSINE Who will take your place?

FATHER TUYISHIME Sister Evangelique. She is being promoted from deputy head nun to head mistress of the school. It will soon be a place run by women. And, personally, I think that is good.

[ALPHONSINE's *eyes begin to well, but she nods her head in understanding.* FATHER TUYISHIME *brings a hand to her face and begins to wipe her tears away.*]

[*Suddenly,* ANATHALIE *shows up at the door. The two jump apart.*]

ANATHALIE Come on, Alphonsine, They're singing the new song! Marie-Clare with her horrible voice is absolutely ruining it.

ALPHONSINE I'll be there in a minute--

[ANATHALIE *runs off.*]

FATHER TUYISHIME You should go now. Join the other girls.

[*Beat.*]

ALPHONSINE Good day, Father Tuyishime. "One who we are thankful for."

FATHER TUYISHIME Good day, Alphonsine Mumereke. "Leave her alone, she speaks the truth."

[*She smiles, bringing light into that tiny office. And then she leaves him.*]

[FATHER TUYISHIME *goes and stands at the doorway of his office.*]

[*They are singing a new song, "Our Lady of Sorrows."*]

[FATHER TUYISHIME *looks out across his country, his land, his people, his heaven on earth, the land of a thousand hills, the land of Rwanda, before.*]

[*Blackout.*]

End of Play

WHEN JANUARY FEELS LIKE SUMMER

by

Cori Thomas

For Chuck Patterson

Production History

World premiere by City Theatre Company Pittsburgh, PA
Directed by Chuck Patterson

Cast

DEVAUN: Joshua Elijah Reese
JERON: Carter Redwood
NIRMALA: Gita Reddy
ISHAN/INDIRA: Debargo Sanyal
JOE: John Marshall Jones

Creative Team

Set: Anne Mundell
Lights: Allen Hahn
Sound: Rob Kaplowitz
Costumes: Ange Nesco
Artistic Director: Tracy Brigden
Dramaturg: Carlyn Aquiline
Opening night March 26, 2010
Closed April 11, 2010

New York Premiere May 28–June 24, 2014
Co-Production Ensemble Studio Theatre and Page 73 at Ensemble Studio
    Theatre
New York, NY
Directed by Daniella Topol

Cast

DEVAUN: Maurice Williams
JERON: J. Mallory McCree
NIRMALA: Mahira Kakkar
ISHAN/INDIRA: Debargo Sanyal
JOE: Dion Graham

Creative Team

Set: Jason Simms
Lights: Austin Smith

Sound: Shane Rettig
Costumes: Sydney Maresca
Artistic Directors:
Ensemble Studio Theatre: William Carden, Artistic Director
Page 73: Asher Richelli and Liz Jones, Co-Artistic Directors
Dramaturg: Michael Walkup

Honors

Edgerton Foundation New Play Award 2010
American Theatre Critics Osborn Award Best New Play 2011

This play was developed with the assistance of the Sundance Institute Theatre
Program and City Theatre's Momentum New Play Festival

Cori Thomas: *When January Feels Like Summer* (2014 Ensemble Studio Theatre/
Page 73/Women's Project Theater NYC, World Premiere—City Theatre Co.,
Pittsburgh); *Pa's Hat* (Pillsbury House Theatre, MN); *My Secret Language of
Wishes* (Mixed Blood, MN); *Akosua Means Sunday; The Princess, the Breast,
and the Lizard; The Unusual Love Life of Bedbugs and Other Creatures; Waking
Up; His Daddy; our lives, our fortunes, and our sacred honor.* Plays developed
and produced at Sundance Theatre Lab, Goodman Theatre, City Theatre Co.,
Page 73, Women's Project, Playwrights Horizons, Lark Play Development
Center, The Ensemble Studio Theatre, Going to the River, Pillsbury House
Theatre, Mixed Blood Theatre, Playwrights Realm, New Georges, The New
Black Fest, Queens Theatre in the Park. Commissions: South Coast Rep, Sloan
Foundation/EST, NYSCA, EST, Page 73, Pillsbury House Theatre. Macdowell
Fellow, Jerome Foundation, American Theatre Critics Association Osborn
Award (*When January Feels Like Summer*); Theodore Ward Prize (My Secret
Language of Wishes), 2nd Place Theodore Ward Prize (*our lives, our fortunes,
and our sacred honor.*)

Production Notes

A statue of Ganesha should be visible throughout the play. Preferably it
should not be an upstaging type thing. A small house-sized statuette placed
somewhere in Nirmala's apartment is fine. It should be noticed at the very
beginning when she touches it and then sort of fade into the woodwork until
the moment when his presence becomes important. It is, however, important
to me that he remain somewhat visible throughout.

Prasad should never be seen. We should hear the hospital sounds, but he
can be placed in the audience or in the wings.

The last scene takes place on a subway platform. Hopefully the stage can be made to look like one as best possible

Text Notes

Didi is an affectionate Hindu term for sister.

Lorrance is pronounced with French accent "Lorons."

ACT I

Scene 1

[*In the dark, we hear the sounds of a subway train approaching and the doors opening. Lights up on a subway car,* ISHAN, *dressed in business suit and tie and carrying a briefcase, exits as* DEVAUN, *age twenty, and* JERON, *age nineteen, enter just as doors are about to close. Both are dressed in light jackets more suited to fall or spring weather. They speak to each other in a loud and animated manner without any consideration for fellow train passengers.* JOE, *an African American man, is sitting reading a paper (or not). He is dressed in a light windbreaker or his sanitation worker's uniform. He has an umbrella with him. From time to time as the boys get very loud, they may bump into him. He looks up at them without really seeing them. He is irritated by them.*]

CONDUCTOR   Stand clear of the closing doors, please.

[DEVAUN *is testing ring tones on his cell phone,* JERON *listens.*]

DEVAUN   Whatchu think about this one?

[*He tries another one.*]

JERON   Naw, man, you got to get somethin' Kanye or somethin'. Those programmable tunes sound wack.

DEVAUN   You know Shirleethia?

JERON   Who?

DEVAUN   Shirleethia.

JERON   I don't know her.

DEVAUN   She work at the Ocean Deli on the corner.

JERON   What corner?

DEVAUN   My corner.

JERON   Beside them subway steps?

DEVAUN   Yeah.

JERON   Why you call it Ocean?

DEVAUN   That's its name.

JERON   It ain't called no Ocean. It's called Oscar, man. Oscar Deli. Why you call it Ocean?

DEVAUN   You sho?

JERON   People name their stores for somethin' and shit. Like, for example, they wives or they daughters or theyselves. That place ain't by no ocean, so why he gon go and call it ocean. His name is Oscar, that's why he named it that way.

DEVAUN   Oh.

JERON   You talking about that place Kareem hang out selling Newports? By the steps to the subway?

DEVAUN   Man, all this time I been callin' it Ocean. It look like Ocean on the sign.

JERON   O-S-C-A-R don't look like no Ocean to me. Can't you read?

[JOE *nods off slightly.*]

DEVAUN   Yeh, yeh, I can read, I just thought it say Ocean.

JERON   Belee me, you ain't gon find no good tunes in that phone. You gotta get a download.

CONDUCTOR   Stand clear of the closing doors, please.

DEVAUN   Yeh, yeh.

JERON   It got a camera and radio?

DEVAUN   Yeh, I think so.

[DEVAUN *hands phone to* JERON, *who begins to check it.*]

JERON   You better figure out how to use this shit.

[JERON *snaps a photo of* JOE *sleeping.*]

JERON   Instagram hashtag sleeping on the train.

[*They laugh.*]

DEVAUN   Yeh. Shirleethia got all them ring tunes. She say she know somebody can do a download and shit.

JERON   I don't know who she is.

DEVAUN   She the one at the Ocean, I mean Oscar Deli.

JERON   Light skin girl, nice rump?

DEVAUN   Yeh, she nice. She real nice.

JERON   I know her, yeh, she nice 'cept for that tooth, man.

DEVAUN Yeh, man, she need to do somethin' bout that tooth.

JERON [*Laughing.*] That shit ain't funny.

DEVAUN She look real nice if she keep her mouth closed.

JERON The minute she open her mouth, Whoa. Stand back!

[*Making sign of the cross.*]

Tooth stick straight out, man. Straight out!

DEVAUN I would get with her 'cept for that tooth. How you gon kiss someone got a tooth stick out like that.

JERON You ain't. What she need to do is go get it fix up. Or get a false tooth or something.

DEVAUN Yeh. She ain't never gon find no man. She could get to be old and unhappiful and what have you. . . .

JERON You gon tell her?

DEVAUN I ain't gon tell her nothin'. I ain't that interested. 'cept for her behind. Girl gotta rump. You gotta hand it to her. Girly gotta rump on her. And she wear them tight jeans so you can see all her curves, and she got a real helpful nature, but then she turn and smile, make me wanna say "Yo, keep yo tooth to yoself. Damn!"

[*They laugh.* JOE *gets up and leaves train.*]

CONDUCTOR Stand clear of the closing doors, please!

JERON You silly. What time you get off tonight?

DEVAUN Seven.

JERON Yeh, me too. Yo, they pay overtime at your Burger King?

DEVAUN Yeh. But I ain't never worked no overtime hours. People say they don't like to pay overtime 'cept it's necessary.

JERON But it's somethin', man, if they got it. We ain't no slaves.

DEVAUN Damn! No. Yeh. You right about that.

JERON Shit! If you work too much or on a holiday they supposed to go overboard with it

DEVAUN Yo, they give it out at your King?

JERON Yeh, but ain't nobody never get it there either. I want to test that shit to see if it's real. I'm trying to figure out how to slide that compensation to myself. Time and a half, man. Time and a half.

[*Lights crossfade to . . .*]

Scene 2

[NIRMALA, *in her convenience store, talking to her brother.* ISHAN *is wearing the same suit we saw in the first scene.* NIRMALA *is wearing a coat. They stand at the counter.*]

NIRMALA   I'm not killing my husband for you, Ishan.

ISHAN   But he's dead already.

NIRMALA   If he was supposed to be dead, he would be dead.

ISHAN   Things would be so much easier.

NIRMALA   I said no. There's plenty of change in the register.

ISHAN   But I need your support.

NIRMALA   What would the people at your job think?

ISHAN   I don't care what they think. If you would just look at the facts, you'd see . . .

NIRMALA   You should look at the facts. How would you be able to help me with the bills without that job? Because I'm not helping you. They'll laugh at you. They'll fire you.

ISHAN   I don't want to think about that stupid job. If you won't take advantage of Prasad's million dollar policy, *a million dollars.* Fine! I've saved some money, and I'll just run up credit card debt!

NIRMALA   Americans are always trying to change everything, their nose, their breasts, everything. You're not an American. Why can't you just continue as you have . . . because to change into a woman . . . you can't go back, you would never be able to go back.

ISHAN   If you don't support me, I'll have to find a way to pay for it by myself.

NIRMALA   And at your age. You're a grown man. Twenty-eight, almost forty. You want to start anew at this age?

ISHAN   Prasad's never going to wake up again.

NIRMALA   You don't know that.

ISHAN   I do.

NIRMALA   Aren't you ashamed? To ask me to do this?

ISHAN   It's what he himself would want.

NIRMALA   How do you know that?

ISHAN   I wouldn't want a machine breathing for me. No one would.

[*Beat.*]

The new year has just begun. I have decided to start it on the right foot. . . . I want us to jump into this new year together, Didi. Think about it. You and I with new beginnings to look forward to and resolutions to keep.

[*Beat.*]

If there was any hope for Prasad . . . I wouldn't ask, you know that.

NIRMALA   If something were to go wrong with this . . . gender reassignment surgery . . . thing, I'd be all alone. Alone in this place by myself.

[*Beat.*]

Do you understand what you have to do here today?

ISHAN   You could try to meet someone new.

NIRMALA   Ishan, please pay attention to me, I'm ready to leave now. They said the bread would come today or tomorrow morning. I don't think it will still come today, because it usually comes at half past eleven, and it's one o'clock now. But just in case, the form is there. . . .

ISHAN   He's just being kept alive.

NIRMALA   Even still, he's alive. If they bring the bread, ask them to please take it downstairs.

ISHAN   All of that life insurance could help you too.

NIRMALA   He's still breathing.

ISHAN   A machine is breathing for him. You just have to ask them to shut it off.

NIRMALA   When the batteries come, count them first. Once you have signed the invoice, I can't complain, and he tried to trick me last month, twenty-five packages were missing. So please, please count them.

ISHAN   I'll count them.

[NIRMALA *picks up a tote bag and drapes a sweater over her arm. SHE goes over to a Lord Ganesha statue and has a small moment of prayer touching her forehead and then his trunk.*]

NIRMALA   [*Long beat.*] Don't tell me what to do, you don't know what I feel.

ISHAN   You don't know how I feel either, so don't you tell me what to do.

[*Beat.*]

NIRMALA   I've got to go and then come back . . . to make dinner . . . for you.

[NIRMALA *exits.* ISHAN *gets his briefcase, he opens it and takes a travel toiletry case out. HE opens it and takes out a small make-up mirror. He sits it on the counter by the register.*]

ISHAN   Good-bye, Ishan.

[*He takes out a lipstick, opens it, and holds it up.*]

Oh my God!

[*He begins to apply the lipstick with trembling hands. He looks at himself in the mirror.*]

This . . . is who you are now. . . .

[*Long emotional beat.*]

Hello, Indira. Hello.

[*Lights crossfade to . . .*]

Scene 3

[DEVAUN *and* JERON *enter a train.*]

CONDUCTOR   Stand clear of the closing doors, please.

DEVAUN   [*Lowering his voice slightly and looking around to see he cannot be heard.*]

Yo, Jeron, yo yo, you know that dude Lorrance?

JERON   Who?

DEVAUN   Lorrance, man, you know Lorrance, tall skinny brotha. He got his hair comb back. Look like he got a relaxer. Look like one of them lollipops.

JERON   No, man, auno know who that is? Whachu mean by he look like a lollipop?

DEVAUN   Them pops they sell for ten cents at the Bodega La Sala?

JERON   What? Whachu talkin' bout, fool?

DEVAUN   Not the round ones, those is five cent, these is long and twisted around, maybe two inches long. Ten cent. They come in all the flavors, in stripes, look like they going down around to the stick. It can almost seem like they twirlin'.

JERON   Yeh, yeh, yeh, hold up, you talkin' bout a tall dude always got a bow tie on. He got a long skinny head with greasy hair.

DEVAUN   That's Lorrance, man.

JERON   I know who you mean now, yeh, yeh, yeh.

DEVAUN   Lorrance.

JERON   He wear them purple suits and pointed shoes look like they hurt.

DEVAUN   Yeh, yeh, that's him. I think he gay.

JERON For his sake, I hope so. Dressed the way that he is? And he got them big white womanly sunglasses with the diamond initials in the corner.

DEVAUN Well, he got the nerve to put his hand on my shoulder, then talkin' bout,

[*Imitating Lorrance.*]

"Come with me, I got something 'special' to show you."

JERON He say that?

[*He cracks up.*]

Don't make me laugh, Devaun. He ain't say that. Tell me he ain't say that to you.

DEVAUN You got my word. I swear it on the Bible. I swear it on two Bibles. I was just mindin' my own business tryin' to find the coldest Pepsi, 'cause, you know, you got to reach way in the back to get the cold ones, and dude step right behind me with his hand, got his glasses on too, touch my shoulder and say in a low quiet voice, "Come with me, I got something 'special' to show you." He say the 'special' just like that, 'special'! Dude gotta nerve to try and homosex me right out in the public eye and what have you?

JERON So then what did you say to that fool?

DEVAUN I turn to him and I say, "Lorrance, you better take yo skank hand off me." He take his hand back quick. Like this.

[*Shows him.*]

Like he touch something hot. Then his mouth drop open, like this.

[*Shows him.*]

Then I bump him hard and said, "You betta fuckin' stay the fuck away from me, you fuckin' fuckhead. I will fuck you the fuck up, if you don't fuck the fuck off, fuckhead!"

JERON Damn! So then what did he say?

DEVAUN He didn't say nothin'. Just look at me with his eyes and mouth

[*Shows him.*]

Like this.

JERON You ain't serious.

DEVAUN I'm serial, man. Only reason I didn't kill that fool is he go to the same church as my moms.

JERON Yeh, yeh, I feel you. But wait, wait, hold up, suppose the dude, Lorrance, suppose he was just trying to Christianize you. He religious. I know you seen him singing them hymns in the street on Sundays, loud and all outta tune and shit. Yo, that shit hurt your ears.

DEVAUN   Yeh, I seen and heard him. But, Jeron, belee me, that ain't it.

[NIRMALA *enters the train. She looks around for a place to sit and sits between the boys. They continue their conversation across her. She closes her eyes to try and escape them.*]

CONDUCTOR   Stand clear of the closing doors, please.

DEVAUN   Why he gon go and pick me? Everyone, man, everyone know I got to get with my woman every day, sometimes two or three times a day even.

JERON   Two or three times a day, Devaun, I know you exaggeratin'.

DEVAUN   Man, I go see Lakwanda, and if she not there or she busy, I get wit Doreen. Yeh you seen Doreen since she lost that weight? She look sweet, man, real sweet.

JERON   Yeh, she look nice. She look real nice, Jamal say he gon get wit her.

DEVAUN   He better stay away from her. She ain't no free agent.

JERON   Yo, yo, yo, you can't be greedy, Devaun, keepin' them two or three women outta circulation just for your own convenience. You got all them women hooked up witchu. How you do that? You should be spreadin' that shit around equanimibly, man.

[NIRMALA *suddenly moans and closes her eyes, the two guys look at her.*]

Yo! You aiight, miss?

[NIRMALA *opens her eyes and notices them staring intently at her.*]

DEVAUN   You aiight?

NIRMALA   Oh, yes, thank you, thank you. Sorry. Sorry.

[*The two boys check her to see that's true. She smiles politely and nods.*]

DEVAUN   [*Lowering his voice.*] Jeron, man, this Lorrance thing has mess me up. I keep thinking about it. Dude had the nerve to try to propose his shit to me while I was in the innocental act of getting my Pepsi. I, a man, he, a man too. My cousin gay and we expect his ass and respectfullin' him how he is. But he don't just go and start feelin' on people less he know first they be the same way. That tell you something important about this.

JERON   I'm tryin' to comprehend the magnitude of the situation. You sho that's all the dude said?

DEVAUN   He had a strange look in his eye, Lorrance. Made the blood in my heart curdle up. This feel like it almost go beyond homosexin'. It's almost like

I can still feel his hand.

Jeron This sound fucked up. Suppose he stop just touchin' people on the shoulder and start layin' in wait to pounce and infest himself on women and children. Man, this here sound like some incredulous shit we dealin' with.

Devaun Wait a minute, Jeron, hold up, he ain't gon be messing with women if he gay.

Jeron I hope he don't come trying to touch on me. Damn! Dude might have STDs, Chlamydia, HIV! All them initials and shit.

Devaun Damn, I ain't even thought about that. Damn! But I think the women is safe.

Jeron Well, boys and men ain't safe. How about they sorry ass?

Conductor Stand clear of the closing doors, please.

Devaun I ain't sleep good last night, Jeron. I don't know what to do.

Jeron What you need to do is speak directly and explicitly to the dude and warn him he playin' with hot fire. You got to tell him to never put his hand on no one no more.

[*Getting loud.*]

Not just you, nobody in the world. Tell him, "This is the United States of America, and people not supposed to do that shit here."

Devaun What's talking gonna do, man? He touched me in the sto. In the sto.

Jeron Well, if he is conducting his homosexual bizness with people in the street, you gotta go warn people about that shit. It's your duty, man. You gotta set the example. 'Cause like you say, innocent children is walking around here. They's easy prey, man. Suppose he try somethin' with one a them next? That's on you. You need to start warnin' these people's ass around here.

Devaun How?

Jeron Auno, maybe we can make some signs to hang in stores so people will know who he is and his mission will fail.

Devaun When?

Jeron Tomorrow. After we get off from work.

Conductor Stand clear of the closing doors, please.

[*Train doors open.* Nirmala, Jeron, *and* Devaun *get off the train. Lights cross as . . .*]

Scene 4

[*At the store.* ISHAN *has applied lipstick and eyeliner. He is still wearing the same casual male clothes he had on before. He is lazily reading a fashion magazine like* Vogue *or some such. The door may jingle as it opens.* JOE, *wearing his sanitation-worker uniform, walks in, the letters J. Patterson are embroidered above the pocket. He does a double take when he sees* ISHAN.]

ISHAN   May I help you?

JOE   Hey. So, where's the . . . lady who's always here?

ISHAN   I'm a lady.

[JOE *looks carefully at* ISHAN *and shrugs.*]

JOE   If you say so.

[*Beat.*]

I mean the one who's . . . who owns . . .

ISHAN   That is my sister, Nirmala.

JOE   How do you say her name again? She told me but I can't . . . and I don't want to keep asking.

ISHAN   Nir, like nirvana, then mala, like whatever.

JOE   Nir-mala. Nir-mala. Okay. You say she's your sister?

ISHAN   Yes, I'm watching the store for her. I quit my job. Accounting. Boring. And I'm going to be working here with her full-time until I get my own business started. My name is . . . Ish . . . Indira, that means bestower of wealth. And you are?

JOE   Joe.

ISHAN   Welcome, Joe. It's a pleasure to meet you. It's my intention to bestow wealth on myself and my didi, my sister.

JOE   You could slide some of it my way too.

ISHAN   I like that attitude. It tells me you have confidence in me. Bless you, Joe. You're the first person to see the real me. It's not the first time of course, but it's the first time I'm . . .

JOE   What?

ISHAN   I'm openly letting the world see me as I really am, in an uncontrolled atmosphere. My therapist told me I have to start. . . . I told Didi but I don't know if she realizes that when she comes home later . . . !

[*Assumes a pose.*]

Joe Huh. Well, congratulations.

Ishan Thank you, Joe. This is such a good omen. You've filled my heart with hope.

Joe I have?

Ishan I just decided to go for it . . . and then you walked in, and just accepted me. You did, didn't you?

Joe [*Beat.*] Look, I told her, your sister? Yesterday, I told her I'd help her haul some crates she was trying to put outside. You can't just put those out on just any old day. She knew, but she had forgotten. I want to put it out so we can pick it up in the morning.

Ishan I don't understand.

Joe I want to pick up her garbage so we can pick it up in the morning.

Ishan That's so nice of you. On her behalf, I thank you. If you don't mind my noticing, I don't see a ring.

Joe Excuse me?

Ishan On your finger. I have a reason for asking this. Are you married?

Joe [*Beat.*] No.

Ishan Are you dating someone?

Joe Why?

Ishan I'm asking because I'm nosy, not interested, don't worry. Although you're lovely, with those big shoulders, but alas, not my type. I am starting a new business, it would be so nice to have a client before I begin.

Joe Client?

Ishan A dating service. Indira's Love Connection! I have made over eight successful matches. So, if you ever want me to fix you up . . .

Joe With your sister?

Ishan My sister? Why, are you interested?

Joe I just . . . I, I . . . what do you mean?

Ishan [*Beat.*] With anyone. A woman, man? Just tell me your type.

Joe [*Gruffly.*] Where are the crates?

Ishan Well! I believe they're probably down in the cellar where she stores her supplies and things.

[Ishan *goes to a door, opens it, and points.* Joe *goes downstairs.*]

[*Calling down after him.*]

I'm very good at what I do, Joe. I've already been doing it for free for years. I'll take you on, half price. No, you're my first real client, I'll take you on for free. Oh, and let me see what I can do about my sister.

JOE   [*Calling up.*] These here in the corner?

ISHAN   Probably.

JOE   These are wood. I can't take these now. You get fined if you leave these out on the wrong day. She's got this box here says trash on it.

[JOE *comes up carrying a pile of crates and a box.*]

ISHAN   I can't promise my sister, she's a little . . . But I can find you someone to love.

JOE   Look, maybe I'm not looking, okay?

ISHAN   That's what she says too, as if it's a ridiculous idea. Everyone needs someone to love.

JOE   [*Beat.*] Tell her I came by.

ISHAN   Has she told you about her husband?

JOE   Husband!?

ISHAN   Um-hum. But from my point of view, she isn't married anymore. Her husband is a vegetable. For three years now. Brain dead. Machines.

JOE   Damn.

ISHAN   She doesn't want to let go. Prasad Kumar, Harlem Hospital, go and see for yourself. I told her to leave the past behind because you can't hold the past against the whole world.

JOE   Yeah . . . well . . . it's not always that easy.

ISHAN   There is no reason a big strong man like you should be alone. You've got to stop hiding and become more forward with your feelings because one of these days you'll get old and you'll be alone and the older you get the harder it is to find.

JOE   Look, you don't know me, and I didn't say anything to you . . . and I don't want to.

[JOE *drops the box, its contents spill out. Pornographic magazines, VHS tapes and DVDs.* ISHAN *rushes to look.*]

Shit!

ISHAN   Heterosexual. Blondes with big boobs. Well, well, well.

[*They silently puts everything back into the box.* ISHAN *gets tape from behind the counter and they tape the box up again.*]

JOE It says trash here.

ISHAN It is that. Please take it outside.

[JOE *takes the boxes and crates out.*]

Thank you. Thank you, Joe.

[ISHAN *is clearly deeply troubled. Lights crossfade to . . .*]

Scene 5

[NIRMALA *stands outside a hospital room. She takes a deep breath before entering. We hear the steady whoosh whoosh of each breath the machine is taking for Prasad. There is a heart monitor keeping a steady beat.* NIRMALA *enters and stands in front of Prasad's bed. She stares at him for a moment, puts her bag down, and sits. She keeps her coat on.*]

NIRMALA Prasad, do you hear me? I wish you could hear me now. At night, when I sleep and dream, I know you hear me. When I sleep, you're awake again. But when I'm awake, and I really need to speak to you, you're the one who's sleeping. Couldn't you show me a sign? I need to know.

[*Beat.*]

It's cold in here.

[*Lights down. We hear the whoosh of the ventilator, the beeping of the heart monitor. She simply sits. Lights crossfade to . . .*]

Scene 6

[DEVAUN *stands on the sidewalk next to the steps leading down to the 157 St. #1 train stop. He is blowing on his hands and rubbing them together to warm up. He wears a light jacket.* JERON *appears, wearing a down jacket and ski hat. It is snowing.*]

DEVAUN Jeron, damn! Where you coming from? I been waitin' since I got off the train from work. It's too cold to stand out here.

JERON You a fool walkin' around like that. I went to my house to get my down, man. Why you dressed like that in the cold and snow and shit?

DEVAUN Weather changed in the day, man. That shit confuse me.

JERON It's the global warming and shit. Soon it might snow and then be a hundred degrees in the same day. If people recycled, we wouldn't have it. You bring the signs?

DEVAUN Yeh, yeh, I got 'em. It's cold, man. Don't know if I can get too far. My fingertips and my ears, man.

JERON   Lemme see the signs.

[DEVAUN *pulls a few pages of copy paper from under his jacket.* JERON *grabs them from him.*]

DEVAUN   I scripted these on my break at work.

JERON   Man, this ain't how you spell freak.

DEVAUN   How it's spelled?

JERON   It got an A in it. That's how it's spelled.

DEVAUN   An A. Where?

JERON   Right here, after the E. Gimme a pen, man. You can't spell for shit. And what is this?

[DEVAUN *hands him a pen.*]

DEVAUN   What?

JERON   This word right here. What is it?

DEVAUN   Lemme see. Oh, that's predictor!

JERON   Predictor? What's predictor?

DEVAUN   You know. Predictor.

JERON   But what is it?

DEVAUN   You know, predictor, man. A predictor and shit.

JERON   Devaun, what is it? What do the muthafuckin' word mean? You the one wrote it. WHAT IS IT?

DEVAUN   Jeron, be cool! Be cool and shit. I'm cold, man. My ear tips, man. Predictor like predictor two. When the creatures start killin' and eatin'. I would have liked to draw a picture but I can't draw, man.

[JERON *looks at him trying to understand.*]

JERON   Devaun, is you talkin' about muthafuckin' *Predator*?

DEVAUN   Yeh, yeh, yeh. *Predator*, that's what I was thinking about. Man, I coulda sworn the word . . .

[JERON *shakes his head and starts fixing the pages.* DEVAUN *stands quietly beside him. teeth chattering.* JERON *fixes the pages.*]

DEVAUN   Yo, you should be a teacher or something. You should be on *Jeopardy* or what have you. You don't need to be taking no class to learn how to fix computers, you should make them.

JERON   I plan to. I'ma invent video games. Do you know how much money I'ma make?

Devaun How much?

Jeron Millions.

Devaun Yo, you gonna give some of it to me, right? 'Cause you know you don't need all that money.

Jeron I'ma send my moms to full-time rehab and I'm a buy me a mansion in Jersey 'cause the taxes are lower. And I'ma send you back to school 'cause, you can't spell, Devaun. That's all there is to it. I can spell and you cannot.

Devaun If I ain't rushin', I can spell. They give us one fifteen-minute break, man. I got to eat, make my calls to my girls, go to the toilet, and write the signs in that time. Where we gon start leavin' them?

Jeron First of all, if people put this on they wall and shit, no one will know what it's all about.

Devaun It say here important and I know that's right 'cause I got it from the choking sign.

[*He hands the sign to* Jeron.]

Devaun Anyway, I put my phone number there for if people have questions and don't understand. I want them to know I will be available to answer any and all questions.

Jeron You got your phone witchu?

Devaun Yeh.

Jeron It got a camera. We need to get a picture of the fool, that way when people call you, you can make an appointment to meet them and show his picture so they will know exactly who it is you is warning them about. There is no name here. No description. Nothing. It's not professional.

Devaun Jeron, you smart, I gotta hand it to you. You smart.

Jeron I got a real good mind. If I think about something, I know all the possibilities. Like, for instance, I know people will not understand this shit the way that you got it.

Devaun How we gon find him to take his picture?

Jeron First we go to your house so we can fix these signs, and you can get a jacket or sweater, and while we doing that you could ask your moms when next he comin' to the church. Then we lay in wait and pounce in front a the sucka. SMILE, MUTHAFUCKA! Snap.

Devaun Hold up! They got choir practice at the church tonight. My moms say she ain't cookin' no dinner. That's what she always say when she got it. We can find him there right now.

JERON I guess we goin' to choir practice.

DEVAUN I guess so.

[*THUNDER!*]

Damn, man, how recyclin' be affecting the weather?

JERON This shit is all hooked up together. The way you dispose of your garbage leads straight up to the weather. The weather is connected to the air. The air is mixed up with the gas and electricity. Fuel and fumes and shit goin' up to mess with the clouds. It's gonna be like this all the time if people keep mixin' up their shit in the wrong bags when they throw it out. Some things you don't think can happen will happen, Iceland will melt, and penguins will die.

[*Lights crossfade to . . .*]

Scene 7

[ISHAN *and* NIRMALA *in their apartment. In the same building as the convenience store.* ISHAN *is wearing a dress. They have just finished dinner.*]

NIRMALA How?

ISHAN I've already begun taking the hormones and my breasts are growing, see? But I can make them even larger with implants if I want. The last step is when they cut my willy off. Praise God!

NIRMALA All right, do it. If you want to do it, do it. You don't have to tell me all about it or show me.

ISHAN All right?

NIRMALA I said if you want to do it, do it. But if you're not happy after, don't speak to me.

ISHAN Couldn't you just try to be supportive? Couldn't you just act as if you are? Do you know what it feels like to have to pretend to the world that everything's okay? And feeling all alone?

NIRMALA Yes.

[*Gentle.*]

I'm sorry.

INDIRA But do you hear my voice? I've been practicing. It's a bit higher already.

NIRMALA Yes.

INDIRA Isn't it great! I feel so happy when I speak these days. I open my mouth and I expect a certain sound to come out and then . . . it's higher. And it's different. And it matches what I used to wish it would sound like. These days, I could hear myself speak all day.

NIRMALA   But do you really feel the same inside?

INDIRA   Didi, I'm the same person. I'm not going to change. The outside's just going to match the inside. I'm going to feel . . . the way you feel.

NIRMALA   Lucky you! Ishan, I just don't want anything bad to happen in this house . . . again.

INDIRA   Don't worry, I know what I'm doing. When this is finally over, I will be . . . ecstatic. When I think about it, it's like fireworks go off in my heart.

[NIRMALA *laughs*.]

What's so funny?

NIRMALA   Fireworks in your heart?

ISHAN   Excitement. Like "YES!" "WHOO!" Like this is what I've been waiting for. Do you know what it is to dream about something? And then you can get it and it could happen?

NIRMALA   Yes. Not that it always does.

ISHAN   I don't mean like waiting for Prasad to wake. I'm sorry, Didi.

NIRMALA   I'm not always talking about that. I waited for things when he was awake too.

ISHAN   I know you love your husband. . . .

NIRMALA   [*Muttering to herself.*] I don't.

ISHAN   What?

NIRMALA   Nothing.

ISHAN   No, what did you say?

NIRMALA   I said . . . I said, I don't love him.

ISHAN   But—

NIRMALA   Never mind.

ISHAN   Didi, was that box of porn in the basement Prasad's?

NIRMALA   [*Shocked.*] You saw it?

ISHAN   Was he hurting you, because I would have kicked his ass.

NIRMALA   No. He was kind. He was fair.

ISHAN   And I thought he was such a catch. The day Daddy told us he had been approached by Prasad's father . . . All the girls wanted to be the one chosen for him. Even me!

Nirmala   You're crazy. They spent everything they had for that wedding. And afterwards it was too late to say anything.

Ishan   You should have said something to me.

Nirmala   I don't want to talk about it, it's embarrassing. And I have to go back downstairs to the shop, Ishan.

Ishan   You're going to have to start calling me Indira.

Nirmala   [*Angry suddenly.*] Can't you just let me get used to one thing at a time!

[Nirmala *gets up from the table and goes to the convenience store. Light's cross fade to . . .*]

Scene 8

[*The convenience store.* Nirmala *straightens up, perhaps sweeping.* Joe *enters.*]

Joe   Hey.

Nirmala   Hello.

Joe   I came by yesterday to put out the crates.

Nirmala   Yes, I know, thank you.

Joe   I met your—

Nirmala   Yes.

Joe   Uh, sister, and your sister explained to me, what he, or I mean she's up to.

Nirmala   Yes.

[*Beat.*]

We've got the ice cream you like.

Joe   Thank you . . . for remembering.

Nirmala   It's a funny thing, I remember what people like to buy. Not always their name, but if you like ten-grain bread, or Breyers vanilla ice cream . . .

Joe   Best vanilla ice cream in the world and I've tried them all.

Nirmala   People buy it quickly. . . . And it's been so hot today. . . .

Joe   Have you tried it?

Nirmala   Yes. It's good. Not so sweet like some others.

Joe   There was a box down there said trash.

NIRMALA   Oh.

JOE   What?

NIRMALA   Those were my husband's belongings.

JOE   Oh.

NIRMALA   It's trash.

JOE   Your sister told me about your husband.

NIRMALA   Yes. He's fine. Thank you.

JOE   It's just that I come in here . . . you see people every day and you don't know . . . I think about that sometimes. Because I see things . . . people throw things out . . . and sometimes I wonder . . . you know . . . why?

NIRMALA   You think about what people throw out?

JOE   Or not.

NIRMALA   I learn about them from what they buy . . . how much they buy, that tells me something too.

JOE   I better get my ice cream.

NIRMALA   You should get two, those run out fast.

JOE   Nah, it's just me.

NIRMALA   I know.

[*He goes to get his ice cream.*]

JOE   [*Shyly.*] Guess I can't fool you.

[*He brings back the ice cream.*]

NIRMALA   Four ninety-nine.

[JOE *hands over a five. He starts to leave, then turns around.*]

JOE   Good night.

NIRMALA   Good night, and thank you for helping . . . with the . . . crates

[*He starts to leave and turns around again.*]

JOE   Listen . . . Uh, well . . . if you ever want to share some ice cream? Because I know it must be lonely.

NIRMALA   [*Beat.*] Thank you. You're very kind.

JOE   Good night.

[JOE *leaves quickly. We may see him pause outside to take a deep breath and then rush off. Lights crossfade to . . .*]

Scene 9

[DEVAUN's *house.* DEVAUN *relaxes as* JERON *studiously rewrites the signs. He shakes his head from time to time.*]

DEVAUN   I'm gon be rich and important like Derek Jeter or someone like that one day. Then I'm gon be with my honeys, yeh yeh, me and they be chillin' in my crib on my skin couch and leopard rug. Music be playin' for the mood. You like to say I'm slow, Jeron. I ain't slow. I'm thoughtful on the question and the plan.

JERON   You see all these signs you got me fixin'?

[*Finishing touches.*]

This is a day's work you got me doing. You owe me.

DEVAUN   OVERTIME! Snap!

[*They laugh and slap five etc.*]

JERON   You better pay up, sucka.

DEVAUN   This is good, what we doin', right, Jeron?

JERON   What do you mean?

DEVAUN   I mean how we warnin' people and shit. I want to . . . I want to . . . do something, you know, like them posters of Malcolm and Martin or Superman?

JERON   What?

DEVAUN   And I wanna teach people wrong from right or somethin' like that. But not like in church, 'cause that shit is borin' and it last too long, and the singin' is wack. But I do like it when Reverend Buford start to clear his throat three or four times in a row, like this.

[*Shows him.*]

And start walkin' back and forth, and speakin' forcible, and his shoulders start goin' up and down like this,

[*Shows him.*]

And he start swingin' one hand with his knees bended. "Yes ah." and the people in the church look like they froze up listenin'. Yeh see, that's what I like to see. How they can listen to that one man and he short and light skinned and plain till he open up his mouth and start speaking forcible. Then it's like he a new man. Like he grew or somethin'. I study that shit, 'cause I like the idea. But it don't have to be in no church. It could be anywhere. I could just say somethin' in a corner in the street, and people will stop to listen and wave they hands 'cause in that moment it will be like they feelin' the spirit of the Lord or the Mighty. If I can figure out how you could get people to sit on a wood bench till they ass burn listening to me. That's when I know I will become a dude with wimmins lining up and down the block waitin' for me. I will walk down the street, and birds will stop flyin' and hang in the sky and look down at me like this.

[*Shows him.*]

Cats, dogs, raccoons, and wimmins and everyone. Just lookin'. At me. Like this.

[*Shows him.*]

Like, this thing we doin' to protect the people from Lorrance is helpful and important. It's a good thing, Jeron, I can feel it. Can't you?

JERON   Yeh, we doin it for the people's safety and good.

DEVAUN   I just want to help the world. I'm looking for the beginning moment to show people the real meaning inside of me so they can say, "Whaaat?" I just want to do something for everyone to know that when we walk down the street and sidewalk, we not invisible.

JERON   I see you. Do you see me?

DEVAUN   Yeh, yeh, that's what I mean. I see you. That's what I mean. Yeh.

[*Lights crossfade to . . .*]

Scene 10

[*Hospital room. Lights up on* NIRMALA *sitting by Prasad's bed.*]

NIRMALA   I've told Ishan that I hate you but I don't hate you. If you hear me, Prasad, I don't hate you. But I hate what you have done to me. You took a young girl from India. And you promised her parents you would be a good husband, but you weren't. How you made me feel. A handsome man like you. And everyone thought you wanted me to be your wife because you thought I was beautiful and suitable. Because my family was low compared to yours, how could I say something. What would my mother think of the real reason I have no children? The doctor says you're not improving. But I can't kill you. I've thought about why I wait. I'm waiting to understand why I wear a bindi and call you my husband, and work at your shop, and cook and clean even though you never . . . On our wedding night, I waited for you. I heard you snore and I knew you were asleep. And I thought it was the days of fun and dancing. And we left India the next day, so then I thought it was the time difference, that perhaps you were tired from the traveling. Every night, I waited for you to turn towards me and enjoy me. And when I used to look at you, I thought . . . I'm lucky. My eyes were very pleased by what I saw,

Prasad. And I could imagine you touching my cheek, or touching my arms, or my legs, and my back, and my neck, and my skin. And I wished you would. Every minute I wished you would, even just once. One night I turned to your back and I put my arm around you and I felt your body pull away from me, and I felt you hold your breath, and I could almost hear you saying, "Don't, don't, don't . . . touch me." And so I turned back to my own side. I took my arm from around you and I turned away to my own side.

[*Beat.*]

After they shot you, I put those magazines and tapes in a box and I closed it. And I wrote the word trash on it. I put away your days and days and weeks and nights and months and minutes of unclothed women who don't look like me at all. Those aren't even real people that you know, Prasad. I'm sure you never knew those people. But you preferred them to me. And now people have seen that box. Ishan has seen it. Joe has seen it, I know he has. And now they know you did not find me pleasing. How can you still be hurting me from there? Well, now, these days, if I want, I can lift your arm and put your hand close to my skin, and make you touch me. And you can't move away. Here is my chance at last to feel your skin next to mine. But it's not the same, is it? What good will it do?

[*Beat.*]

But I can't let these people unplug this machine. Even though I have a good reason, I can't do it. Every morning I wake and I wash my face, and I brush my teeth, and I comb my hair, and I place the bindi to my forehead and I remember what it means to wear one. It means that I'm your wife, Prasad, whether or not you liked it. It means that I'm your wife until you die.

[*Lights crossfade to . . .*]

Scene 11

[INDIRA. *She is wearing a dress and makeup. She is at the store, maybe reading a magazine or eating. Anything except working. The door jingles and* DEVAUN *and* JERON *walk in.*]

JERON   Yo, you the proprietor?

DEVAUN   Yeh, 'cause we need to speak to the person who own this sto.

INDIRA   Well, you can't.

DEVAUN   Whatchu mean.

INDIRA   The actual person who owns this shop has been in a coma for three years.

JERON   Damn! So who are you?

DEVAUN   [*Overlapping.*] Damn!

INDIRA   I'm his sister-in-law.

JERON   Where you from? You Spanish?

INDIRA   I'm from India. My name is Indira.

JERON   Aiight, that's cool. Listen up, we got a sign we want to hang on the wall.

INDIRA   A sign?

DEVAUN   About a prederator trying to infest himself on some children.

INDIRA   A what?

DEVAUN   I got his picture right here.

[DEVAUN *takes his cell phone out of his pocket and tries to get to the picture.*]

Right here. Wait, Jeron, how you find it again?

JERON   Man, gimme that thing.

[*Grabs phone.*]

You got to get to the picture section first.

DEVAUN   Oh snap, yeh, yeh, yeh.

[JERON *holds the phone up so* INDIRA *can see the picture.*]

JERON   That's him. You seen him around here?

INDIRA   No, I don't know this . . . person. But what did you say he is doing to children?

DEVAUN   Man come up to me in a sto like this one, not too far from here and try to homosex me while I was mindin' my bizness gettin' my Pepsi.

INDIRA   Oh?

DEVAUN   I'm serial. In the sto.

INDIRA   Well . . . , perhaps he found you appealing?

DEVAUN   Naw, naw naw naw naw.

INDIRA   But you are not a child. You look like a man to me.

DEVAUN   Yeh, yeh, but see, he might be ready to start on the children next seein' as I stopped him in the instant of the crime. He won't mess with me no more. It's the children of the world I'm thinking of.

INDIRA   I see.

DEVAUN   So you need to help us.

INDIRA   Me?

JERON   Yeh, we belee he dangerous, and we want to warn people. To do our duty and shit. That's all. You gotta do whatchu gotta do. If you help us, that might help.

DEVAUN   It's important to tell people if something is wrong. And it's our justiful dutiful and shit. And I can explain it to them, see I got my number right here. I can show them the picture so they'll know who it is.

INDIRA   Well . . . First, I'll have to ask my sister. Leave it here. I'll ask her when she comes.

[*She picks up the sign and begins to examine it. The door jingles and* JOE *walks in.*]

Joe! Hello.

JOE   Hey.

JERON   Aiight, so if your sister has questions, she can call Devaun's number right there, or if you see anything.

JOE   What's going on?

DEVAUN   We tellin' people about some dangerous danger. This man in my cell phone is infestin' himself.

JOE   What?!

[INDIRA *raises her eyebrows and hands the paper to him.* JOE *reads it and hands the sheet back.*]

INDIRA   Young men, this is . . . serious. But I must wait for my sister to return before I can agree to hanging this on the wall.

JERON   It's crucial.

DEVAUN   Yeh, tell her it's very cruserus. I got the picture here in my phone? Jeron, find the thing.

[*He hands the phone to* JERON, *who shakes his head, finds the picture, and holds the phone up for* JOE. DEVAUN *holds up sign.*]

JOE   I know this guy. He wears purple suits.

DEVAUN   That's him. You got the nail from the head.

JOE   I've seen this man around the neighborhood for years. What did he do?

JERON   He gon made a move on my man Devaun here in the Bodega La Sala.

JOE   What?

DEVAUN   And he might have LSD, SUV, A-I-Dees and everything.

JOE   What!? He messed with you?

DEVAUN   Naw, naw, man. Whatchu sayin'? Don't even think about it. Naw . . . I ain't let that fool . . . I would run away . . . them shoes, man . . . he can't catch me. I ain't but let him touch my shoulder before I realize . . . Jeron, tell him.

INDIRA   It's all right. We understand, no need to—

JERON   We just trying to stop him . . . before he goes one step further. None of us want to experience that.

DEVAUN   [*Getting very worked up.*] If that fool touch me again, I will bust him up and dial the digits. Let them shoot the muthafucka. I will hurt his fuckin' ass up so good he will never sing or walk again. He ain't got no right to try to touch on people don't want him to. He just ain't.

JERON   Devaun, please remember that Lorrance is not here right now.

INDIRA   Well, I will certainly inquire.

DEVAUN   This is the United States of America. You ain't supposed to touch on people unless they ask you to first!

INDIRA   You are quite right about that.

JERON   Devaun don't usually get this upset about just nothing. That means some serious shit is goin' down.

INDIRA   Young men, I wish to thank you very much for your . . . diligence. I will definitely speak to my sister about hanging this beautiful sign in here. Thank you and good evening.

JERON   Thanks, miss.

INDIRA   Now, Joe, is there anything I can help you with, because I am closing the shop right now.

DEVAUN   We appreciate the support and everything.

INDIRA   You're welcome.

[*Turning to* JOE.]

I'm going to hang a sign for my own business here.

JERON   What kind of business you got?

INDIRA   I run a dating service to make matches between people. Not like those cheap internet places.

JERON   How much you charge for that?

INDIRA   I will start with a flat hundred-dollar fee. That is a bargain, some services charge a thousand dollars.

JERON   One thousand dollars!

DEVAUN   People gotta pay to go witchu?

INDIRA   I'm not the one they pay to go with.

DEVAUN   Why not, you gorgeous, miss.

INDIRA   [*Beat, shocked.*] I am?

DEVAUN   I could get witchu.

INDIRA   You could?

JERON   But not for no thousand dollars, damn! Even a hundred is high.

DEVAUN   We gotta do mad overtime for that.

[*They laugh.*]

INDIRA   I am sure I'm a little too . . ..old for you.

[JOE *is watching the whole thing amused.*]

DEVAUN   You mature, but you real nice. I look at you and I like what I see.

INDIRA   Well . . . I don't know what to say. Thank you . . . gentlemen.

DEVAUN   Gentleman, I like that. I really like that.

JERON   Can you find me a woman know how to present herself? Aun care if she from India or Egypt or what have you.

DEVAUN   I ain't never paid for no date.

JERON   Devaun, you got to pay for the business this woman's got. And it don't pertain to you anyway. It's for single people.

DEVAUN   You ain't got to tell me like that. I got ears and I hear.

[*To* INDIRA.]

But I could get the hundred dollars.

JERON   Where you gon get it from?

DEVAUN   Excuse me, but every Thursday is pay day.

INDIRA   [*Interrupting.*] Gentlemen, if you are looking for a woman to love, who will love you back, that is what you will pay me for. Joe here is my client.

[*The two men turn and look at* JOE, *who has been amused and is suddenly not.*]

JOE   Hey, wait a minute . . . I never said—

INDIRA   Yes, I know, I know. You want to keep it a secret. Please don't tell anyone about Joe, young gentlemen. But spread the word. Tell everyone you know that Indira is operating from here until I can rent an office.

[*She takes a business card out of her pocket and hands it to* JERON.]

WHEN JANUARY FEELS LIKE SUMMER 323

JERON If you want to pay me a percent of your bizness, we goin' around the neighborhood now. I can hook you up so they will put it on the wall and shit.

INDIRA Would you do that for me?

JERON Why not? But you got to pay me for my time. These ain't the slavery days.

INDIRA If you bring people to me. I will surely give you a commission.

DEVAUN When I take my honeys to the movies I pay for they ticket and what have you. If they go wit me, you don't gotta pay.

[*As they start to leave,* DEVAUN *turns back.*]

And yo, yo, yo! Please make sure y'alls got your garbage in the right bags, because of the weather and the dead penguins!

[*Everyone looks blankly at* DEVAUN.]

JERON Watchu talkin' bout, Devaun?

DEVAUN I'm just sayin', just sayin'.

[*They leave.*]

JOE I seen that guy around the neighborhood for years. I've never heard about him doing anything.

INDIRA I did not know if I should be afraid or flattered.

JOE Listen . . . the last time . . . you mentioned something about dating your sister. . . .

INDIRA Shhh. Shhh, La la li la la la.

[NIRMALA *enters.*]

Look who's here.

NIRMALA Hello.

JOE Hello . . . Nirmala. How are you?

[INDIRA *picks up on* JOE *and* NIRMALA'S *shyness, she looks from one to the other.*]

NIRMALA Fine. Thank you, and you?

JOE I'm fine. Thank you.

INDIRA I'm fine too. And, how is . . . Prasad?

NIRMALA There's no change.

INDIRA Which is good and bad, depending on how you look at it. Didi, you have an important decision to make right now.

NIRMALA   About what?

INDIRA   Two young men from the neighborhood would like for you to put their sign on the wall.

[INDIRA *hands* NIRMALA *the sign.*]

NIRMALA   What is this?

JOE   That is trouble!

[*Blackout.*]

End of Act One

ACT II

Scene 1

[*One week later. In the dark, we hear the sound of a TV news cast. Lights fade up on* INDIRA *in the store watching.*]

NEWSCASTER   There is breaking news in the case that is shocking the Harlem community. Officers say that when they searched Lorrance Dupois's apartment they found seventy-four Polaroid photographs of buttocks with various sharp objects stuck into them. It seems Dupois did not discriminate. Women and men were both stuck by him. According to the victims who have come forward, Dupois lured them to his apartment, stuck them, then paid them to keep their mouths shut.

[*Lights up on* JOE *in his apartment watching intently to the same newscast. He is dressed to go out; heavy jacket, wool cap in hand.*]

Detective Helizondo Barranco says the investigation is ongoing.

[*Lights up on* DEVAUN *and* JERON *posing for the press. Camera's flash.*]

NEWSCASTER   And the mayor said today that the two young men, Devaun Jenkins and Jeron Smith, who alerted members of their community to stay clear of Dupois, after Jenkins himself was approached by Dupois are heroes and examples of what it is to be a true citizen of New York City.

[JOE *switches the TV off. Meanwhile,* ISHAN *continues watching.*]

The New York City Hero Incentive Program is rewarding both men with a year's worth of MetroCards. Both men are employed by Burger King, who is so proud of their hero employees, they get burgers for free anytime they want, for life. Lorrance Dupois is being held without bail. Meanwhile, it pays to be a hero. This is Milton Jacobs, gimme a large fries with that.

[*Lights crossfade to . . .*]

Scene 2

[JERON *drinking from a Burger King cup and straw. He wears a light jacket or hoodie.* DEVAUN *appears in a down jacket.*]

DEVAUN   Yo, Jeron, what's up, man!

JERON   It's seventy degrees, whatchu got your down for, Devaun?

DEVAUN   I ain't takin' no chance these days.

[*It begins to rain.*]

[*Pulling out umbrella.*]

See?

[DEVAUN *and* JERON *huddle under umbrella.*]

JERON   Yo, yo, Devaun, you seen yoself on Fox News last night?

DEVAUN   Yeh, I seen it. You seen yoself? My phone ain't stop ringing, man. On the train this morning, conductor come up to me. Say she proud. The conductor! I don't know her, but she be actin' like she know me. Took me a minute to realize she must have saw the news.

[*Rain stops. The umbrella is collapsed and put away.*]

JERON   I can figure most things out but that one had even me surprised. You could have knocked me down when I heard about that fool. And he ain't even gay, he just like sticking people. He gon fry. They gon fry his sorry ass. The detective came to my King today to ask me some more questions.

DEVAUN   He came to mines too.

JERON   What he say?

DEVAUN   He ain't say nuttin' speticular. Just ask me do I have more information. All I keep thinkin' is what if Lorrance try to stick some shit in my ass, and then take my picture! When I heard about it! I was like damn and shit! And I'm only safe because when he touched me, I jumped back 'cause I was nervous, and 'cause my innerition knew it was something very very bad. I bet he thinkin' that in jail right now. "I should have stayed the fuck away from Devaun Jenkins."

JERON   What your moms and them church folk say?

DEVAUN   Reverend Buford and some of the deacons come over and they all start hollerin' and screaming and praying in the living room while I was in the other room on the phone with Doreen, man. She axed me what all the noise was.

JERON   Why?

DEVAUN   'Cause she heard it, that's why.

JERON   No, why all them folks be hollerin' in the living room.

DEVAUN   Lorrance, man, Lorrance. They is shockified and electrified. When they heard that shit, it mess up the church. Stickin' things in people ass! That shit ain't funny. Yo, you remember that ole lady used to play the organ? Stuck. And I heard one of the pictures had some little toe nail scissors stuck in somebody ass.

JERON   Damn! That shit is terrible. No joke. It is terrible. Damn!

DEVAUN   The whole neighborhood heard about it. My moms, man, my moms and all a them church folk, man, what your moms say?

JERON   She out of it. My uncle the one who came wit me to City Hall.

DEVAUN   Yeh, I saw that.

JERON   He say now I should give him half my MetroCards and I told him to step back and keep on dreamin'. Damn! That sign was a good muthafuckin' idea.

DEVAUN   Jeron, when you right, you right. I hand it to you right in your hand. And you heard me say it on the news too in front of the mayor and all a them people. "The sign was my man Jeron's idea. We wouldn't be here 'cept it wasn't for him."

JERON   I appreciate you givin' me my props in public that way.

DEVAUN   Yo, yo, Jeron, when they gon send our MetroCards?

JERON   They just told us about it yesterday, that shit take time with the red tape and what have you. I can't wait, though, I can't wait. I might try and get me a lil side business selling rides for a discount or something. That shit is worth a lot.

DEVAUN   No, man, you can't do that. People looking at us. We gotta be cool.

JERON   Yeh, man, when you right, you right. I never could have dreamed I would one day meet the mayor, man. The mayor!

DEVAUN   We somethin' now. We really somethin'. It's real nice the mayor did that shit. Real nice. I got his number too. I could call him. My manager and co-workers at Burger King today, they like,

[*Chanting.*]

"We seen you on the news. And you a celebrity. It's your birthday. It's your birthday. You ain't even gotta mop the floor today. It's your birthday. It's your birthday. You ain't even gotta mop the floor today." I can get wit that.

[*Lights crossfade to . . .*]

Scene 3

[INDIRA *and* NIRMALA *stock the shelves.*]

INDIRA The heroes of New York City were standing right in this shop. And guess what? One of them even flirted with me.

NIRMALA Ishan, stay away from them.

INDIRA What do you mean?

NIRMALA They are the same kind of people who shot Prasad.

INDIRA Just because the man who shot Prasad is black does not mean—

NIRMALA I know. I know. . . .

[*Beat.*]

I know.

[*Beat.*]

Did he know you were a man when he was flirting with you?

INDIRA I'm not a man.

NIRMALA You are . . . sort of . . . still. Aren't you?

INDIRA Forget it, okay? I don't think he's quite ready for Indira anyway.

NIRMALA I'm sure . . . you'll meet someone . . . very nice soon.

INDIRA I wish you weren't alone.

NIRMALA I'm not. I've got you to bother me all the day long.

INDIRA Ha-ha, very funny. Okay, listen to me because I have the most amazing idea.

[*Beat.*]

Suppose I send you out . . . on a date? I know about a big shouldered someone who has the hots for you. Say yes, say yes, please say yes. Do it for me?

NIRMALA No.

[*Beat.*]

Who is it?

INDIRA I'm not saying.

NIRMALA Is it Joe?

INDIRA I'm not saying. Why? Do you like him?

NIRMALA Of course not.

INDIRA Well, then, suppose I say, sorry, not Joe.

Nirmala   That would be . . . good. Very good.

Indira   Um-hmm.

Indira   Didi, you've locked yourself up like a Hindu widow. Locked yourself away from life, from society. You used to have friends. . . .

Nirmala   I have friends.

Indira   When was the last time you had tea with one?

Nirmala   I don't . . . remember. I met most of them through Prasad . . . he knew them. Most of them were older than me. Like him. Anyhow, how would I explain this thing you are doing to them? And I'm too busy to have tea. They know I'm busy.

Indira   Do you want me to leave?

Nirmala   No, of course not! Ishan, Indira . . . it's hard to get used to the name. . . .

Indira   At least you're trying.

Nirmala   Anyway, I have to watch this shop. I have to make sure everything is all right. I didn't ask for any of this, Ishan. It's just happened to me. So please just please stop putting so much pressure on me . . . about everything. There's so much . . . noise . . . here all the time . . . everywhere I go. Every day. Everything I do, and you keep reminding me . . . and pushing me . . . and pushing me, and pushing me to do things. I don't want to do anything. Sometimes I feel as if Prasad's hospital room is the only place where there's any . . . peace. Couldn't we just talk about . . . the weather. It's been so strange recently, hasn't it? One minute hot. One minute cold.

Indira   There is absolutely nothing wrong with going out to dinner with someone. Dinner. Maybe a movie? Harmless.

Nirmala   Nothing is harmless. No, I'm sorry. I won't.

Indira   You've got to.

Nirmala   I don't.

Indira   This Friday, I promised.

Nirmala   What! How could you do that? Well, I won't go.

Indira   Give me one good reason why you can't just go out to dinner with . . . Joe. You said he's nice.

Nirmala   I'm married.

Indira   That's a pretty good reason. Usually. I would pay money for what you have, Nirmala. In fact, I am paying money for it. At least be proud.

NIRMALA   I don't know . . . how to do that.

INDIRA   Go back to your first days with Prasad, in the beginning he must have appreciated . . .

NIRMALA   He did not.

INDIRA   What do you mean?

NIRMALA   [*Beat.*] Prasad never touched me.

INDIRA   Never, Didi? Never?

NIRMALA   No. I'm a virgin! So now you know.

[NIRMALA *turns and goes out the door, leaving* INDIRA *open mouthed and in shock. Lights crossfade.*]

Scene 4

[DEVAUN *and* JERON *play ball in T-shirts.*]

DEVAUN   Man, that wind last night feel like it want to blow the whole city away, man.

JERON   It should have blown your sorry ass away.

DEVAUN   That shit was serial.

[*They laugh.* DEVAUN *sees someone littering.*]

DEVAUN   [*Yelling.*] Yo, yo! Pick that shit up from the street and put it in the garbage. You ever had a January feel like summer? It's your fault. Pick it up, 'fore I kick your ass. Thank you and look where you throwin' things from now on.

[*To* JERON.]

Damn! These fools don't care about the global. Throw they garbage in the street. Yo, I'ma start making signs about that. I ain't playin'. These days the weather is wack.

[*The wind starts and stops abruptly.*]

Jeron, man, listen up. Snap! I almost forgot, you know that Chinese girl they got working there?

JERON   Where?

DEVAUN   Her name, Larissa, Larana, somethin' like that, you seen her, right? At my King, not yours. She cute, she got them lips, she say she want to get witchu.

JERON   With me?

DEVAUN   Yeh, man, I was like you know, kinda interested myself, but she ain't never spoke to me, and suddenly after all the news and what have you, she start speakin'. I look at her like this.

[*Shows him.*]

'Cause she say "Hi," real friendly when she see me today, and that make me look twice at her, 'cause I ain't never really looked at her before, and I see her lips and shit and it look nice, And she say,

[*Imitating her with a real high voice.*]

"Your friend, the one was on the news witchu. He gotta girlfriend?"

[*It begins to rain lightly.*]

[*The boys pull their T-shirts over their heads so they look like turtles and continue speaking. The rain stops sometime after it began. They will uncover their heads when* JERON *says "What? Devaun, what?" and continue as if nothing out of the ordinary has occurred.*]

JERON   Devaun, she ain't say that. Tell me, did she say that shit?

DEVAUN   Man, I'm telling you.

JERON   So what did you say?

DEVAUN   I say, "He single. Why?" That's when she say "Oh." and start to giggle and shit.

JERON   What she gigglin' for?

DEVAUN   You know.

JERON   What? Devaun, what?

DEVAUN   Man, if I gotta tell you . . .

JERON   You ain't gotta tell me, just making sure. That's all. She did that?

DEVAUN   They do that when they wanna, you know, git witchu and shit.

JERON   She give you her number?

DEVAUN   Why she gon do that?

JERON   So I can call her.

DEVAUN   Man, I ain't thought about that, I'll give you her number later tonight.

JERON   Let me ax you something, Devaun, who school you on all this shit about wimmin?

DEVAUN   Auno, ain't nobody school me 'bout nothin. If I like 'em, I just know what to do. "Cause like, if you take 'em to a movie, you say, "Yo, you can pick the one you wanna see." They love that. Even if it something wack and stupid.

JERON   Well, tell me this, how long 'fore you . . . you know, 'fore you can git wit 'em?

DEVAUN   Auno, ten or fifteen minutes.

JERON   You git wit 'em while you still inside the theater? Damn!

DEVAUN   Naw, man, that's against the law. After the movie I go to they house, and then I give 'em ten and maybe fifteen minutes to run they mouth. They will talk about this and that and everything they ever heard about. When I ready, I look at 'em, look at 'em all over, wit my eyes like this.

[*Shows him.*]

Yeh, behind my eyeball feel hot. I make my eyes look like a flashlight.

JERON   Whatchu mean like a flashlight?

DEVAUN   I mean like this.

[*Trying to show him.*]

Like, I make 'em look like a light, warm and soft, like this, like they can flow like a blanket or somethin' you trying to cover 'em all over wit. See?

[*Showing him.*]

And you better shower and put your deodorant on that morning too. Let your shoulders and your knees and back relax. Like this. If you let your body get too tighted up, you scare 'em. And your eyes gotta be soft when you look at 'em, 'cause that make 'em look back, and when you git close to 'em you touch their cheek like it somethin' smooth. That make 'em lose they fears and shit and in that exact moment, you know you got ='em in your power, and you better grab them and kiss them 'fore it's too late.

[**JERON** *is listening intently.*]

JERON   How do you know all about doin' alla that?

DEVAUN   Auno, Jeron, how you know whatchu know?

JERON   Auno, I just know it.

DEVAUN   Well, that's what I do and it work.

JERON   Whatchu say her name is?

DEVAUN   Larissa Shing, or Shang, or something like that. Call her and redruce yourself and be upfront and forceful and let your interest be shining in the moment of the instant.

[*It begins to snow hard.*]

DEVAUN What the . . . SNOW!

[*The boys run to get out of the snow. Lights crossfade to . . .*]

Scene 5

[NIRMALA *enters and finds* JOE *standing in front of Prasad's bed at the hospital.*]

NIRMALA What are you doing here?

JOE I just wanted to see. . . .

NIRMALA Wanted to see what?

JOE I don't know—I—was walking by and your sister had told me where . . . I don't know why I came.

NIRMALA Please leave.

JOE I'm sorry.

[*He turns to leave, then turns around.*]

JOE It's just that I keep thinking about how alone you must feel. . . . I wondered why . . . it's not my business I know, but I couldn't help—

NIRMALA Do you agree that I should kill him?

JOE You mean unplug.

NIRMALA It's the same thing.

JOE If he's not going to get better.

NIRMALA This man is my husband.

JOE I understand, but—

NIRMALA But what?

[JOE *doesn't answer.*]

They say he can't hear me. But I don't know if that's true. How do they know? Perhaps he can't speak, and he can't move, but he can hear. Unless they can go inside his head and prove it to me, I don't know anything.

JOE I know what it is to hold on to something because you think it's the right thing to do. It never is.

NIRMALA I promised to honor him . . . I believe in promises. My husband is still breathing.

JOE I know, but—

NIRMALA He's the reason why I wear this.

[*Pointing to bindi.*]

JOE   I see. I know what you feel.

NIRMALA   [*Angrily.*] You don't know anything. It's not what you think. This man. He never touched me like a wife.

JOE   He never touched you? He never touched you.

NIRMALA   I don't know why I just told you that, I don't even know you.

JOE   You know I eat ice cream alone.

NIRMALA   Yes, I do know that. And I even know the kind you like.

JOE   Yes, you do. And you know that I'd like to share some with you.

NIRMALA   Yes.

JOE   So then . . . why? If he never . . . why?

NIRMALA   When you do something. You just do it. When you promise something. You promise it. I agreed many years ago to leave India and come here with him. And he had my hope. I let him have my hope. And he sponsored my brother so he could come here. And he helped him to go to school. And when my parents died he sent money home. He took my hope into one hand like this, but he kept giving things with the other one like this.

JOE   I've been thinking about how things end up in the garbage, 'cause there's a chain of events that has to take place. First, you gotta determine if it's broken or outlived its usefulness. Then it's got to be sorted and put in the right bag. After you've done that, people like me come and pick it up. Once we've done the house to house and the truck is filled—and it can hold the ten, twenty thousand pounds or so you and your partner picked up. And it's a dangerous job. People don't always think about wrapping things right. If you don't wear your gloves, if you don't look at what you about to pick up before you actually do, even if you do, you can get hurt. Cut by rusted metal, burned by all kinds of putrefying substances. But I'm not just talking about garbage you find in the street 'cause it was thrown out. Janice, my ex, for instance . . . we had ourselves some nice times, seemed to want the same things . . . But seem like I had just barely got my tuxedo off and climbed into the bed to warm it up for my new wife. I had just finished exhaling a breath of relief because now I was a man with a job what's got benefits and a pension, and stability; a breath carrying with it the fact I was now looking forward to a future with my wife I could see myself enjoying . . . babies and children and a house and . . . a life. A real life . . . I should have known that something was broke that no account of trying was going to fix. I could have saved myself a lot of time . . . years full of trouble. I could have stopped holding on to my dreams so tight they had to be pried from my hands still trying and trying to hold on to them. . . . Every time she came out after staying too long in the bathroom. I should have known because she always seemed nervous and couldn't settle down, and started going out and staying late . . . and . . . in and out of rehab and finally she run off and took all the savings. The first time I saw that white powder on my blue sink, I should have known that she was garbage and just accepted it. That experience made me feel that maybe because of my job, there's something in me that's gonna attract garbage, even though it's the opposite of what I want, because I want jewels, I want gold and treasure, but seem like I'm scared to try again to look for it. I'm just scared now. But when I see you tending to the store, I want to pick you up . . . and handle you carefully because you're so beautiful. You're like a flower. You're like that gold earring I saw shining on the sidewalk last Thursday. Shining in the dirt, and I couldn't help but reach down and pick it up to see if it was real. I didn't know you were married. But I do know that I want . . . I want to be here for you.

NIRMALA Listen. Do you hear his heart beating?

JOE I hear it.

NIRMALA Could we go out even if we still hear it?

JOE Yes.

NIRMALA Good.

[*Beat.*]

Good.

[*They sit quietly and watch Prasad, who sleeps. As lights fade, we hear the whoosh of the ventilator, the beeping of the heart monitor. Lights crossfade to . . .*]

Scene 6

[JERON *and* DEVAUN. JERON *is examining one of* DEVAUN'S *global warming signs.*]

JERON I'm not convinced this make sense.

DEVAUN People will read this the same way they read the Lorrance sign. If two people throw they garbage away the right way, that might save the weather for one or two days. Even one day of normal weather will be worth it after this shit we been having. If ten people do it, it might be ten days, and if everyone in the neighborhood do it, it will change a lot of days of weather and what have you.

JERON I'm not saying it won't do something, it don't hurt and it might help.

DEVAUN Put it there in big words: DON'T HURT and MIGHT HELP.

JERON   Naw, it should say: Don't Hurt to Help!

DEVAUN   So do that then, man.

[*Beat.*]

I'ma go get me a date with that woman and how I'm even supposed to know what to wear.

JERON   What woman?

DEVAUN   You remember the one from the sto?

JERON   Damn, Devaun, how you gon get a mature woman like that to go witchu? You can't even spell nor nothin'. I can't even get Lucy Ming to talk to me.

DEVAUN   Who?

JERON   You the one told me she was so interested and want to get wit me, and then come to find out she don't.

DEVAUN   Wait, you mean Lips from my King? She is interested.

JERON   She ain't.

DEVAUN   Jeron, she is interested. I been with too many mature and young wimmin in my life. I even been wit a few of my mom's friends and what have you. . . .

JERON   Your mom's friends? Them church ladies?

DEVAUN   . . . I been gittin' wit wimmin since I was eleven and a half.

JERON   Whatever.

DEVAUN   . . . So if I say she is, she is. She speticularly axed me about you, two or three times. You two would like each other. She prolly like to spell like your ass. She always reading. What did you say when you call her up on the phone?

JERON   Auno, shit! I said, "Hi."

DEVAUN   That's it? Maybe she think your phone disconnect.

JERON   No, I dial. She answer. I say, "Hi, is this Larissa Shang?" And that's another thing, that name you gave me is wrong. Larrisa Shang don't sound like Lucy Ming, Devaun. The woman's name is Lucy. So the shit was confusing right there at the jump point.

DEVAUN   It sound confusing the way she say it to me.

JERON   She say, "Who?" I tell her I got the number from you. She say "yeh?" I say "yeh." She say, "My name is Lucy." I say, "Oh." I want to punch you in your mouth right then. But then, she ax me how it feel to be on TV? So I say, "It cool. I'm kinda like a celebrity. Do you want to git wit me?" And then I hear some quiet silence so that I can hear her breathe over the phone. But I remember how you said to keep talkin' and to put your interests up front and shit, so I ax her again forcefully if she want to git wit me. She silent. I don't know if maybe she don't speak English good or she slow, but then she say, "What do you mean?" So I say, "what do you mean, what do I mean?" She say, "What. Do. You. Mean?" In a real nasty tone, in a low voice sound, almost like a man. So I say, "I mean git wit me. To git. Wit. Me. Git it? You know about that, right? 'Cause if your moms and pops ain't git together, you and all human beings might not be born." So I repeat it one more time, I say, "Do. You. Want. To. Git. Wit. Me?" That's when Lucy Ming scream, "I'MA SEND SOMEONE TO FUCK YOU UP!" in my ear so loud it vibrate like a bell was ringing inside my head. But I say to myself, well, at least I know she understand me. Shit! But then, she hang the muthafuckin' phone up on me. And when I call back, she hang up soon as I said "Hello." And this right here is exactly why I don't like to do this shit. Wimmin is stupid. Some of 'em git pregnant and you gotta spend alla your lil money on Pampers. Then some of 'em want for you to pay for them to do they nails every week. Why I want to spend my money on they nails? For what? I got more important things in the world to think about. I don't need to be talkin' on no phone to no stupid-ass punk-ass Lucy Ming. That's on you, telling me some lie on her. That girl ain't interested in me. And you made me call her like a damn stupid-ass fool. I oughta whup you, Devaun. I oughta whup your fuckin ass.

DEVAUN   First of all, if you use rubbers they won't git pregnant. Jameeraquoin tell me his girlfriend git pregnant and he was using the rubbers faithfully, so he belee she might have cut some lil holes in it first, because otherwise that shit is not humanly possible. Secondly—

JERON   My pops warned me to stay away from wimmin, 'cause they will tie you to the wall and suck your last drop of blood if you let 'em and you won't even know it's happenin' till it's too late and you're dried up like a branch from an old tree. Then he said to me, "You need to make sure you stay rooted in the ground, boy. Keep your leaves green. Let the sun and the rain reach your roots so you can grow tall and strong." He told me that shit expressively and looked straight into my eyes while he said it.

DEVAUN   He was talkin' about your moms, man.

[JERON *turns away hurt.*]

You and I both know your pops and your moms ain't see eye to eye from the time you was born, and she been messed up most of the time, from way back. People talk like that when they want you to understand something. It's like a . . . example. But it don't mean all wimmins is the same. Look, I think I can fix this Lucy thing for you if you want me to.

JERON For real?

DEVAUN Yeh, I can do something 'bout it. Give me about a day.

JERON Belee me, I ain't losin' no sleep over her. There are plenty of women in the world. When I'm hooked up with my video game corporation, I won't have to call them, they'll be making appointments to see me and I might be too busy for them.

DEVAUN You think she cute?

JERON She aiight.

DEVAUN But do you think she cute and shit?

JERON I said she aiight.

DEVAUN But I ain't wastin' my time if you gon mess it up. Or if you are not interested.

JERON Whatever. She aiight. If you can fix it so I can git wit her, that would be aiight.

DEVAUN Jeron, it ain't all about only gittin wit her. You didn't even say, "Hey. How you doin'?" "Whassup?" Damn! Those are the words to say in the beginning. The way you call and reproached her sound rude and you prolly scare the daylight out from her.

JERON You the fuckin' shithead fool told me to be up front and make my eyes like a muthafuckin' flashlight. Shit! I would not have called that girl and said a thing if it had not been for you advising me.

DEVAUN You got to use soft words on wimmin. You got to calm 'em down. They is nervous. If you follow my path, you will git to where you are going.

[*Lights crossfade to . . .*]

Scene 7

[INDIRA *as she minds the shop.* DEVAUN *comes in wearing a T-shirt.*]

DEVAUN Yo, miss.

INDIRA Well, hello again, and congratulations, I understand you are now a hero.

DEVAUN That's what the mayor said.

INDIRA It seems you must have done something good to invite him to say such a thing.

Devaun   Yeh, but none of us knew that Lorrance was stickin' people and what have you.

Indira   Well, you did a good deed. Where I come from God rewards you for that.

Devaun   Where you come from again?

Indira   India.

Devaun   Yeh, yeh, I remember that. So listen up, whachu think if I put up some signs about the global.

Indira   The what?

Devaun   The global, on account a garbage and what have you. It's serial, and people don't seem to care. When I heard about that shit I said Whaat!? You mean it got a reason? You mean there is some way to stop the shit and people don't want to do nuthin' about it? We, and that means you and me, are all sufferin' on account a some stupid-ass people's ways. I'm the first to say I ain't always carefulintal with it and shit, but it's important and everyone should know and do they best.

Indira   I don't know if I actually understand what you are talking about, but if you want to hang a new sign, that's fine. You seem to have a good success rate with yours.

Devaun   Thanks. I appreciate the support.

Indira   My pleasure.

Devaun   So what about that date?

Indira   Do you want me to find someone for you?

Devaun   Whatchu mean, naw, baby, I want you to go wit me.

Indira   You want me . . . to go with you? You're serious?

Devaun   I'm serial. I could take you to a movie or what have you, and you can pick the one you want to see. We could go to Burger King if you want. They give me a little card say I can eat for free.

[*Shows it to her.*]

Indira   Burger King! Wow!

Devaun   Yeh, so like I said, I'll show you a real nice time. I was thinkin' about how you call me gentleman and I like that. I really like it. Nobody usually call me that before.

Indira   How old are you?

Devaun   I'm twenty. How old are you?

INDIRA   Don't you know it's bad manners to ask a lady how old she is?

DEVAUN   I ain't never heard that before.

INDIRA   Well, it is.

DEVAUN   Sorry, I don't meant no disrespect.

INDIRA   I'm very flattered. You have really made my day, but alas, I don't think it would be wise. Firstly, I am a little older than you. . . .

DEVAUN   I don't care about any and alla that.

[*Stepping up close and looking* INDIRA *right in the eye in an extremely seductive way.*]

You beautiful and smell sweet as perfume.

[INDIRA *backs away, totally under his spell.* DEVAUN's *slightly goofy self-confidence rectifies itself totally when he's in the act of conquering a female. His ability to charm and seduce a woman is unsurpassed. While* INDIRA *is usually the dominant personality, she is no match for* DEVAUN *on the make.*]

INDIRA   I . . . I . . . I don't think that would be a good idea.

[DEVAUN *gets right back in her face. His eyes hold her in an almost hypnotic trance. His voice has lowered so that he speaks in a soothing confident tone.*]

DEVAUN   Why not? . . . an, you a woman.

INDIRA   Whaaa?

DEVAUN   So we belong together.

INDIRA   We?

DEVAUN   And I know you feel what I feel.

INDIRA   I . . . I . . . just don't think it's—it's a good. . . .

DEVAUN   I can't take no for an answer. It's Wednesday now, I'll pick you up Friday at seven-thirty to show you a real good time.

[*He begins to back away, still holding her gaze.*]

And I'll bring the sign. We can put it up together befo we go out.

[DEVAUN *leaves the shop.* INDIRA *is left speechless, and in total leg buckling shock! It begins to hail.* DEVAUN *runs. Lights crossfade to . . .*]

Scene 8

[JOE, *who is in his apartment. He turns the radio on and some . . . oldie song comes on. He looks at himself in the mirror. He examines his chin carefully to see that he has shaved close enough.*]

JOE What you so nervous for, huh? What are you so nervous about?

[*He turns back to the mirror. He applies cologne. Maybe too much cologne. He examines his hair carefully and closely. He bends over to re-tie his shoes. Straightens up and looks at himself in the mirror again. Takes a deep breath and exhales.*]

Okay. Okay . . . Okay. Okay.

[*Beat.*]

Okay.

[*He leaves.*]

[*Light's crossfade to . . .*]

Scene 9

[*Lights up on* NIRMALA *and* INDIRA's *apartment.* INDIRA *holds a mirror and* NIRMALA *tries to apply eye shadow.*]

INDIRA My hands are trembling.

NIRMALA You look fine.

INDIRA Thanks, I was hoping for pretty.

NIRMALA For Burger King, you look more than fine.

INDIRA Is that what you're wearing?

NIRMALA I'm not wearing that dress you bought. It looks awful and it's cut too low. You wear it if you think it's so nice.

INDIRA All right, all right. You look like a nun. Oh my God! I don't know why I accepted. Actually, I didn't. He just insisted. . . . It's not even him, but, Didi, the fact that he, that anyone could look at me and . . . Look at me. Look at you. Look at my neck. Look at yours. Look at my wrists. Look at yours. I can't believe he looked at me and saw something that said, "I want to go out with you."

NIRMALA [*Beat, looking at her brother.*] Well, why not.

INDIRA I know you're just saying that, so never mind.

NIRMALA I'm not just saying it.

[*Changing the subject.*]

If one goes out to eat dinner with someone. Is there anything . . . expected?

INDIRA How would I know. I know it the other way around. Of course not, Didi. Not unless you want it.

Nirmala   I don't know why I agreed to this.

Indira   I know why.

Nirmala   Why?

Indira   For the same reason I agreed.

Nirmala   I did not say I wanted to go, you arranged it. And the only reason I'm going is because I feel sorry for him.

Indira   For him? For Joe?

Nirmala   His wife was not good.

Indira   Well, maybe he feels sorry for you! Oh my God, I know next to nothing about this man-child except that he hates homosexuals. No. Nothing's ever expected. It's hoped for, of course. But, expected . . . no. And Joe is a nice man.

Nirmala   And what about if your . . . date is expecting something?

Indira   Thank you!

Nirmala   What are you complaining about. You wanted this. All you talk about is dates. Dates. Dates. Well, now you're going on one. And you've talked me into one too. I hope you're satisfied. Neither one of us should be going on a date.

Indira   [*Yelling.*] I deserve to go on a date!

Nirmala   Okay. Yes, you perhaps . . . I didn't mean . . .

Indira   OH MY GOD, I must be attracted to danger or something. What if he wants to sleep with me. He could kill me!

Nirmala   Don't! Not the first time you go out with him anyway. Anyway, not till you know.

Indira   Isn't that one of the things I'd want to know?

Nirmala   I don't know.

Indira   Anyway, I want it, Didi. I long for it. I don't know how you've lasted so long.

Nirmala   Ishan!

Indira   But just sleeping with someone does not compare to someone looking at you with admiration, and affection, accepting you and wanting you. . . . He looks at you and you can look at him straight on. He puts his hand on your shoulder, or around your waist. He holds your hand. He strokes your cheek, he looks into your eyes, and touches your hair, and almost blinds you with the intense light of his gaze. But then there will come a moment, when I will have to tell him . . . and the look will go away, just like that. I know it will. It will be switched off. Like someone blew out the candle and all that will be left is that little bit of smoke looking for the fire that was burning so brightly there one second before. I will want to die when I see that look.

NIRMALA   Don't say that.

INDIRA   I will want to disappear. And I won't be able to blame anyone but myself, because my own light goes out when I look at myself in the mirror, or when I touch myself down there. Or when I think about it at all.

NIRMALA   Stop now. Let me help you with your lipstick. No, that one is too bright. This one. This one will look good on you.

INDIRA   One day, it'll happen, won't it? Someone will want to be with me?

NIRMALA   [*Applying lipstick carefully.*] Of course. It's happening tonight.

[INDIRA *stares at herself in the mirror.*]

INDIRA   But I mean it'll happen and I won't feel like I'm a fraud. I'll feel real?

NIRMALA   Yes, of course. Because anyway, you are quite real.

INDIRA   Not yet.

NIRMALA   Indira, I can't unplug him, okay. But let me look into borrowing against the life insurance policy.

INDIRA   Would you do that for me?

NIRMALA   Yes.

INDIRA   Thank you

[*A buzzer sounds. They start.*]

I wonder which has come first, your date or mine?

NIRMALA   [*Weakly.*] I don't know.

INDIRA   Would you get the door?

NIRMALA   Me? I've never even gone on a date.

INDIRA   But I need two minutes. Look at me, I'm a wreck.

NIRMALA   If it makes you feel so bad, you don't have to go. I could tell him you're ill. And I can stay with you.

INDIRA   [*Fiercely.*] You have to go. And I have to. If I don't give it a chance, it won't ever happen. And anyway, even though it will feel horrible when the light goes out, the moments leading up to it will be spectacular.

[*The buzzer sounds again.*]

NIRMALA and **INDIRA**   [Yelling.] Coming!

[NIRMALA *begins to leave but stops to pat* INDIRA's *cheek.*]

NIRMALA   You look very pretty.

INDIRA   You're just saying that.

NIRMALA   I mean it.

INDIRA   So do you.

[NIRMALA *rushes to the door and opens it.* DEVAUN *and* JOE *both stand there.* JOE *holds flowers.* DEVAUN *has his rolled-up signs.*]

DEVAUN   You the lady own the sto? Got some signs, India say I can put them up.

NIRMALA   Oh? Well, let me get my . . . sister, for you.

[*Calling.*]

Indira, come!

JOE   These flowers are for you.

[JOE *hands her the flowers.*]

NIRMALA   Oh. Thank you.

[INDIRA *appears. She seems perfectly calm and together.*]

INDIRA   What have we here? Two dates for the price of one.

DEVAUN   [*To* JOE.] You payin' for yours?

[*Proudly.*]

Mines is free.

I didn't bring you flowers, but I did bring this sign I told you about.

[*He shakes the rolled-up sign.*]

You 'bout as gorgeous as a movie star.

INDIRA   Thank you! Well, let's put it up, shall we?

[*To* NIRMALA.]

Have a good time.

NIRMALA   Yes, you too.

[INDIRA *and* DEVAUN *leave first.*]

JOE   You look beautiful.

NIRMALA   Thank you.

[JOE *and* NIRMALA *leave.*]

[*On another part of the stage we see* JERON *pacing. He holds a cell phone. He takes a deep breath and dials.*]

JERON   [*Nervously.*] Hello, is this Lucy? Yo, it's me, Jeron, the real one. Devaun say he explained that shit to you. Yeh, it was wack. I didn't know that fool got your number and pretended to be me. He just sound like me 'cause he my cousin, but he a little disabled, if you know what I mean, and he like to overhear stuff when me an Devaun be speakin'. He movin' next week to California so he'll be gone for good and shit. I apologize, though. Yeh. Yeh. Yeh. I ain't mean no disrespect, yeh. Yeh. Yeh.

[*Lights crossfade and . . .*]

Scene 10

[*. . . up on* NIRMALA *and* JOE. *They are leaving a restaurant.*]

JOE   Did you enjoy your dinner?

[*Beat.*]

NIRMALA   Yes.

JOE   Best Indian restaurant in the neighborhood.

NIRMALA   Actually, it is Bangladeshi, their curry was a little too spicy.

JOE   Oh?

NIRMALA   But it was nice. Thank you.

[*Beat.*]

I hope Indira's okay.

JOE   She looks like she can handle herself okay. I gotta admit, I was surprised to see her going out with that guy. . . . But I guess she knows what she's doing.

[*Awkward date beat.*]

So, what would you like to do?

NIRMALA   What would I like to do?

JOE   Because see . . . as you know, I've got some Breyers vanilla bean ice cream. I've got some bananas, chocolate syrup, cool whip, chopped up nuts, and maraschino cherries. What say you let me make you one of my famous banana splits?

NIRMALA   You want me to go to your house?

JOE   Yes, I do.

NIRMALA   I'm sorry I can't do that.

JOE   Look, it sounds like my wife and your husband belonged in the trash, and you're still attached to him, and that's your business. I am a gentleman, and I have no interest in taking advantage of you, but it would make me happy if you'd let me fix us a banana split.

NIRMALA   [*Beat.*] All right.

JOE   All right?

NIRMALA   Yes.

JOE   Wow! All right, then. All right!

[*They exit to the subway.*]

[*On another part of the stage we see* INDIRA *and* DEVAUN *arriving from their date. They each wear Burger King crowns. They are laughing and clearly had a good time.* INDIRA *enters the apartment with* DEVAUN.]

INDIRA   I wonder if they're back yet.

[*Calling.*]

Nirmala!

DEVAUN   Don't sound like she home.

INDIRA   I hope it means she's having a good time.

DEVAUN   Maybe she went to a movie. You sho you don't want to go see one?

INDIRA   No. No, thank you. I've had a lovely time.

DEVAUN   Yeh, me too.

INDIRA   I would offer you some wine, but I don't think we have any. So thank you and good night.

DEVAUN   That's it?

INDIRA   What do you mean?

DEVAUN   I mean, I'm not ready to leave yet, India.

INDIRA   Oh. Would you mind taking off your shoes?

[DEVAUN *does this, may smell and hide shoes after she goes.*]

I could get you a beer from the shop.

DEVAUN   That sound aiight. I'll take two.

INDIRA   All right. I'll be back.

[INDIRA *leaves.*]

[JOE *and* NIRMALA *arrive.* JOE *gestures to a chair. There should be something unfancy about his place. Mismatched furniture as if he found pieces in the garbage.*]

JOE   Please.

[JOE *begins to leave.*]

I'll be right back. Make yourself at home.

[JOE *leaves.* NIRMALA *sits.* DEVAUN *gets up to look at a statue of Lord Ganesha. He picks it up, examines it carefully.*]

DEVAUN   [*To Ganesha.*] Yo, you got too many hands doin' too many things.

[INDIRA *returns with two beer bottles. She opens the two bottles and hands them to* DEVAUN.]

INDIRA   Do you want a glass?

DEVAUN   Nah. The shit taste better in the bottle.

[*He drinks, there is a beat.*]

This elephant with so many hands you got here?

INDIRA   Oh, that is Ganesha, the God of Good Fortune who . . . who removes all obstacles.

DEVAUN   God?

INDIRA   My religion has many gods.

DEVAUN   For real? You all don't go to church and belee in Jesus and what have you?

INDIRA   No.

DEVAUN   I ain't never heard of nobody praying to no elephant.

INDIRA   Ganesha was originally a real boy. But then by mistake his head was cut off and the only replacement head was an elephant's. It was attached, life was breathed into him again and after overcoming this huge obstacle, everyone lived happily ever after.

[*Beat.*]

Devaun, I think you like me.

DEVAUN   Yeh, I like you.

INDIRA   Do you really?

DEVAUN   Yeh, I feel peaceful tonight, right here. I feel peaceful witchu. I like how you talk and call me gentleman.

INDIRA   You are a gentleman, aren't you? Because if you're not you should leave right now.

DEVAUN   Yeh. I'm real gentle. Yeh.

[*He gently touches* INDIRA'*s shoulder. She closes her eyes briefly.*]

INDIRA   Do you want to make love to me?

DEVAUN   Yeh, I could git wit you. Damn, usually I got to make all the moves first. You don't play. I like that. I like that a lot.

INDIRA   Well, finish your beer, because we must pray together to Lord Ganesha if you want to do that to me.

DEVAUN   You want me to pray to that elephant?

INDIRA   Yes, because there's something . . . he must help us with.

DEVAUN   Aiight, that's aiight wit me. But I ain't gon tell my moms about prayin' to no elephant. She will shit for real. She religious wit the church and alla that. India, you somethin' else.

[JOE *presents* NIRMALA *with a big bowl of ice cream.*]

NIRMALA   My goodness, that is a big bowl of ice cream

JOE   That's why I have two spoons. You dig in there, and I'll work this side.

[NIRMALA *tastes.*]

NIRMALA   Mmmm! This is good.

JOE   This—is perfection!

[*They eat.*]

[INDIRA *stands before the elephant. She beckons for* DEVAUN *to join her. He puts his beer bottle down and does so.* INDIRA *places a little bell beside her on the floor.*]

INDIRA   Do you have a key?

DEVAUN   A key? Yeh, these the keys to my house.

[*He removes a key from his pocket and hands it to* INDIRA. *She places it in front of the elephant. She picks the bell up and rings it.*]

INDIRA   [*Ceremoniously.*] This bell which I ring will get the attention of my Lord Ganesha. Hello. I ask Ganesha, the gatekeeper, to use this key to remove all hindrances to my happiness.

[*Beat.*]

Thank you, Lord Ganesha. Thank you. Thank you.

[*To* DEVAUN.]

Say thank you.

DEVAUN   Thank you.

[INDIRA *beckons for* DEVAUN *to join her. He does. She picks the bell up and rings it again.*]

INDIRA   Good. Now that we have begun to pray, the miracles will begin.

DEVAUN   Miracles?

INDIRA   Shhh, don't interrupt. Yes. If you believe in miracles, they happen. What do you wish for?

DEVAUN   I wish for the weather to be normal again.

INDIRA   Okay. Fine. That's a good wish. It depends on a lot of things, but fine. Close your eyes and feel it happening in your heart. And then thank Ganesha.

DEVAUN   Thank you!

INDIRA   The weather is a big thing to wish for. You may have to do this a few more times for it to come true. But this is a very good beginning. The weather feels better already. Don't you feel it?

DEVAUN   Yeh, I feel it. Damn!

INDIRA   You do?

DEVAUN   Yeh. Don't you?

[INDIRA *realizes she does feel something.*]

INDIRA   Yes. Yes, I do. Now for mine. And for my sister Nirmala as well.

[INDIRA *rings the bell throughout next few lines.*]

Close your eyes, please. My magic is happening.

[*Adding quickly.*]

It's happening right now, all over New York, because you and I believe in the goodness of our Lord Ganesha. . . .

NIRMALA   [*Fanning herself.*] I feel slightly . . . odd.

JOE   Are you okay?

NIRMALA   Yes. Yes. Thank you.

[*Beat.*]

Do you hear something?

DEVAUN   I ain't never heard of this before now. But if you say it can do things, I ain't got no problem wit that.

INDIRA   Just the fact that you are willing is already a miracle. Now listen carefully, in India, a child is frequently born with a trunk—like Ganesha. Especially if this child is a boy.

DEVAUN   A trunk?

INDIRA   Yes. And every now and then, a girl gets one too.

DEVAUN   Shit!

INDIRA   But the trunk is usually down here.

[*She points down to her crotch area.*]

DEVAUN   Daaaamn!

INDIRA   Shhh. Shhh. Be calm. Be calm. Be calm and listen. Listen and be calm. If a boy has it, you Americans sometimes call it a penis. But if you are a woman, and you have one, it is useless, do you understand me?

DEVAUN   You tellin' me that some wimmin got a useless . . . dick down there?

INDIRA   [*Beat.*] Yes.

DEVAUN   You tellin' me you got one?

[*There is an awkward beat.* INDIRA *does not answer at first,* DEVAUN *waits for* INDIRA *to answer. Finally . . .*]

INDIRA   Yes.

[*There is an even more awkward beat as* DEVAUN *registers this.*]

[*Beat.*]

INDIRA   But remember that it's a trunk. So please do not call it that again!

[*Beat.*]

My breasts are not large, but they're real because I am real.

[DEVAUN *listens and hears* INDIRA *and understands what she is saying.*]

DEVAUN   You ain't gotta tell me.

[*Reaching for her.*]

INDIRA   I promise you, I am a woman in every way.

DEVAUN   I can see that. India, aun care about your trunk or nothin' like that. But do you got a bedroom? Or do we have to do this right here in front of this elephant?

INDIRA   [*Faces Ganesha and has a brief emotional silent beat which* DEVAUN *does not see. She then turns to* DEVAUN,]

Thank you. Thank you so much!

[*Taking* DEVAUN's *hand.*]

Come with me.

[*They start to exit.* DEVAUN *turns back.*]

DEVAUN   [*Mouthing to Ganesha.*]

Thank you!

[*Music begins playing as* DEVAUN *and* INDIRA *begin to exit, it is Al Green singing "How Can You Mend a Broken Heart." As the lights crossfade, the song plays from a radio in* JOE's *apartment.*]

[JOE *and* NIRMALA *react to the music. Not a huge reaction, but they notice it and notice how comfortable they are with each other.*]

NIRMALA   This is . . . nice.

JOE   I haven't sat across from a woman since *2006.

[**Insert correct year eight years prior.*]

That's eight years.

NIRMALA   My goodness, that is a long time.

JOE   I want you to know it's a little piece of heaven to see you in my house. It's the sun and the moon and the stars in the sky. It's the whole world!

NIRMALA   I'm also pleased to be sitting here.

[JOE *gets up suddenly.*]

JOE   That song . . . Would you like to . . . could we . . . dance?

[*He holds out his hand to* NIRMALA.]

NIRMALA   Dance!

JOE   Yes.

NIRMALA   [*Tentatively.*] All right.

[JOE *holds his arms out to* NIRMALA, *she awkwardly moves into them, giggling.*]

JOE   You put your hand here, and I'll put my hand there.

[*They begin to dance. The following conversation takes place as they dance.*]

NIRMALA   What I've told you about my husband.

JOE   Yes.

NIRMALA   I thought there was something wrong with me.

JOE   There's nothing wrong with you. What I've told you, about my wife, I've never told anyone.

NIRMALA   You shouldn't have been alone for so long.

JOE   I thought there was something wrong with me. You know. I guess we're a pair, aren't we.

[*They continue dancing a little more.*]

NIRMALA   [*Stopping suddenly but still in* JOE's *arms.*]

I feel strange. I feel so strange.

[NIRMALA *bursts out laughing. She laughs hysterically, and then she begins to cry very hard. She cries and holds on to* JOE *as if he is her very lifeline.* JOE *holds her.*]

JOE   I'm here, Nirmala. I'm right here.

[NIRMALA *moves away and then pauses and reaches her arms back out to* JOE.]

NIRMALA   I want you to touch me.

JOE   [*Gently.*] You sure about that?

NIRMALA   No, I'm not sure about anything.

[JOE *begins to move towards* NIRMALA.]

NIRMALA   Wait.

[NIRMALA *removes her bindi and makes a big deal of placing it on the table.*]

Do you see what I've done?

JOE   I see.

[JOE *and* NIRMALA *resume dancing. Lights begin to cross as* JOE *and* NIRMALA *dance towards their exit.*]

[JERON *speaks into his phone.*]

JERON   Devaun, man. Yo, yo, man, I left you so many messages. Where you at? Check this out, I got a date with Lucy tomorrow, man. I did it! I did it! I ain't playin' witchu. Call me!

[*We hear the whoosh of Prasad's breathing, the beeping of his heart. The sounds continue and underscore, as the lights cross fade to . . .*]

Scene 11

[NIRMALA *standing beside Prasad's hospital bed. She is wearing a winter coat, buttoned up. She is not wearing a bindi. There is a beat of her simply standing and watching Prasad, before she speaks.*]

NIRMALA   Prasad, I have gone on a date and I now know what you have kept from me. I could pull this plug out right now. And I'm not wearing my bindi, you wear one!

[*The rest happens quite quickly.* NIRMALA *leaves Prasad's hospital bedside. The whoosh of Prasad's breathing and the beeping of his heart underscore as she walks to the subway platform and waits for the train. Maybe we hear a subway announcement about a train approaching, or the sound of a train leaving while she gets into waiting mode. This may merely be a light shift and* NIRMALA *may simply be leaning forward to see if she sees a train approaching*] *as the sound shifts to subway sounds.* DEVAUN, JERON, INDIRA, *and* JOE *each enter separately to the same platform, and stand somewhere around* NIRMALA. *They all wear the proper seasonal winter outerwear. They do not notice each other. They each stand lost in their own thoughts while waiting for the train to arrive. As lights begin to fade, we hear the sound of a train approaching. They each step towards the yellow line and stop. The approaching train's light illuminates the faces of the five individual characters as if they are a skyline.*]

[*Blackout.*]

[*Silence.*]

End of Play

YEAR OF THE ROOSTER

by

Eric Dufault

Production History

Year of the Rooster premiered in New York City with the Ensemble Studio Theatre. It was directed by John Giampietro; the set design was by Alexis Distler; the costume design was by Sydney Maresca; the lighting design was by Greg MacPherson; the sound design was by Shane Rettig; and the production stage manager was Eileen Lalley. The cast was as follows:

GIL PEPPER: Thomas Lyons
DICKIE THIMBLE: Denny Dale Bess
LOU PEPPER: Delphi Harrington
ODYSSEUS REX: Bobby Moreno
PHILIPA LONG: Megan Tusing

Eric Dufault is a graduate of Sarah Lawrence College. His plays include *Year of the Rooster* (*New York Times* Critics' Pick), *The Tomb of King Tot*, *American Girls*, and *The Last Great Telemarketer*. His plays have been performed at the Ensemble Studio Theatre/Youngblood as part of their "34th Annual Marathon of One Act Plays" and Mainstage series. Additionally, his work has been performed at the Flea Theatre, the 52nd Street Project, the Magnet Theatre, the Theater for the New City, the Lark Play Development Center, and the Great Plains Theatre Conference. He is the recipient of a 2013 Sloan Commission, the 2013 David Colicchio Emerging Playwright Award, the 2010 Lipkin Playwriting Award, and the 2008, 2009, and 2010 Harle Adair Damann Playwriting Award. His play *Something Fine* will be published in the *Best Ten-Minute Plays of 2014* anthology. He is a member of the Obie Award–winning Youngblood Playwriting Group.

Characters

GIL PEPPER—Mid-thirties, he wears old clothing, an eye patch.
DICKIE THIMBLE—Mid-forties, he wears expensive clothing, a cowboy hat.
LOU PEPPER—Mid-sixties, she wears a nightgown.
ODYSSEUS REX—Mid-twenties, he is a rooster.
PHILIPA LONG—Late teens, she wears a McDonald's uniform.

Round 1

[*The sun is coming up.* ODYSSEUS *enters.*]

ODYSSEUS   Get on up now. Come on, ya big celestial ball a' light and crap. Come on, Sun! Get your ass up and come on down here'n face me. 'S'been eight months since I came into this cocksucker of a world, and I been calling you out every day since. Each morning ya rise and each night ya fall and yet ya never got the balls to come down and fight! Come on now, Sun! Get your ass up and get ready for your beating!

[ODYSSEUS *waits. Nothing. He breaks out a knife. He swings it in the air.*]

ODYSSEUS   Come on! I'll peck out yer eyes, tear off yer feathers! I'll cut open yer belly and light will spill out! I'll break yer neck with my beak and they'll throw yer corpse in the goddamn bucket! And I will make this world night eternal! Yer a coward! Yer a coward and this is my goddamn year!

[ODYSSEUS *crows. His crows become louder. We begin to hear more cock crows and squabbles.* ODYSSEUS *exits.*]

[*The noise of a cockpit before a fight. About a hundred or so men talking, laughing.* DICKIE *enters.*]

DICKIE   Settle down now! Settle down! Shut the fuck up!

[*The noise dies down.*]

DICKIE   It's good to see this kind of turnout, lotta friendly faces out there, huh? Rodney, Stu, Mattie, that your boy there? Buy 'im a hot dog for me. To the rest a y'all: take off yer coats, take out yer betting cards, and take a good look at those birds over there 'fore they tear each other apart! But look, fellas, 'fore we start, I gotta say somethin' real important. There's gonna be lotsa money bein' tossed around tonight. And we all gots to get what we gots to get, and I will throw down with the best of 'em. But if you really want money, rob a bank! Get up tomorrow morning, walk up one floor above us, talk to my secretary, Doreen, and I will give you a job! That is how little I give a shit about money!

What we are really here, for men—and women, I see you back there Agnes, don't you try and hide—is much older than money. And as a little reminder of why you called up a sitter and came out tonight, I give you:

[DICKIE *pulls out two eggs from his pockets.*]

The bastard boys of Cassidy Coltrane!

[*Lots of whoops and hollers.*]

Yes! Cassidy Coltrane, the motherfucking meanest son-of-a-bitch cock to end all cocks! You put your ear against these shells you can hear his boys, and lemme tell you, these things want out! They got road salt and hot sauce in their veins, they're headbuttin' these prison walls a'theirs so as to rip your goddamn throat out! And I got the only two Coltranes in all the land. So let's follow their fucking example and fight!

[*Roars and applause.*]

Fight 'til yer hair falls out! Fight like a killer, fight like a crook, fight like you ain't ever fought before!

[*Wild noise.* DICKIE *exits. A fighting bell sounds. All noise stops.*]

[GIL *stands wearing a McDonald's uniform punching numbers into a cash register.*]

GIL   Thass' a bacon double cheese, extra cheese, a McRiblet, large fries, large cola, two apple pies, and a Butterfinger Flurry. That right? Yer total comes to seventeen eighty-five, cash or credit? You have a good night.

[DICKIE *enters.*]

DICKIE   Well, well, if it ain't Mr. Pepper himself—

GIL   Dickie—I told you guys, I can't have you coming here—

DICKIE   What, a man works as hard as I do can't get hungry? That's not right, Gil, that's not what this place is about, is it?

GIL   We can't talk business here—

DICKIE   What business? The only business is that I'm fucking starving. I want it my way. Now listen up, you gimme a Quarter Pounder—throw some extra onions on there, I'm a man who likes his onions—small fries, nah medium fries, hell gimme a large, and why don't you take off those onions—fuck onions, I hate onions, make me sick—and change those fries for a couple hash browns—

GIL   Dickie—

DICKIE   Hey, you still make those riblets? You do, I'll have one of those, you don't, get rid of the Quarter Pounder, take a chicken sandwich, heavy on the mayo, onions 'til it stinks. Cool? Say it back to me.

GIL   Man—

DICKIE   Say it back to me.

GIL   I don't know—

DICKIE   You don't know what I want? That seems to be your job. And seems to me, you can't do your job, I should alert your manager, right?

GIL   Dickie, I'm serious right now, look me in the eye, don't you do that—

DICKIE   Hey, man, I'm just fucking with you. We're all pals here! I'll have a chicken sandwich and a Diet Coke.

GIL   Comes to six sixty-five—

DICKIE   Hey, hey, no need to rush, no one's here, huh? I haven't seen you in forever, man. So I hear you got a fancy new chicken little. Is that right?

GIL   I don't talk business here. You know that.

DICKIE   What is he? A topknot? A Claiborne? I bet he's an Irish Gray—

GIL   Dickie—

DICKIE   Aw, he is an Irish Gray, isn't he? Because my sources tell me he's a bit of a battle stag, and I said, Gil Pepper? Pepper's got himself a battle stag? That guy—bless his soul and all, but that guy's been out of the game for like ever, only brought out these little scrubs shit themselves soon as they enter the pit. Well? You got something special?

[GIL *glances around for his superiors.*]

GIL   Maybe I do.

DICKIE   Ya didn't ask to put him in the bracket.

GIL   Well . . . he's only eight months old. . . .

DICKIE   I mean, not that I'm overly eager, seeing as your birds generally got the strength of a three-legged rat.

GIL   Well, we don't all have enough money to buy the latest top bird now, do we? Here's your food, Dickie, have a night.

[GIL *hands* DICKIE *his food.*]

DICKIE   I didn't order this.

GIL   What?

DICKIE   This ain't what I ordered.

GIL   You didn't even look—

DICKIE   Excuse me, is the manager back there?

GIL   Hey. Stop it.

DICKIE   'Cause my needs are not being met! Manager?! Yo, Manager!

GIL   Please, man! I'm serious.

DICKIE   MISTER MANAGER!

GIL   Please!

DICKIE   I didn't order this but I'll take it, 'cause I'm a good guy. Now say thank you.

GIL   What?

DICKIE   Say "Thank you, Mr. Thimble. Thank you for covering up for my stupidity."

GIL   Thank you, Mr. Thimble.

DICKIE   For?

GIL   For . . . covering up for my stupidity.

DICKIE   You are very welcome, Gil. And hey, for your exceptional service: a crisp fifty.

[GIL *considers. He tries to take the fifty-dollar bill, but—*]

[DICKIE *tosses the bill on the ground and begins to exit.*]

[GIL *bends down to pick up the bill.*]

GIL   Wait! I want in on that bracket.

DICKIE   Calm down, big balls. There's a ritual to this kinda shit. You see this ring? Bought it after I won me my one-hundredth fight. Why don't you kiss it. Go on. Kiss it. Kiss it like it was a baby.

[GIL *kisses the ring.*]

DICKIE   You're a good sport, Gil. What I'm gonna do, I'm gonna start you off in a low tier. Up against Rabbit Season, maybe Heavy Leonard. Work your way up.

GIL   I'm not fightin' you?

DICKIE   What, you got some kinda death wish?! I got this bird, he's a Berdugo Black. Been training him for damn five years now. Took out both his eyes. Uses his hearing to fuck up anything gets in his way. Like a bat, or a dolphin. 'Is name's Bat-Dolphin. He'd eat yer little boy up. You gotta learn to piss before you can shit, man. You gotta learn to piss before you can shit.

[DICKIE *begins to exit.*]

DICKIE   Three weeks 'til fight night, champ! My warehouse, 8 p.m., Wortham's Rules. This here's your personal special invitation! Bring your little chickadee!

[DICKIE *sings the McDonald's "Doo Doo Doo Doo Doo" theme song.* DICKIE *exits. A fighting bell rings.* GIL *takes the bill out of his mouth.* GIL *picks up two large McDonald's bags. He walks over to his home.* LOU *is sitting, reading a* People *magazine. In her lap is an incredibly old lapdog represented by an inert rag of hair.*]

LOU   Yer late!

GIL   Hey, Ma, what were you reading about?

LOU   The Fifty Most Beautiful People on Earth! Did you bring the honey mustard?

GIL   Ma, you know the managers won't let us take condiments.

LOU   But, Gil . . . the honey mustard . . . I love the honey mustard. . . .

GIL   They already gave me a written warning. Said I could get fired.

LOU   So you didn't get me any?

GIL   Of course I got you some.

[GIL *produces honey mustard;* LOU *squeals with joy.*]

GIL   But we gotta be careful, because I think they're getting suspicious—

LOU   Hey, Gil? I got a question for you—

GIL   So I'm thinkin' maybe at the end of the month I'll just stockpile like hundreds of 'em and we can put 'em in the fridge—

LOU   Do you think Bo is dead?

GIL   What?

LOU   He hasn't moved for the last three hours.

[*Beat.*]

LOU   Wait. Wait, no. He breathed. I just felt him breathe.

GIL   Jesus, Ma.

LOU   Sometimes it's real hard with him to tell—

[LOU *puts Bo on the ground.*]

GIL   Ma! Yer robe! Bo peed on you!

LOU   He does that sometimes. Gil? Gimme a foot massage.

GIL   Ma. I'm tired.

LOU   Gil. My leg's been asleep for like two hours. I need a foot massage. It's a medical emergency.

[GIL *reluctantly begins giving* LOU *a foot massage.*]

LOU   Thassit. Yeeeeah. Thassit. Also, Gil, ya gotta clean the house. When yer daddy made this house they called it the crown jewel of Oklahoma. And they called me its Queen.

GIL   They never called you that, Ma.

LOU   Gil, don't be mean to me. I'm disabled.

GIL   You're not disabled.

LOU   Yes I am! And the government agrees with me, so if you got a problem with it, don't talk to me, talk to them! Look, Gil, I'm done. Okay? I worked for thirty-five years, I raised my kid, I played my game, and I got my prize. Let me enjoy my prize.

[*A bang on a door.*]

GIL   What's that?

LOU Your rooster was making noise, so I locked it in the laundry room.

GIL What?! Ma, I told you—if he gets into the bleach—!

[GIL *rushes out.* LOU *takes a packet of McNuggets from the bag and begins eating.*]

GIL Odie?! You okay?!

LOU You gotta be careful to lock the door whenya leave, okay? 'Cause it's a little loose and—

[GIL *laughs offstage.*]

GIL You gotta see this, it's unbelievable!

[ODYSSEUS *enters with a mangled red towel. He dumps it on the floor, as if it were prey.* GIL *follows.*]

ODYSSEUS Motherfucker didn't stand a goddamn chance.

LOU That's my only towel.

[GIL *picks up the towel.*]

GIL Look at the precision on these cuts!

LOU Now I'll just stand around wet.

ODYSSEUS Hey, what the fuck you lookin' at?

[ODYSSEUS *notices Bo. He moves closer to him.* LOU *is visibly scared.*]

GIL Ma, he won't hurt him—

ODYSSEUS When I see things that move it makes me the angriest motherfucker lived.

GIL He's a sweetie, ain't ya, Odie?!

ODYSSEUS If somethin' moves, I take it as them tellin' me: "I wanna die."

LOU What time is it?

GIL Two o'clock

LOU AM or PM?

GIL AM.

ODYSSEUS An' if somethin' doesn't move, I take it as it them tellin' me: 'I wanna die, but not right now.'

LOU Bo and I are going to sleep.

GIL Ma, you've lived with these guys before—

LOU This one's different. And I know you like it—

GIL "Him," Ma, "him"—

LOU —but I can't help but feel that one day it's going to kill me.

[Lou *exits.*]

Gil   Look at the number you did on that thing! Goddamn, son! Now that calls for a victory snack!

[Gil *puts the second McDonald's bag in front of* Odysseus. Odysseus *voraciously eats the chicken McNuggets.*]

Gil   I tell ya, there're days, Odie, days when you think the world was designed to fuck you up. Like it was all a machine, a big fuck-you machine. Fuck people, you know what I mean, Odie? Sometimes, I wish I could go back to the Garden of Eden, before man, before even Eve, just me and God and the animals.

[Odysseus *has finished his meal.*]

Odysseus   I want more meat.

Gil   So, hey, I don't want you to get too nervous, but I got a little surprise . . . we're in the bracket! Facing off against some bird named "Heavy Leonard." So we gotta up our training! Here's the schedule: half-hour warm-up, hour dummy-work, two hours mirror-work, spin cycle, vitamins. And, hell, maybe we'll see what else we got around here for you to fuck up.

[*A fighting bell. A transition.* Gil *sits in his McDonald's uniform, eating McNuggets.* Philipa *enters.*]

Philipa   Hey, Girl!

Gil   Shit! Philipa.

Philipa   Stanley know you're stealing all those condiments?

Gil   Hey, Philipa, don't talk about the condiments-

Philipa   You wanna get your ass fired over honey mustard, you be my guest, dude. But, uh, you're not gonna have to worry about Stanley much longer. If you get my meaning. You wanna know why?

Gil   Why?

Philipa   Turns out Stanley's got a case of ball cancer. Cancer of the balls.

Gil   No shit.

Philipa   Yes shit. He's got to go to Tennessee to see some ball specialist. Get his balls chopped off. Apparently he's moving to Mexico after. I think he's gonna start a bar called, like, One-Ball's or something.

Gil   So there's an opening for manager?

Philipa   There would be. But turns out they already had their eye on someone. A real up-and-comer, kind of a genius when it comes to fries and shit, dope as hell doesn't hurt either—

GIL   What? You? How old are you, like twenty-two?

PHILIPA   Motherfuckin' nineteen, motherfucker!

GIL   I been working here for five years—

PHILIPA   See, the thing is, I'm a go-getter! I go, and I get! You don't need to be a dude, you don't need to be a slut, you don't need to graduate high school, all you need to know is what you want and go get it! I don't do coke, I don't do smack, and, now, man, everything's coming up Philipa. Ten years from now, I'm gonna be like the manager of all McDonald's, and you know where I'm goin' after that?

[*Beat.*]

Walt Disney World Resort. You ever been to Walt Disney World Resort?

GIL   Nah—

PHILIPA   Course ya haven't. I have literally met no one who went to Walt Disney World Resort. But that is when you know you have made it! I got this Disney autograph book when I was five? And when I go to Walt Disney World Resort, I'm gonna meet the dude who plays that little naked kid in *The Jungle Book*? Mowgli? And I'm gonna fuck the shit out of him.

GIL   Wow.

PHILIPA   And after we've finished, I'll get him to sign my autograph book. And then whenever any basic bitch tries to shame me or make me feel lesser than her or whatever, I'll show them the autograph book and be like: What've you done, bitch?! And that's when I'll know I've made it.

GIL   . . . It's good to have dreams.

PHILIPA   But hey, you wanna know the first thing I'm gonna do when I'm manager? I'm gonna can your ass for stealing all those condiments.

GIL   You serious?

PHILIPA   If I were you I'd start workin' on your resume.

GIL   Woah, look, Philipa, you remember when the kid puked? I covered for that!

PHILIPA   You wanna keep your job? Show me your eye.

GIL   Wh-what?

PHILIPA   You don't know much about women, do ya, Pepper?

GIL   I know a lot of stuff.

PHILIPA   Uh-huh. You know what the women that work here say about you?

GIL   What?

PHILIPA   They say you have got a really, really tiny dick.

GIL   Yeah, well, uh, that's not true.

PHILIPA   Like, an anti-dick, a micro-dick—

GIL   That's not—

PHILIPA   A dick the size of the pencils they give you for mini-golf.

GIL   Look, I don't have a small dick; I have a medium-sized dick!

PHILIPA   Prove it.

[*Beat. They stare at each other.*]

PHILIPA   See ya later, Pepper. Try not to get your balls chopped off.

[PHILIPA *exits.*]

GIL   The fuck?

[*A transition. A fighting bell.* GIL *puts on mitts, preparing train* ODYSSEUS.]

GIL   Was a time, Odie, when you were a cocker, you were a king. Only the best and brightest got in on the sport. Whole theaters were built for it! You know who invented cocking? The Greeks. You know what else they invented? Democracy.

[GIL *hits* ODYSSEUS *in the head with the mitt.*]

ODYSSEUS   The fuck. ·

GIL   Okay, Odie, remember, you gotta move to the side, not down.

[GIL *hits* ODYSSEUS *again.*]

ODYSSEUS   The fuck!

GIL   The side, not down.

[GIL *hits* ODYSSEUS *again.*]

ODYSSEUS   The fuck?!

GIL   The side, Odie! We've gone over this! Sorry. I didn't mean to raise my voice, I'm not upset, I'm just . . . I think we should move on.

[GIL *takes out a mirror.*]

ODYSSEUS   Sometimes I think about what the largest thing I could kill is. I think I could kill a cow. If I put my mind to it. I think I could kill a car. A house. I like to think a' these things sometimes.

GIL   Today, Odie, I saw a woman with no nose. Just no nose, like a skeleton or somethin'. I was lookin' at her, and she gave me the finger.

[GIL *shows* ODYSSEUS *the mirror. He immediately assumes a battle stance.*]

ODYSSEUS   Who the fuck are you?!

[Odysseus *attempts to attack his reflection.*]

Gil   Did ya know they misspelled my name tag? 'Stead a "Gil" it says "Girl."

Odysseus   This is the motherfucking place I call home!

Gil   And I told 'em to change it. I told 'em.

Odysseus   I will eat yer teeth.

Gil   But they didn't listen, Odie. We gotta make 'em listen.

Odysseus   I will make yer skin look like the inside a yer mouth.

Gil   We gotta make 'em know our name!

Dickie   [*Offstage.*] Knock, knock.

[Gil *quickly puts away the mirror.*]

Odysseus   Hey, where the fuck'd he go?

[Odysseus *wanders away.* Dickie *enters.*]

Dickie   Door was open so I came on in.

Gil   Dickie, what the hell?

Dickie   Hey, pal. Yer house looks like real shit.

[Lou *enters.*]

Lou   Gil? Who is this?

Gil   Ma, this is Dickie Thimble—

Dickie   And you must be Mrs. Pepper! Damn if you are not the picture of sweet maternal nurturance. Pleasure to meet you, ma'am, I own the second largest beef jerky factory in the state, maybe you've seen us, Herky Jerky?

Lou   No—

Gil   What're ya doin' here, Dickie?

[Dickie *pulls out some jerky from his pocket and offers it to* Lou.]

Dickie   [*To* Lou.] So hey now, why don't you sit in that kitchen, enjoy some samples while your son and I talk shop?

Lou   Is this about McDonald's?

Dickie   Ohhh, no, ma'am, this here's your boy's other business venture.

Lou   It's . . . it's about the chickens?

Dickie   'Fraid so, ma'am.

Lou   Gil, I don't want this person in my house—

Gil   Ma, it's okay, just wait in the kitchen with Bo—

Lou   Gil. I do not want this person—

GIL   Ma. The kitchen. Please.

[*Beat.* Lou *takes the jerky offered by* DICKIE, *then exits.*]

DICKIE   And enjoy the jerky, Mrs. Pepper. Nice lady.

GIL   Why the hell're you here? Scaring my mom like that—

DICKIE   Okay, show me the goods.

[GIL *takes* DICKIE *over to see* ODYSSEUS.]

DICKIE   Hey there, little fella.

[ODYSSEUS *makes a noise and lashes out at* DICKIE.]

GIL   Here, lemme calm him down—

[GIL *places a blinder over* ODYSSEUS's *eyes.* ODYSSEUS *becomes still.*]

ODYSSEUS   Damn. 'S nighttime. Son of a bitch really sneaks up on ya.

DICKIE   What kinda steroids he on?

GIL   Six milligrams Bolazine, five a' Dianabol, twelve Trestolone.

DICKIE   Hm. Diet?

GIL   Starve 'im for two weeks, then strict courses a' extra-strength feed, vitamin mash, and McNuggets.

[*Beat.*]

DICKIE   Nuggets?

GIL   Sure.

DICKIE   That's chicken nuggets, yeah? Those got real chicken in them?

GIL   'Course, why?

DICKIE   Nothing, no reason. Hey, where's your training oven at?

GIL   I just use the washing machine.

DICKIE   The washing machine?

GIL   Sure, set it on spin, put 'im in there for an hour or two. He tries to bash himself on the sides just like if he was in an oven. Also gets him used to disorientation on account of all the spinning.

DICKIE   Hm. That's smart. You think of that on your own?

GIL   Yeah.

DICKIE   Lemme take a look at this killer a' yours.

[DICKIE *bends down and expertly examines* ODYSSEUS.]

DICKIE   You are a goddamn fool, Pepper. Sure, he's got some nice thighs, a good neck, but this is the secret goddamn weapon the boys have been pissing themselves over? Why're you smiling? Why're you grinning like you fucked my girlfriend?

GIL   Guess who his daddy is?

DICKIE   No fucking way. I didn't notice it, but damn. He looks like him. This bitch is the spitting image of—

GIL   He's not a bitch. His name is Odysseus Rex. And when his blood spills in the pit, that's the blood of Cassidy Coltrane.

DICKIE   Did you get him from Big Papa Headcase?

GIL   Nope.

DICKIE   'Cause that's where I got my eggs. . . .

GIL   You got Coltrane eggs?

DICKIE   Two of 'em.

GIL   Two?

DICKIE   Where the hell did you find him?!

GIL   I got my secrets.

DICKIE   Fuck. How much is he?

GIL   Not for sale.

DICKIE   Two thousand.

GIL   Not for sale.

DICKIE   Five thousand.

GIL   Not for sale.

DICKIE   Ten thousand.

GIL   No.

DICKIE   Damn, you love this bird, don't you? You are an interesting character, sir, I will give you that. All the fuckheads I deal with, they got their brain located next to their wallet. . . . Few good men these days. You get me, man?

GIL   I get you.

DICKIE   I'm not gonna lie to you, bein' rich as fuck gets old, even if you were poor as shit like me. But you, you are a man of a different age, Gil Pepper. You inspire somethin' between pity and honor! And honor's the meat in my goddamn sandwich! I'm giving you a compliment, asshole, say thank you!

GIL   Well, thank you.

DICKIE   Somethin' you may have noticed, Gil. Long as I've been running these games, I've never lost. Not once, not ever. You're so excited about your little pal, I'm gonna be like *The Jeffersons*; I'm movin' you on up. Title match. Fuck Rabbit Season. Fuck Heavy Leonard. You're facing down Bat-Dolphin. You're facing down death. 'Cause I'll tell you right now, Gil, that's a nice cock, but he's no champion.

Maybe in three years, five, he'll be ready. But look at him: too young, too confident. The best gamecocks are the old ones who been fucked over too many times to count. The best gamecocks ain't got no eyes.

[Dickie *pokes at* Gil's *good eye,* Gil *grabs it in pain.*]

Gil   What say we bet yer eggs on it?

Dickie   What?

Gil   The Coltranes. If yer so sure you'll win.

[*Beat.*]

Dickie   I'll tell ya what. I'll put up the eggs, but in return, I want somethin' a yours.

Gil   I'm not bettin' Odie—

Dickie   Fuck the bird. I don't want the bird. I want the house.

[*Beat.*]

Gil   This is my ma's—

Dickie   You don't haveta be a gynecologist ta tell that broad's gonna drop dead tomorrow, Pepper. Now, this is a nice piece of property, I mean, I assume it is when it don't smell like the inside of a pig's anus. I think I'm gonna turn it into a jerky store.

[Dickie *extends his hand.* Gil *shakes it.*]

Dickie   Damn but I do love business! One week 'til fight night, muchacho.

[Dickie *exits.*]

Dickie   Mrs. Pepper? Real nice meetin' ya, ma'am. Ya got yerself a real dickhead of a son.

[Gil *stews. He goes over and organizes a series of needles.*]

[*He takes the blindfold off of* Odysseus.]

Gil   We don't have to listen to him, Odie. The only ones we have to listen to are each other.

[Gil *injects* Odysseus *with the needles. It's clearly painful.*]

Odysseus   I am making a list of everything I hate in this world. One: the sound'a people talkin'. Two: the sound'a myself talkin'. Three: silence.

GIL   Ya feel it, Odie? That's the breakfast of champions running right through yer veins.

ODYSSEUS   Four: words. Five: numbers. Six: anythin' that happens when you put those fuckers together. Seven: the motherfucking sun.

[GIL *gives* ODYSSEUS *an especially violent injection.*]

ODYSSEUS   Why the fuck are you doing this to me?!

[LOU *enters.*]

LOU   Gil, stop playing with your bird. I wanna talk to you.

[GIL *groans and leads* ODYSSEUS *off, then returns.*]

[LOU *is sitting, with Bo on her lap.*]

LOU   See, what it is—wait.

[*Beat.*]

LOU   I think Bo might be dead.

[*Beat.*]

LOU   No, no, there it is. Anyway, Gil. I wanted to say: I was a good hairdresser. And I think that's all we can ask for, to be good at something, at anything. I cut people's hair, I made 'em happy, and I finished. Life is real easy when you think of it that way.

GIL   Sure.

LOU   What's wrong with you, Gil?

GIL   What? Nothing's wrong—

LOU   How many hours do you sleep a night?

GIL   I don't know—

LOU   Do you ever—I mean, I never see you go out, do you ever go out?

GIL   Sure, I . . . I go to the store, and I get stuff—

LOU   You don't sleep, you don't go out. How many people have you talked to, Gil, like really talked to, in the last year?

GIL   Ma—

LOU   I've been thinking maybe we should take you to a doctor. Like maybe we missed something, maybe you're mentally disabled—

GIL   Ma, I can name all fifty states! Now, I don't have time for this—

[GIL *begins to exit.*]

LOU   Why aren't you with a woman, Gil?

[*Beat.*]

GIL   Well, I'm sorry that I don't bring home girls to screw in the tub.

LOU   Gil? Are you a faggot?

GIL   Excuse me?

LOU   In some of the magazines, they say that people can do weird things when they're lying about being a faggot. It's okay. Just tell me that you're a faggot and go live in a motel for a little while—

GIL   What time is it, Ma? That's a real easy question, right? What day of the week is it? What month is it?

LOU   Well—

GIL   See, if you can't answer these questions, I don't see why I should answer yours. How many people've you talked to this year? When was the last time you changed yer clothes? And when was the last time you showered 'cause you smell like shit!

LOU   Your rooster destroyed my towel.

[*A transition.* GIL, *in McDonald's uniform, eats chicken nuggets.* PHILIPA *enters wearing a new uniform.*]

PHILIPA   Check this shit out. "Manager," motherfucker! I manage. Shit happens and I manage.

GIL   Yeah, that's pretty cool, Philipa. So I just wanted to tell you, that I'm not comin' in tomorrow-

PHILIPA   Mmmnope.

GIL   I haven't taken a sick day in—

PHILIPA   As a highly respected leader of the McDonald's family, I got a commitment to maintaining our particular brand of restaurant excellence. Request formally denied.

GIL   Philipa. Seriously, no joking, this is actually really important to me.

PHILIPA   . . . Huh. Well, this is interesting. What could you possibly be doing that would warrant time off?

GIL   I'm not really at liberty to say. . . .

PHILIPA   Yeah, I'm gonna be honest with you, Pepper, I don't think there's anything you could ever say to convince me of anything.

[*Beat.*]

GIL   Walt Disney World Resort.

PHILIPA   Where are you going with this?

GIL   Tomorrow is my Walt Disney World Resort.

[PHILIPA *considers this.*]

PHILIPA   I'll tell you what. Show me your eye.

GIL   Philipa . . .

PHILIPA   Show me your eye, and I'll let you ditch work.

[GIL *awkwardly turns around and lifts his eye patch so* PHILIPA *can see.*]

PHILIPA   Holy shit! That is fucking disgusting! What happened?!

GIL   Aw, a rooster clipped me.

PHILIPA   A fucking rooster?

GIL   Yeah, I got a rooster.

PHILIPA   Let me see that thing again.

[*He shows her his eye again.*]

PHILIPA   Well . . . I think it's kinda cool. It's like you're a fucking Cyclops. Livin' in a cave. Eatin' sheep.

[*Beat.*]

PHILIPA   Hey. On a scale of one to ten, how would you rank your physical body, with ten being like, Steven Seagal, and one being a sack of moose shit?

GIL   Wh-what?

PHILIPA   Tell me.

GIL   . . . Three. I don't know. Three.

PHILIPA   . . . Three?

GIL   Two?

[*Beat.*]

GIL   . . . One?

PHILIPA   Enjoy your day off, Pepper. Try not to hurt yourself when you're jerking off to pictures of cats or whatever. I just hope you know what you're doing with your life. 'Cause I got the feeling you ain't got a clue.

[PHILIPA *exits. A transition.* ODYSSEUS *is asleep, his eyes covered.* GIL *enters and sits.*]

GIL   Hey, Odie. I'm sleepin' here tonight, okay? Slumber party, just us guys.

[GIL *knocks on the floor.*]

GIL   My dad built this house, ya know. That's why it's so strong.

[*Beat.*]

Man. Tomorrow. Tomorrow.

[ODYSSEUS *twitches in pain as he sleeps.*]

Sometimes, man, I wonder what you dream about. You must dream about the pit, right? Even though you've never been. You dream about that moment when the other bird falls and you first notice the cheers. . . . Maybe you dream about me. I dream about you, man. And I dream about . . . I dream about so many fucking things.

[*Beat.*]

When I was young, I used to, uh, I used to have these night terrors. Where there were all these monsters and they would just sit on my face. And I would wake up screaming, just yelling at the top of my lungs. And my ma . . . she'd tell me to shut up, but my dad, he'd get up, and he taught me this mental trick. Whenever I had a nightmare . . . I'd just imagine I was a rooster. Nothing can hurt you when you're a rooster.

[*Beat.*]

Tomorrow, Odie. Tomorrow.

[GIL *sits, unable to sleep. A transition. The noise of a cockpit before a fight. About a hundred or so men talking, laughing.* DICKIE *enters.*]

DICKIE   Settle down now! Settle down! Shut the fuck up! There are days when I wake up and wonder why shit is the way it is. Why we got death and disease and why my first wife turned out to be such a bitch. Well, let me tell you, boys: it all comes down to tonight. This is the reason your mommy left when you were three years old! This is the reason Rome fell! This is the reason man was made and the dinosaurs all blew up! So that we could be right here right now watching these two great beasts do terrible things to each other! Odysseus Rex! Bat-Dolphin! Life! Death! Love! Hate! This fuckin' night is the reason why Earth has always existed!

[GIL *enters, sharpening* ODYSSEUS's *blade.* ODYSSEUS *follows.*]

GIL   Okay, Odysseus Rex. I'ma call you Odysseus Rex 'cause it's game time and that's your game name. Here, eat this. You nervous? Nah, yer not nervous, I'm not nervous either.

[GIL *shoves a nugget into* ODYSSEUS's *mouth.*]

ODYSSEUS   My heart feels like it's gonna explode with hate.

[GIL *pours liquor into* ODYSSEUS's *mouth.*]

GIL   Here, drink this. Odysseus Rex, Odysseus Rex, baddest battlecock ever born, that's you, that's your name, Odysseus Rex. You done slain armies, you done murdered monsters, ruled cities, ran countries, King Odysseus Rex.

[GIL *puts lamp black under* ODYSSEUS's *eyes.*]

ODYSSEUS   It's beating like a goddamn fool. Is this what fear tastes like?

[GIL *hands* ODYSSEUS's *his knife.*]

GIL   Remember side, not down! Side, not down! This thing's sharp enough to shave the hairs off God's back, look at all these fools, look at all these shits, I'm not nervous, you nervous, Odie? Fuck no, you're not. You ready?

ODYSSEUS   I am ready.

GIL   You ready?

ODYSSEUS   I am ready.

GIL   You ready?

ODYSSEUS   I am ready!

[*A fighting bell sounds. Unbelievable noise.* ODYSSEUS *is alone in a combat stance.*]

ODYSSEUS   I don't know where I am! I don't know who you fuckers are or what the fuck you want! WHAT THE FUCK DO YOU WANT?! All I know is that my whole life's been building up to something and this's sure as hell gotta be it!

[*Blackout. Lights return.* BAT-DOLPHIN *has entered the arena. He is painted and scarred up. He wears a blindfold around his eyes. He's played by the same actor who plays* DICKIE. *He is old and calm.*]

BAT-DOLPHIN   Hello, little one. It is I, Bat-Dolphin.

ODYSSEUS   Jesus. Yer a blind motherfucker, ain't ya?

BAT-DOLPHIN   Oh, little one. Don't be so scared.

ODYSSEUS   I ain't little and I ain't scared.

BAT-DOLPHIN   I can hear your heart beating like a little frog. I remember when I was like you, with dogs running around inside my brain. Now look at me. Older than the sky. Older than the sea. When the mountains broke open and made the earth as we know it, I was there. I am five years old.

ODYSSEUS   I wanna tear off what's left a'yer face—

BAT-DOLPHIN   Oh, little one. You're barely a baby, and this is your very first fight.

[BAT-DOLPHIN *pops open a knife.*]

ODYSSEUS   Guess it goes without saying that I hate you more than anything ever was.

DICKIE'S VOICE   Pit 'em!

[*Incredible noise.* Odysseus *and* Bat-Dolphin *rush at one another. They kick and slice.* Bat-Dolphin *appears clearly more experienced.* Odysseus *is on his back. He scrambles back up.* Odysseus *and* Bat-Dolphin *separate.* Odysseus *is breathing more heavily.*]

Bat-Dolphin   It feels different, doesn't it? It feels different than you thought it would feel.

Odysseus   I WANNA SEE YA FALL APART IN FRONT OF ME!

Bat-Dolphin   It's okay to be scared. We're all scared just a little bit. We are such strange creatures, you and I. It was only upon killing my one true foe that I realized this. And now, I am free to see us as we are: the ultimate of contradictions! I am both ugly and beautiful! Loathed, like a bat, and loved, like a dolphin.

Odysseus   I wanna see ya weep!

Bat-Dolphin   It is best to just lie down. Lie down, and offer up your belly. I have already faced down the impossible foe, and I have won. I am the one who killed the Sun.

Odysseus   What?

Dickie's Voice   Pit 'em!

[Odysseus *and* Bat-Dolphin *rush at each other again. Brutal fighting.* Bat-Dolphin *scores a deep gash.* Odysseus *bleeds.*]

[Odysseus *and* Bat-Dolphin *separate.*]

Odysseus   Aw, fuck! What're ya talking 'bout with the Sun?!

Bat-Dolphin   Do you ever wonder why it's no longer here?

Odysseus   You didn't kill the Sun.

Bat-Dolphin   Of course I did—

Odysseus   I see that son of a bitch every day.

Bat-Dolphin   When I was young, I woke up every morning and hated all that I saw. Especially that big bright face who made the whole world up. And then one day, I woke, and I didn't see anything anymore. So you see? I killed him. I had to have killed him. Why else would the world be so dark?

[*Beat.*]

Odysseus   You poor blind fucker. Yer just as weak as the rest of 'em.

Dickie's Voice   Pit 'em!

[Odysseus *and* Bat-Dolphin *rush. A death blow.* Odysseus *holds in his hands an unidentifiable part of a rooster.*]

ODYSSEUS   You see this, Sun?! This is what I will do to you! This is what you will become! I will dump your corpse in the bucket, and the bodies of my brothers will cover you up!

GIL   [*Offstage.*] Odie!

ODYSSEUS   Night eternal! Night forever! Sleep for always!

GIL   [*Offstage.*] Odie!

ODYSSEUS   Come on down, you sonofabitch! Come on down here and face me!

[GIL *enters, he is sweaty and out of breath. He grabs* ODYSSEUS.]

GIL   I fucking love you.

[*Blackout. End of Round 1.*]

Round 2

[GIL *enters, drunk. He's deliriously happy. A few cars honk.*]

GIL   When I was small I studied U.S. geography! My teacher said would you stand up and list the states for me! My knees began a-knockin'! My words fell out all wrong! Then suddenly, I burst out with a silly little song! Oooooh . . . Alabama and Alaska, Arizona, Arkansas! California, Colorado, and Connecticut and more!

[*A big honk;* GIL *almost gets hit by a car.*]

Hey! Hey, watch where yer going! Delaware, Florida, Georgia, and Hawaii, Idaho! Illinois, Indiana, Iowa, thirty-five to go! Kansas then Kentucky—

[*The buzzing noise of someone talking over a McDonald's drive-through intercom.* GIL *mimes speaking into it.*]

Hello? Hello, I would like to place an order! Let me see, okay, hm, okay, I want a Big Mac. And on the side, I would like an order of respect! Because I won! Pepper wins! Fuck you, Ronald McDonald! Fuck your white clown ass in the butt! Fuck your Grimace, fuck your Fry Kids, fuck your Play Place, I feel INCREDIBLE! I'm better than you. MY NAME IS GIL, NOT GIRL, AND I'M A FUCKING WINNER! Kansas then Kentucky, Louisiana, Maine! Maryland, Massachusetts, then go to Michigan!

[*Angry intercom buzzing.*]

What's that? Oh yeah? Do you want to come out here, Ronald? Because I am the best goddamn cocker in the—Oh yeah? How many states can you name, asshole?! Minnesota, Mississippi, Missouri, Montana, and Nebraska is twenty-seven, number twenty-eight is Nevada!

[GIL *is beginning to feel sick.*]

Next New Hampshire and New Jersey . . . and we're down in New Mexico. . . . Next New York . . . North Carolina . . .

[GIL *begins to retch. He continues to sing.*]

North Dakota . . . Ohio, Oklahoma . . . Oregon, Pennsylvania, now let's see . . . Rhode Island, South Carolina . . .

[GIL *stops retching and begins to sing again.*]

South Dakota, Tennessee! Texas and there's Utah, Vermont, I'm almost through, Virginia and there's Washington, and West Virginia too! Could Wisconsin be the last or it's only forty-nine, no Wyoming is the last one in the fifty states that rhyme! YES, WYOMING IS THE LAST ONE IN THE FIFTY STATES THAT RHYME! I WIN!

[GIL *laughs and exits. A transition.* LOU *looks at an incubator holding the eggs.* GIL *enters, less drunk.*]

LOU   [*Referring to the incubator.*] Gil. What is this thing? Is this something to do with drugs?

[GIL *goes over to the incubator, takes out the eggs very delicately.*]

GIL   Nah, Ma. These have to do with something else entirely.

LOU   Are those chicken eggs?

GIL   Nah, nah, these are Minotaur eggs. sphinx eggs. The eggs of a Pegasus!

LOU   Can any of those actually lay eggs?

GIL   'S'all gonna be different now, Ma.

LOU   I thought a Pegasus was a horse.

GIL   Dad built this house. And ya know what? I'm gonna build a house too.

LOU   Gil, you can't build a house. You're not physically capable a' that—

GIL   I built a birdhouse once. A birdhouse is just like a regular house, except smaller. And this new house, Ma? It's gonna be a cocker's dream. A big old training room. Seven different washing machines—

LOU   But who would bring me my honey mustard?

GIL   I guess you'll have to go to the restaurant yourself—

LOU   No. No, Gil, I don't like this, I don't think this is a good idea. I'm getting very agitated; I need you to rub my feet—

GIL   I'm not doing that, Ma—

LOU   Gil, rub my feet!

GIL   No.

LOU ... Suddenly you're too good to rub my feet? What, you think you're the president of the United States or something?

GIL Maybe I am. Maybe I woke up this morning and realized I just got elected by a landslide.

LOU Gil. I promise you. No one would ever vote for you to be president of the United States.

[LOU *exits.* DICKIE *enters.*]

DICKIE Y'gotta learn to lock your door, Pepper, no idea who could come in.

GIL Dickie—

DICKIE Look. I know what I am. I'm an asshole. I'm an asshole now. I was an asshole as a kid. I was an asshole as a baby. But I'm fucking smart and I'm fucking honest, and what I saw last night? Fuck. That was real impressive.

GIL Well, thank you.

DICKIE Yeah. So I'm just gonna say it. Gil. I'd like to formally offer you a job.

GIL ... What ya mean?

DICKIE One of my trainers, he's a real idiot, thinks a wattle is somethin' a penguin does. Faggot. Now, I don't let just anyone touch my cocks. But I look at you and I just think ... goddamn. Together? Imagine the things we could accomplish. So what ya say, man? You wanna conquer the world with me?

[*Beat.*]

GIL No.

DICKIE ... You're turning me down?

GIL Uh-huh.

DICKIE No one turns Dickie Thimble down!

GIL Well, Dickie, I was looking in my mirror today, and I swear I grew an inch. I don't appreciate how you've treated me, and I don't think I need your help. 'Cause I'm in possession of the three deadliest cocks on this planet. I'm gonna learn how to make a website. It's gonna look amazing. I'm gonna sit in the bathtub in my swimsuit and finally like the way I look.

DICKIE Congratulations, Pepper. Ya hear that? That's the sound of your balls descending. There's just one problem: they dropped right into a fucking bear trap.

[DICKIE *exits.* ODYSSEUS *enters. He's all bandaged up; he's in a strange state.*]

GIL There he is! There's the champion!

ODYSSEUS I feel weird-like.

GIL All hail the king!

ODYSSEUS Think I got about half the blood I had in me last night.

GIL Hey! Guess what I got later? An interview! With *Cockfighting Quarterly*! Lead feature! I'm gonna buy a suit! And when people hear my name, they will cheer. And I will stand in my suit and I will listen ta the most beautiful sound on goddamn planet Earth.

ODYSSEUS Thought after last night I was s'posed to be satisfied. . . .

GIL And I been thinking about the future, Odie. We're gonna start breedin' ya, and before ya know it, we'll have a dozen different little Odysseus Rexes tearin' this place to hell! I got this idea, right, I go to one of the McDonald's farms, pick out the most beautiful chicken they got. Can ya imagine it, Odie? Damn. You'll be a father.

ODYSSEUS So why ain't I satisfied?! Just don't get it.

GIL Man, Odie. I can't stop smiling. I tell ya. It's like I'm starin' straight into the future, and it's just covered in feathers and love.

[*A transition. McDonald's.* PHILIPA *enters, pissed off, with a mop.* GIL *enters holding his folded uniform.* PHILIPA *hands* GIL *the mop.*]

PHILIPA Here ya go, Cocknugget.

GIL What is this?

PHILIPA Some asshole vomited outside the drive through last night.

GIL Nah, I'm not doing that.

PHILIPA What?

GIL I came to drop this off.

[GIL *places down his uniform.*]

PHILIPA I look like your fucking dry cleaning?

GIL No. I'm quitting. I quit.

[PHILIPA *laughs, then stops.*]

PHILIPA You serious? Why?

GIL I deserve more.

PHILIPA . . . Fuck. Jesus, Girl—

GIL 'M'not a girl.

PHILIPA What?

GIL 'M'not a girl. I'm a man.

PHILIPA . . . Okay.

GIL   I got you a gift. For your promotion.

[GIL *takes out a little box and hands it to* PHILIPA. *She looks at it skeptically, then opens it.*]

GIL   Tickets. To Walt Disney World Resort.

PHILIPA   . . . Are you making fun of me?

GIL   But they're not just for you. They're for us. We'd go together. We'd ride the Teacups. We'll ride the Splash Mountain and buy the photos they take, and we'll look at them, and we'll look so fucking happy. We'll find Mickey and Minnie Mouse. I'll give them five hundred dollars each. And they'll take off their costumes, and loan 'em to us.

PHILIPA   . . . What would we do with them?

GIL   I dunno. Just put 'em on. Sit in our hotel room.

PHILIPA   . . . Nah. We could do anything we wanted. If you're Mickey Mouse and Minnie Mouse? You can do whatever the fuck you want.

[*Beat.*]

PHILIPA   You'd wear the Minnie Mouse.

GIL   No, I'd be Mickey—

PHILIPA   You'd definitely be Minnie.

GIL   Are you saying you'll come with me?

[*Beat.*]

PHILIPA   . . . I know what people say about me, you know. I'm not stupid. Like, I know this isn't the most glamorous . . . whatever. But I don't care. Because I try harder than anyone I've ever met. And I don't think there's anything funny about that.

GIL   Philipa, I'm pretty sure one day you're going to run the whole world. And I'm going to be honest with you. I know I'm not a good-looking guy. But I've got a heart like a fucking fire truck.

[*A transition.* GIL *enters.*]

GIL   Man, Odie, those Mexican fellas at the McDonald's farm are some genuinely swell folks! You know how to say "chicken" in Spanish? "Pollo!" "Pollo." It's a beautiful word. Just when you feel like you've given up on all of humankind, they go and make something beautiful. So, hey! I got you a little gift! She's in the other room; I gave her a name. Lucky Lady. Now, she's been specially designed by McDonald's to be like two times the weight of a normal chicken, so she can't really walk right. . . . But before ya meet her proper, I just wanted to . . . I know you didn't ever get to know your father.

And I am so sorry about that, Odie. But it's okay. You have a family now.

[GIL *takes the two eggs out of the incubator.*]

GIL   Little brothers just waitin' for you to show 'em how to live right. What you think we should name 'em? Ajax? Agamemnon? Ah, we'll figure it out later. Right now, we're gonna be adding a couple new branches to our family tree. 'Cause this whole thing . . . it isn't just about sex, or breeding it's . . . I'm giving you the gift of fatherhood. I'm giving you the gift of being the most important part of someone else's life.

[*Beat.*]

GIL   Okay. Let's get you laid.

[GIL *puts away the eggs. He exits, and returns with* LUCKY LADY. *She's played by the same actor who plays* PHILIPA. *She collapses in a heap.*]

GIL   Here she is!

ODYSSEUS and **LUCKY LADY**   What the fuck are you?

[*Beat.*]

ODYSSEUS   So what? We supposed to fight or something?

LUCKY LADY   Don't know.

ODYSSEUS   You sent here by the Sun? What, you one a his generals or somethin'?

LUCKY LADY   Don't know what that means—

GIL   Let's get some music goin'!

[GIL *turns on romantic music.*]

ODYSSEUS   This what you got for me, Sun?! Look at you! Like a fuckin' basketball made outa' meat. Can't even stand. Can't even fucking breathe. I'd sneeze and you'd start bleedin'. I'd blink and your head would fall off.

LUCKY LADY   Then do it.

ODYSSEUS   'Scuse me?

LUCKY LADY   Blink or sneeze or take a shit, I don't care. I've been through a hell the likes you couldn't ever imagine, so why don't you just do whatever you wanna do.

ODYSSEUS   . . . You think you had it worse than me?

LUCKY LADY   I know I had it worse than you.

[ODYSSEUS *approaches* LUCKY LADY *violently. A beat. They both stare at each other.*]

ODYSSEUS   . . . I am feeling incredibly aroused right now.

LUCKY LADY   That's pretty fucked up.

GIL   Now don't mind me, just pretend I'm not here—

ODYSSEUS   What are ya anyway?

LUCKY LADY   I have no idea.

ODYSSEUS   Yeah. Yeah, I know exactly what ya mean.

GIL   Come on, Odie, ya gotta touch her. . . .

ODYSSEUS   Lemme ask you a question.

LUCKY LADY   Okay.

ODYSSEUS   You ever killed something before?

LUCKY LADY   Not that I know of.

GIL   You gotta touch her in her hen places—

ODYSSEUS   But you wanna, right? Like you dream about it? Like you can't stop dreamin' about it? Even when yer awake?

LUCKY LADY   . . . No.

ODYSSEUS   Fuck. Fuck.

GIL   Shit. Do you not like her? Is that it? Damn it! I messed it up again! I'm sorry, Odie. I'm gonna fix this. I swear to you.

[GIL *exits, frustrated.*]

ODYSSEUS   . . . See, I. I got an anger inside me. An anger shaped like a fucking anvil inside a' my chest. And sometimes I wanna rip it out and leave it soaked in my guts on the floor! . . . My words ain't right. I never really talked to anyone that much before.

LUCKY LADY   What's yer name?

ODYSSEUS   To be honest? I got no fuckin' idea.

LUCKY LADY   I know what you mean, creature-with-no-name.

ODYSSEUS   Really?

LUCKY LADY   Yeah.

ODYSSEUS   Do you think . . . I don't know if this is too . . . Would you help me rip that anvil outta my chest?

LUCKY LADY   I don't know how to do that.

ODYSSEUS   Well, first I think you gotta reach into here and just sorta . . . pull.

LUCKY LADY   Okay—

ODYSSEUS   But I should. I should warn you. I got, uh, I got like, some serious issues with self-control.

LUCKY LADY   What do you mean?

ODYSSEUS   It's just . . . everything that touches me always ends up . . .

[*Beat.*]

LUCKY LADY   Well, I figure I been through so much already? I must be pretty much immortal.

[LUCKY LADY *reaches towards* ODYSSEUS, *but he pulls away.*]

Hey. 'S'all okay.

[LUCKY LADY *touches* ODYSSEUS. *He is awed. This awe leads to peace.*]

ODYSSEUS   . . . Fuck.

LUCKY LADY   Did I get it?

ODYSSEUS   I think you got it.

LUCKY LADY   Wow.

ODYSSEUS   Can I tell you a secret?

LUCKY LADY   Okay.

ODYSSEUS   I'm not sure what exactly you are, but I think I might love you forever.

[*A transition. Night. A moment of calm.* ODYSSEUS *sleeps.* LUCKY LADY *sleeps next to him.* GIL *enters, picks up the sleeping* LUCKY LADY, *and exits.*]

[*A transition. The next day.* ODYSSEUS *wakes, doesn't see* LUCKY LADY, *and begins to search for her.*]

GIL   Odie, I am so sorry, buddy, I learned my lesson—

ODYSSEUS   Where is she? Come on. Where she at?

GIL   Hey, calm down, she wasn't your type. I get ya, pal, I will not let you down again—

ODYSSEUS   I'm tryin' to be calm, but oh fuck, I feel it. I feel the anvil in my chest again.

GIL   Plus, those things are probably pumped so full a' poison, baby would come out with eyes on its feet. So I sent her back to where she came from.

ODYSSEUS   Sun? What the fuck'd you do with her?! 'Cause I'll find her! I'll tear this fuckin' world apart! I'll drain the damn oceans, I'll fuck up the forests, I will open up every animal and look inside 'em until I find out where the fuck she's at!

GIL   And don't you worry! I'm already on the lookout for an even Luckier Lady! Because, Odie? You deserve the best. The best that anyone's ever had.

[GIL *exits.* ODYSSEUS *notices Bo.*]

ODYSSEUS   Hey. Hey, you. You weird fuckin' thing. You were around these parts last night. You see anything?

[*Beat.*]

ODYSSEUS   I'm talkin' to you, shithead.

[*Beat.*]

ODYSSEUS   Look, assfuck, you better answer me right the fuck now.

[*Beat.*]

ODYSSEUS   Why won't you fuckin' answer me?!

[*Beat.*]

ODYSSEUS   Oh fuck. Oh holy fuck. It's been you all along. Sittin' there! Watchin' me! Plottin'! You a fucking spy of the Sun, ain't ya?

[ODYSSEUS *violently grabs Bo.*]

ODYSSEUS   Where is she?! What the fuck did you do with my mate?!

[*Beat.*]

ODYSSEUS   Oh, you fool. You poor fuckin' fool. You got no idea, do ya? You got no idea what you just did.

[ODYSSEUS *exits with Bo. A transition.* GIL *sits, mid-interview.*]

GIL   I mean, yes, of course the breeding's important, and the diet, and the training, but you know, it's the love, man. You gotta love it. Love the sport, love the bird, love it when ya win, love it when ya lose. And I love it. I can honestly say I've never been happier in my life.

[*Pause while* GIL *listens to a question.*]

Ah, wow, good question. Let's see, uh, it must've been when I was like, seven, eight. My dad and I went to—you remember Pittsworth Arena? Near the shopping strip? So we enter, and I look over the stands and it's just people, people I know, and my dad's patting everyone on the back and I look into the pit, I see the cocks all tied up, the barrel, and I realize the referee is the guy that drives my school bus. It begins, and everyone's shouting, calling out bets. We put twenty on Spoilsport and he got a lucky swipe, took the other guy down in under thirty, and my dad raises me up over his head and he goes, "Winner! Winner! Winner!" And maybe that's when I knew. That answer the question? Yeah, yeah, of course. You want me to like, pose or—?

[GIL *poses. A camera flash. Blackout. Lights up.* LOU *is still sleeping.* GIL *enters, smiling. He takes off a jacket, he sees Bo in some unusual place: halfway under a chair or something.*]

GIL   Bo? What're ya doing there?

[GIL *begins to clean up around the house.*]

Well, I tell ya, guy, they liked me. It's been awhile; I sorta forgot what it's like, when you enter a room, and just, they like you. And more'n that, they respect you. Just by entering a room—

[GIL *picks up a blanket or something. Beneath it, he sees another piece of Bo. He freezes. He looks at the first piece of Bo. He looks at the second piece.*]

Oh shit.

[GIL *attempts to push the two pieces of Bo together.* LOU *enters.*]

LOU   Gil . . . I don't know about these eggs. Look at that machine—

GIL   Ma—

[LOU *picks up both pieces of Bo. She begins to pet him.* GIL *is frozen.*]

LOU   I don't trust anything that's gonna grow in that machine. Since when've you heard of an animal bein' born in a machine? That doesn't seem right, so when they come out—

[LOU *makes a motion, disconnecting the two pieces of Bo. She freezes. Beat. She places her piece of Bo down on the ground.*]

LOU   Please throw out this magazine.

[LOU *begins stomping the floor.*]

My leg's asleep. My damn damn leg is asleep goddamnit! It did it!

GIL   Ma . . . let's think about this, I mean, he was pretty old, right? We had him for a very long time, he was basically already dead.

LOU   He was supposed to die in a blanket, in my arms, without either of us realizing. I want it out of my house, Gil!

GIL   No.

LOU   You sure you want to do this, kid?

GIL   Ma—

LOU   You said you want out, Gil? Then get out. Go build your own damn house. You say you're here to help me. You're not here to help me. I don't care what's wrong with you, I don't care if you're lonely, I don't care if you're sick. This is my house. Get out of my house! Why the hell is my leg still asleep?!

GIL   I'll clean this up, okay? And it will be like nothing happened at all. 'S'just a dog, Ma. Plenty more where that came from.

LOU   You got no idea what you just did.

[LOU *exits.* GIL *goes to the incubator and looks at the eggs.*]

Gil   I know what I'm naming ya. You're Uncle Remus. And you're one's Uncle Romulus. Two brothers sucking dog milk.

[Dickie *enters.* Gil *quickly puts the eggs in his pockets.*]

Dickie   Knock-knock, I don't give a fuck. I'm pissed off, Pepper, let me tell you why. Since I saw you last it's like the fucking universe hasn't been operating right. Up is down, left is right, pussies are dicks, dicks are pussies, and I just found out my secretary Doreen is fucking about ten people other than me.

Gil   What do you want?

Dickie   I'm here to right fucking wrongs. Gimme back the eggs.

Gil   What?

Dickie   The eggs.

Gil   Why would I ever do that?

Dickie   Those eggs were for winners. Not cheaters.

Gil   How the hell did I cheat?!

Dickie   You can only have one bird in the ring at a time. Any more, and it's cheating.

Gil   So?

Dickie   Did you or did you not feed that cock McDonald's brand Chicken McNuggets?

Gil   Sure—

Dickie   And did he or did he not have a bowel movement before the fight?

Gil   No, he did not.

Dickie   Then I count two of your birds in the ring. One on the floor. And one in his stomach.

[*Beat.*]

Gil   That's some creative motherfucking bullshit—

Dickie   The eggs. Give 'em to me.

Gil   Hey, look, I'm real sorry that Dolphin-Bat wasn't what ya hoped for—

Dickie   Bat-Dolphin! You say 'is goddamn name right!

Gil   —but ya gotta have winners and losers in this world—

Dickie   You keep this up you're gonna end up just like your daddy—

Gil   Don't you fucking dare.

[Gil *pushes* Dickie.]

DICKIE   You suicidal or something?

GIL   You don't get to talk about my dad.

DICKIE   Your dad was an annoying as fuck drunk who died with a shitty haircut and no friends.

[GIL *tries to punch* DICKIE. DICKIE *grabs* GIL *and throws him to the ground.*]

GIL   Shit!

DICKIE   Where the eggs?

[DICKIE *kicks* GIL *in the stomach.*]

DICKIE   Where the eggs?

GIL   Stop it!

[DICKIE *kicks him again.*]

DICKIE   Where the eggs?

[DICKIE *kicks him again.*]

GIL   In my . . . in my pocket.

[DICKIE *stops kicking* GIL.]

DICKIE   Huh.

[GIL *stands up, panting. He puts his hand in his pocket, he removes it; it's covered in egg.* GIL *and* DICKIE *stare at it.*]

DICKIE   Fuck you, Gil! You coulda been my friend!

[DICKIE *exits.* GIL *holds his ribs in pain. A transition.*]

[ODYSSEUS *speaks to the Sun.*]

ODYSSEUS   I'm comin' for you next, ya big bright fucker! Floatin' in the sky like an organ on fire! And yer gonna tell me where the fuck she is! I don't care how far I gotta travel! I don't care the lands I gotta cross or the creatures I gotta kill! I will march to the highest mountain, I will launch myself from its peak, and I will fuck up your face 'til it's all but unrecognizable!

[LOU *enters. Beat. She and* ODYSSEUS *stare at one another for a moment.*]

LOU   You think I'm scared a' you?

ODYSSEUS   The fuck is this?

LOU   I'm not scared a' you.

ODYSSEUS   This your final fucking trial, Sun?

LOU   I been through seventy years of bad friends, bad news, bad health, bad husbands, and bad sons. I'm not scared a' anything anymore.

ODYSSEUS   Just another shit-written chapter in my long and fucked-up history.

[ODYSSEUS *brings up his knife. A transition.*]

[DICKIE *exits.* GIL *holds his ribs in pain. A transition.* GIL *enters McDonald's.*]

PHILIPA   Hey. Check it out.

[PHILIPA *reveals that she's wearing a Minnie Mouse shirt under it.*]

GIL   . . . Wow.

PHILIPA   I got one thing to say: Motherfucking aisle seat, motherfucker! So, hey, I got like fifty packs of gum 'cause I hear you're supposed to chew 'em when the plane goes up or else you get like a seizure—hey. Where's your crap?

GIL   Yeah. About that—

PHILIPA   'Cause you can use my gum, but you're sure as shit not using my gum-flavored toothpaste!

GIL   I can't go with you to Walt Disney World.

PHILIPA   What are you talking about?

GIL   Just, I need to get my bearings, I need to show certain assholes that things are different now! And I need to get another chicken, the biggest, the most muscular, and the, the sexiest—

PHILIPA   You want a sexy chicken?

GIL   No, I'm just . . . I can't go.

PHILIPA   . . . But . . . the costumes. The fire truck . . . You were gonna be Minnie Mouse. I can't just be Mickey standing there alone. That would look stupid.

GIL   Take Stanley—

PHILIPA   I'm not taking fucking One-Ball Stanley—

GIL   Well, take someone else then. I mean, don't you have like other friends?

PHILIPA   . . . Of course I have fucking friends. I'm incredibly popular.

GIL   Then you're fine.

PHILIPA   Yeah. Yeah, I am fucking fine. I'm the finest thing in the world.

[PHILIPA *begins to exit.*]

GIL   . . . Hey, are you . . . are you okay?

PHILIPA   I showed you my Minnie Mouse T-shirt. I don't fucking do that for just anyone.

[PHILIPA *exits. A transition.* LOU *sits.* GIL *enters his home.*]

GIL   Ma? Odie? Anyone home?

[*Beat.* LOU *enters, she collapses into her chair.*]

GIL   Ma?

LOU   I was gonna be in beauty school, Gil, you know that?

GIL   Uh, nah, Ma—

LOU   I was real good at making ugly people look pretty. It was 'cause a my sister. 'Cause she was real ugly. But then I met your dad. And I ended up just being a regular hairdresser rather than a beauty school one.

GIL   Ma, what're you—

LOU   I used to put makeup on you. When you were little and Dad wasn't home. I'm sorry. It probably wasn't right to do to a little boy. God, I'm sorry, Gil.

[LOU *begins to cry a little.*]

GIL   Why you sorry? Hey. Why you crying? Ma? Is this about Bo?

LOU   I'm sorry about the makeup, and, and just everything, you know? I just wanted to be done.

GIL   Hey, no worries, I don't remember it. Ma? Hey, Ma. Where's Odie?

LOU   I'm sorry, honey.

GIL   Mom. Where is Odie?

[GIL *stands up and begins to look around.* LOU *is crying.*]

LOU   Your dad was a good guy, more or less. And I did my best, I really did.

[GIL *exits, alarmed. We hear him yell. He reenters holding an empty bleach bottle and supporting* ODYSSEUS, *who teeters into the room.*]

GIL   Oh fuck, holy fuck—

ODYSSEUS   I feel as if I am on the edge of something great.

[ODYSSEUS *falls down on the ground. He stands back up.*]

GIL   Oh God, Odie. Don't move, don't move, I'm gonna call Poison Control—

[GIL *rushes offstage.*]

ODYSSEUS   I have killed many things in my short, strange life. Someday, I will write a book about it. And then I will kill the book. See, I realized today, that there's somethin' deep an' true that unites each and every thing in this world. From the blades a' grass to the raindrops to the rabbits an' the people diggin' ditches on the side a' the road. And that's that I can kill 'em. I can kill 'em all.

[GIL *rushes back onstage.*]

GIL Okay, they don't know much about roosters, so just, you just keep calm—

ODYSSEUS I think I'm gettin' sentimental in my age.

[ODYSSEUS *slumps to the ground.*]

GIL Odie. Don't you go and do this—

ODYSSEUS Man. My insides feel wrong. What kinda beast am I? Body like a beat-up truck. Face like a knife. Heart like a nuclear bomb!

GIL You're the strongest motherfucker I know, Odie! Fight this!

ODYSSEUS Sun? You asshole. You shithead. Why the fuck did you make me? See, sometimes I think I'm the Devil, and I been around since the world began. 'N'sometimes I think I'm a baby, an' I don't get what the fuck is goin' on.

GIL You fight like a goddamn man!

ODYSSEUS An' the only thing I can think of. Is that I was made to end you. I am the Sun's suicide pact. That lazy motherfucker is sick of it all and sent me to do what he ain't got the courage to do. To which I say . . .

[ODYSSEUS *suddenly violently surges upward.*]

Fuck you!

[ODYSSEUS *begins swinging his blade about madly, thrashing.* LOU *screams and stands on a chair.*]

LOU Gil! Gil! Gil!

ODYSSEUS Fuck you for makin' me! Breakin' me up and turnin' me inside out!

[ODYSSEUS *clips* GIL *in the leg with his blade.*]

GIL Shit!

ODYSSEUS Fuck you for makin' me what I gotta be!

[GIL *manages to cover* ODYSSEUS's *eyes with the blinder.* ODYSSEUS *suddenly stops.*]

ODYSSEUS Shh. Shut up. Everyone shut the fuck up.

[*Everything is still.*]

ODYSSEUS Ha. Haha. Look at that. I got 'im. I finally got that coward! I did it. I fucking did it. I feel sick.

LOU Gil, your leg—

GIL Shut up, Odie. Odie, you hang on.

ODYSSEUS   He's gone. Ain't he? Oh God. Oh God. It's over. He's gone.

GIL   I love you, Odie.

ODYSSEUS   I don't need to be here.

GIL   You listen to me! I love you!

ODYSSEUS   The Sun done gone and got extinguished.

GIL   And I know you love me, man! I know you love me so motherfuckin' much!

ODYSSEUS   And now nothin' can hurt nothin' no more.

[ODYSSEUS *dies.*]

LOU   Gil—

GIL   You shut the fuck up.

[GIL begins stomping ferociously on the bleach bottle. LOU is crying.]

GIL   Stop crying! Why the fuck are you crying?!

LOU   I've never killed something before.

[*Beat.*]

GIL   You ever seen a man kill himself?

LOU   N-no—

GIL   I ain't ever seen that either.

[*Beat.* GIL *picks up a discarded item from* ODYSSEUS—*a piece of his costume, his knife—and treats it as his body.*]

Where'd you bury your dog?

LOU   In-in the back. Near the garden.

GIL   Well, I'm gonna take this body. I'm going to the cemetery. I'm gonna bury it next to Dad.

LOU   Gil—

GIL   I'm gonna take a shovel, I'm gonna dig up whatever asshole's buried next to Dad, I'm gonna throw 'im in the back of the car, I'm gonna put Odie in that hole, and then cover it back up.

LOU   I don't think they'll let you do that.

GIL   Don't say a fucking word.

[GIL *exits.* LOU *sits.* GIL *returns. He's crying. He hugs* LOU.]

Shit. I'm sorry, Ma. I'm sorry. Oh shit.

LOU   It's . . . it's okay.

GIL   Fuck you. How could you?

LOU   I just think that you should give cock-fighting a little break. I mean, it was Mexicans who made it, right? Why not try something that was made in America? Like baseball. Or bowling.

GIL   Wasn't Mexicans, Ma. Was the Greeks. Was the Greeks who invented it.

[*A transition. The noise of a cockpit before a fight.*]

[DICKIE *enters.*]

DICKIE   God, we got a weird-looking group out there tonight, huh? Now, folks, we are entering a bold new period of history. The Age of Coltrane is over, and I got a special request for you all: we got us the oldest game in the world gonna be playin' out before our eyes, so let's treat it with some dignity, huh? This sport was here long before we arrived and it's gonna be here long after we've gone. So show it respect. Show it honor. And I guarantee it will break your heart and love you forever. Now fuck this romantic bullshit, let's see these fuckers bleed!

[*A transition.* GIL *stands at the cash register.* DICKIE *enters.*]

GIL   So that'll be two cheeseburgers, one with extra mayo, large fries—you wanna super-size that?—one super-size fries, a medium Sprite, extra ketchup packets. That all? Cash or credit?

DICKIE   Gil Pepper, goddamn sir! Looks like somebody fucked you up, what happened there?

GIL   Dickie, I don't want trouble—

DICKIE   Trouble? All I want is food, not trouble! That's all anyone really wants. A little more food and a little less trouble. Damnedest thing: on the way here, I passed a lady with no fuckin' nose! Great bod but freaky as fuck! Wrote her a check for a thousand fuckin' bucks, told her to get some goddamn surgery. Which reminds me, hey, what you think about breedin'?

GIL   What?

DICKIE   Breedin'. You know, like some people think training is useless; a bird's only as good as its parents. And I'm not sure, 'cause you look at where I came from, bumfuck fuck-all, and then you look at me now, and well, goddamn, right? But then I look at you and yer parents and think: Damn, son, sometimes no matter how hard you try to train them, a scrub is always gonna be a scrub. So anyway, I just wanted to come by and tell you, ya know that trainer job I mentioned a way's back?

GIL   Sure.

DICKIE   You want it?

GIL   You serious?

DICKIE   Always.

GIL   Well, uh, hell yeah, I do.

DICKIE   Well, too the fuck bad! That ship done gone and sailed! I'm outta here, Pepper. This place's food makes my asshole scream.

[DICKIE *makes the McDonald's "doo doo doo" sound effect.* PHILIPA *enters as* DICKIE *exits.*]

GIL   Hey, Philipa . . . I, uh, I wanted to thank you. For giving me my job back.

PHILIPA   . . . You are a sad, stupid creature, Pepper. So I got a question for you. You wanna see my autograph book?

GIL   Uh—

PHILIPA   Read it.

[PHILIPA *hands* GIL *her autograph book;* GIL *reads it.*]

GIL   "Mickey Mouse."

PHILIPA   Mhmm.

GIL   "Ariel."

PHILIPA   Yup.

GIL   "Mowgli.

PHILIPA   We fucked. He's my boyfriend now. I got another question for you, Pepper. You a man?

GIL   What?

PHILIPA   Before. You said you were a man. But I think maybe you misspoke. What do you think, Girl?

GIL   Philipa . . . please—

PHILIPA   Empty your pockets.

GIL   Why—

PHILIPA   Empty your fucking pockets!

[GIL *pulls up his pockets; they're empty.*]

PHILIPA   I catch you with a single ketchup packet, a single red stain in your pocket, I don't give a shit it's your time of the month; you're gone.

GIL   Please, just—

[PHILIPA *knocks condiment packets on the ground. She points to* GIL *to pick them up. He does so.*]

PHILIPA   Guess what? I'm getting another promotion. Regional motherfucking manager. I changed my mind. I'm gonna run this company in five years, and then sell the whole thing to Wendy's. Until then, you're my bitch. That's your job. That's your life. You're a burger bitch.

[PHILIPA *exits. A transition.* LOU *sits reading a magazine.* GIL *enters with two McDonald's bags; he hands one to* LOU.]

GIL   Honey mustard.

LOU   How was yer day?

GIL   'S'okay.

LOU   I've been reading this article. Some actress I never heard of says the only thing you need to do to get pretty and be happy is to eat, like, three grapefruits and then clean your house. You ever eaten a grapefruit?

GIL   Nah.

LOU   Me neither. I'd like to look pretty again, though. I remember when this town looked pretty. Now it looks like crap.

GIL   Huh.

LOU   Gil? Things are gonna change around here. Okay?

GIL   Mm.

LOU   You can stay here. I've decided that. But you gotta help out around the house. I'm gonna make a chore schedule for you. And you're gonna buy a new dryer. There's bird flesh in the old one. And in return, I' gonna try ta be better, to know what time it is, okay? Look. I bought a new towel.

[LOU *takes out a new towel.*]

I'm disabled, so you gotta be nice to me. And I'm gonna be nice to you. And we're gonna love each other. Okay?

GIL   Okay.

LOU   I talked to your McDonald's people today. Called 'em up to see how things were going. They said that you were real good at making the Flurries. That's great, Gil. That's all we can hope for. I'm telling you, we just gotta get good at what we do. Doesn't matter what we do, we just gotta get good at it, and then everything just falls into place. I'm proud of you. Okay? I'm real proud.

GIL   Ma?

LOU   Yeah?

GIL   I'm getting another bird.

Lou   What?

Gil   You heard me.

Lou   No. No, you are not.

Gil   I went to this farm yesterday. I found one.

Lou   Gil—

Gil   He's big. Like the size of a dog. I went to touch him and he broke one of my fingers.

Lou   Gil, I swear to God if you buy another fuckin' chicken—

Gil   And he's gonna be meaner. And madder. And he's gonna make the whole damn world afraid.

Lou   Gil, listen to me. This is an opportunity. Please. Do not fuck yourself up any more than life already has.

Gil   I'm pickin' him up Thursday.

Lou   You leave the house, I'm locking the door, I'm changing the lock; I'm not letting another chicken—

Gil   It's not a motherfucking chicken! You lock the door; I break it down. You call the cops; I torch the house. You never touch a thing I love ever again. And if you got a problem with who I am or what I do, you shut your ugly mouth, you go to your ugly room, and you cry! Sometimes, Ma, I think we're just made for one thing. One thing only, and we can't help it. It's just what we are.

[*Beat.*]

I went to the farm, Ma. And at the farm, there's a room a' chicks and it sounds like death when you enter. I walk in, and I see this bird standin' atop a pile a' pig corpses. I looked in his eyes, and I saw something. His eyes looked like a man's. Like he was the very first man, and this was his Garden of Eden. I think I'm gonna call 'im Adam. This is it, Ma. This one's it.

[Lou *exits without* Gil *noticing.* Gil *gradually removes from the McDonald's bag the same war paint he put on* Odysseus *prior to the fight. He puts it on.*]

Gil   This is the year. And if anythin' tries to stop me, I'll break its face. I'll tear out its teeth. I'll set it on fucking fire! And when the cheering fades and the bucket's full, I will feel the hands of God lift me up and shout, "Winner! Winner! Winner!" 'Cause this is my year, goddamnit! This is my year!

[*Blackout. The End.*]

Play Sources and Acknowledgments

The Country House © 2014 by Donald Margulies. Reprinted by permission of Derek Zasky, William Morris Endeavor. For performance rights, contact Dramatists Play Service, 440 Park Ave. S., New York, NY 10016 (www.dramatists.com) (212-683-8960).

Dinner with the Boys © 2014 by Dan Lauria. Reprinted by permission of Dan Lauria. For performance rights, contact StageRights (www.stagerights.com).

Mala Hierba © 2014 by Tanya Saracho. Reprinted by permission of Mark Orsini, Bret Adams Ltd. For performance rights, contact Mark Orsini (morsini@bretadamsltd.net).

Our Lady of Kibeho © 2014 by Katori Hall. Reprinted by permission of Olivier Sultan, Creative Artists Agency. For performance rights, contact Dramatists Play Service, 440 Park Ave. S., New York, NY 10016 (www.dramatists.com) (212-683-8960).

When January Feels Like Summer © 2014 by Cori Thomas. Reprinted by permission of Ron Gwiazda, Abrams Artists. For performance rights, contact Ron Gwiazda (ron.gwiazda@abramsartny.com).

Year of the Rooster © 2013 by Eric Dufault. Reprinted by permission of Leah Hamos, Abrams Artists. For performance rights, contact Playscripts, Inc. (www.playscripts.com)